ROUTLEDGE LIBRARY EDITIONS: LIBRARY AND INFORMATION SCIENCE

Volume 93

SERIALS TO THE TENTH POWER

SERIALS TO THE TENTH POWER
Tradition, Technology, and Transformation

Edited by
MARY ANN SHEBLE AND BETH HOLLEY

LONDON AND NEW YORK

First published in 1996 by The Haworth Press, Inc.

This edition first published in 2020
by Routledge
2 Park Square, Milton Park, Abingdon, Oxon OX14 4RN

and by Routledge
52 Vanderbilt Avenue, New York, NY 10017

Routledge is an imprint of the Taylor & Francis Group, an informa business

© 1996 The Haworth Press, Inc.

All rights reserved. No part of this book may be reprinted or reproduced or utilised in any form or by any electronic, mechanical, or other means, now known or hereafter invented, including photocopying and recording, or in any information storage or retrieval system, without permission in writing from the publishers.

Trademark notice: Product or corporate names may be trademarks or registered trademarks, and are used only for identification and explanation without intent to infringe.

British Library Cataloguing in Publication Data
A catalogue record for this book is available from the British Library

ISBN: 978-0-367-34616-4 (Set)
ISBN: 978-0-429-34352-0 (Set) (ebk)
ISBN: 978-0-367-36966-8 (Volume 93) (hbk)
ISBN: 978-0-367-36983-5 (Volume 93) (pbk)
ISBN: 978-0-429-35218-8 (Volume 93) (ebk)

Publisher's Note
The publisher has gone to great lengths to ensure the quality of this reprint but points out that some imperfections in the original copies may be apparent.

Disclaimer
The publisher has made every effort to trace copyright holders and would welcome correspondence from those they have been unable to trace.

SERIALS TO THE TENTH POWER: TRADITION, TECHNOLOGY, AND TRANSFORMATION

Proceedings of the
NORTH AMERICAN SERIALS INTEREST GROUP, Inc.

**10th Anniversary Conference
June 1-4, 1995
Duke University, Durham, NC**

Mary Ann Sheble
Beth Holley
Editors

The Haworth Press, Inc.
New York • London

Serials to the Tenth Power: Tradition, Technology, and Transformation has also been published as *The Serials Librarian*, Volume 28, Numbers 1/2/3/4 1996.

© 1996 by The Haworth Press, Inc. All rights reserved. No part of this work may be reproduced or utilized in any form or by any means, electronic or mechanical, including photocopying, microfilm and recording, or by any information storage and retrieval system, without permission in writing from the publisher. Printed in the United States of America.

The development, preparation, and publication of this work has been undertaken with great care. However, the publisher, employees, editors, and agents of The Haworth Press and all imprints of The Haworth Press, Inc., including The Haworth Medical Press and Pharmaceutical Products Press, are not responsible for any errors contained herein or for consequences that may ensue from use of materials or information contained in this work. Opinions expressed by the author(s) are not necessarily those of The Haworth Press, Inc.

The Haworth Press, Inc., 10 Alice Street, Binghamton, NY 13904-1580 USA

Library of Congress Cataloging-in-Publication Data

North American Serials Interest Group. Conference (10th : 1995 : Duke University)
    Serials to the tenth power : tradition, technology, and transformation : proceedings of the North American Serials Interest Group, Inc., 10th anniversary conference. June 1-4, 1995, Duke University, Durham, NC / Mary Ann Sheble, Beth Holley, editors.
    p. cm.
    Includes bibliographical references and index.
    ISBN 1-56024-840-8 (alk. paper)
    1. Serials control systems–United States–Congresses. 2. Serials control systems–Canada–Congresses. I. Sheble, Mary Ann. II. Holley, Beth. III. Title.
Z692.S5N67 1995
025.3'432–dc20   96-2320
                                                                                    CIP

Serials to the Tenth Power: Tradition, Technology, and Transformation

CONTENTS

Introduction   1
    Mary Ann Sheble
    Beth Holley

PRECONFERENCE PROGRAM: GOPHERS AND WEBS: A CYBER SAFARI

GENERAL SESSION

The Internet Information Delivery Revolution   7
    Ann Ercelawn

BREAKOUT SESSIONS

Gopher Gold and Gopher Gears: Using and Maintaining Gophers   11
    Betty Landesman

Electronic Dream Catchers and Spinning Charlotte's Web: Using and Maintaining World Wide Web Services   17
    Steve Oberg

NASIG Tenth Anniversary Conference Panel   23
    Tina Feick

PLENARY SESSION I: APPROACHING THE PRECIPICE–RE-ENGINEERING THE STRUCTURE OF THE SCHOLARLY INFORMATION UNIVERSE

From Serial Publications to Document Delivery to Knowledge Management: Our Fascinating Journey, Just Begun   37
    Paul Evan Peters

The ACM Electronic Publishing Plan and Interim Copyright Policies   57
    Peter J. Denning

PLENARY SESSION II: COPYRIGHT CAMPS–ELECTRONIC FAIR USE IN THE CROSSFIRES

Copyright in an Electronic Age: Making New Vintages from the Great Old Grapes   63
    Gale Teaster-Woods

Whose Work Is It Anyway? Perspectives on the Stakeholders and the Stakes in the Current Copyright Scene   69
    Ann Okerson

PLENARY SESSION III: VISIONS FOR A NEW DECADE OF 21ST CENTURY SERIALS

The Transformation of a Nation: The Impact of Politics and the Potential of Technology on Information Access in South Africa   89
    Dianne Leong Man

Security and Uses of the Internet   105
    Steven M. Bellovin

Serials in the Networked Environment   115
    Carroll Davis

CONCURRENT SET I: ELECTRONIC PUBLISHING–HOT PROJECTS IN PROGRESS

PROJECTS SESSION 1

SCAN: Scholarship from California on the Net 123
    Rebecca Simon

Resources for Mathematicians: The Evolution of e-MATH 129
    Ralph Youngen

PROJECTS SESSION 2

Electronic Journal Update: CJTCS 135
    Janet H. Fisher

Developing an Electronic Journal: A John Wiley & Sons
  Project 139
    Melissa Nasea

PROJECTS SESSION 3

Carnegie Mellon University and University Microfilms
  International "Virtual Library Project" 143
    Charles B. Lowry
    Denise A. Troll

Recent Steps Toward Full-Text Electronic Delivery
  at Elsevier Science 171
    John Tagler

PROJECTS SESSION 4

Springer-Verlag's Electronic Projects 181
    Beatrice L. McKay

CONCURRENT SET II: SERIALS AND SERIALISTS ON THE MOVE: ISSUES AND CHALLENGES IN THE ELECTRONIC AGE

SESSION 1: ROLES IN TRANSITION

The Alarmists versus the Equilibrists: Reexamining the Role of the Serials Professional in the Information Age   187
Thomas W. Leonhardt

What If They Started Talking? New Roles for Staff in Change Management–A Case Study   197
David S. Goble
Kathleen Brown

SESSION 2: CONVERSATIONS WITH E-EDITORS

The Rhetoric of Serials at the Present Time   209
Eyal Amiran

Five Years of *Bryn Mawr Classical Review*   223
James J. O'Donnell

SESSION 3: CATALOGING ON THE EDGE: PROVIDING ACCESS TO REMOTE RESOURCES

Mr. Serials Revisits Cataloging: Cataloging Electronic Serials and Internet Resources   229
Eric Lease Morgan

U-R-Stars: Standards for Controlling Internet Resources   239
Priscilla Caplan

NASIG WORKSHOPS

WORKSHOP SET I

Trading Back Issues on the Internet   249
Joseph P. Hinger

New Technology and Traditional Sources 257
Sandy Gurshman

Cataloging Electronic Journals: The University of Virginia Experience 263
Mary Ellen Soper

Optimizing Serials Access in the Online Catalog 269
Patricia M. Wallace

Truck and High-Tech: Document Delivery in the '90s 275
Gail Julian

Serials Interfaces: Planning and Implementation 283
Roger L. Presley

Preparing Tomorrow's Serial Leaders: Creating New Alliances Among Library Schools, Libraries, and Serial Professionals 291
Katy Ginanni

Change and the Impact on Serials Staff 297
Jay Harris

CONSER Live: A Conversation with CONSER Coordinator 305
Sally Sorensen

Making the Most of Electronic Journals–Library and Secondary Publisher Perspectives 311
Judy Luther

WORKSHOP SET II

What's in It for Us? Internet Use in Technical Services 317
Lauren Noel

Using the RFP Process to Select a Serials Vendor: A Work in Progress 325
Bill Willmering

Cataloging Computer Files as Serials 331
Cathy Kellum

Training Aid in Cataloging Gopher Sites
and Electronic Serials 337
Beverley Geer

Transformation in the Library Bindery Through Increased
Preservation Awareness 343
Marilyn P. Fletcher

Automating Journal Use Studies: A Tale of Two Libraries 349
Karen Cargille

Scholarly Journals at the Crossroads 355
Rita Echt

Implementing Teams for Technical Services Functions 361
Cathy Tijerino

Changes to the Serial Item and Contribution Identifier
and the Effects of Those on Publishers and Librarians 367
Cindy Hepfer

If Publishers Perished, Just What Would Be Lost? 371
Barbara Woodford

10th Annual NASIG Conference Registrants,
Duke University, June 1995 377

Index 397

IN MEMORIAM
FREDERICK (FRITZ) SCHWARTZ
1949-1995

These proceedings are dedicated to the memory of Fritz Schwartz who died of AIDS-related lymphoma on November 9, 1995. Fritz was a frequent speaker at NASIG annual conferences, having most recently conducted a workshop at this 10th Annual Conference. Fritz was a well-known and highly respected authority on EDI (Electronic Data Interchange), the Internet, and library standards, and actively participated in various committees within SISAC (Serials Industry Systems Advisory Committee), NISO (National Information Standards Organization), and ICEDIS (International Committee on EDI for Serials). At the time of his death, Fritz was Manager of Electronic Services and Standards at the Faxon Company. Prior to that he worked for six years at CLSI. Fritz's friends and colleagues will greatly miss his energy, warmth, humor, and passion for standards, to which he devoted so much of himself. NASIG dedicates these proceedings to honor Fritz and to recognize his many contributions to the serials information chain.

Introduction

The theme of the tenth annual conference of the North American Serials Interest Group (NASIG) was "Serials to the Tenth Power: Tradition, Technology, and Transformation." The conference was held from June 1-4, 1995 at Duke University, Durham, N.C.

The conference opened with a celebration of the tenth anniversary of NASIG. A panel of NASIG founders and participants from the first conference reminisced about the initial conference and discussed the evolvement of NASIG into a significant international organization.

The opening conference plenary session addressed the impact of electronic publishing on the dissemination of knowledge. As more publishers move toward electronic publication, libraries will need to develop strategies to meet the challenges of a completely network-based information environment. The second plenary session focused on copyright law. Developed primarily as a form of legal protection for printed works, copyright law has expanded to apply to new types of works. Respect for copyright is as important in the digital world as in the more traditional environment. As information is increasingly available in electronic format, new copyright issues need to be resolved. The closing plenary session presented an overview of visions for the future of information dissemination. This session included a presentation on the relationship between politics, technology, and information access in South Africa, a discussion of Internet security issues, and a summary of the issues that serialists must resolve to ensure continuing access to information in the coming decade.

Speakers in the concurrent sessions brought many of these ideas to the day-to-day level. Publishers, vendors, and librarians involved in Internet publication projects, and editors of electronic journals provided a diversity of perspectives on the challenges that they face in their innovative approaches to providing information in electronic format. Another set of sessions focused on several recent library efforts to deal with these innovations. These sessions addressed standards for identifying and citing electronic resources, bibliographic control for Internet resources, and organization of service delivery to meet the challenges of evolving technology.

Twenty workshops covered a broad array of concerns, ranging from trading back serial issues on the Internet, Internet use in technical services, and ANSI/NISO standards for identifying serially published materials in a machine-readable context.

The NASIG Electronic Communications Committee sponsored a preconference, "Gophers and Webs: A Cyber Safari." Preconference attendees explored the pros and cons of the two basic navigational tools of the Internet: Gopher and World Wide Web. The keynote speaker, Richard W. Wiggins, discussed each tool from the perspective of user friendliness, access to resources, and maintenance. This presentation was followed by two breakout sessions, covering each of the tools in depth.

The conference drew close to 600 attendees. A large North American contingent was joined by participants from Europe and Africa. Attendees represented all areas of the serials spectrum.

This volume includes papers from the plenary and concurrent sessions, along with summary reports of the panel discussion, preconference, and conference workshops. We hope that these papers will provide readers with practical ideas on managing the challenges of the electronic information environment.

We would like to thank our NASIG Board liaison, Beverley Geer, for guiding us through the editorial process, and Robert Persing for preparing the index. We also acknowledge Karen Garrison for her expert secretarial help, and the University of Detroit Mercy Libraries/Media Services, and the University of Alabama Libraries for their support of the project. Our greatest debt is to the individuals who gave willingly of their time to share their expertise by speaking at the conference and preparing contributions for this volume.

Mary Ann Sheble
University of Detroit Mercy Libraries/Media Services

Beth Holley
University of Alabama Libraries

PRECONFERENCE PROGRAM: GOPHERS AND WEBS: A CYBER SAFARI

GENERAL SESSION

The Internet Information Delivery Revolution

Richard Wiggins
Workshop Presenter

Ann Ercelawn
Recorder

SUMMARY. Information delivery via the Internet has changed dramatically since 1991. Wiggins's presentation provides an overview of recent developments in information delivery with an emphasis on the explosive growth of the World Wide Web, and offers comments on a number of areas that pose significant challenges for users of the Internet. *[Article copies available from The Haworth Document Delivery Service: 1-800-342-9678.]*

New Internet protocols and applications are revolutionizing the process of information delivery. In the opening general session of

---

Ann Ercelawn is Original Cataloger for Vanderbilt University, Nashville, TN.
© 1996 by the North American Serials Interest Group, Inc. All rights reserved.

[Haworth co-indexing entry note]: "The Internet Information Delivery Revolution." Ercelawn, Ann. Co-published simultaneously in *The Serials Librarian* (The Haworth Press, Inc.) Vol. 28, No. 1/2, 1996, pp. 7-10; and *Serials to the Tenth Power: Tradition, Technology, and Transformation* (ed: Mary Ann Sheble, and Beth Holley) The Haworth Press, Inc., 1996, pp. 7-10. Single or multiple copies of this article are available from The Haworth Document Delivery Service [1-800-342-9678, 9:00 a.m. - 5:00 p.m. (EST)].

the preconference, Richard Wiggins, well-known Internet lecturer and author of *The Internet for Everyone: A Guide for Users and Providers*, observed that just two years ago no one would have predicted how quickly the World Wide Web (WWW or Web) has caught on as a method of information delivery. Wiggins provided historical context to the recent revolution in information delivery by demonstrating retrieval of the Library of Congress's Vatican exhibit files utilizing different Internet protocols. Before 1991, document retrieval was accomplished by means of anonymous file transfer protocol (FTP), using a non-user friendly, command-driven interface to retrieve documents with cryptic file names. In 1992-1993, the Gopher protocol came into widespread use. Gopher allows for more descriptive document titles and easier document navigation and retrieval, but is limited in its inability to deliver multiple document types simultaneously, and in its non-sophisticated presentation of text (mono font ASCII). Since 1993, the WWW, developed by Tim Berners-Lee at the European Organization for Nuclear Research (CERN) prior to Gopher, has gained increasing popularity as an information delivery tool, due to the introduction of simple-to-use, graphical interface browsers designed for multiple platforms. These browsers, such as National Center for Supercomputing Applications' (NCSA) Mosaic and Netscape, offer significant advantages over other methods of online information retrieval in that they are "multi-lingual" clients, allow for simultaneous delivery of text and images, provide for some degree of user control over document presentation, and simplify navigation of the Internet via Uniform Resource Locators (URLs) and hypertext links.

After demonstrating how to navigate the WWW and providing a quick overview of Web-related terminology, Wiggins observed that business has become an increasingly active player on the Web. Companies are selling access to the Internet and to online databases, mounting product catalogs, and providing form capabilities for placing orders. Advertising in particular is a high growth area, with both positive and negative outcomes. Wiggins demonstrated a number of business Web pages and applications, developed by such companies as IBM, Federal Express, and the Digital Corporation. Of particular interest to librarians is the Web version of *Encyclopaedia Britannica* sold on a campus licensing model. Britannica

Online effectively utilizes Web information delivery capabilities by providing continuous updating of information, 24 hour database accessibility with simultaneous use, a sophisticated search engine, and linkage of standard articles with related external resources on the Web at large.

Wiggins concluded his survey of business applications by noting that expanded commercial capabilities are contingent upon improved system interoperability and better security tools to protect financial transactions. Trends that he noted in the business sector include providing information "by the sip" versus bulk purchase, and the sale of access to information as well as to goods.

In spite of the enormous potential of the Internet as an information delivery medium, the online environment poses a number of challenges in the areas of navigation and organization of resources. The multiplicity of Internet indexing tools (Archie, Veronica, WAIS, etc.) is daunting to information seekers, and efforts to organize Internet resources have been largely dependent on uncoordinated, individual efforts to date. While Wiggins noted several useful pioneering attempts to bring order out of chaos (the OCLC Internet Cataloging Project, and the University of Michigan's Clearinghouse for Subject-Oriented Internet Resource Guides), he predicted that manual cataloging efforts would be overwhelmed by the sheer volume of available resources, and that document retrieval will become more dependent on automated indexes such as Lycos and publisher-initiated self-cataloging efforts in the future. Wiggins offered a "wish list" for the ideal Internet index tool. Such a tool would cross all publishing media (Gopher, Web, FTP), incorporate author or publisher supplied document abstracts, and allow for sophisticated searches, structured as well as free-form.

Wiggins identified document navigation as a challenge for both information providers and information consumers. Providers must decide how to organize their documents; today's documents have little structure. Users of Internet documents must cope with increasingly unmanageable personal hotlists of favorite resources.

Other problematic information delivery issues addressed by Wiggins include insufficient bandwidth as the multimedia content of documents increases, as well as charge-back issues for Internet use. Content quality is also a serious concern. Wiggins described our current online information environment as "brochure mode," i.e., lacking in substantive content compared to traditional print media. Permanence of documents is problematic, as documents tend to vanish or migrate over time; a persistent naming scheme (Uniform Resource Identifier) is needed. Currency of documents is also an issue, as information tends to go stale over time, and Hypertext Markup Language (HTML) coded documents are cumbersome to print and view offline compared to other media.

The revolution in online information delivery that we are experiencing offers challenges on a number of different fronts. But as Wiggins observed in closing, our current environment offers much excitement and potential for the future of information delivery.

BREAKOUT SESSIONS

Gopher Gold and Gopher Gears: Using and Maintaining Gophers

Donnice Cochenour
Marilyn Geller

Workshop Presenters

Betty Landesman

Recorder

SUMMARY. Gophers provide a means of finding and retrieving information stored on the Internet. Based on a hierarchical, menu-driven client/server model, gophers allow maintainers to present information in an organized manner and users to sift through these menus in a methodical way. This session introduces the general capabilities of gopher clients, demonstrates some of the ways to use gopher clients, and explores some of the interesting sites in gopher space. It also covers what is needed in terms of systems, knowledge, and time to set up and

---

Betty Landesman is Coordinator for Systems Planning, Gelman Library, George Washington University, Washington, DC.

© 1996 by the North American Serials Interest Group, Inc. All rights reserved.

[Haworth co-indexing entry note]: "Gopher Gold and Gopher Gears: Using and Maintaining Gophers." Landesman, Betty. Co-published simultaneously in *The Serials Librarian* (The Haworth Press, Inc.) Vol. 28, No. 1/2, 1996, pp. 11-16; and *Serials to the Tenth Power: Tradition, Technology, and Transformation* (ed: Mary Ann Sheble, and Beth Holley) The Haworth Press, Inc., 1996, pp. 11-16. Single or multiple copies of this article are available from The Haworth Document Delivery Service [1-800-342-9678, 9:00 a.m. - 5:00 p.m. (EST)].

maintain a gopher server. *[Article copies available from The Haworth Document Delivery Service: 1-800-342-9678.]*

This breakout session introduced attendees to the history of gopher development, the client/server model as it relates to gopher software, ideas for organizing a gopher menu, technical requirements for establishing and maintaining a gopher, and how we can apply all of the above to our own NASIGNET gopher.

Donnice Cochenour began the sessions with the "Gopher Gold" portion, i.e., what is a gopher and how do we use it. She began by determining how many people in the audience had used gophers and Gopher client software. She then gave a brief description of how Gopher was developed at the University of Minnesota in 1991 as a simple way to publish information to help people use the campus computing services, and quickly grew into a worldwide information system. Items on a gopher menu can, in fact, be on many different computers in many different places.

Donnice explained how a gopher uses the client-server model, which divides the work between the user's PC (the "client") and the host computer (the "server"). She then reviewed different Gopher client software available for DOS, Unix, Windows, and Macintosh computers as well publically-available text-based clients accessible via Telnet.

The original Gopher software was designed to handle primarily text documents. However, users needed the ability to handle other types of files. This resulted in the development of Gopher Plus in 1993. Gopher Plus allows the user to store and transmit information ("attributes") about an item, such as the file size and type and the last date it was modified. Some of the "smarter" clients will automatically invoke appropriate "helper applications" to view the file. The features available to users depend on their expertise in setting up the client software.

The "Mother Gopher" at the University of Minnesota provides information about Gopher developments and the latest version of available public domain clients.

There are several public clients available, the most common of which is the Unix Curses client. Public clients enable users to access a gopher server without a client installed on the local workstation. Two examples of Gopher Plus clients are HGopher (for Windows) and TurboGopher (for Macintosh). Donnice illustrated what is involved in configuring a client by showing screens from the HGopher software. She then explained "viewers," which are "helper applications" invoked automatically by a Gopher Plus client to display a document. Text and image viewers show information on the screen; sound viewers will play the sounds if the workstation is equipped with the necessary hardware. Some viewers might also decompress a file. Donnice's HGopher example had been configured to open the "write program" (provided with Windows 3.11) and display the text within this program to provide full editing capabilities. Gopher allows the user to save the location of any gopher menu item found in navigating "gopherspace" as a *bookmark*, thus eliminating the need to retrace steps to get to that item again. Bookmarks can be created either by marking the item while there or manually. Donnice showed the audience how to parse out Universal Resource Locator (URL) information to create a bookmark for the "Gopher FAQ" (Frequently Asked Questions) file listed in the handout.

Gopher menus are designed in a hierarchical fashion through which the users browse. There are some navigational tools that assist users looking for specific information. *Veronica* is a keyword index to the words in gopher menus, developed in 1992 at the University of Nevada. It has some limitations: gopher menus lack a controlled vocabulary; items removed from their original hierarchical context may be difficult to understand; menu titles are not always descriptive; and user demands on the available Veronica servers often exceed capacity. *Jughead* is similar to Veronica in indexing gopher menus, but it is most often used to index a single gopher server or collection of servers.

Donnice then shared with the audience some of the "Gopher Gold" that she has found at particular gopher sites. Rice University uses the "subject tree" approach. Listings of resources are organized by broad subject areas. The "tree" is created automatically by running a program called "linkmerge" which merges selected directories from other gopher sites into the Rice subject menus. Gopher Jewels also uses a subject tree approach, but it is created manually by one person. This person is no longer able to keep up this project and so Gopher Jewels is regrettably no longer being maintained.

Gophers are used by many organizations and associations. Donnice reviewed the NASIG gopher resources available to members, the *Directory of Electronic Journals* and the *NewJour-L* listserv on the Association of Research Libraries' gopher, the USMARC documentation on the Library of Congress's LC Marvel, and information on the American Library Association and National Library of Canada gophers. She then reviewed the different organizational approaches to information provided on three library gophers. The InfoSlug gopher at the University of California at Santa Clara (named after the school's mascot, the banana slug) is a joint development effort between the University Library and Communications and Technology Services. The electronic journal collection is alphabetically arranged with cross-references created though the addition of menu items. The gopher at the University of Houston Library has menus phrased in terms of users' needs and organized by type of resource, e.g., "Looking for Articles." Finally, the "Library Without Walls" at the North Carolina State University Library gopher is organized around functions similar to the physical library, e.g., the reference desk, study carrels (a subject arrangement of resources), and full-text resources (journals and books).

Marilyn Geller then proceeded to take the audience through the technical requirements for setting up and maintaining a gopher server; the "Gopher Gears" portion of the session. She conveyed this technical information in terms that were accessible to the lay audience. There are three basic requirements: hardware, or a computer connected to the Internet and running all necessary protocols; software (in this case Gopher *server* software, not *client* software), which is available for free from the University of Minnesota via anonymous file transfer protocol (FTP) at boombox.micro.umn.edu/pub/gopher; and, of course, the data! Marilyn emphasized that this is where library skills come into play as decisions are made about what information will be on the machine.

Gopher administrators need a basic knowledge of their operating system, the necessary "root privileges" to get to the heart of the operating system and tell it what to do, and good organizational skills. To install the server, the administrator unpacks (decompresses) the software, configures the server by editing the Makefile.config and conf.h files, and starts the server to enable the Internet protocols.

To determine what data to put on the server, it is necessary to identify bodies of information, then select, acquire, and organize pieces of information. In other words, it involves having librarians do what they do for a living!

Marilyn gave some valuable guidelines on organizing gopher menus. First, divide information into broad categories. Within categories, identify forms, functions, and similarities. At the lowest level, create an order, e.g., alphabetical, numerical, or chronological. Marilyn illustrated these principles with the NASIG gopher, which has the following menus: Bylaws (a file); Procedures (a directory); Newsletters (a directory); Instructions (a file); Welcome (a file); and Nasignet (a directory).

Marilyn explained how links to local resources are created. Every menu item has a "shadow" which controls how it will be named and displayed. For Gopher 1.x servers ("plain," not Gopher Plus), a .cap directory is created with files that have the same name as items in the directory that contains resources. For Gopher 2.x servers (Gopher Plus), a .names file is created in the same directory where resources are located. These files contain the menu name and number of the menu item.

To create a link to non-local resources, define the *type* (what kind of document the object is, e.g., text file, directory, searchable index, telnet); the *path* (the directory names leading to the resource); the *host* (the name of the machine on which the resource resides); and the *port* (the place on a machine where a "service" listens). This information is then copied to a .links file. If you are using the Unix Curses client to access a gopher, you can see this information for any resource on the menu by moving the cursor to the spot on that menu and pressing '='.

The link in the NASIG gopher that appears on the menu as *Library Catalogs via Telnet* actually looks like this:

Name=Library Catalogs via Telnet

Numb=5

Type=1

Port=70

Path=1/Libraries/Card Catalogs via Telnet

Host=gopher.micro.umn.edu

Administrators need to ask some important questions when they consider adding non-local resources to the gopher menu. Is this the authoritative version? Is it reliably published? Will it always be there? Is the server readily available and well-maintained? How is it displayed?

Having revealed the nuts and bolts of establishing a gopher server, Marilyn opened the floor to a hands-on exercise for audience input. She showed the existing NASIG gopher menu and invited suggestions on how it could be organized differently. She showed one possibility of reorganizing the menu that had resulted from discussion among the members of the Electronic Communications Committee (ECC). This invited some lively comment from members of the audience! Comments given at both of the gopher sessions were summarized and considered by the ECC in a discussion of reorganizing the NASIG gopher.

Two handouts were distributed. Donnice's handout provides an outline of her presentation, the URL's of the gophers visited during the demonstration, and a bibliography consisting of print and electronic references. Marilyn's handout consists of an illustrated outline which includes the details about FTP and file information given during her talk and the NASIG gopher menus (current and proposed).

Electronic Dream Catchers and Spinning Charlotte's Web: Using and Maintaining World Wide Web Services

Birdie MacLennan
Maggie Rioux
Workshop Presenters

Steve Oberg
Recorder

SUMMARY. The World Wide Web (WWW) is an Internet organizing tool that combines text and multimedia resources and, through embedded hypertext/media links, enables users to find a wealth of information from computers around the world, display it in an attractive "desktop" format, and often interact with it. This workshop focused on the web-threads that can be spun for useful applications in serials work. The workshop included a behind-the-scenes look at how the WWW is spun, including an in-depth look at Hypertext Markup Language, the mark-up languages that hold it all together. *[Article copies available from The Haworth Document Delivery Service: 1-800-342-9678.]*

Interest in the World Wide Web (WWW or Web), a navigational tool which uses hypertext and hypermedia links to access and inte-

---

Steve Oberg is Head of Bibliographic Control at the University of Chicago, Chicago, IL.

© 1996 by the North American Serials Interest Group, Inc. All rights reserved.

[Haworth co-indexing entry note]: "Electronic Dream Catchers and Spinning Charlotte's Web: Using and Maintaining World Wide Web Services." Oberg, Steve. Co-published simultaneously in *The Serials Librarian* (The Haworth Press, Inc.) Vol. 28, No. 1/2, 1996, pp. 17-22; and *Serials to the Tenth Power: Tradition, Technology, and Transformation* (ed: Mary Ann Sheble, and Beth Holley) The Haworth Press, Inc., 1996, pp. 17-22. Single or multiple copies of this article are available from The Haworth Document Delivery Service [1-800-342-9678, 9:00 a.m. - 5:00 p.m. (EST)].

grate text, video, sound, and graphic resources available on the Internet, still remains high two years after the introduction of the National Center for Supercomputing Application's (NCSA) Mosaic. NCSA Mosaic was the first easy to use, widely available geographical Web "browser" software that popularized the Web and demonstrated its potential as a new medium for the delivery and retrieval of information. Many libraries and commercial organizations that serve the library market are extensively involved in developing Web-related services to exploit this potential. Yet many persons who have only heard of the World Wide Web or who have seldom used it remain unclear as to what exactly the Web is, how it works, how it can be used, and how one creates a Web page. This presentation by Birdie MacLennan (Serials Coordinator, University of Vermont) and Maggie Rioux (Information Systems Librarian at Marine Biological Laboratory/Woods Hole Oceanographic Institution (MBL/WHOI) Library), addressed these issues as well as other aspects of the World Wide Web by combining a "guided tour" of Web space with an overview of how to build and maintain a Web site. Both presenters have extensive experience in using, developing, and maintaining World Wide Web services.

In order to provide a context for their points, and also as a live demonstration of Web capabilities, Rioux and MacLennan presented their talk by accessing via the Internet an excellent set of Web pages residing at host computers at the University of Vermont and at MBL/WHOI which they designed specifically for the preconference. To view the Web "home page" for their presentation, point your Web browser to the following URL:http://www.uvm.edu/bmaclenn/NASIF/index.html. Handouts provided for the participants were derived from these Web pages, making it easy to follow along throughout the presentation. Each handout had two components: a representation of the screen displays from the presentation's Web pages, and a corresponding "behind the scene" view of each screen showing how the screen display was created using Hypertext Markup Language (HTML). Participants were encouraged to use the handouts as guides for creating their own home pages. It was noted that one way to learn more about HTML and how to use it to set up one's own home page is to view what another person has created via the source document and use it to get ideas or modify it for local use. It is easy to use a command in a browser program to view the "source" document or HTML version of a particularly innovative home page in order to see what tricks or techniques have been used by its creator.

Before starting her part of the presentation, MacLennan asked the audience whether there was anyone present who had never used the Web. Three participants (out of a total of about 150) answered in the affirmative; a fourth participant indicated that he had only used the World Wide Web one time. MacLennan then began by defining basic characteristics and definitions relating to the World Wide Web. Some of these characteristics include the use of hypertext and hypermedia (defined by MacLennan as "a collection of multimedia documents connected by hyperlinks"); the ability for users to seamlessly move around the Internet by pointing or clicking to view documents or files on computers around the world; ease of use; and growing popularity for use in electronic publishing initiatives and other applications. In order to illustrate these characteristics, MacLennan took the audience on a tour of various Web sites around the world by clicking on embedded hypertext links on the Web page she created. The first place visited was a Web page promoting tourism for Vermont that included links to graphic images of tourist spots and other images such as a United States postal stamp commemorating the founding of the state of Vermont. From there, various other Web pages were shown to the audience, including one at Cape Cod, the Web page of the University of British Columbia (in honor of NASIG's 9th annual conference held there last year), and a site in Australia.

MacLennan discussed basic pointers for getting started with using the Web. One of the most fundamental steps to take when learning to access the Web is to choose a browser, or client software program, of which there are two broad categories: browsers with a graphical user interface or GUI (examples include Netscape, NCSA, Mosaic, Cello, MacWeb); and text-based browsers such as Lynx or Line Mode (the original WWW browser developed at CERN). The main distinction between text-based and graphical oriented browsers is the ability of graphical browsers to access and display multimedia information such as video, graphics, and sound. For more information on various available browsers, MacLennan referred participants to an article in the April 1995 issue of *Internet World* that compared twenty-four browser applications.[1]

Three core components of the Web were briefly explained, including HTML, hypertext transfer protocol (HTTP), and uniform resource locator (URL). MacLennan closed her section of the presentation by highlighting several important Web sites relating to cataloging, acquisitions, and collection development. These included a well-developed Web site of links to serials-related information which she created, called "Serials in Cyberspace" (URL: http://www.uvm.edu/-bmaclenn); a demonstration World Wide Web gateway to the DRA OPAC of North Carolina State University Library, which offers a prototype in linking MARC catalog records to two complete electronic journal archives via URLs embedded in the recently approved 856 field (URL:http://ncsulib4.lib.ncsu.edu/drabin/niso_forms); a Web page created by Ann Ercelawn of Vanderbilt University entitled "Tools for Serials Catalogers" (URL: http://www.library.vanderbilt.edu/serials.html); and a Web site of acquisitions and collection development links called "AcqWeb" and maintained by Anna Bell Leiserson (URL:http://www.library.vanderbilt.edu/law/acqs/acqs.html). Web sites of general interest were also mentioned, as MacLennan concluded with a demonstration of the Shakespeare Homepage, containing the complete works of Shakespeare marked-up in HTML, with links to a dictionary of terms used in Shakespeare's plays (URL:http://the-tech.mit.edu/Shakespeare.html).

Having provided participants with an overview of using the Web, the second half of the session, presented by Maggie Rioux, focused on providing an introduction to methods for creating and maintaining Web services. Rioux introduced her topic by using E. B. White's classic children's story, *Charlotte's Web*, as a metaphor for the World Wide Web. Wilbur the pig was saved from injury by Charlotte the spider who spun words ("hypertext") into her web which told the world ("hyperspace") that he was "some pig." Rioux likened Charlotte to the World Wide Web server software which sits in the background waiting for a request from a client, or browser, somewhere in hyperspace. Her spinnarets are the tools needed to create the web, while Wilbur the pig represents the content of the web. Rioux described each of these components in more detail, beginning with Web server software. This is the software that makes Web pages accessible for viewing by browser software. It is available for several operating systems including UNIX, VMS, and Macintosh, although most sites on the Internet use a UNIX server called httpd (Hypertext Transfer Protocol Daemon) due to its ease of configuration, availability as freeware, and capability for handling heavy traffic twenty-four hours a day. In discussing various tools for creating and maintaining a Web site, Rioux described various aspects of HTML in more detail, for example the difference between using logical HTML tags (e.g., title, list) versus tabs for format (e.g., italic, bold), and the need for writing HTML documents that are able to be interpreted by a variety of browsers. Several programs for creating HTML documents were mentioned, including HoTMetaL and Microsoft's Internet Assistant. Another important part of Web authoring is the use of images, including use of images for display within the text (also known as "inline" images) versus creation of hypertext links to images residing as separate files. More advanced Web authoring techniques such as forms-based searches, Common Gateway Interface (CGI) scripts, and new features developed for the next version of HTML were also described.

Rioux offered several pointers about Web content. She emphasized the importance of clear and logical design for Web pages, since they represent the author and his or her affiliated institution to a worldwide community of users. Two sound principles for creating a Web page espoused by Rioux are "think (at least) twice, type once"; and, "quality, quality, quality." Rioux also outlined several other useful suggestions for beginning Web spinners: search other organizations' home pages and "What's New" announcements at Web sites for relevant links; adhere to a regular maintenance schedule to ensure that all hypertext links remain current and useable; access your Web page using several different browsers to ensure the widest possible uniformity and usefulness of information presented in your Web page; clearly label each Web page with information about when it was last updated and who is responsible for it as well as how to contact that person; be prepared to answer requests for help by users of your Web page; and use graphics sparingly. Rioux also emphasized the need to be aware of and adhere to copyright laws. She displayed a prototype copyright statement developed for use by her library to protect information contained in its own Web pages. This statement was designed for inclusion in her library's home page, and was developed in response to an actual case of potential copyright infringement involving information residing on Web pages at MBL/WHOI which another organization wanted to repackage and distribute commercially.

At the close of the presentation, Rioux and MacLennan provided answers to questions from participants. One participant asked for suggestions to deal with a situation in which she is discouraged by her superiors from getting involved in setting up a Web page. Both presenters described their situations which are opposite to this in that they have been encouraged to experiment with this new technology. One suggestion was to request the formulation of policies and procedures for creating and maintaining Web pages. It was also suggested that the participant should seek to educate and inform her superiors about the potential for added value and skills gained in participating in developing web sites. Many participants expressed their appreciation for the thorough and informative handouts. Included in the handouts were several bibliographical references to resources providing more information about the World Wide Web, thus providing another kind of "link" to further discovery and exploration.

NOTE

1. Peter Kent, "Browser Shootout," *Internet World* 6, no. 4 (April 1995): 46-59.

NASIG Tenth Anniversary Conference Panel

Tina Feick

SUMMARY. In 1986, the first annual North American Serials Interest Group (NASIG) conference took place June 22nd through June 26th at Bryn Mawr College in Bryn Mawr, Pennsylvania. Amidst the Gothic towers and the grassy lawns, NASIG became a reality and grew to be a major organization in the library/serials world. In honor of our tenth anniversary in 1995, we go back in time to explore the people, the places, the motivation, and the influences that made NASIG what it is today. *[Article copies available from The Haworth Document Delivery Service: 1-800-342-9678.]*

Following the first successful conference at Bryn Mawr, NASIG enhanced the formula to organize nine additional conferences at various college campuses throughout North America:

- 1st - 1986 - Bryn Mawr College, Bryn Mawr, Pennsylvania
- 2nd - 1987 - Denison University, Granville, Ohio
- 3rd - 1988 - Oglethorpe University, Atlanta, Georgia
- 4th - 1989 - Scripps College, Claremont, California
- 5th - 1990 - Brock University, St. Catharine's, Ontario
- 6th - 1991 - Trinity University, San Antonio, Texas

Tina Feick is Sales Manager–North America for Blackwell's Periodicals Division, Oxford, England.

© 1996 by the North American Serials Interest Group, Inc. All rights reserved.

[Haworth co-indexing entry note]: "NASIG Tenth Anniversary Conference Panel." Feick, Tina. Co-published simultaneously in *The Serials Librarian* (The Haworth Press, Inc.) Vol. 28, No. 1/2, 1996, pp. 23-35; and *Serials to the Tenth Power: Tradition, Technology, and Transformation* (ed: Mary Ann Sheble, and Beth Holley) The Haworth Press, Inc., 1996, pp. 23-35. Single or multiple copies of this article are available from The Haworth Document Delivery Service [1-800-342-9678, 9:00 a.m. - 5:00 p.m. (EST)].

- 7th - 1992 - University of Illinois at Chicago, Chicago, Illinois
- 8th - 1993 - Brown University, Providence, Rhode Island
- 9th - 1994 - University of British Columbia, Vancouver, British Columbia
- 10th - 1995 - Duke University, Durham, North Carolina

In addition, the membership has skyrocketed to over one thousand from three hundred in 1986, and conference attendance has climbed to over six hundred (tenth conference) from two hundred fifty at the inaugural meeting. In 1985/86, there was no budget, no money at all; now, in 1995, there is a healthy balance to ensure ongoing sponsorship of various NASIG activities. Our publications encompass *The NASIG Newsletter*, the conference proceedings (in *Serials Librarian* plus as a separate monograph), and NASIGNET (communication over the Internet). Various committees have been established to carry on the spirit of the organization, such as Student Grant, Horizon Award, Continuing Education, Database and Directory and other committees and task forces. Throughout these ten years, NASIG, even as the organization has grown in numbers and complexity, has striven to maintain the essential ingredient of "people."

The NASIG Tenth Anniversary Panel is comprised of five people that played a major part in the formative years. John Riddick, co-chair of NASIG during 1985/86 and the primary marketing strategist, reminisces about the beginnings of NASIG–why and how NASIG was created. Founder of the United Kingdom Serials Group (UKSG) and advisor to NASIG, John Merriman, current editor of *Serials,* provides insight to the UKSG and how UKSG influenced NASIG. As a publisher and speaker at the inaugural conference, Keith Courtney presents his perspective on NASIG over the past ten years. Tina Feick, president during the second and third years of NASIG, comments on the first conference and the first years with a look to the essence of the organization. Speaking from her extensive background in the library world, Becky Lenzini, co-chair first year, discusses NASIG's place today in the serials information chain. The following pages cover the major points of these five talks.

JOHN RIDDICK, Head, Acquisition Services, Central Michigan University

We celebrate in this conference the tenth anniversary of the birth of the North American Serials Interest Group. A birth suggests an act of creation–an act of love. That might be an apt description of the feelings embraced by a very special group of platform guests, numerous individuals seated in our audience, and others unable to join us this evening. Contrary to common thought, no single individual created NASIG. Rather, it was the amalgamation of ideas mutually shared; of interests jointly held, and common goals sought by several individuals bonding together and working in a spirit of consensus. And thus there was no heroic figure–no bigger-than-life individual. NASIG was conceived and brought forth through the efforts and dedication of many individuals.

By attending the UKSG Conference in 1984, a group of brash Americans marveled at the flow of ideas, talked with publishers, librarians and subscription agents, shared in good drink, and returned to brood upon the experience. With informal meetings in Charleston and Dallas, this group of American serials librarians debated an American styled UKSG. Some asked "why" and others "why not." And so it came to pass that from the latter response NASIG was to emerge.

THE START

Have Americans ever accomplished anything without a committee? Of course not, and so it was with NASIG that a study team was formed to examine the potential of a UKSG-like organization. The exact composition of that group after ten years is difficult to reconstruct–but it certainly included the strong quiet guidance of John Merriman, Becky Lenzini's grace and diplomacy, Marcia Tuttle's enthusiasm, and Tina Feick's organizational ability, but also the help and encouragement of many of you.

From the work of the team emerged several guiding principles– many of which were graciously given or blatantly stolen from the UKSG. These were:

1. Solicit the representation of all members composing the serials information chain and insure an organizational governance which included all the constituencies.
2. Avoid the acceptance of commercial financial support. No handouts and no special interests. One member and one membership payment prevailed.
3. Keep the administrative costs as low as possible thus making possible an inexpensive membership fee to make joining NASIG especially attractive to the younger professional.
4. Construct an organizational administration which would insure a rotation in office and thus eliminate the semblance of an inner administrative clique.
5. Accept as many ideas from the UKSG as possible–after all they had an immensely successful product.
6. Provide some strong learning or educational opportunities wrapped in a fun social environment.

EARLY PROGRAMS

As NASIG took form, a flood of ideas and programs emerged for consideration, some of great value and others of none whatsoever. Obviously the strength of the annual conference and its published proceedings have proven their value. Other aspects such as *The NASIG Newsletter*, the Student Grant program and other ideas have taken root and attained success.

Some of the failures include the job trading program, the house exchange, and the NASIG logo without the country of Mexico. And so in the fullness of time in those early halcyon days, NASIG experienced its ups and downs, but mostly success as a highly complex marketing scheme engaged a growing membership.

MARKETING

The technique of personal contact, hand typed letters, the personal visit or individual telephone call brought in a strong initial membership. The selling of NASIG spread the intent and meaning of NASIG . . . and the process was great fun, especially a Midwestern chap's influential dancing technique.

CONCERNS

Before ending there are two subjects which need to be seriously addressed. First, throughout the initial period of organization and extending even unto today, the relationship of NASIG and the American Library Association (ALA) has been misconstrued. At no time was it our desire to create a substitute or competitor to ALA for the serials' profession. NASIG could not and did not want to assume the essential roles played by ALA in the areas of library school accreditation, legal support of its members, or the representation of its interests to state and national governing bodies. The basic intent of NASIG embraced the offering of a three-day conference for the discussion of serials issues on a level playing field in academic surroundings. It was hoped that NASIG might be a provider of well-informed young professionals ready to move up in their career and to make positive contributions to their national professional organizations.

Finally, we are gathered here to enjoy our tenth birthday. However, have not many of us in this room taken youngsters through their teenage years, a sometimes daunting task? If this analogy holds any truth, may the NASIG leadership in the years which follow be blessed with vigilance, thoughtfulness, and dedication for it is no time to lean on the oars.

JOHN MERRIMAN, Editor, *Serials*

It is wonderful to have this opportunity to return to a NASIG conference. As the roots of NASIG lie with UKSG and being the so-called "grandfather" of NASIG, I wish to reminisce about the beginnings of UKSG and also NASIG.

In 1975, "forklift" librarianship prevailed in the United Kingdom caused by the isolation of librarians. It was obvious that there was little communication among the various parties within the serials industry. With the permission and sponsorship of Richard Blackwell, I organized a serials conference at Christ Church College in Oxford, England. Sixty-nine librarians attended with the feature speaker being Robert Maxwell, the founder of Pergamon Press. The second conference was at Trinity College and was again supported by Blackwell's.

After the success of these two conferences, the United Kingdom Serials Group was formed in 1978. The group was created for all parties involved in the serials information chain, especially as one had to be a certified librarian to be a part of the Library Association. In the beginning the following tenets were in operation: (1) total independence of the UKSG from any other library organization; (2) no barriers to membership; (3) free membership as the conference produced the funding for the organization; and (4) university campuses to be the site of conferences.

Eventually, as the UKSG grew in numbers and complexity, the organization changed to accommodate the needs of the current membership. A membership fee was charged to cover increased expenses. Trade exhibitions were added, but publishers and vendors were still treated as equals within the group. A part-time administrator was hired to handle membership and conference matters. In addition, the UKSG sponsored travelling sideshows to library schools with the purpose of informing the students about the serials information chain. Much effort has been put into publications including the journal *Serials* and various indexes. The major activity continues to be the conference which generally takes place in the Spring of each year. Besides the annual conference, UKSG also participates in organizing the European Serials Conference which will be in Ireland next year (1996).

It was in 1984 that sixteen American librarians, as part of a tour, set off to attend the UKSG Conference at the University of Surrey. The tour's leader abandoned the group at Heathrow Airport, so Marcia Tuttle took the lead. This group, after some assistance, had a wonderful time and came back to the States with the idea of forming a North American counterpart of the UKSG. The "Class of '84" went on to found NASIG and the rest is history.

Both the UKSG and NASIG foster the concept of mutual respect and promote informed debate among the participants of the serials information chain. In this vein, NASIG and UKSG will continue far into the future. Many happy returns on this tenth anniversary and thank you for inviting me to be part of the celebration.

KEITH COURTNEY, Director, Taylor and Francis Ltd.

My association with American librarians really started in earnest in 1984. The place was the University of Surrey, England, and the occasion was the 8th UKSG. It was here that I was "tuttled" by Marcia Tuttle. Little did I realize that my rather boring talk about journal publishing would lead to an invitation to address the inaugural conference of NASIG.

Mind you, I did not at that time give too much thought to what I was going to Bryn Mawr to do; and, by the time I realized it, it was too late to back down. Would anybody in their right mind agree to give a paper on Discriminatory Pricing of British Scholarly Journals for the North American Market?

Imagine my dilemma when I sat down to decide what to say about journal pricing policies. Anyway, who is this chap 'Chuck Hamaker' who is on the program with me? (NOTE: Chuck Hamaker, along with Deana Astle, was awarded the Bowker Award for his research into journal pricing.) Well, I wrote the paper; however, I soon realized that presenting the paper was one thing and answering the difficult questions that would follow had the potential to bring my downfall. I duly gave the paper and sat back to listen to Chuck and thought to myself how glad I was that I had gone first because he raised a number of interesting points which would have stretched me to the limit to give a plausible answer.

The moment of reckoning came, question time. Marcia Tuttle, who was chairing the session, stood up and to my utter relief announced that we had run out of time and lunch was now served. I had survived and I have been paying Marcia ever since.

I suppose that I must have enjoyed it because I returned for more in 1987. The venue was Denison University in Ohio. As a reward for surviving Bryn Mawr, I was appointed Chief Bartender, a position that I was more comfortable to fill. My lasting memory of Denison was cursing the idiot who had left the lights on all night in the men's bathroom, with the windows open. The following morning it was the perfect site for the Entomologists Convention.

The caravan then headed south for Atlanta and Oglethorpe University for the 1988 Conference. At this point I would just like to say that during the many hours of reminiscing over NASIG conferences in order to try and fill a few minutes addressing you, I have to say that I have no recollections of any former speakers or papers presented at previous conferences, but I do have many thoughts on people, informal discussions, and events. In essence, that statement sums up what NASIG is really all about—people and memories.

Oglethorpe was renowned for the "Brits" throwing a late night party which went on to the dawn when the janitor arrived to check out the noise and everybody ran away. That, incidentally, was unofficially declared as the first NASIG fun run. If that was not bad enough, the "rent a mob" returned the following evening.

And so to California and Scripps we went. What a wonderful conference, wonderful venue, and wonderful speakers, although I confess I cannot remember their names. Remember the Acacia trees? It was great fun and I would certainly love to return there.

Soon it was 1990 and NASIG was going "international"—crossing frontiers and even changing money. My very special memory of NASIG at Brock University was the total surprise and indeed embarrassment at being presented with a rather lovely paperweight in recognition of the three years I had just completed on the NASIG Executive Board.

So after five years of NASIG conferences, what was happening to serials? In spite of considerable advances in technology, the 'print-on-paper' journal was still with us. Indeed, the number of titles was actually increasing rather than decreasing. The economic debate continued, library budgets and publishers' pricing were still high on the agenda; but, we were still together as a group, looking for answers and endeavoring to steer the serials industry through turbulent times.

We went from Canada to just North of the Mexican border (San Antonio, Texas) for the 1991 conference. It was becoming increasingly difficult to convince my wife that I really was attending a 'library' conference. Put your hands up if you stayed dry in San Antonio. Who in their right minds would take a river boat trip in a thunderstorm?

Coming from a country (England) that plays cricket, I was extremely surprised when NASIG visited Comisky Park in Chicago in 1992, to see the batsman wielding a rather primitive looking stick and the fielders wearing a huge glove, which I can only assume is to protect their manicured nails. I must tell you that it is just not cricket to catch a ball with anything but bare hands, and I thought baseball was a game for men.

With a visit to Rhode Island in 1993 and a return to Canada (Vancouver) last year, I have to look back and say how fortunate I have been to belong to such a vibrant group as NASIG. How fortunate I have been to have visited so many wonderful places in North America; how fortunate I am to have had so much fun doing it.

So, has anything changed in the last ten years? In publishing there is no doubt that print-on-paper journals continue to survive; indeed, there appears to be no let up in the number of new journals being launched. Papers continue to be submitted at an unprecedented rate and academic editors continue to pressure publishers to publish more. In our experience rejection rates have continued to rise, and with many journals it reaches a point where the editors refuse to reject good quality material. Hence, here comes the pressure to increase pages and to increase frequency with the inevitable increase in price. It does not take much intelligence to understand that if library funding increases by 3 percent and the cost of maintaining a collection increases by 10 percent, then ultimately we have a problem and we have to tackle that problem if we want our industry to survive.

This organization can and should play a significant role in effecting the transition. NASIG is about people, but its particular strength is that its members represent all parts of the serials industry.

Ten years ago at Bryn Mawr I was one of only three publishers at the conference. If there were more, they certainly maintained a low profile and possibly with some justification. The fear amongst publishers in the early days was that this conference was an opportunity for publisher bashing. I am pleased to say that NASIG now has many more publishers as members; indeed, many of us have been bashed and lived to tell the tale. What is more, we publishers have bashed a few librarians and vendors, and NASIG is a better organization for it.

We live in an exciting time, and I do believe that the next ten years will see significant changes in our industry. If we continue to work together as we have in the past ten years, we will have an industry and an organization of which to be proud.

TINA FEICK–Sales Manager–North America, Blackwell's Periodicals Division (Oxford, England)

Going through my files, I came across a letter written by John Riddick. It was addressed to me and was dated 10 September 1984.

In the letter, John invited me to become part of a study group to determine if there were a need for a North American serials group similar to the one in England (UKSG). I was to represent subscription agencies. I was ecstatic; and in accepting his invitation, I never dreamed how dramatically an organization called NASIG would affect my personal and professional life, and that of the library/serials world.

As John has described, many of us went out and promoted the new organization. John's infamous letters travelled the countryside and soon we saw our membership grow as the word was spread. John and I and many others spent long hours on the phone promoting; we needed proof positive that there was a need for a serials group where all parts of the industry could meet and talk together. The response was a resounding "yes," and we were off and running.

In the background, we were also planning the first conference, for that is where we saw our role–to hold a three day conference discussing the serials issues of the day among the various constituencies–librarians, publishers, subscription agencies, automation vendors, authors, readers, editors, etc. From the beginning, the NASIG Study Group felt that we played a different role than the American Library Association. In no way was there ever any intention of competing or replacing ALA. Each organization has its place. I wish to add that neither is NASIG involved in setting nor implementing standards nor are we the arbiters of disputes, that is left for other associations. We are willing, however, to hold a forum where all parties can discuss any issue or concern.

In August 1985, John Riddick, Lenore Wilkas, and I toured various sites in the Philadelphia area. Our plan for the first conference was to have the site near New York City, where the 1986 ALA conference would be held. That way NASIG attendees could easily go on to ALA to which we even provided transportation.

Our Site Selection Committee ended up selecting Bryn Mawr College, not only as it is one of the most beautiful campuses in the Philadelphia area, but also as the dates suited our plan of action. Oh yes, I was appointed chair of the Local Arrangements Committee–at first, a committee of one.

So, we selected a site. Where do you go with no budget/no staff/no volunteers? We created a budget and used registration monies to pay off ongoing expenses. Fortunately, Bryn Mawr had a conference director, who helped us through many a trying moment. In addition, we received valuable assistance from Bryn Mawr College Library–Jane McGarry and Penny Schwind. I was fortunate to have the support of staff within my company and in particular, the support of John Merriman, who was my immediate boss at the time. How wonderful to have an expert at arranging UKSG conferences right within your own organization? I was very lucky.

It is now history that the conference was a smashing success with 251 registrants, though we thought we would only get 150. No one will ever fully know the problems that we encountered. As time goes on, the negatives seem to dissipate, but at the time the problems seemed overwhelming. One point that most of you probably do not know–two weeks before the conference began, we still could not obtain the required $1,000,000 worth of insurance. No one would insure us as we were so new as an organization plus we had no money. I was in total denial about the insurance; I just knew everything would work out. John planned for the worst. Eventually Bryn Mawr, without any charge, arranged for a rider to be put on their policy. What a relief that was!

Just as a reminder of the conference, I have a few slides that were taken by Penny Schwind, the Assistant Director of Technical Services at Bryn Mawr College. What is missing in these slides? The beautiful buildings do not represent the true essence of NASIG– people. People are the essence of NASIG; the synergy that develops when you work within this organization is amazing. We must keep the people energy flowing in order for NASIG to continue to be an important part of our lives.

We learned so much from this first conference. We developed a site selection checklist and a calendar of conference planning activities. We actually took the UKSG checklist and altered and expanded to suit our needs. Each year, we have revised and refined our documentation to ensure that we continue in the NASIG tradition.

During Ann Okerson's tenure as president, NASIG began strategic planning. The first step was determining what NASIG was all about. Under the tutelage of the Association of Research Libraries (ARL), the Executive Board divided up into teams; the teams were given an assignment to draw NASIG. Each of the teams sketched a map of North America with ties to the United Kingdom (UKSG) and several groups placed stick figures, to represent people, across the continent. It was not until the last moment that we noticed that the one factor that binds us together–the journal–was missing from the diagram. So, we quickly drew a "magazine." That point illustrates that what is important within the NASIG organization is the interaction of all the participants.

In those beginning years, other events occurred. We developed a database for membership; we became incorporated; we obtained not-for-profit status; we surveyed the membership to make sure we were meeting the needs of everyone. One important point was the overwhelming need to change the bylaws to permit staggered terms and also for the Vice-President to move into the Presidency slot. The original bylaws resulted in a total change of the Executive Board every year. There was a transition year, 1988/89, where the complete Board stayed in place for another nine months in order for the staggered terms to become effective.

As Keith alluded to in his talk, people from outside the organization saw us as a group of librarians out to bash publishers and vendors. So much so, that the *Library Hotline* in promoting our conference noted that NASIG would be discussing "predatory pricing policies of vendors." In response to this comment, the Executive Board requested that a position statement be developed. Keith Courtney and Rosanna O'Neil wrote the following:

> The North American Serials Interest Group (NASIG), Inc. is an independent organization established to provide for the exchange of information amongst participants of the serials information chain. The membership consists of publishers, librarians, subscription agents and others interested in being a part of this open forum.

It neither represents nor favors by its actions any segment of the information chain. A statement that I hope we continue to abide by forever.

I have one last comment about the people within NASIG. At the second conference at Denison University, Ford LeMay of Yale University stopped me as I was going up the aisle of the auditorium. He said, not knowing me at the time, "Thank you, blue dot," for my badge had a blue dot indicating that I was involved in the planning of the conference. I concluded that conference by reminding everyone to thank the blue dots. So much hard work has gone into the preparation of each conference. Please always remember to THANK THE BLUE DOTS. And, I thank all of you for giving me and this panel an opportunity to share our memories of NASIG.

REBECCA LENZINI–President, Carl Corporation

As we need to move on to other festivities, I will keep my remarks short. It was great to see the slides of Bryn Mawr and be reminded of the exhilarating feelings of that first conference. There are so many positive memories of those beginning times.

Getting NASIG going was an interesting experience. We needed to be so diplomatic in order not to offend nor to be misunderstood. In no way were we ever a threat to the ALA Serials Section. We are totally different organizations, but it was a concern that we addressed and continue to do so.

Well, what are my predictions for the next ten years? The view is very optimistic, certainly based on past performance. Everything was done just right, especially following our well-thought out marketing plan:

1. Target market–We focused our promotion to members of the serials information chain with an initial major push among academic serials librarians.
2. Delivered value for cost–The NASIG Conference continues to have one of the lowest registration fees with housing/food, program, and social activities for $300 or less.
3. Attention to details–This can be seen by all the planning for this conference.
4. Very strong leadership–Our early leaders provided direction that continues today.
5. Meet real need–There was a vacuum within the serials industry that needed a NASIG to pull the various parts together.

Happy tenth birthday and may NASIG have many more!

PLENARY SESSION I: APPROACHING THE PRECIPICE– RE-ENGINEERING THE STRUCTURE OF THE SCHOLARLY INFORMATION UNIVERSE

From Serial Publications to Document Delivery to Knowledge Management: Our Fascinating Journey, Just Begun

Paul Evan Peters

SUMMARY. Experience with internet information resources and services suggests the creative destruction of the classical, paper-based process of scientific and scholarly communication, and of the professions and enterprises that realize that process. A modernized, at least partially network-based process is rapidly, if unevenly, becoming established. The characteristics of an emergent, completely net-

---

Paul Evan Peters is Executive Director of Coalition for Networked Information, Washington, DC.

© 1996 by the North American Serials Interest Group, Inc. All rights reserved.

[Haworth co-indexing entry note]: "From Serial Publications to Document Delivery to Knowledge Management: Our Fascinating Journey, Just Begun." Peters, Paul Evan. Co-published simultaneously in *The Serials Librarian* (The Haworth Press, Inc.) Vol. 28, No. 1/2, 1996, pp. 37-55; and *Serials to the Tenth Power: Tradition, Technology, and Transformation* (ed: Mary Ann Sheble, and Beth Holley) The Haworth Press, Inc., 1996, pp. 37-55. Single or multiple copies of this article are available from The Haworth Document Delivery Service [1-800-342-9678, 9:00 a.m. - 5:00 p.m. (EST)].

work-based process is the subject of a growing number of digital library research and development initiatives. These processes are discussed in the context of the transformation, real and imagined, of the value-chain of productive relationships between authors and readers of intellectual works. *[Article copies available from The Haworth Document Delivery Service: 1-800-342-9678.]*

INTRODUCTION

The contemporary context of "networking" can be summed up in three simple observations:

- The Information Highway is hot.

Although there is ample reason to worry that the Nation is working harder on its information "hype-way" than it is on its information "highway," the fact of the matter is that the US Congress, the Federal Communications Commission, the Clinton Administration, and uncounted numbers of other public and private agencies and actors are hard at work on the laws and regulations, the programs and projects, and the many other things we need to stimulate and manage life and commerce in the new communications environment that will be enabled by wide-spread use of high performance, interactive, digital technologies.

- The Internet is red hot.

Generally speaking, speculative interest in the information highway is being converted into real usage of the Internet, and one of the greatest stories of human immigration is now under way in the Internet. The Internet is the "place" in which for at least five years now the resident population has been joined by an immigrant population equal to its numbers. And the Internet population is not only getting bigger, it is getting much more diverse at the same time. All human communities undergoing these sorts of population pressures face problems with civility and with, in general, what constitutes acceptable behavior, and the Internet community is no exception to this rule.

- The World Wide Web is white hot.

And the hottest thing in the Internet for coming on to two years now is the World Wide Web, a client/server environment that enables proficient as well as expert Internet developers to use capable and affordable as well as powerful and expensive hardware and software platforms to create multi-media networked information resources and services that can be linked to each other and to other resources and services. The World Wide Web has changed the look and feel of the Internet forever, and in so doing it has also raised the expectations and educated the habits of Internet users by the hundreds of thousands, if not millions. Many, perhaps even most, users are now focused on the "content" rather than the "conduit" aspects of the Internet, and they are able and willing to analyze and code the structure of the content that they make available on the Internet.

Another feature of the contemporary scene is the growing number of futurists and social commentators who believe that access to communication networks and digital resources will be as important to social and economic well-being in the 21st century as access to transportation routes and natural resources were in the 19th and 20th centuries. They believe that historians will come to regard the last half of the 20th century as the start of a new "Information Age," which will constitute as distinct and important a period of human development as the Industrial Age and the Agricultural Age did before it. The Internet shows us the way ahead to this new world and away from a world dominated by broadcasting technologies (including "print" broadcasting technologies) that treat everyone the same and telephonic technologies that are optimized for relatively short voice conversations among relatively small numbers of people.

THE LIFE OF THE MIND IN THE INFORMATION AGE

The coming Information Age promises much to the "life of the mind," i.e., the things we do to create, disseminate, and use ideas and their expressions (e.g., words, graphics, and sounds). But we should not take the happy realization of these promises for granted.

Librarians in particular need to translate their long-standing and well-practiced commitment to intellectual freedom and participation, among many other professional principles and skills, into the new "knowledge milieu" generated by these technological, social, and economic developments. We need to take stock of our progress as we enter the Information Age in terms of what that progress, however preliminary, implies for the life of the mind. We also need to plan our next steps with the aim of supporting the life of the mind under these new conditions. It will be some time until we can do a good job at this; just keeping up with technological and related changes is difficult enough. But "practice makes perfect," and there is no better place to begin than with the research, teaching and learning, and community servic emissions of the life of the mind, which are also the missions of the institutions and professions that support that life.

RESEARCH IN THE INFORMATION AGE

We know quite a lot about the impacts of networking and, particularly, networked communications and publications (i.e., "networked information") on the research mission of the life of the mind. Indeed, we know much, much more about the research mission than we do the other two missions. Researchers, research communities, and their funding agents (particularly the science agencies of the federal government) literally invented the type of networking and many of the networked resources and services that the information highway will make commonplace. They were compelled to move in this direction by their need to use information technology to control their ever more complex instrumentation (as well as to visualize and analyze the resulting data), and by their need to share ever more rare and expensive scientific equipment and facilities. However, it is premature, even "reckless," to draw strong conclusions about the life of the mind in the Information Age solely on the basis of researcher and research community experience to-date with networks and networked information. We even still have more to learn about research itself in the Information Age than we have learned so far.

By definition, the way research information is rendered will change in the Information Age: instead of all information being rendered in analog formats (such as printed books and journals, audio and video cassettes, and the like), some (perhaps even most) information will be rendered in digital formats (such as magnetic and optical tapes and disks, servers on local and wide-area networks, and the like). We are already well into the "modernization" of the research communication and publication process by incorporating digital technologies and techniques to improve efficiency and effectiveness. What's more, some well-funded and equipped scientists and scientific communities are making rapid progress with establishing an "emergent" system in which networks and networked information are used throughout their communication and publication process, using network technologies and techniques to drive the research information forward to its actual users rather than to printed pages delivered to those users. But, much more is going on than a change in the way research information is rendered. If such a change was all that was at stake, then libraries and librarians would make short work of it, as they did with microforms, sounds recordings, films, and numerous other format innovations and changes before this one.

At least three other things seem to be going on as a result of the impact of the growth of networks and networked information on research communication and publication. First of all, readers clearly want to use network technologies and techniques to obtain journal articles without having to acquire the associated journal titles, to obtain monograph and report chapters without having to acquire the associated monograph or report titles, and to otherwise reach into the usual packages by which research publications and communications are produced, distributed, and used so as to pluck out just the information they want at just the time they want it. Said otherwise, readers want to use these technologies and techniques to pulverize the packages that publishers, librarians, and even authors have been using to produce and distribute research information. Information products and services are being repackaged, therefore, to cater to this desire. Some commentators have observed that these new products and services point in the direction of future "high volume, low cost / margin" information markets that will function quite differently from the "low volume, high cost / margin" ones that presently serve the research communication and publication process. Network technologies and techniques seem to be having this effect on markets in general. Moreover, where the "main" information market will be found in any given research specialty in the future is a profoundly open question. The rethinking of this question and related macro-marketplace questions is another important thing (the second on this paper's list) that seems to be going on as a result of the rise of networked research communication and publication.

It used to be that individual researchers, organized into "invisible colleges" of interactive and collaborative relationships, were responsible for the "before-market" of proposed and draft findings, publications, and other "informal" communications and publications, that, primarily, commercial publishers, disciplinary societies, and university presses were responsible for the "main-market" of journals, monographs, reports, proceedings, and other "formal" communications and publications, and that a mixed bag of individuals, publishers, academic departments, secondary publishers, libraries, bookstores, photocopy shops, etc., were responsible for the "after-market" of compilations, anthologies, course-readings packs, and other "derivative" communications and publications. In large measure, the costs, profits, and other rewards (including tenure and other forms of recognition) of the entire system of research communication and publication have been generated by the main-market. But, it is by no means certain that this will continue to be true in the networked environment. The rapid emergence of document delivery services, and of products and services that place specific communications or publications in quite different contexts than their authors and publishers originally had in mind, suggest that "back-end" costs, profits, and rewards will be much more important to the system than they have been to-date. The future marketplace for research information might even come to resemble the current market for music, film, and other entertainment, a marketplace in which back-end money (from video rentals, and from cable, hotel, and airplane viewings) accounts for more than half of the revenue earned by the average offering.

The rise of networked preprint services and the surge of interest in them, not only by practitioners of a given research specialty but by others with a stake in that specialty (such as cross-disciplinary researchers and students), demonstrate that the before-market is growing in importance as well. Some commentators have suggested that the traditional main-market will disappear entirely in the future research communication and publication system, because it is responsible for nothing more than packaging strategies and distribution channels that are generally unnecessary and mostly unneeded in the networked environment. This is the third of three things, other than a change in the way research information is rendered, on this paper's list of what's really going on as a result of the impact of networks and networked information on the research communication and publication process: the rethinking of the chain of operations and actors that link authors with readers in this process. It is important to keep in mind that this chain is responsible not only for packaging and distributing research information but for adding intellectual value to that information as well. Network technologies and techniques seriously erode the position of actors in this chain who are involved only in packaging and distribution, but they reinforce the position of those actors who contribute unique intellectual value. They also enable such actors to add new sorts of value to the research communication and publication process, principally by tailoring communications and publications to the specific interests and capabilities of individual researchers and research communities. These new opportunities are consistent with another general effect of network technologies and techniques: they drive markets away from mass production and toward mass customization.

TEACHING AND LEARNING IN THE INFORMATION AGE

We currently know very little about what specific network technologies and techniques have to offer the teaching and learning mission of the life of the mind. Determining this, at all levels of education, has recently become a high priority for both the networking and education (especially, the higher education) communities. It is clear that in the Information Age educational products and services will be delivered via networks as well as via campuses, and that students will access those products and services via workstations as well as via classrooms. It is also clear that information products and services in support of teaching and learning will be accessed and delivered in the same ways. However, the technological platforms needed to realize this vision are still being developed and tested, and the pedagogical justifications for adopting these platforms are still being formulated. Networked teaching and learning are attractive primarily because of the large increase in the number of people who would seem to be able to conveniently avail themselves of educational opportunities over the course of their entire lifetime. Being able to accommodate a larger (and more diverse) number of learners over a longer period of time (i.e., not just when they are young) is a pressing national priority due to normal population pressures (particularly in those regions of the Nation experiencing major in-migrations) and to the rapid rate of change in various job markets. Network technologies and techniques also seem attractive for accessing and delivering educational products and services for the first time in rural and other population-sparse regions of the Nation. But networked teaching and learning will never establish itself if it costs more than conventional approaches or if it produces inferior educational outcomes. This is why pedagogical justifications are now beginning to garner as much attention as delivery systems and access methods. Network technologies and techniques enable relatively more open interaction among students, between students and teachers (among other experts), and between students and the information resources and services that support the course of study. They also allow an individual student to be tested and evaluated as often as he or she finds it useful to her or his learning. And, they can be used to construct certificated programs of study that span the offerings of multiple educational providers. These and other pedagogical opportunities and challenges define the leading edge of work on networked teaching and learning, and they will in short order shed powerful light on the teaching and learning mission of the life of the mind in the Information Age.

COMMUNITY SERVICE IN THE INFORMATION AGE

The community service mission of the life of the mind in the Information Age hinges entirely on the ability of those who live the life of the mind, and of the institutions and professions that support them, to appreciate and contribute to the networking goals and objectives of their situating communities. Investments in network technologies and techniques for research and education communities are frequently justified by the increases in research and educational productivity (increases in benefits as well as decreases in costs) that can be attributed to those investments. These investments can be linked to the community service mission by explaining how increases in research and educational productivity translate into progress on a given community's networking goals and objectives. This can be done, for instance, by drawing the connection between research and educational productivity, on the one hand, and economic development and competitiveness, government accessibility and accountability, community and individual identity and heritage, and even retail and entertainment services, on the other. Those who live the life of the mind, and the institutions that support them, have to become adept not only at explaining what investments in network technologies and techniques mean for research and for teaching and learning, but also what they mean in terms that resonate with the community of which they are part.

THE FUTURE OF KNOWLEDGE MANAGEMENT

In summary, we may (think we) know a lot about the impact of network technologies and techniques on the three missions of the life of the mind, and of the institutions and professions that support the life of the mind, but any honest assessment must conclude that we know much less than we need to if we are to manage the scientific and scholarly communication and publication process in this new environment at least as well as we currently do. Librarians, publishers, and other experts in knowledge management have been trying to use networks like the Internet for these purposes for not even ten years yet. This is not enough time, to say the least, for the full promise of network technologies and techniques to reveal itself, let alone for that promise to be proven and made widely available. What's more, as mentioned above, the population of the networked environment is (at least) doubling every year. The communication and publication priorities and activities of this rapidly expanding community will provide the strategies, resources, and services that need to be addressed by the new knowledge management system. Networked information programs should include assessment and evaluation components that capture and analyze these user strategies, resources, and services. And the results of this process should provide insight for and guidance to the development of the sorts of value-adding strategies, resources, and services that only institutions and organizations can provide (due to their scope, expense, or some other characteristic).

While the future of knowledge management will flow in large measure from what users do with network technologies and techniques, it will be determined by an enormous number of other variables as well. Right now a lot of the drive behind networking is coming from the attention that national governments are paying to the "Global Information Infrastructure." In due course (perhaps as soon as the next year or two) this attention will likely wane. The interest being shown by telecommunications, broadcasting, media, publishing, and many other industries is currently greater than it has been in over fifty years. No one knows for sure whether this interest will increase or decrease in the months and years ahead. Unless "Moore's Law" is repealed, hardware will continue to give us much more power for much less money. But, it is an open question whether software will advance apace to make that power usable and to manage the exploding complexity of networked resources and services. The future does not have to be the same as the past in these and many other respects, and the future of knowledge management will go in a very different direction if historical patterns change radically. The future of specific knowledge management institutions and professions, like libraries and librarians, is also intertwined with that of other institutions which may (as in higher education) or may not (as with state and local governments) be themselves involved in knowledge management. And, even though the roles of all of these institutions with respect to basic knowledge production, distribution, and utilization functions in society remain to be determined, it is a safe bet that they will be very different from what they are at present.

One good way to aid thinking about a future with so many variables is to formulate a set of narrative scenarios, each of which tells a defensible, but not necessarily convincing, story about how the future "turned out," and all of which, taken together, cover as wide a range of alternative outcomes as possible. A set of four such scenarios, written from the specific perspective of higher education institutions and their libraries, is attached. These scenarios can be summarized as follows:

- Another Marketplace for Global Enterprises

This scenario images a future in which knowledge management is but one marketplace, and a relatively minor one at that, targeted by large, global enterprises that seem to compete with each other but which have long since mostly retreated to their respective areas of strength, and to defending their positions, rather than creating new value, in those areas.

- Mass Customization for and by Individuals

This scenario imagines a future in which knowledge management is a highly individualized activity performed primarily by (ad hoc teams of) people working on their own and affiliating themselves as needed with a broad and frequently changing array of very flexible and tightly focused institutional and organizational structures and processes.

- Knowledge Guilds Reign Supreme

This scenario imagines a future in which knowledge management is primarily the responsibility of scholarly and scientific societies that have in general succeeded in leveraging their traditional role in assessing, recognizing, and rewarding excellence into major new roles as providers of the network servers used by their members, and as managers of actual research and education programs and their budgets.

- Ivory Towers in Cyberspace

This scenario imagines a future in which knowledge management is primarily the responsibility of higher education institutions and their libraries that have in general parlayed their considerable experience with networking and their near-monopoly position as proven providers of advanced research and education services into an even stronger position in the networked environment.

DIFFERENTIAL RATES OF CHANGE

Why some people and communities change more quickly than others is a difficult question that calls out for answers regardless of whether the focus is on the impacts of networks and networked information on the research, teaching and learning, and community service missions of the life of the mind, and of the institutions and professions that support the life of the mind, or on speculative, but defensible, scenarios of the future of knowledge management in society. No matter how emotionally satisfying they may be to invoke, we should not rely solely on stereotypes like "so and so is unable to change" or "those people are threatened by the mere idea of change" to explain differential change rates. Even though such stereotypes often have some basis in fact, they do not offer useful guidance regarding how to encourage or to facilitate change. They imply instead that change can be made only by replacing the people involved, and such implications are rarely more than wishful thinking. Differences in the degree of access that different people and communities have to network technologies and techniques provide a much more adequate way to explain why some of those people and communities are changing faster than others. But a given person or community can be positively disposed toward change and have the means to change at its disposal and still exhibit a slow rate of change from the existing analog toward the emerging digital system of communication and publication.

The reason why this is the case is that different people and communities are focused on different system performance factors, and they will not change from one system to another until they can see that the new system is clearly superior to the old one in the performance areas with which they are most concerned. For instance, some people and communities value ease-of-use above all other performance factors; they will not change until they are sure that the new system is easier to use than the existing one. Other people and communities value accuracy and precision above all other knowledge management system performance factors; they are willing to run the risk that the information they are receiving is not as timely or as comprehensive as it could be in order to rest assured that it is accurate and relevant to their interests. Still others place the highest value on timelines, and they are drawn to new knowledge management systems that offer superior performance in that area. The current Internet information environment cannot be said fairly to offer superior performance across the entire spectrum of factors of concern to various people and communities; far from it. Until it does, many people and communities will show interest in and be willing to experiment with network technologies and techniques, but they will be not be willing to commit to using them in any serious, binding way.

CONCLUSION

The ultimate test of whether network technologies and techniques make things better or worse for the life of the mind, and the institutions and professions that support the life of the mind, in the Information Age is whether they allow us to close the gap between creators and users of intellectual works. We should not rush to judgment regarding this extremely complicated and important matter. And we will not find the answer to this question by worrying about what the impact of these technologies and techniques will be on knowledge management institutions and professions. The two most basic questions that all users ask about networks are who and what can I find on them? We need to work as hard as we can to make sure that the answers to those questions are "all the people that you want to reach" and "all the resources you want to use." But we also need to keep our minds open to the surprises ahead, and to the possibility that network technologies and techniques will not always be the right tools for the right job. We need to continue on our fascinating journey, just begun.

SCENARIO A:
ANOTHER MARKETPLACE FOR GLOBAL ENTERPRISES

Although government efforts to stimulate the development of a ubiquitous, high-performance, and affordable Global Information

Infrastructure (GII) were very successful in the last half of the 1990s, and the telecommunications industry continued to make steady progress across the entire front of related technologies and markets, the scholarly and scientific communication and publication process has become even more concentrated into and dominated by large, commercial firms than it was before these developments. This is due in part to the high cost and complexity of configuring and operating servers capable of reliably delivering a common, very high (as compared with other GII applications) level of service to all points on the very complicated and ever-changing fabric of networks that constitute the GII. It is also significantly due to the fact that commercial firms were willing and able to continue investing in networked information research and development long after the financial and other resources of government agencies, higher education institutions, and scholarly and scientific societies, among other non-commercial actors, had been exhausted.

In general, higher education institutions have not recovered from their financial and political lows of the 1990s, and most such institutions are very much smaller and more dependent on tuition revenues than they were before the onset of these difficulties. The flow of research dollars and talent from such institutions to the corporate sector that started in the 1980s and became a virtual flood in the 1990s has re-enforced the influence of commercial publishers in strengthening both technical and legal measures for protecting intellectual property. In addition, only large, multi-national firms have the resources to understand and observe the complex local "content" and "culture" rules and regulations that many nations, and even some states in the United States, have enacted.

The programs of higher education libraries are carefully crafted to serve the particular interests of their parent institutions, reflecting the priority-consciousness of those institutions, but inter-library programs still extend the coverage of library budgets and the reach of library services. Higher education libraries are very involved in the organization of scholarly and scientific information and in the training and support of scholars and scientists, and both activities are widely recognized as essential for the cost-effective acquisition and utilization of networked information in this commercialized environment. Selected commercial publishers and higher education libraries co-operate in the funding and operation of a consortium of facilities for preserving networked resources, but most publishers do not see the need for and do not participate in this effort.

SCENARIO B:
MASS CUSTOMIZATION FOR AND BY INDIVIDUALS

Government efforts to stimulate the development of a ubiquitous, high-performance, and affordable Global Information Infrastructure (GII) were wildly successful in the last half of the 1990s, and the telecommunications industry has continued to make steady progress across the entire front of related technologies and markets. Access to networked resources and services is now commonplace, and such resources and services cost less than most users paid for cable television *and* their television sets as recently as the early 1990s. The first widespread, commercially successful applications of artificial intelligence now enable these users to configure and stretch the performance of their individual hardware and software platforms to interact with a spectacularly heterogeneous and distributed network environment.

In general, higher education institutions did not recover from their financial and political lows of the 1990s, and the most successful of the ones that did now concentrate almost exclusively on a relatively small number of disciplines and subject areas. Many individual scholars and scientists affiliate with specific home institutions, but many more prefer to affiliate with institutions on a project by project or a course by course basis and they engage in many such ad hoc affiliations at the same time. Most, if not all, scholars and scientists are also involved in the advanced research and educational activities and offerings of the large and still growing set of new virtual institutions and organizations that emerged in step with the growth of the GII. Student preferences and behaviors show a similar pattern, as most choose the certificated offerings of a variety of advanced educational service providers rather than the degree offerings of a single provider. The higher education institutions that do best in this environment are not only those that are the most focused; they are the ones that have been able to leverage their historic reputations for quality into a competitive edge against the unproven capacities and performances of a large and still-growing set of alternative providers.

Higher education libraries have mainly suffered the fates of their parent institutions. But, many have drawn upon their long tradition of inter-library cooperation to consolidate their resources and services, and some have even merged into subject-defined consortia. Although most authors retain personal control of their intellectual property, these consortia are generally quite effective at negotiating very favorable use terms and conditions for the communities that they serve, and some consortia even function as repositories and service agencies for the disciplines and subject areas that they cover. All higher education libraries are intimately involved in organizing access to networked resources and services, and they routinely provide evaluative as well as descriptive information about such resources and services. They also have very active and well-respected preservation programs which they try, with uneven success, to leverage into the early deposit and management of the works of particularly well-regarded authors.

SCENARIO C:
KNOWLEDGE GUILDS REIGN SUPREME

Although government efforts to spur the development of a ubiquitous, high-performance, and affordable global information infrastructure waned in the last half of the 1990s, the telecommunications industry has continued to make steady progress on providing very attractive technologies and strategies for building mission-oriented, wide-area networks. As a result, networks that serve specific, carefully defined industries and other communities of interest have proliferated. Applications housed in these networks inter-operate across network boundaries in accord with bilateral and occasionally multi-lateral agreements and partnerships. The technological price / performance of server and client workstations has continued to improve in step with historical trends, and most scholars and scientists now routinely access a rich array of networked resources and services through very powerful client workstations. However, the complexity of configuring and operating the server workstations that house those resources and provide those services, together with the strain of keeping up with the frequently changing technical requirements of connecting to and communicating with individual (sets of) networks, has ruled in favor of most servers being built and operated by organizations rather than individuals.

Scholarly and scientific societies have generally succeeded in leveraging their traditional role in assessing, recognizing, and rewarding excellence into a major new role as the key providers and operators of the network server(s) used by their members. They also usually jointly own the intellectual property they manage with the creators of that intellectual property, and many are now very actively involved in formulating and managing actual research and educational programs and their budgets. Higher education institutions have struggled to recover from their financial and political lows of the 1990s, and the ones that have succeeded the best now concentrate almost exclusively on the needs and capacities of a relatively clearly defined and generally proximate geographic area. Most institutions subscribe and integrate access to numerous subject-oriented networks, but they do not generally control access to the resources and services available through those networks.

Higher education libraries have generally followed the course of their parent institutions. On campus, these libraries manage the complex portfolio of contracts and payments that govern access to and use of the networked information resources and services provided by scholarly and scientific societies. They take a special interest in enabling and supporting access by students and across disciplines at their parent institutions. This role entails the development of access strategies and mechanisms that are tailored to interests and abilities of these individuals, who are not practitioners of particular disciplines or members of particular scholarly and scientific societies. Many higher education libraries have also evolved into very significant regional players in the provision of scholarly and scientific information to the full range of research and educational institutions. On a selective but very real basis, moreover, individual higher education libraries have formed partnerships with groups of scholarly and scientific societies to preserve the works distributed by those societies, and such libraries have frequently been able to leverage this role to the general advantage of the communities and regions that they serve. But, in general, the societies themselves have assumed responsibility for preservation.

SCENARIO D:
IVORY TOWERS IN CYBERSPACE

Government efforts to spur the development of a ubiquitous, high-performance, and affordable global information infrastructure waned in the last half of the 1990s, but the telecommunications industry has continued to make steady if uneven progress. Although the technological price/performance of server and client workstations continued to improve in step with historical trends, the complexity of configuring and operating these workstations together with the cost and complexity of network connectivity ruled in favor of most scientists and scholars gaining access to these workstations through their affiliations with or employment by research institutions. These institutions recovered from their financial and political lows of the 1990s to build the Global Research and Education Network (GREN) and to strongly reinforce their traditional position as nearly monopoly providers of advanced research services and educational experiences.

The GREN is modeled upon the prior experience of these institutions with the global Internet, and it technically inter-operates with the Internet. Full participation in the GREN, however, requires joint ownership of the intellectual property produced by GREN member institutions as well as the sharing of costs, user support, and standards development with the GREN community. Intellectual property is used and reused within GREN member institutions according to academic rather than commercial protocols and standards. Access to intellectual property outside of GREN member institutions, and access to the intellectual property of GREN member institutions by non-members, is through specific project and partnership agreements, or through a complex variety of commercial discovery, access, and use product and service offerings. The GREN is used to provide access to GREN resources and services well beyond the confines of GREN member facilities and campuses but always as the result of the direct involvement of one or more GREN member institutions.

The libraries of GREN member institutions now play a major new role in the creation, production, and distribution of new intellectual works. This role developed in step with the growth of "life-cycle" information resource management principles, policies, and practices in GREN member institutions. Libraries continued to play their historically important roles in acquisition, organization, and utilization of scholarly and scientific information, updated to reflect the fact that most of these activities are now done in an inter-institutional context among GREN members and entail the development of "locator" and "helper" network servers and services rather than the building of individual institutional collections and the direct provision of user support per se. The libraries of GREN member institutions are also deeply involved in the preservation of not only scholarly and scientific but administrative information.

The ACM Electronic Publishing Plan and Interim Copyright Policies

Peter J. Denning

SUMMARY. Publishing has reached an historic divide. Ubiquitous networks, storage servers, printers, and document and graphics software are transforming the world from one in which only a few publishing houses print and disseminate works, to one in which any individual can print or offer for dissemination any work at low cost and in short order. This poses major challenges for publishers of scientific works and for the standard practices of scientific peer review. The Association for Computing Machinery (ACM) aims to be one of the first scientific society publishers to cross the divide. ACM has embarked on an ambitious electronic publication plan, co-authored by Peter Denning and Bernard Rous, Deputy Director of ACM Publications, and has established new copyright policies to accompany it.

For the past three years, the ACM Publications Board has been developing its vision for the future of publication in the electronic age and a program to achieve it. We envisage a diminishing role for print journals and exciting new programs around an ACM digital

---

Peter J. Denning is Chair of the ACM Publications Board. He was formerly the editor-in-chief of the ACM Communications and was president of ACM 1980-82. He is Associate Dean for computing in the School of Information Technology and Engineering at George Mason University, where he is also Chair of the Computer Science Department and Director of the Center for the New Engineer.

© Copyright 1995 by ACM, Inc. Permission to copy and distribute this document is hereby granted provided that this notice is retained on all copies and that copies are not altered.

[Haworth co-indexing entry note]: "The ACM Electronic Publishing Plan and Interim Copyright Policies." Denning, Peter J. Co-published simultaneously in *The Serials Librarian* (The Haworth Press, Inc.) Vol. 28, No. 1/2, 1996, pp. 57-62; and *Serials to the Tenth Power: Tradition, Technology, and Transformation* (ed: Mary Ann Sheble, and Beth Holley) The Haworth Press, Inc., 1996, pp. 57-62.

library and new copyright practices. As we move aggressively into electronic publishing, we will preserve and extend the traditional openness of ACM publications in the new media. Authors and readers should find the new framework at least as hospitable as the traditional one.

Publishing has reached an historic divide. Ubiquitous networks, storage servers, printers, and document and graphics software are transforming the world from one in which only a few publishing houses print and disseminate works, to one in which any individual can print or offer for dissemination any work at low cost and in short order. This poses major challenges for publishers of scientific works and for the standard practices of scientific peer review.

The scientific publishing tradition, in which ACM founded its publication program, has two central tenets. The first is that manuscripts are published only after careful and deliberative review by experts. The second tenet is that every published paper is a permanent member of the library of all scientific literature. In this tradition, a journal paper passes through the four phases of preparation, review and revision, publication processing, and archiving and indexing. In the new practices that are arising in the Internet, a moment of publication occurs with posting on a home page and is much sooner than the moment of imprimatur given by an editor who accepts the paper after successful review. Authors invite comments on their papers posted in this manner, and some will produce improved versions after official publication.

Although less visible, the policies and practices of archiving and indexing are as critical as publishing. A society's imprint would be worthless without reasonable assurances that the published work will be preserved for posterity and that readers can locate the work without having to locate the author. Even though digital libraries will offer new possibilities for archiving and indexing, the responsibility of the society to assure the archiving and indexing of its own authors' materials will not diminish.

ACM has a broad range of programs to disseminate information in various forms to people who can use it. ACM's publication program includes the traditional journals of scholarly research ("Track 1"). It includes magazines and other services specifically designed to communicate with those who develop computing hardware, software, and services ("Track 2"). ACM's strategy is based on two principles:

- ACM is a membership organization charted to promote the free flow of information about information technology not only among members but to the public.
- The value that ACM members will be willing to pay for will be in the form of services, not copyrighted information objects.

Consistent with these principles, ACM expects to realize most of its revenue from three principal, value-added businesses:

- Guided access to literature through search and access to the ACM Digital Library. Individual members can be notified of new entries matching their profiles. Nonmembers can obtain access licenses or pay per item retrieved.
- Continuing education through professional knowledge certificate programs. These programs are designed to make available the information donated by authors for further education of wider groups of people.
- Conferences, including new forms on Internet.

ACM's publications strategy is designed to facilitate all three businesses. The technological heart is the digital database of all ACM literature. The strategic directions are:

- Establish an ACM digital library database containing the entire ACM literature in SGML formatted files.
- Acquire and process all manuscripts into SGML format for storage in the database and for rapid translation into printer's codes. (Operational summer 1995)
- Establish tools that support review processes so that the turn-around time will normally be under 2 months and the reviewing load of any given individual does not exceed that person's capacity. (Experimental version operational by end 1995)
- Maintain the health and vitality of the tradition Track 1 research-oriented publications by constantly repositioning them, by introducing new ones, and by offering electronic access.
- Expand the line of Track 2 publications for practitioners and developers.

- Unleash the creativity of the SIGs and other elements of ACM to experiment intensively with prototypes of new services that would be of value to members and authors.
- Work closely with libraries and institutional members to facilitate the dissemination of ACM works to their users and employees.
- Design and implement a professional knowledge program that offers reading programs in selected areas and certificates of completion of those programs.

COPYRIGHT POLICIES

Under the traditional ACM copyright policies, documents were considered as property whose value had to be protected by release fees and permissions. Authors did not mind transferring copyright to ACM, since ACM was an author's principal agent for bringing material to readers; copyright transfer was a reasonable price to pay for dissemination. ACM allowed authors to retain the right to reuse any portion of the work in a future work with only a proper citation to the ACM published version. Many of these assumptions are changing in the Internet. It is cheap and easy to copy an electronic document and thus nearly impossible to protect an electronic file as property. Authors are beginning to post manuscripts on their home pages and servers, making it seem to them that publishers are less relevant as agents of dissemination; the primary functions of a publisher now are to give an imprimatur of quality to a work, to find more readers than the author might find alone, and to maintain archives of ACM works. New situations not anticipated in the original policies have posed new questions. One is whether posting a document on an Internet server constitutes prior publication and thereby disqualifies the author from submitting it to ACM for publication. Another is whether an author who implants a hyperlink to a copyright document is effectively incorporating that document and needs to get the copyright holder's permission.

The ACM publications board has developed and issued a set of new copyright policies. They are labeled "interim policies" because they are subject to review and revision as we gain experience with them. As in the past, the ACM will hold the copyright on items it accepts for publication; this allows it to freely disseminate on the author's behalf without having to check with the author in each instance, and it will protect the ACM digital library as a whole from expropriation by those who might attempt to reproduce the same service for free. The principal assumptions are:

1. ACM grants authors liberal rights, including the right to reuse the copyright material in any future work provided that proper citation of the copyright work is given, and the right to post preprints and revisions on home pages for noncommercial purposes and personal use by others in the Internet.
2. ACM will define and store definitive versions of works, including eventually dynamic objects, warranting them against unauthorized changes. Authors will be asked to store the definitive versions on ACM servers with pointers from their personal collections.
3. Anyone obtaining an ACM copyright object may use that object only for personal use unless explicit permission has been granted for other use. This limits third parties (i.e., non-authors) from distributing ACM materials freely in the Internet without ACM permission.
4. Libraries will have general licenses that permit their users to examine ACM materials and print copies for personal use.
5. Authors' employers will have permission to distribute copies of their works within their organizations.
6. A link to another document is treated as a citation. It is a matter between the individual attempting access via the link and the copyright holder what fee, if any, must be applied. An author does not have to obtain permission to include a link.
7. Servers from which ACM copyrighted objects can be downloaded must display to browsers a general notice advising that copyright materials are posted and are subject to copyright limitations specified by their individual holders.
8. ACM assumes that most revenues will come primarily from value added services such as database access, conferences, and professional knowledge certificates. Copyright release fees will not figure significantly in business plans.

NOTE

Denning, Peter J., and Bernard Rous. 1995. "ACM Electronic Publishing Plan and Interim Copyright Policies." Communications of ACM (April), p97ff. These documents plus an author's guide are available on the server <http://www.acm.org/pubs>.

PLENARY SESSION II: COPYRIGHT CAMPS– ELECTRONIC FAIR USE IN THE CROSSFIRES

Copyright in an Electronic Age: Making New Vintages from the Great Old Grapes

Isabela Hinds

Workshop Presenter

Gale Teaster-Woods

Recorder

SUMMARY. New technology alone does not promote or hinder the progress of science and the useful arts. Technology is a democratizing influence, allowing more management by individuals and creat-

---

Gale Teaster-Woods is Head of the Serials Acquisitions and Cataloging Department, Dacus Library, Winthrop University, Rock Hill, SC.

© 1996 by the North American Serials Interest Group, Inc. All rights reserved.

[Haworth co-indexing entry note]: "Copyright in an Electronic Age: Making New Vintages from the Great Old Grapes." Teaster-Woods, Gale. Co-published simultaneously in *The Serials Librarian* (The Haworth Press, Inc.) Vol. 28, No. 1/2, 1996, pp. 63-68; and *Serials to the Tenth Power: Tradition, Technology, and Transformation* (ed: Mary Ann Sheble, and Beth Holley) The Haworth Press, Inc., 1996, pp. 63-68. Single or multiple copies of this article are available from The Haworth Document Delivery Service [1-800-342-9678, 9:00 a.m. - 5:00 p.m. (EST)].

ing the need for more precision on the part of all constituencies involved in the publishing system. How do publishers and librarians realize the promise of these changes without sacrificing their valuable roles in selection, validation, dissemination, and preservation? How do publishers and librarians advance the promise of the digital environment in which all intellectual properties, text, photographs, images, software, and sound become interchangeable objects? Can publishers and librarians ally in this new environment to ensure great new vintages? *[Article copies available from The Haworth Document Delivery Service: 1-800-342-9678.]*

Isabela Hinds, Director of Professional Relations for the Copyright Clearance Center, Inc. (CCC), gave the publisher's view of copyright during her presentation at the tenth annual NASIG conference. She began her presentation on copyright by reinforcing a statement made by Peter J. Denning, Chair of the Association for Computing Machinery (ACM) Publications Board. According to Denning, ACM's publishing future rests on the organization's ingenuity, creativity, and its ability to add value. Hinds believes that many other publishers are looking in these same directions. Hinds also reiterated a statement made by Ann L. Okerson, Director of the Office of Scientific and Academic Publishing for the Association of Research Libraries. Okerson said that the point of copyright is to promote the progress of science and the useful arts. According to Hinds, it will be important to keep this point in perspective in order to get through the next forty or fifty years of evolution of the copyright law.

Copyright, as set down in Title 17, is a monopoly right and, as stated by Hinds, is "a fairly jolting statement" for individuals of the 20th century to accept. Intellectual property is fragile and the value of that property is especially important to the scholarly publishing area. Through copyright, the quality of intellectual property in scholarly publishing can be protected, developed, nurtured, and the peer review and editing processes can take place. These processes, however, would not be able to work successfully if some flexibility or "wiggle room" did not exist. Fair use in the copyright law serves the purpose of providing that "wiggle room." Fair use is the defense that keeps copyright's monopoly right from constraining the system. This "wiggle room" needs to be preserved.

Section 107 of the copyright law provides fact-specific criteria for determining fair use. However, it also leaves a great deal of discretion to individuals involved in dissemination of information. Fair use relies on an individual's ability to think, make judgments, differentiate among activities, and take risks about information. The rules developed in Title 17 were developed 20 years ago when the copyright law was revised. It is important not to get so caught up in the rules that the reasons for the rules are overlooked. For example, the fair use limit of five copies is a somewhat arbitrary number, but the principle behind the number which states that a certain number of uses is fair is important.

One problem with copyright compliance that Hinds sees is that seeking copyright compliance is a cumbersome process. CCC was created as a collaborative effort among authors, publishers, and users. Better efficiency in copyright compliance was one of the problems addressed in this effort. One of the daunting possibilities of authors retaining copyright, an idea expressed by Okerson, is that the process of obtaining copyright could become even more complicated. Copyright transactions can now be reported online through the CCC's World Wide Web site. Using the online process for reporting copyright transactions will save time and labor for both the user and CCC. Hinds referred to two aspects of the system she considers important. First, the system is voluntary. The user chooses whether or not to go to the Web site and once there, whether to use the information it contains. Second, it is a trusted system. Over one million titles are included in the database. The information needed to complete the transaction, for example price, is included. The user is also trusted to pay the bill for the copyright permission.

An added advantage to this online process is that it provides CCC and publishers with information on the relationship between the number of requests for materials and the number of aborts to these requests. Transactions can be aborted at the point where the user checks the price of an article. Royalties are set by publishers in the CCC system, due to anti-trust considerations and other laws. CCC has no impact on establishing royalty fees.

Publishers, libraries, and users view Section 108 of the copyright law in different ways. Section 108 contains the seven privileges specific to libraries. The publishing community views this as a powerful set of privileges. Libraries are viewed as having powerful institutional and collective support behind them and being much more influential than a single user. However, experts in copyright from the library field do not believe that Section 108 precludes any restrictions placed on libraries by Section 107.

How far can libraries and librarians "push the envelope" and not unbalance the system? Unfortunately, not very far. Journal subscription rates are falling at about 6% per year. While this may sound like a small percentage, the cumulative effect can be disastrous for the publishing community. Paper costs and other expenses are rising. These trends are not comforting. In the midst of these concerns, it is understandable that fair use copies are viewed by publishers as "giveaways." Publishers consider these uncompensated copies. One reason that fair use is being examined so closely at this point is that nobody knows how much uncompensated copying is done. Hinds compared these uncompensated copies with the "leakage" that occurs in other markets, such as the cellular phone market and credit card transactions. This leakage is a cost that publishers want to understand, as they review all of their costs during this period of subscription reduction. Publishers are investigating encryption as a possible method for reducing leakage. But encryption is absolute and Hinds expressed concern that encryption of documents may affect fair use activities.

Hinds discussed some of the unresolved issues discussed at the fair use conference. The fair use conference has been conducted fairly informally under the auspices of the Intellectual Property Working Group. The informality is intentional because it enables discussions of copyright issues without bureaucratic involvement by the federal government. The meetings have been in process since September 1994, and have a balance among the interested constituencies of rights holders and users. Meetings are held once a month, and distance and expense can be prohibitive for some interested organizations. Therefore, it is a small group. It is, however, growing and interest from groups representing music, museums, and video media are becoming part of the conference meetings. This is important because copyright discussions need to focus on more than copyright for print-on-paper publications. Copyright law covers all media. As stated by Hinds, "the big boys are in," referring to what she called "Hollywood interests." It is important that the interests of scholarly research do not get lost in the quagmire of the "Hollywood interests."

Hinds believes that it is important for the group to finish its work expeditiously. Unavoidably, the membership of the group will change as members drop out or new members are added, and this could affect the continuity of the group's work.

Although the White Paper from the group has yet to be published, the meetings have been beneficial. The discussions at the meetings have emphasized practical issues in their focus on fair use and copyright. The fate of new technologies, developed, but not covered and protected by existing interpretations of the copyright law, has been a focus of several meeting discussions. Distance learning and electronic reserves are examples of some of these new technologies. While recognizing the rights of authors and publishers to withhold use permission, Hinds believes that it is necessary to develop reasonable systems of acquiring copyright permission.

The arena of site licensing has been an additional focus. Contracts will increasingly be substituted for copyright. Licensing has the potential for narrowing fair use. At one of the conference meetings, Robert Henderick of Educom asked if everything could be licensed forever at a nickel, would a fair use problem still exist? The librarians in the group said yes, because more is at stake than just an economic issue.

Problems related to copyright for multimedia packages have also been discussed. When intellectual property is digitized, it is still the same stream of bits. However, multimedia packages have distinctive properties and create their own copyright problems. For example, if a user has copyright permission to show a video but has textual material to go with it, which set of copyright guidelines pertains? What if the showing of the video and use of the text material is part of a distance learning project?

Although many unresolved problems still exist, there are signs of progress. An informal set of guidelines has been established for multimedia. There has been agreement in developing guidelines for copies made for preservation purposes. In the area of translation of information into digital format for the visually impaired, fair use seems to be moving in the direction of "fair use is good use."

Discussion and argument related to the number of digital copies of software programs that are produced in the process of manufacturing commercial software could have been lengthy and mind boggling. The fair use conference has decided to accept the fact that these copies exist as a "byproduct of transient activity."

Many obstacles and opportunities exist as information is transferred from print and other more traditional formats into digital format. Discussions of copyright issues will be at the center of many of these obstacles and opportunities. Not all information will be in digital format in five years, but constituencies are becoming serious about the quality, business, technology, and copyright issues relating to electronic information.

Whose Work Is It Anyway?
Perspectives on the Stakeholders
and the Stakes
in the Current Copyright Scene

Ann Okerson

SUMMARY. Today the subject of copyright, one that five years ago did not fill up even a small room at such meetings as this, draws standing room only audiences. Why has copyright become so compelling? This talk considers the groups that have a particular interest and substantial activity in the current copyright discussion: the U.S. government; the public interest/user groups, often represented by the library associations; author interests (e.g., National Writers' Union, Authors' Guild); and the publishing industry. Why they care, how they express their interests, and a modest attempt to suggest where the activity might take, form the center of this paper. *[Article copies available from The Haworth Document Delivery Service: 1-800-342-9678.]*

Copyright has been a vexing topic throughout the centuries. Michael Giesecke in his book entitled *Der Buchdruck in der freuhen Neuzeit*, published in Germany in 1991, writes, "From the beginning, printing is accompanied by complaints over the effects of illegal reprinting which God will surely punish and which is seemly for no honorable Christian man." Giesecke is writing about

---

Ann Okerson is Director of the Office of Scientific and Academic Publishing, Association of Research Libraries, Washington, DC.

© 1996 by the North American Serials Interest Group, Inc. All rights reserved.

[Haworth co-indexing entry note]: "Whose Work Is It Anyway? Perspectives on the Stakeholders and the Stakes in the Current Copyright Scene." Okerson, Ann. Co-published simultaneously in *The Serials Librarian* (The Haworth Press, Inc.) Vol. 28, No. 1/2, 1996, pp. 69-87; and *Serials to the Tenth Power: Tradition, Technology, and Transformation* (ed: Mary Ann Sheble, and Beth Holley) The Haworth Press, Inc., 1996, pp. 69-87. Single or multiple copies of this article are available from The Haworth Document Delivery Service [1-800-342-9678, 9:00 a.m. - 5:00 p.m. (EST)].

the dawn of the age of printing. But even before that St. Columba, in the sixth century in Ireland, copied a Psalter and was told by the arbiter to give it up. The king who heard the case said, "As the calf belongs to the cow, so the copy belongs to the book." Columba went on to fight a war about this. He left Ireland and moved to Scotland where he is thought to have discovered the Lochness monster, a story that shows that copyright can have numerous unanticipated social consequences.

Today more often than not, our information about copyright comes through the popular press (see Figure 1). This is because copyright permeates not only the work of those in the information chain (the people who gather at North American Serials Interest Group (NASIG)) but also much of daily life: education, entertainment, and bestsellers. We hear about copyright in the nightly news,

FIGURE 1

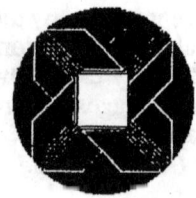

Whose Work Is It Anyway?

- **Copyright Is a Hot Topic**
- **Litigation = Negative Awareness (Kinkos, Texaco)**
- **Technology Raises New Situations and Questions**
    - **Are Electronic Formats Protected? How?**
    - **How Are Collaborative Works Owned?**
    - **What Are Transborder Implications?**
    - **What Liability for Conduit Providers?**
    - **How to Keep Track of Rights in a Time of Segmentation and Fragmentation and Change?**

Association of Research Libraries   Ann Okerson–NASIG 6/95

for instance, when Viacom tries to buy Paramount at huge prices in order to own content. Or, we read reports of celebrated court cases, some of which play out in research and education. For example, a couple of cases settled in the 90s (Kinko's and Texaco) have taught academics, librarians, and publishers a great deal about copyright. For the most part it has been a negative awareness that makes educators and librarians say, "We are already short of funds to buy what we need for our organization; why do publishers want to be paid so much and so often for information?" and rightsholders such as publishers say, "Librarians and academics simply do not understand copyright or that publishers need to earn an income in order to continue their value-adding work."

Without being aware of it, we find ourselves entwined with copyright even here, at this meeting. The topic of copyright has come up many times from various presenters. Peter Denning of the Association for Computing Machinery (ACM) offered us one society publisher's highly creative copyright policy. In his elegant and witty talk at the conference opening, Keith Courtney adapted and showed cartoons from the New Yorker–and we could have a productive discussion about whether his use of those cartoons was fair use (I believe so) and what he and NASIG will do (if anything) in order to reproduce those cartoons in the proceedings (if they try at all). All your speakers have signed three sets of permissions: one, allowing NASIG to tape the talks for its use (but not to sell the tapes); another, allowing NASIG the rights to post the papers on NASIG-Net as part of the record of the conference proceedings; a third allowing Haworth Press, the publisher for this conference's proceedings, the necessary rights to produce the print publication and to carry out the related parts of its work as a publisher. That is, the author owns the copyright but has assigned various permissions or licenses to the paper.

Copyright affects us in the workplace as well, teasing us with questions about using new electronic technologies. Such questions include: are electronic formats protected? How do we attribute ownership to new collaborative works that have been created electronically by a number of people at a number of institutions over time? What are the international implications for copyright over a world which is electronically globally linked? What is the liability for conduit providers? In the past week, we have heard one judge's ruling on Prodigy's liability, a ruling perhaps not without implications for educational sites. How does one keep track of rights in a time of rights segmentation and more frequent needs for clearing rights? What works can one hyperlink to, and is hyperlinking a copyright matter at all? Recently, I heard an entire session for copyright lawyers devoted to an analysis about whether six seconds of green grass from a Wisconsin dairy association was allowable in a video.

Copyright is a legal construct that ascribes ownership to a particular kind of intellectual form: any expression of an idea in a "fixed" form on, for example, paper, canvas, celluloid, tape, or other formats that are identified in the Copyright Act (see Figure 2).

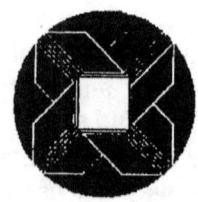

FIGURE 2

US Copyright Law: Balance for Owners and Users

- **Authors have initial rights to their work, e.g.**
  - Keep the rights
  - Transfer them to publishers
  - Divide or segment them (retaining some)
  - Place in public domain
- **Owners have basic rights:**
  - Reproduce copies
  - Prepare derivative works
  - Distribute the work
  - Perform or display it
  - Economically benefit, for Progress of Science & Useful Arts

Association of Research Libraries　　　　　Ann Okerson–NASIG 6/95

Because the law says that such a work is owned, it is possible to treat that work as property. Owning the copyright to what the law characterizes as a work "fixed in a tangible medium expression" gives the owner five exclusive rights: (1) the right to reproduce copies, (2) to prepare derivative works, (3) to distribute the work, (4) to perform the work, (5) to display the work. All in all, copyright owners may economically benefit from their ownership.

U.S. law balances owners' economic rights with the rights of readers or users to be informed. Thus, information users also have a number of rights in the copyright law, even though the owners do have the exclusive rights above. In fact, having defined the exclusive rights early on, in Section 106, the U.S. Act then comprises a number of sections titled: Limitations on Exclusive Rights. These limitations include rights for citizens, libraries, and archives. The most famous limitation on owners' exclusive rights is the theme of this panel session: fair use. Section 107 defines this concept, which allows readers to copy works for personal use, education, scholarship, and criticism, using a set of four criteria that are applied on a case by case basis. Because, in effect, fair use is a provision for users to copy for free, it is indeed the focal point for many of today's current copyright disagreements between different stakeholders.

What I will discuss are not so much the technical and legal aspects of copyright which you will read and hear about from people more qualified than I. Instead, let us briefly consider the social and political aspects of copyright: why it is important and who cares about it these days–for a great many people do.

THE PLAYERS

Government

A cornerstone promise of the Clinton administration is to hasten the coming of the NII (the National Information Infrastructure), and a number of national working groups have been addressing matters vital to the progress of the NII. The administration has charged groups in areas of privacy and security, interoperability, and standards. One of the NII committees that has received national coverage is the NII Working Group on Copyright, whose purpose is to make the SuperHighway safe for information and commercial content, for without substantial content, the NII will be limited or hollow. A task force comprising twenty-five government agency representatives, chaired by Bruce Lehman, the Commissioner of Patents in the Department of Commerce, released a draft report in July, 1994. It is affectionately (?) called the "Green Paper." To convey its message, the authors have traveled and discussed the report with a number of societies, organizations, and publishing groups across the country and have made representations at a number of intellectual property and copyright venues overseas (see Figure 3).

Although the NII working group draft calls its proposals a "tweaking" of the law and argues the law does not need major changes at this time, many critics, particularly user-rights advocates (librarians among them) believe that some of the proposed changes go beyond tweaking.

FIGURE 3

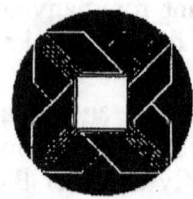

Copyright Pro-Activists:
• U.S. Government

- NII Working Group on Copyright "Green Paper" July 1994
- Final Report ("White Paper") due Summer 1995
- "Tweaking" of Copyright law proposed?
- A national, open process
- http://www.uspto.gov/niiip.html
- WG sponsors Conferences on electronic fair use (ConFU)

First is the Green Paper's affirmation that any information alighting in a computer's memory, for any amount of time—however fleeting—is "fixed." The definition of fixation is important, because the Copyright Act governs, as previously mentioned, only those ideas "fixed in a tangible means of expression, when its embodiment . . . is sufficiently permanent or stable to permit it to be perceived, reproduced, or otherwise communicated for a period of more than transitory duration" (Section 101). By the Green Paper's reasoning, copying occurs each time information is transferred between computers. Every chip could potentially deliver countless numbers of copies per second, and the user who transfers copyrighted information between computers through a network, without permission of the copyright owner, would be breaking the law.

Consequently, the Green Paper proposes an additional right within the Act's current distribution right: the Transmission Right. According to the Green Paper:

> In the world of high-speed communications systems, it is possible to transmit a copy of a work from one location to another . . . When the transmission is complete, the original copy remains in the transmitting computer and a copy resides in the memory of, or in a storage device associated with, each of the other computers. Therefore, this transmission results essentially in the distribution of a copy of the work. The Working Group recommends that Section 106 of the Copyright Act be amended to reflect the fact that copies of works can be distributed to the public by transmission, and that such transmissions fall within the exclusive distribution right of the copyright owner.

The Green Paper also states that the so-called Doctrine of First Sale in the Act is not applicable to electronic media. First Sale (Section 105) means that when one buys a piece of intellectual property, one is the owner of that particular artifact and can read it, donate it to someone, sell it on the street, burn it, do whatever one likes with it. The Green Paper reasons that the situation for electronic information is different. In addition to transmitting a copy, the sender has a copy in his or her own hard disk or memory, even if for a short time. By this logic, the transmitter has at least two copies of the work; if there is no explicit definition of electronic fair use (a drawback to the document is that no such definition is proposed), then the transmission is likely infringing.

The Green Paper is important, disturbing in some places, and well worth reading, although it is supposed momentarily to be eclipsed by the final White Paper, an as yet unknown quantity which will go directly to judicial committees in the Senate and House with proposed changes to the current 1976 Act.

Publishers

As of the early 90s, the core copyright industries of the U.S. (including publishing, film, music), accounted for $206.6 billion in value added to the economy, or 3.6% of the Gross Domestic product. According to the International Intellectual Property Alliance, the copyright industries contribute more to the U.S. economy than most industrial sectors and more than any single manufacturing sector including aircraft and aircraft parts, primary metals, fabricated metals, electronic equipment, industrial machinery, good and kindred products, and chemicals and allied products. These risk-taking industries (they invest heavily in bringing information products to market) are vital to the financial, social, and intellectual well-being of the United States and they stand to benefit financially if electronic copyright protection evolves in their best interests—or, to economically suffer if it does not. At meetings of publishers, exhilaration about the opportunities offered for multi-media creation and transmission, rapid information delivery, creating new products, reaching ever new markets and marketing strategies—is damped by the countervailing fear that a single sale (to a library or even an individual) could, at least in theory, result in a document or product transmitted over the global Internet like an unbroken chain letter.

For the most part, the copyright industries create mass market items such as movies, trade books, and related items (the novel *Jurassic Park*, for example, spawned a major movie, videos, tapes, tee-shirts, toy dinosaurs, and other derivatives), while, according to some estimates, book publishing represents about 10% of that market and "serious" publishing about $1 billion, or 0.5%. That tiny subset embraces the scientific, scholarly, critical, artistic, and literary record of human knowledge—a record all of us here are committed to preserving, and one that is as much governed by copyright as mass market works.

Publishers–particularly such well-organized groups as the Association of American Publishers (AAP) and the Scientific, Technical, and Medical (STM) group based in Europe, have adopted a strong pro-owner stance about their copyrighted property. The publishing community's positions are clearly and powerfully articulated in many different settings–through court actions such as Texaco; position papers such as the AAP Statement on Document Delivery (1992, rev. 1994) which argues that ILL and resource sharing as currently constituted are systematically infringing on the letter and spirit of the Copyright Act and the CONTU guidelines; and in a series of Electronic Fair Use discussions currently taking place among about 50 or so stakeholders in Washington, DC under the aegis of the Department of Commerce, e.g., the Green Paper group. In the CONFU (*Con*ferences on *F*air *U*se) sessions, representatives publishing groups are reluctant to concede, at least right now, any electronic fair use to educators and librarians, arguing that the technology is not yet ripe enough to appreciate the dangers that any early agreements might invite. Of course, it is fair to add that the user community is equally careful not to give up rights it currently has in the Copyright Act.

Authors

Authors obviously have keen interests in copyright–in fact, without authors there would be nothing to copyright, so one would expect authors to have more power than they currently seem to have or feel they have (see Figure 4). From the authors' perspective, however, primary power lies in the hands of the publishers/producers who bring their work to market. (It has ever been thus, since the days of patronage and then of booksellers' guilds.) Two main types of authors are those who earn a living through their work, i.e., journalists, and novelists; and academic authors whose primary purpose in writing is to share their scholarship as far and wide as possible. While their interests are not identical, they are in the end not so different after all.

Representing several thousand professional writers, the National Writers Union (NWU) launched a lawsuit in December 1993

FIGURE 4

Copyright Pro-Activists:
• Authors

- **National Writers' Union – more rights and royalties**
  - http://ccat.sas.upenn.edu/jod/nwu.html
  - Lawsuit December 1993; Position Paper September 1994
- **Researchers and Faculty – wide copying and access on the Internet for scholarly works and scientific research**
  - Electronic Journal Copyright Statements Permissive
  - Preprint Servers Accessible to Everyone

Association of Research Libraries Ann Okerson–NASIG 6/95

against a number of major information producers such as the New York Times, IAC, and Mead Data Central. Essentially, the NWU argues that in the new-tech age, authors can add a great deal of value to their own publications; publishers add less value than they used to in paper, for authors can more readily revise, enhance, and add value to their own works. Therefore, authors–the argument runs–are entitled to the maximum economic benefit from their work, certainly a larger share of the proceeds than they are getting now in print media. The NWU affirms that owners or vendors do not have the right to sell authors' works without an explicit agreement and without paying appropriate royalties. Part of the problem is, of course, that many agreements within the copyright period of 50 years plus the lifetime of the author were signed before certain new media existed. Authors may not feel that publishers have a right to their works in these new forms, while producers may assume that initial copyright transfer granted them the rights to media as they are created.

Now take the case of the academic authors whose salaries are paid by their institutions rather than from their publications. During a productive lifetime, such an author is likely to create many works: articles, books, videos, code, CDs, and so on. More than anything, such authors desire their works to be disseminated widely and read by as many students and peers as possible. According to U.S. copyright law, all authors are the initial creators and owners of their works. The way the publication system currently works for journals is roughly this: academic institutions generally cede to academic creators the rights to do whatever they choose with their creations. Authors, in turn, tend to transfer all rights to articles to journal publishers as a condition of having their articles published. The majority of journal copyright transfer forms say (more or less), "I attest that this work is mine, and I assign and transfer my rights to the publisher for the duration of copyright in any and all media which may exist or which may be created."

Even though the incentives for the commercial and academic authors are not identical, these days academic authors also believe they have an interest in changing traditional practices. We know this for a fact because academic researchers have started retaining more rights to their published works and where they have begun Internet e-journals and preprint servers, they generally advocate new kinds of copyright policies, ones that allow for wide copying and use, provided the work is properly attributed and that it is not re-sold.

Universities

Another group of players interested in copyright is universities (see Figure 5). In July of 1993, a working committee from the Triangle Research Library Network, a group of North Carolina Universities, published a model copyright policy. It recommends that academic authors publish in reasonably priced journals (generally from societies and university presses), and that if or when they transfer copyrights to publishers, they retain rights to use the work for themselves, as well as permission for any research or educational uses of the work.

Next, a task force of the Association of American Universities

FIGURE 5

Copyright Pro-Activists:
* **Universities**

- **Triangle Research Libraries Network Model Policy July 1993 – recommends faculty copyright retention**
  - http://ccat.sas.upenn.edu/jod/trln.html
- **Association of American Universities IP Task Force April 1994 – recommends author ownership or shared ownership of copyrights**
  - http://arl.cni.org/aau/IPTOC.html
- **Campus faculty committees reviewing copying and copyright management policies: Iowa, MIT, Delaware, Rice, Columbia, and others**

Association of Research Libraries   Ann Okerson–NASIG 6/95

(AAU) met for a year and a half and wrote a report for university presidents in Spring 1994. Laura Gasaway and I had the opportunity to serve with about 16 people representing administrators, faculty, librarians, and legal scholars of these universities. The Task Force was charged by the 60 AAU university presidents to recommend what they should do to most effectively deploy academic information in an electronic era. Our task force agreed that copyright was a more complicated issue than members of the university community generally realize. That is, members of universities have different copyright interests at different times. As teachers, they want the widest and freest possible use of copyrighted works for their classrooms and their students. As authors, academics generally desire their work to be widely read; more often than not they are not directly paid when the work is accepted for publication. However, the possibility of payment for their copyrighted work can markedly influence their perspectives of copyright and control. Finally, universities as publishers (that is, through their university presses) need the revenue that copyrights generate to continue their existence as publishers.

The Task Force examined copying as well as copyright ownership policies at many universities and found that faculty and researchers are rarely part of the policy creation process, they seldom know what policies are in place, and many of the policies are hard to understand. More often than not, there are no identified sources on campus for help or questions in this complicated area.

The Task Force report recommended that authors and universities begin to consider different copyright transfer agreements than the types that are currently signed; it recommended considering either copyright retention by authors (with limited or licensed rights to publishers or some shared ownership of copyrights between faculty and universities, provided the university in turn offers incentives for that (e.g., copyright management services, or publishing sites). As a result of or contiguous with those recommendations, a number of campuses have begun reviewing intellectual property management and copyright policies. Meanwhile, the Task Force has begun the second phase of its work: planning resources to support universities in educating campuses about effective, legal uses of copyrighted works.

Librarians

Librarians believe it is part of their responsibility to represent the interests of users of library materials, and it is in the users' interests that the library community carries out an advocacy role for the widest possible access to information (see Figure 6). Researchers, teachers, students, and the citizenry rarely have the deep pockets that would enable them to pay for the rich, wide range of information resources they need to go about their daily pursuits. To meet the informational needs of society, libraries have evolved as the collectives that house, organize, and service information. However, for economic reasons, this role may be in jeopardy. (ARL library data show that serial prices double about every seven years and that monograph purchases have

FIGURE 6

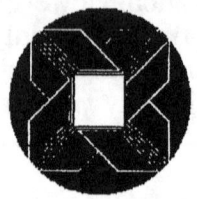

Copyright Pro-Activists:
• Libraries and Info Users

- **ARL "Statement of Rights and Responsibilities of the Research Library Community in Copyright"**
  - http://arl.cni.org/scomm/copyright/principles.html
- **Six library associations: "Fair Use in the Electronic Age: Serving the Public Interest"**
  - http://arl.cni.org/scomm/copyright/uses.html

Association of Research Libraries   Ann Okerson–NASIG 6/95

been severely reduced–even as the price of electronic formats is even greater than the paper media they are replacing.)

A number of library associations, with support from groups of scholars, have advanced strong pro-user documents including "Intellectual Property; An Association of Research Libraries Statement of Principles," and "Fair Use in the Electronic Age: Serving the Public Interest." This same community has made representation to the Lehman Green Paper group asking that the White Paper should recognize a set of user rights to balance the owners' rights that were so clearly articulated in the Green Paper. These organizations attend the Fair Use meetings and speak clearly to the Constitutional mandate behind the copyright law: to promote the progress of science and the useful arts.

Copyright Skeptics

Our quick review would be incomplete if it omitted the viewpoint of a growing number of voices that say copyright is an idea whose time has passed (see Figure 7). Jerry Campbell, University Librarian at Duke, made that statement here during his welcome at the NASIG opening. Peter Lyman, a political scientist and University Librarian at the University of California, Berkeley, believes that the 90s could be thought of as a renaissance, a time in which technology and imagination intersect to redefine the way a culture creates and represents knowledge (Educom Review, Vol. 30/1, January/February 1995: 32-35). Lyman is concerned that copyright law could be shaped so as to impede innovation by being too narrow and technical a context for the social policy debate it merits. He and many other advocates of networked communications doubt whether

FIGURE 7

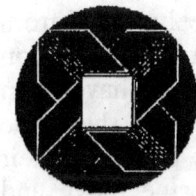

Copyright Skeptics

- **Peter Lyman, *Educom Review* (Jan/Feb. 1995)**
  - "It isn't clear to me that networked information can be regulated the way print commodities are . . ."
- **John Perry Barlow, *Wired* (March 1994)**
  - "All the goods of the Information Age . . . will exist either as pure thought or something very much like thought . . . [that we can] never touch or claim to own in the old sense of the word."
- **Thomas Jefferson, letter to Isaac McPherson, 1813**
  - "Inventions then cannot, in nature, be the subject of property."

Association of Research Libraries   Ann Okerson–NASIG 6/95

traditional copyright mechanisms can be scaled up to a global information society in which every electronic lookup, transfer, or download becomes a copy in the legal sense of that word.

The most famous 90s Copyright Skeptic is probably John Perry Barlow, formerly of the Grateful Dead and today an advocate of freedom in cyberspace. "All the goods of the information Age," he wrote in the cyberage magazine *Wired* (March 1994: 84+), "will exist either as pure thought or something very much like thought: voltage conditions darting around the Net at the speed of light, in conditions that one might behold in effect, as glowing pixels or transmitted sounds but never touch or claim to own in the old sense of the word."

Barlow, in turn, traces his philosophy back to Thomas Jefferson, one of the fathers of this country. In 1813 in a letter to Isaac McPherson, Jefferson wrote, "That ideas should freely spread from one to another over the globe, for the moral and mutual instruction of man, and improvement of his condition, seems to have been peculiarly and benevolently designed by nature, when she made them, like fire, expansible over all space, without lessening their density at any point, and like the air in which we breathe, move, and have our physical being, incapable of confinement or exclusive appropriation. Inventions then cannot, in nature, be a subject of property."

Interestingly, the Jeffersonian theme was picked up recently by Barbara Ehrenreich in her review of Alvin and Heidi Toffler's newest book, the *Politics of the Third Wave*. In a May issue of the New York Times Book Review, she writes:

> But the Tofflers do pull one highly significant punch. They fail to mention that the very basis of power, as all civilizations so far have known it, is crumbling within our hands. Power inheres in property, meaning, in First Wave societies, the factories, machinery, etc., required for production. But, as they point out, the basis of wealth and power in the Third Wave is information (including images and "knowledge"), and this is a slippery substance indeed. Land and factories are easy to fence off and defend, but information, as the Tofflers briefly acknowledge, is "intangible," "inexhaustible" and capable of being used by many people at once. Which means, although

they do not come out and say it, that information cannot easily be "owned."

You can copyright it, of course, and surround it with electronic passwords and codes, but sooner or later some hacker, like Kevin D. Mitnick, the recently apprehended computer security breaker, will come along and set it loose just for fun. The Tofflers pooh-pooh the opponents of the trade agreement with Mexico as Second Wave troglodytes, but a true Third Waver should have equal scorn for, say, the opponents of Chinese software piracy. Though the Tofflers seem not to notice it, the struggle is already going on between those who would keep information frozen as property and those–including the poor and merely playful, who would let it flow free.

CONCLUSION

Let us speculate on the conclusion of the copyright matter. Simply put, there will not be a definitive conclusion. Copyright will continue to evolve as it has been doing since the days of Columba in the sixth century. There will be periods of peace, of war, and of monsters, which may be mythical or real. The 1990s uncertainty is not whether copyright will disappear, but to what extent will the copyright law be changed in the short term and how will it–or will it?–as effectively balance the interests of authors, producers, and readers as it has done fairly well for the print medium?

There are certainties as well. One certainty is that the ways that authors in research and academia are now applying the copyright law, that is the social, and economic practices and relationships that surround the creation, distribution, and ownership of their created works, are definitely changing. Today, authors are making different choices about how to assign their copyrights and how their work shall be published or disseminated. They are beginning to retain some rights to their own works and do some of their own distribution–which can make a permission-seeking process more difficult for users who need to ask permissions. Another certainty authors like is this sense of greater control over what happens to their work and that this movement will gain more momentum.

John Perry Barlow is dismissed by the mainstream legal community; however, my recommendation is that we should not be quick to join in that censure. It is not impossible—in fact it is highly probable—that the copyright law we seek to update now will evolve into a different and barely recognizable set of practices 50 years from now.

My advice about copyright is that we inform ourselves (see Figure 8). Whichever position we take in the Great Copyright Debates of the 90s must be firmly grounded in the law and in an awareness of current issues and practices. All of us need to read and understand the copyright policies of our organizations and institutions, to help shape them, and to pay close attention to any legal documents such as licenses or contracts. I recommend joining the national copyright conversation. The NII copyright process, for example, has been open to everyone. We can also participate in copyright discussions with other players in the information chain, ones who do not share our positions, to see if there is room to come together and to craft new understandings and practices. This is a dialog that we must have; we opt out to our own disadvantage.

FIGURE 8

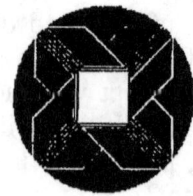

Copyright Turmoils
- **What to do?**

- **Know the law and articulate your own position**
    - http://www.law.cornell.edu/
- **Use value-adding talents of publishers & libraries; Re-define the value that libraries & publishers add**
- **Develop good mechanisms to identify owners of works in the electronic environment**
- **Experiment rather than litigate**
- **Embrace Change -- things will never be the same as they were in the paper-centered universe?!**

Association of Research Libraries   Ann Okerson–NASIG 6/95

Finally, most of the people in this room do not have many hours to invest in copyright, and that is why, whatever your affiliation, you pay association staff in Washington to sit on top of these issues, worry about them, respond to them, and attend the meetings on your behalf. That said, everyone in this auditorium makes a statement in the way that they manage their own created works and in the choices you make about copying day by day. Our daily copyright practices support or complement discussions at the policy level and are no less clear and no less powerful in their own way than the national debates. Our actions are the way the market speaks each and every day and they help to shape and influence the law.

PLENARY SESSION III: VISIONS FOR A NEW DECADE OF 21ST CENTURY SERIALS

The Transformation of a Nation: The Impact of Politics and the Potential of Technology on Information Access in South Africa

Dianne Leong Man

SUMMARY. The year 1994 marked a period of radical political transformation in South Africa with the election of a Black majority government. Information is seen as a strategic resource for social transformation and "empowerment." Traditional South Africa is expected to extend its resources inside and outside its boundaries and to serve as the technological springboard. The political situation before and

---

Dianne Leong Man is Assistant University Librarian (Technical Services) for the University of the Witwatersrand, South Africa.

© 1996 by the North American Serials Interest Group, Inc. All rights reserved.

[Haworth co-indexing entry note]: "The Transformation of a Nation: The Impact of Politics and the Potential of Technology on Information Access in South Africa." Man, Dianne Leong. Co-published simultaneously in *The Serials Librarian* (The Haworth Press, Inc.) Vol. 28, No. 1/2, 1996, pp. 89-104; and *Serials to the Tenth Power: Tradition, Technology, and Transformation* (ed: Mary Ann Sheble, and Beth Holley) The Haworth Press, Inc., 1996, pp. 89-104. Single or multiple copies of this article are available from The Haworth Document Delivery Service [1-800-342-9678, 9:00 a.m. - 5:00 p.m. (EST)].

after 1994 is examined, along with the impact of politics on information access, and the role of technology in facilitating access to information and fostering resource sharing. *[Article copies available from The Haworth Document Delivery Service: 1-800-342-9678.]*

INTRODUCTION

Traditional South Africa is identified with the policy of "apartheid" or enforced racial segregation, resulting in an unequal society where lavish wealth and abject poverty exist side by side.[1] During the 1980s we saw the further political polarization of the Black majority and an intensified struggle against apartheid by a mass democratic movement. The rest of the world became involved, and South Africa found itself subjected to political ostracism, sanctions, boycotts, and problems with the free flow of information.

The release of Nelson Mandela from prison in February 1990, and the unbanning of Black political parties set the wheels in motion for political change through negotiation. In April 1994, the country's first all-race elections were held, and we saw the radical, but peaceful, changeover from White minority rule to Black majority rule under an internal constitution. Such reform aimed at democratizing the nation is referred to as "transformation."

South Africa is an example of only a minority of countries which have, in recent times, been able to *negotiate* a transition in governance, rather than have it occur through civil war, military conflict, or economic collapse.[2] We are proud of this achievement, and have passed our first anniversary. There are still many hurdles to overcome, but at least there is a significant degree of political stability.

The aim of this paper is to examine how politics and technology are influencing information provision and access in the new South Africa and Southern Africa, under the following headings:

The Impact of Politics on Information Access

- The RDP
- Implications for library and information services
- Changes in government structure
- Impact on serials

The Potential of Technology for Information Access

- New government and information
- Telecommunications
- Sanctions and technology
- Relationship with Southern African neighbours
- New technological developments
- Some concerns

THE IMPACT OF POLITICS ON INFORMATION ACCESS

The RDP

Besides the word "transformation," the next most-used buzzword is "RDP" or "Reconstruction and Development Programme." The African National Congress (ANC) produced a document entitled *The Reconstruction and Development Programme: A Policy Framework* before the April, 1994 elections in consultation with its political partners and other mass organisations, in preparation for its major role in government. In its own words:

> The RDP is an integrated, coherent socio-economic policy framework. It seeks to mobilise all our people and our country's resources toward the final eradication of apartheid and the building of a democratic, non-racial and non-sexist future.[3]

As a party-political manifesto, it is a detailed and well-structured document of 147 pages which has now been incorporated into national policy via a parliamentary White Paper on Reconstruction and Development. The five key programs of the RDP are as follows:

- *Meeting basic needs.* Aims at eradicating poverty and deprivation in terms of jobs, land, housing, water, electricity, telecommunications, transport, the environment, nutrition, health care and social welfare.[4]
- *Developing our human resources.* Concentrates on education and training from cradle to grave, and rectifying the inequalities wrought by racially based education systems.[5]

- *Building the economy.* Although there is a good infrastructure, there has been domination by the white minority and an unequal distribution of wealth. There is also domination by a few large conglomerates in the public and private sectors. Worker rights, collective bargaining, and affirmative action are important aspects under this heading, as is the stress on a Southern African regional policy.[6]
- *Democratising the state and society.* This is integral to the RDP. One person one vote, as well as transparent and accountable government. All public services need to be restructured from national government downwards to local government and to the public sector itself.[7]
- *Implementing the RDP.* How it is going to be done, and who is going to pay.

The RDP as national strategy has gained support from virtually all sectors. " ... No one rejects its ideals, or the real need in South Africa for some sort of restructuring and development programme," and there was fear of the RDP becoming a 'holy cow' with no criticism of it being brooked.[8] A year has now passed and there have been positive and negative comments on what has been achieved. This is in the spirit of transparency and accountability which the new government has been at pains to encourage. Escalating crime, unemployment, homelessness, and the delay in setting up local government structures are cited as examples of the RDP's failure, while the RDP Ministry point out the need to develop criteria and infrastructure for many of the projects, e.g., housing has to be combined with provision of water, electricity, sanitation, health clinics and schools.[9] Many Blacks feel that the new government has brought no change whatsoever into their disadvantaged lifestyles, but the government has repeatedly warned against unrealistic expectations. Changes are, however, occuring almost on a daily basis.

A 1994 study by the Canadian-based International Development Research Centre found that there was insufficient information to support the implementation of the RDP because of the fragmented information-gathering approach adopted by the previous government. A lot of data had been gathered over the years by government departments, non-government organisations, research organisations and universities for their own use. These needed to be co-ordinated and integrated to assist decision-making. They recommended that a small Information Policy and Coordination Unit be set up to harness available data with the use of appropriate technology.[10]

IMPLICATIONS FOR LIBRARY AND INFORMATION SERVICES

So within the wide-open agenda offered by the key programmes of the RDP, how and where do library and information services fit in? In the words of the Director of our State Library, Dr. Peter Lor, what is lacking is the L-word:

> The word 'libraries' occurs twice in the RDP policy framework. In both cases libraries are mentioned in the context of arts and culture and in association with institutions such as museums and art galleries . . . Nowhere are libraries and information referred to in the same context. There is no evidence that the compilers of the report have any appreciation of the role LIS can play in national reconstruction and development.[11]

With regard to information, he adds further:

> The word 'information' occurs quite frequently in the RDP policy framework. However, the word is used loosely, with connotations ranging from telecommunications and data to the mass media, publicity and propaganda. In many contexts where information services can make a significant contribution to national reconstruction and development, no mention is made of them. More seriously, the RDP policy framework offers no coherent treatment of information as a national resource in support of reconstruction and development.

Like education, library services for the so-called non-White groups had historically always been separate and unequal to those of the White group. From 1928 onwards when the Carnegie Corporation organised a conference to study the position of libraries in South Africa, there is documentary evidence of the inadequacies of public library services for Black users, and these worsened progressively under the period of 'grand apartheid' when facilities were racially segregated by law in terms of the Separate Amenities Act. The legacy of apartheid is not only a gross imbalance in library provision between White and Black, but also White librarians who have had to learn to adapt their service to Black users, and to acquire material for a multilingual and multicultural society.

Librarians and information workers have naturally been disappointed about the scant recognition afforded them in the RDP document. Even before the release of Nelson Mandela and the repeal of the Separate Amenities Act in 1990, librarians had begun to realise that they needed to play a greater role in development programmes. Since 1990, there have been major reports issued by bodies such as the National Education Policy Initiative (NEPI), Transforming our Library and Information Services (TransLis), Centre for Education Policy Development (CEPD) and Community Library Information Services (COLIS). All these documents point out the important role that libraries can play in redressing past imbalances and assisting with the education of the disadvantaged communities.[12] Much criticism has been levied against the document drawn up by the ANC-backed Centre for Education Policy Development which recommends a system of centralised government control over library and information services.[13]

So why, despite all this activity and the important role that they need to play in the New South Africa, are the librarians still receiving such scant recognition from the government? The major problem is that, if you want to lobby the government you have to speak with one voice, and the library and information profession cannot do so. It is represented by no less than three library associations and urgently needs to get itself unified. The three library associations are:

- *SAILIS* The South African Institute for Librarianship and Information Science, formed in 1980 but has been in existence since 1930 as the South African Library Association
- *ALASA* African Library Association of South Africa
- *LIWO* Library and Information Workers Organisation

The root cause of this unhappy situation is the fact that the forerunner of SAILIS, the South African Library Association, took a decision in 1962 to terminate Black membership. This was done voluntarily, even before apartheid legislation required them to do so. ALASA was then formed in 1963, and they have operated separately ever since. LIWO was formed in 1990 as an alternative multiracial organisation which represented both qualified and non-qualified librarians, and has been strongly critical of SAILIS which it sees as an "establishment" organisation.

A ground-breaking conference of librarians, regardless of their affiliation, was held in January, 1995 under the banner of LISDESA, or Library and Information Services in Developing South Africa. It took four years to plan and was conceived as a conference to address the role of LIS in the development of South Africa. IFLA, Unesco, and some Dutch companies gave generous sponsorships to ensure that the conference had a broadly-based representative attendance from all three groups. There were many agreements and disagreements, but the conference was cathartic. In the end the 200 or so delegates unanimously adopted a resolution to form a Steering Committee, with the mandate to organize a conference within 12 months at which a national library association is to be formed. This will probably take place in September, 1996.[14]

In the meantime, the future structure and governance of LIS still hangs in balance because it is not a top priority with the Government of National Unity, and there is uncertainty over which State Department or Departments they are to fall under. Academic libraries could fall under the Department of Education, or even under the Department of Art, Culture, Science and Technology. Little consideration seems to have been given to the link between an academic medical library and the Department of Health, which controls the medical schools.[15] The most uncertainty lies with the public library system as the provincial and local government structures have not yet been finalised. Literacy and education are important facets of the RDP Program, but in the meantime the libraries are running the risk of developing uncoordinated plans and policies.

CHANGES IN GOVERNMENT STRUCTURE

What changes have been brought into being by the interim constitution and the Government of National Unity? In 1984 a racially-based Tricameral (or three-chamber) Parliament was created after an election which excluded the Black majority. In addition to a large Cabinet, there were separate houses for Whites, Coloureds (or mixed races) and Indians.

After April 1994 we had a completely changed multiparty government of Blacks and Whites. Parliament consists of a Cabinet, a National Assembly, and a Senate. In addition, there is a Constitutional Assembly which will oversee the adoption of a new constitution to be adopted by 1999. Voting took place in November, 1995 for local government within the nine provinces.

In the past, South Africa had four provinces and ten separate territories or homelands for the different Black ethnic groups in South Africa. Four of them were granted independence, while the remaining six were self-governing territories. None of these were recognised by the United Nations on the grounds that their creation was contrary to a number of norms in the field of self-determination and human rights.[16]

From 1994 onwards the physical boundaries have changed. We have nine provinces and all the homelands have been incorporated. We have nine sets of provincial governments, some with new names, some with existing names. The local government elections are problematical, as voter registration is low and millions of people do not understand why they have to vote again, or are just not interested.

THE IMPACT ON SERIALS

A government publications collection mirrors the system of government at any one time, so the bigger and more complex the system, the more publications it will produce, especially in serial form. The previous system of government with the tricameral parliament, four provinces and ten homelands was a nightmare for serials librarians. They had a constant battle with cataloguing backlogs, claiming missing issues of gazettes and reports from eleven government printing departments and escalating binding costs. In addition, the cataloguers were constantly arguing over the authority forms of names because only South Africa recognised the sovereignty of the four "independent" homelands of Transkei, Bophuthatswana, Venda, and Ciskei.

LCNA   Bophuthatswana (South Africa). Dept of . . .

SANB   Bophuthatswana. Dept of . . .

LCSH   Venda (South Africa). Economic conditions

SANB   Venda. Economic conditions

The dilemma was: do you follow the Library of Congress (LC) conventions where sovereignty is not recognised, hence South Africa in parenthesis, or do you follow what your own country says? The SANB is the South African National Bibliography, and in recent years they have had to capitulate, particularly with subject headings, because of conflict when downloading LC records. The problem is now over, but our national database, SABINET, reflects this dilemma as its authority file is full of inconsistencies which need to be ironed out.

Under the new government, the serials catalogers will continue to be fully employed. They have to wrestle with new titles, changes of title, title merges, closing off the serials records of the homelands, and multilingualism because of the eleven official languages. Often it is not possible to distinguish a new title from a merged title because of the new geographical boundaries.

We have also seen the end of censorship, sanctions, and the cultural boycott, where information was withheld by the government within the country, and prevented from coming into the country by outside parties. Censorship was used by the previous government to suppress anti-apartheid viewpoints, and serials were particularly vulnerable because they could be suspended or banned before publication. This happened whenever the parent organisation of a serial was banned, or when a newspaper received a suspension for periods varying from one to three months.[17]

In theory, information should now be flowing freely into and inside South Africa, and we should now be able to buy anything we want, including pornography. Our political problems, however, have left us with a weakened economy, a very weak currency, and diminished budgets. Our neighbours in Southern Africa, however, consider us as "information rich" and are beginning to make extensive use of interlibrary loan facilities.

THE POTENTIAL OF TECHNOLOGY ON INFORMATION ACCESS

New Government and Information

To its credit, the ANC has led the new government into a strong awareness of the value of information, and is exploiting the power of technology to disseminate information. Political transformation must be accompanied by "transparency" and the free flow of information, and there is creative use of media other than radio and television for this. Here are a few examples:

- An ANC archive is available for searching on the World Wide Web (WWW) and by gopher:
  (http: //www.anc.org.za/;gopher://wn.apc.org:70/11/anc/)
  It contains historical documents, policy documents, press statements, speeches, and Constitutional News, a fortnightly serial.
- The writing of a new constitution is underway, and the public is encouraged to give input. The documents and minutes of the Constitutional Assembly are available on a WWW site. A bulletin board is also being planned, as well as extensive television coverage. Messages calling for public participation in the constitution-making process have been placed on the automatic teller machines of various banks.[18]
  (gopher://constitution.org.za:70/1/)
- The Constitutional Court has been set up to rule on issues such as the death penalty. The proceedings of the Constitutional Court are available on a WWW site which is administered by the School of Law, University of the Witwatersrand.
  (http://www.law.wits.ac.za/)

Some of these developments bear out the shift from an information environment that is geared towards *informing* to one that is *involving*, as discussed in a recent issue of ASIS Journal.[19]

The RDP argues that in order for a society to advance, it requires informed government and citizenry, and that this is a two way process.[20] Naturally this type of hi-tech information dissemination will only reach a few of the privileged citizens, so it is being argued that making people FTP information from the Web is not democracy. There is a definite need for low-tech print as well, and there is some resentment against the use of scarce resources on sophisticated technology.

TELECOMMUNICATIONS

While the richly endowed urban areas may be looking at telecommunications in terms of the Information Superhighway, the RDP views it simply in terms of telephones. "Under apartheid the provision of telecommunications was racially distorted. For black people it is estimated that less than 1 line per 100 persons is in place compared with abut 60 lines per 100 white persons."[21] There is a close linkage between telecommunications and democracy, as an authoritarian state can use telecommunications to control citizens and to deny access to information, especially to economic and political resources.[22] One understands this concept in terms of the mass media, but seldom thinks about the common telephone as a political instrument.

SANCTIONS AND TECHNOLOGY

Sanctions and the anti-apartheid movement had both a negative and positive impact on information technology in South Africa. Computer companies such as IBM and Apple pulled out. Other companies refused to supply equipment, spares or software. South Africa had to become more self-sufficient, and had to buy out many of the companies that withdrew. Many libraries, and even SABINET, the South African bibliographic network, only had a handful of locally supported systems to choose from for their library packages. Whatever aid money came into South Africa went to alternative organisations or non-government organisations (NGOs), as a form of protest against the policies of the Nationalist government. Donating to NGOs was often the only way in which foreign governments were willing to contribute towards the development and resistance cause in South Africa.[23]

This aid money gave rise to some important developments in information access, such as:

- *SANGONET.* The Southern African Nongovernmental Organisations Network not only publishes information required by development workers, but provides e-mail links to facilitate communication among them. It also provides full Internet access to subscribers, and stores information on development and the RDP from the NGOs, the government, and the private sector. Grants from foundations in the United States and South Africa establish and subsidize the service, e.g., from the Ford, Mott, and Kellogg Foundations, and some costs are recovered through subscriptions.
- *INFOACT DATABASE.* This database is published by the Institute for the Study of Public Violence, which was established by the Goldstone Commission. It is funded by foreign donors. The level of violence is a major concern in South Africa, and the purpose of InfoAct is to contribute to the peace process through the systematic collection and dissemination of information related to public violence. It provides dial-up access to the full text of the Goldstone Commission reports as well as a variety of other NGO's and human rights organisations.

This protest money is either drying up completely, or else is now being channelled into the RDP, which is being given aid by many foreign governments. It would be a pity if such important databases were to close down because of lack of funds. SANGONET is struggling for funding, and has had around 80 cancellations from NGO organisations that closed down after the elections.

RELATIONSHIP WITH SOUTHERN AFRICAN NEIGHBOURS

In the past, South Africa could barely cope with its own information needs and struggled to meet its own priorities, yet the transformed South Africa is expected to extend its resources inside and outside its boundaries. South Africa joined the Southern African Development Community (SADC) as its eleventh member in August, 1994, but warned that it had no desire to become the dominant partner and that it had no illusion of becoming the regional benefactor. Such capacity it did not possess, even though its gross domestic product is four times that of all the other SADC countries combined. "South Africa will be unable to match the West in development capacity–it may have the know-how and appropriate technology, but it has neither the skilled manpower nor the capital resources to do so. . . . South Africa does not have the capacity to deal with its own hardship, let alone alleviate the region's tribulations."[24]

NEW TECHNOLOGICAL DEVELOPMENTS

Overseas technology companies who disinvested during the 1980s are flooding back, trying to pick up where they left off. They have an additional agenda item–to use South Africa as a springboard to the rest of Africa. The International Development Research Centre found that South Africa had a unique combination of a small highly developed and technologically sophisticated sector alongside large underdeveloped and underprivileged regions, and that this was attractive to information technology suppliers worldwide.[25]

New companies are setting up. In the library world, we saw two well-known United States library software vendors exhibiting at our annual conference for the first time. Even OCLC has set up trial evaluations to FirstSearch.

UNINET, the universities network, is the main supplier of links inside South Africa, although there are also a few commercial suppliers. Uninet is providing access via leased lines to the rest of Southern Africa, including Mozambique and Namibia. Zambia has a dedicated line via a commercial supplier. Other countries are interested, but cannot afford the costs.

An interesting plan is the ambitious Africa One Project by AT&T and the International Telecommunications Union (BDT). They want to raise funds among United States and South Africa companies to install telecommunication access throughout the African continent by encircling it with an undersea fiberoptic cable. This Africa One network will connect all African countries with coastal access, and then link inwards deeper into Africa and outwards to the rest of the world. The reasoning behind this is that underdeveloped country has to have telecommunications in order to have economic growth.[26]

SABINET, the South African Bibliographic and Information Network, has a database of South Africa holdings and provides access to overseas databases such as LC, Inside Information, as well as gateways to Uncover and OCLC. Its role as an information provider and as a national resource is expected to increase.

There are excellent databases on South Africa and Africa, with maps, that have been developed by institutions such as the University of Pennsylvania and Yale University. (http://www.sas.upenn.edu/African Studies/) (http://minerva.cis.yale.edu/~jadwat/me/sa-resources.html)

SOME CONCERNS–OR PARANOIA?

Technology is fine and well, but gives rise to some problems when one views information access on a national level. When one has lived through a prolonged period of sanctions and boycotts, one is forced to think in terms of building up a national collection and being nationally self-sufficient. In the 1980s we worried about not cancelling the last remaining subscription to a title in South Africa. It is difficult now to change to a mind-set of access rather than ownership of information and I have some concerns:

- *Print vs. electronic.* Is the high cost of electronic access, such as multi-user license fees for CD-ROMs, a luxury? Should we not rather spend these large sums of money on original material which can add to the national bookstock?
- *Just in case vs. just in time.* Just in case or ownership of information will help a country far more when it is hit by sanctions and boycotts. Political affiliations can change very quickly–one minute a country is a friend, next minute it is an enemy and vice versa. Russia, Iraq and South Africa are prime examples of this type of change.
- *The imposition of sanctions and boycotts is so much easier with technology.* All you have to do is turn off the switch to the network and you have an information black-out.

CONCLUSION: A DIFFICULT FUTURE AHEAD

Politics and technology separately have tremendous power to control the lives of people. When used together, the control is magnified, and one only has to look at the fight for control of the media to appreciate this. Democratic processes and the free flow of information can be either retarded or advanced. In South Africa, over the past decade, we have gone from one end of the pendulum's swing to the other. In the mid-1980s, we had tight censorship and dissenters and organisations were partially or totally banned. Then the world got involved, and through sanctions and boycotts further restricted the free flow of information.

Since the release of Nelson Mandela and the unbanning of anti-apartheid organisations in February 1990, South Africa has opened-up and we have witnessed the dismantling of apartheid. The election in April 1994 was an emotional event for all of us. In his inaugural speech, President Mandela proclaimed us to be a rainbow nation. The pot-of-gold at the end of the rainbow holds our hopes and dreams, but one thing is certain: freedom of information is much in evidence. We sincerely hope that this is here to stay, but we know that information and politics will always remain closely interwoven, and that politics is fickle.

NOTES

1. *African National Congress, The reconstruction and development programme: a policy framework.* Johannesburg: Umanyano Publications, 1994, p. 2.

2. Robin Lee, Library and information services as part of South Africa's transition to democracy. Keynote address to SAILIS Conference, 20 September 1994, p. 1.

3. RDP, p. 1.

4. RDP, p. 7-8, 14.

5. RDP, p. 8, 58.

6. RDP, p. 10-11, 110.

7. RDP, p. 12, 119-125.

8. RDP monitor 1(1), June/July/August 1994, p. 1.

9. Assessing the performance of the RDP. *New Nation*, April 13, 1995, p. 6-7.

10. International Development Research Centre. National Information Management Project South Africa, Report of the Preparatory Mission, Johannesburg, May 16-31, 1994, 34 p.

11. P. J. Lor, RDP and LIS: an analysis of the Reconstruction and Development Programme from the perspective of library and information services. *South African Journal of Library and Information Science* 62(4), Dec. 1994, p. 128-135.

12. C. M. Walker, Dreams, policies, problems and practitioners: learning to provide information for all. *South African journal of library and information science*, 62 (4), Dec 1994, p. 117-126.

13. Centre for Education Policy Development. Implementation plan for education and training. 11: Library and information services (LIS), 51 p.

14. Unification of Library and Information Services. ULIS information sheet, no. 1, March 1995. 2 p.

15. G. Myers. Health information delivery in post-apartheid South Africa. *In print*, 1995.

16. John Dugard, Recognition and the United Nations. Cambridge: Grotius Publications, 1987, p. 103.

17. D. L. Man, The serials collection as a reflection of social and political change. *Serials*, 4(2), July, 1991, p. 36.

18. Bank on ATMs for constitutional info.; SA notches up a first in constitution-making. *The Star*, 24 January 1995.

19. Leah A. Lievrouw, Information resources and democracy: understanding the paradox. *Journal of the American Society for Information Science* 45(6): 1994, p. 350-357.

20. Lee, Robin. Library and information services as part of South Africa's transition to democracy. Keynote address to SAILIS Conference, Kempton Park, 20 September 1994.

21. RDP, p. 34.

22. J. Hills, Telecommunications and democracy: the international experience. *Telecommunication journal* 60(1), 1993, p. 21-29.

23. B. Davies, Funding for NGOs: a lost cause? *Sash* 37(2), Jan 1995.

24. D. Venter, Comment: some thoughts on South Africa and Southern Africa. *Africa insight* 24(3), 1994, p. 158-9.

25. International Development Research Centre, p. 13.

26. Africa ONE connection, September 1994.

Security and Uses of the Internet

Steven M. Bellovin

SUMMARY. The Internet is a very powerful tool. Nevertheless, security problems are crippling it, and–if matters continue as they have been going–will ultimately drive away serious information providers and users. This presentation explores some of the problems and their causes, and sketches some palliative measures. *[Article copies available from The Haworth Document Delivery Service: 1-800-342-9678.]*

INTRODUCTION

Scarcely a day goes by without mention of the Internet in the mass media. Everyone, from researchers to politicians to Madison Avenue, finds it essential–or rather, they say they do. Resources, from the trivial–promotional pages for the latest summer movie–to the sublime–catalogs of the world's largest libraries–are readily available, often for free. Why? Why should the Internet suddenly have become so important?

Part of the reason, of course, is precisely because of the attention. On the one hand, people who might always have had a need for the Internet but did not know of it can scarcely avoid hearing of it now. They are thus prompted to seek access. On the other end of the spectrum, information providers, from the most arcane scientific researchers to the traditional bottom feeders of the popular media,

---

Steven M. Bellovin is a distinguished member of the Technical Staff, AT&T Bell Laboratories, Murray Hill, NJ.

Copyright © 1996 by ATT. All rights reserved.

[Haworth co-indexing entry note]: "Security and Uses of the Internet." Bellovin, Steven M. Co-published simultaneously in *The Serials Librarian* (The Haworth Press, Inc.) Vol. 28, No. 1/2, 1996, pp. 105-113; and *Serials to the Tenth Power: Tradition, Technology, and Transformation* (ed: Mary Ann Sheble, and Beth Holley) The Haworth Press, Inc., 1996, pp. 105-113.

are now familiar with a new outlet for their wares. The Internet is seen as one of the most effective ways to distribute certain types of information.

Implicit in the above statement is a change in the nature of the Internet: much of what is now available is, by some standards, frivolous. People are using the Internet for fun. This is quite a change from its early days, when only bona fide research organizations were even allowed to connect! (To be sure, many of the early denizens of the Internet found it fun even then, but in a rather different–not to say odd–sort of way . . .)

The Internet has always been a good way for researchers to communicate and to share resources, indeed, that was among its original purposes. What has changed now is the fields of study to which the Internet is relevant. Once, it was almost exclusively for computer scientists or–somewhat later–physical scientists and mathematicians. Today, even such organizations as the Vatican Library are going online. Naturally enough, that attracts the sort of scholars who need such information.

This last point illustrates the final reason for the explosive growth of the Internet: it is growing rapidly precisely because it has grown. Expansion fuels expansion, and the Internet has reached the take-off point on an exponential growth curve. Such a rate cannot be sustained forever, of course, but there is still plenty of headroom left. There is no possible doubt: for the foreseeable future, more and more of us will do more and more on the Internet.

Unfortunately, this democratization of the Net has not been without its price. In any population, some percentage will have criminal or otherwise antisocial tendencies, and the larger the group, the more nasty folks there will be. The user population of the Internet is now estimated at over 20,000,000 people, and no community of that size is free from crime.

So it is on the Internet. It has its own set of undesirables, popularly known as hackers. For assorted reasons, the hackers have been breaking into various systems around the Net, and in doing so have made life unpleasant for legitimate users. What are these hackers after?

Some claim they only want information. This may very well be, though one might prefer that they asked permission from the owners of the systems–and information–concerned. But some hackers appear to have more sinister aims in mind. The very spread of the Internet has created new targets. When no one did business on the Internet, there were no credit card numbers there to steal. Now there are–and those who prey on such things have followed close behind. Willie Sutton is widely (though apparently falsely) reported to have said that he robbed banks because that is where the money is. Now there is money on the Internet, too.

Other targets are more subtle. After all, information has value. Sometimes people want to get the information without paying the requested fee. But there are more sinister forms of information gathering, such as industrial or foreign espionage. Is this taking place on the Net? Apparently it is, though it is very hard to judge the extent of such activities; professionals are much harder to detect than the joy hackers who are only interested in carving extra notches into their terminals.[1]

Although it is clearly improper to blame the victims for being attacked, in one important way the environment of the Internet has made widespread attacks easier: it lacks genetic diversity. The vast majority of machines on the Internet today run one of only half a dozen or so different operating systems. Worse yet, many of these share a common ancestor, the networking code developed at Berkeley in the early 1980s. A design or implementation flaw that affects one machine will likely affect very many. Biodiversity is nature's way of protecting against threats; the Internet lacks it.

Finally, the hackers themselves are getting better. Ten years ago, breaking into systems was easy; one simply guessed at logins and passwords, as in the movie *War Games*. Most such doors have been closed now, but the hackers have not given up; instead, they have learned to exploit subtle flaws in the programs and network protocols that actually implement Internet services. In one recent incident, an attacker used a sophisticated technique previously demonstrated only in the laboratory to break into some computers belonging to security expert Tsutomu Shimomura.[2,3] And as a direct consequence of that attack, the Bad Guys now have an even more powerful tool that most experts had thought was only a theoretical possibility.[4] (A second consequence of the Shimomura incident provides graphic testimony to how newsworthy the Internet is.

When he helped track down the alleged attacker, Shimomura was reportedly rewarded with a lucrative book and movie deal. Not very many years ago, the phrase "Internet break-in" would have sounded like something that happened to a tennis player, and a hacker was a bad golfer.)

PROBLEM AREAS

Suppose that a computer system is successfully penetrated. What are the consequences?

The first and most obvious consequence is that the machine itself may become unavailable for some period of time. That may happen because the hacker has caused some damage, intentionally or not. But even if the hacker has not caused any harm, the owners and administrators do not know this. An infested machine must be thoroughly sanitized, if only to remove any back doors the hacker has installed. During this process, the computer is generally unavailable to legitimate users.

Sometimes, unavailability is the hacker's intent. We have all seen calls to suppress or ban certain books. What might be the fate of an Internet site that published such a book electronically? For that matter, will hackers trash machines belonging to some organization they dislike?

Hackers have been known to change data stored on a machine. In one reported incident, a U.K. Government computer was successfully attacked within seven minutes after it went online on the World-Wide Web.[5] The perpetrators found the Web pages–and improved them!

Clearly, one cannot count on such benevolence. The hacker was not so much trying to help as showing off; this and other manifestations are really a form of graffiti, and graffiti rarely improves its substrate. More to the point, what if substantive changes were made to the data being provided? The government minister concerned noted that possibility, and wondered about liability. Is an electronic library responsible for the accuracy of the files it contains? What if the operators did not take sufficient care?

One very important type of modification is a malicious change to a program being distributed via some archive. This may be done out of pure malice; more likely, the modified version contains a back door intended to let the hacker into some new computer system. This has happened at least twice, and it is virtually certain to happen even more often in the future.

In a different vein, computer systems often contain sensitive personal information that must not be disclosed to unauthorized personnel. This may range from credit card numbers to financial information to library records. There are documented instances of the first two classes being stolen by hackers; it is only a matter of time before the third class is compromised as well.

There is an obvious defense, of course: do not put sensitive information on a networked computer. But that denies legitimate users the benefit of the network connection. Computers are interconnected for a reason, but we are often faced with the dilemma of being able to protect information regardless of the owner's intent. Also, the Internet is world-wide in scope, and in many countries the import, export, and even use of cryptography is restricted by law.

WHAT CAUSES SECURITY PROBLEMS?

Given that there are serious security problems, and given that they have serious consequences, what can we do about them? Put another way, what causes them? We cannot fix problems if we do not understand the cause.

Approximately half of the security problems encountered are caused by failures of the authentification mechanisms. That is, users or computers use various methods to persuade another computer who they are. These range from sophisticated cryptographic techniques to simple passwords to reliance on a computer's network identity or address. If the methods used are inadequate, an intruder can subvert them. Passwords, for example, can be guessed or picked up by so-called network "sniffers"–eavesdropping programs. The attacker who penetrated Shimomura's machine had his computer impersonate the network address of a computer Shimomura's computer trusted.

Cryptographic protocols are much harder to fool. To be sure, their design is a subtle and tricky business;[6] often, years elapse between the development of a cryptographic mechanism and a demonstration of its inadequacy. In practice, though, the deployment of cryptography on the Internet has been so hindered by the legal factors mentioned earlier that we do not yet know if the designs are adequate.

The second major cause of security breakdowns is buggy code. That is, the programs that offer network services do not function as intended, generally because of errors by the programmers responsible. Some of the best-known security failures have been caused by bugs. A major way the Internet Worm of 1988 spread was due to careless programming; a network server was willing to read data without checking the size of the input. This allowed the worm to overwrite crucial information and execute its own code instead.[7,8,9,10] Nor was that an isolated failure; indeed, a popular Web browser triggered a security alert recently because of the exact same program flaw.

Cryptography is no defense against inadequate code. The most private, best-authenticated connection possible is no protection if it is a private, authenticated connection to a hacker, and the program on your end will invite the hacker in. How to prevent such problems is a very active research area–but as we all know, computer programs are often buggy, and the state of the art of software engineering is quite abysmal. For now, the best defense known is a firewall, an electronic barrier between the outside and the inside.

Firewalls work because of what they are not. That is, they run very little code, and if you do not run a program you do not have to worry about whether or not it is buggy. In a similar vein, they block outside access to almost all inside machines. Again, if an attacker cannot communicate with a buggy program, he or she cannot exploit any possible security flaws. I am not saying, of course, that one should be sloppy about internal security procedures–attacks can come from insiders, too–but firewalls can deflect the very considerable threat from the outside.

A final major cause of security problems is a lack of security awareness by users. This may manifest itself by poor password selection; experimental evidence shows that at typical sites, 20-25% of users will choose passwords that are easily guessed.[11,12] Passwords are a technology that is obsolescent at best, and arguably obsolete as a reliable authentication mechanism; still, we should avoid making the problem any worse than necessary.

A more subtle user problem is known as social engineering. A social engineer essentially pulls a con game on a victim. The attacker generally poses as an insider, citing enough names that most people do not realize they are being fooled. A call that arrives around 4:55 p.m., and cites a vacationing boss as an authority figure can be terribly convincing.[13]

Phone calls are not the only ways to trick people; attractive Web pages can serve as well. For example, there is one page that offers to show weather movies on your terminal. That sounds innocent enough–but to receive them, you have to grant their machine permission to connect to yours via X11. Giving such permission is tantamount to giving any user on that system free access to your keyboard, mouse, and screen. That is, that user can see your display, and can monitor your keystrokes as you type them. But the Web page has no Surgeon-General's warning at the bottom, no cautions to unwary users. Even assuming that the administrators of the site are completely honest–and I believe that they are–oh, what a magnet for hackers. They can penetrate that system first, and use it as a stepping stone to go after folks who blithely follow the instructions on the Web page.

IF THIS GOES ON

Security problems on the Internet are a serious concern for everyone, not just system administrators. Information providers will not put their wares or computer systems at risk if cyberspace remains such a bad neighborhood. For that matter, users will be scared away, too, if not by the lack of the information they need then by the danger to themselves. Most of us try to avoid walking through dangerous areas; in the future, many people will avoid the so-called Information Superhighway if all of the exits lead to Web sites of dubious repute.

The Internet itself, of course, will not go away. But it may become a glorified form of interactive television instead, where the Web links sites dedicated to music video stars rather than libraries and databases. Not that it will help to withdraw from the Internet in favor of specialized networks; the problems are inherent to any sufficiently powerful network.

Is the situation hopeless? No, though we should not be complacent. Firewalls are not a perfect solution, but they are a powerful defense mechanism. Critical servers can be run on dedicated machines; while this does not reduce the need to make sure the server code is absolutely secure, it does mean that other, potentially dangerous programs can be eliminated. Again, if you do not run a program you do not have to worry about whether or not it is buggy, and hence insecure.

Users bear some responsibility, too. Social engineering cannot be prevented by technical measures, but the potential victims can be wary. But there is another, more important measure: users must demand more secure systems from their vendors. Today, most systems are purchased because of their features, their abilities. But this powerful functionality—the Web comes to mind—often comes at a price: security was not adequately considered during the design. This will change if and only if users start demanding something different.

And that is the real message here: that we will not have adequate security, on the Internet or anywhere else, until everyone wants it enough.

NOTES

1. Cliff Stoll, *The Cuckoo's Egg: Tracking a Spy Through the Maze of Computer Espionage* (New York: Doubleday, 1989).

2. Robert T. Morris, "A Weakness in the 4.2BSD Unix TCP/IP Software," *Computing Science Technical Report 117* (Murray Hill, NJ: AT&T Bell Laboratories), February 1985.

3. Steven M. Bellovin, "Security Problems in the TCP/IP Protocol Suite," *Computer Communications Review*, 19, no. 2 (April, 1989):32-48.

4. Laurent Joncheray, "A Simple Active Attack Against TCP," In *Proceedings of the Fifth Usenix UNIX Security Symposium* (Salt Lake City, UT: 1995).

5. Radford, "The Minister, the Mints, and the Net with a Hole Big Enough to Let in a Hacker," *Guardian*, 8 December 1994.

6. H. Abadi and Roger Needham, "Prudent Engineering Practice for Cryptographic Protocols," In *Proceedings of the IEEE Computer Society Symposium on Research in Security and Privacy* (New York: IEEE, 1994): 122-136.

7. Eugene H. Spafford, "The Internet Worm Program: An Analysis," *Computer Communication Review*, 19, no. 1 (January 1989): 17-57.

8. Eugene H. Spafford, "An Analysis of the Internet Worm," In *Proceedings of the European Software Engineering Conference*, ed. C. Ghezzi and J. A. McDermid, *Lecture Notes in Computer Science*, no. 387 (Warwick, England: Springer-Verlag, September 1989): 446-468.

9. M. W. Eichin and J. A. Rochlis, "With Microscope and Tweezers: An analysis of the Internet Virus of November 1988," In *Proceedings of the IEEE Symposium on Research in Security and Privacy* (Oakland, CA: IEEE, May 1989): 326-345.

10. J. A. Rochlis and M. W. Eichin, "With Microscope and Tweezers: The Worm from MIT's Perspective," *Communications of the ACM*, 32, no. 6 (June 1989): 689-703.

11. Daniel V. Kelin, "Foiling the Cracker: A Survey of, and Improvements to, Password Security," In *Proceedings of the USENIX UNIX Security Workshop* (Portland, OR, August 1990): 5-14.

12. Eugene H. Spafford, "Observations on Reusable Password Choices," In *Proceedings of the Third Usenix UNIX Security Symposium* (Baltimore, MD, September 1992): 299-312.

13. Ira S. Winkler and Brian Dealy, "Information Security Technology? . . . Don't Rely on It: A Case Study in Social Engineering," In *Proceedings of the Fifth Usenix UNIX Security Symposium* (June 1995): 1-5.

Serials in the Networked Environment

Clifford Lynch

Workshop Presenter

Carroll Davis

Recorder

SUMMARY. There is no doubt that serials are in a period of rapid transformation. Many different aspects of the change that we are facing as serials librarians, vendors, and publishers have been discussed at this conference. This presentation will summarize the various themes that have been discussed, and offer a look into the future. *[Article copies available from The Haworth Document Delivery Service: 1-800-342-9678.]*

In the closing address of NASIG 1995, Clifford Lynch undertook to weave a synthesis of themes from the meeting together with his own thoughts and ideas about the future. He explained that he was not a serialist, but was surprised at how much the "hot" issues of NASIG 1995 overlapped his own active interests.

Library and information professionals need to stop focussing narrowly on scholarly publishing alone, Lynch emphasized. Rather, they must study and understand scholarly communication, for which publishing is only one approach. It is important to remember that the current changes in scholarly publishing which concern us are being driven by changes in the overall scholarly communication process and its needs.

Carroll Davis is Serials Cataloger for Columbia University Libraries, New York, NY.

© 1996 by the North American Serials Interest Group, Inc. All rights reserved.

[Haworth co-indexing entry note]: "Serials in the Networked Environment." Davis, Carroll. Co-published simultaneously in *The Serials Librarian* (The Haworth Press, Inc.) Vol. 28, No. 1/2, 1996, pp. 115-120; and *Serials to the Tenth Power: Tradition, Technology, and Transformation* (ed: Mary Ann Sheble, and Beth Holley) The Haworth Press, Inc., 1996, pp. 115-120. Single or multiple copies of this article are available from The Haworth Document Delivery Service [1-800-342-9678, 9:00 a.m. - 5:00 p.m. (EST)].

Lynch discerned two "cultures of change" or tracks of development in present trends and discussed key issues and visions in terms of them. One was innovation, the application of technology to do better the things that you do already. The other was transformation, technology changing fundamentally what is done, or applied to do new things. He described how both are emerging, but said he could not offer a prediction of whether, when, or how the vectors of innovation and transformation will converge.

Innovation was first evident in the application of new technologies to produce journals and other print publications by different, computerized means. From the resources those developments created, different ways are emerging to deliver, store, and display the same documents as are available in print. An obvious example is journals on CD-ROM. Most interesting in this area are numerous pilot projects making print journals available in online form. Noteworthy examples include the TULIP Project (undertaken by Elsevier with cooperating institutions), the Red Sage Project (started in 1992 by Springer, AT&T Bell Laboratories, and the University of California, San Francisco), and a partnership of the University of California and the Institute of Electrical and Electronics Engineers to put IEEE publications online.

Collectively, these pilot projects are generating a lot of experience and useful data, Lynch said. They may be described as technological successes and are doing a good job of revealing the problems of such undertakings. As open-networked systems, these projects are hard to accomplish in actual practice, it turns out. They are encountering and addressing problems with standards, authentication, and distributed printing. They are confirming that substantial upgrades or replacements of infrastructure are necessary for large-scale distribution of any of them. Lynch predicted that Ethernet technology's ability to support development in this area cannot last more than ten more years.

Lynch questioned the significance of the pilots in the long run because they have not addressed other issues convincingly. These implementations have tended to be stand-alones, with little range of content and generally narrow in aim. Consequently, Lynch said he expects user acceptance problems when their models are adopted more broadly. Evaluating success with a general population of users may be difficult or impossible in projects involving the literature of only one publisher. Users will not accept many services with limited ranges, Lynch predicted, only integrated models that support their information-seeking success on a general scale.

Centralized versus local storage of networked data remains an unresolved dilemma. Undertaking these pilot projects requires huge upgrades and commitment of storage capacity. In larger implementations of any them, many institutions will be unable to store all the resources they need to access. On the other hand, too much centralization is dangerous. Storage centers are only as secure as their computer systems and the organizations that operate them. Both remain highly vulnerable.

The pilots have not tested economic models seriously, Lynch said. In fact, it still remains unsettled how to test economic models for networked resources. One key question Lynch identified was how acceptable transactional pricing systems will be to end users or to producers, suppliers, and rights holders. Will such models cause streams of income and expenditures to become unworkably erratic?

Turning to visions of transformation, Lynch described evidence of it occurring already. Informal scholarly communication has become increasingly prominent, as opposed to formal, structured discourse. Mostly, this is happening spontaneously over networks.

Styles of scholarly writing have changed in networked settings and will continue to do so. A style for desirable World Wide Web (WWW) pages is emerging and is not the same as for traditional print documents. The structure of the latter generally works poorly for networked users, unless they print out a document before reading it. Similarly, long logical analyses are less effective in Internet-based communication than are back-and-forth exchanges of short messages. New values are being discovered and new conventions developed for what it means to write well. It remains to be seen how these will influence scholarly discourse in the long run.

Along with writing, reading may be transformed. Different readers accessing the same hypermedia resources navigate them differently. They may find it hard to decide when they have "finished" reading. Consequently, it becomes increasingly uncertain that they come away from the same sources with the same content.

Lynch warned against assuming that the WWW represents the

end of development in networked information. He reminded listeners of comparable claims about gophers. Technology will continue developing and changing; the transformation process never really ends. Information professionals must bear this in mind when thinking about committing resources.

Past complaints about lack of organization and review will finally produce results and more order will come to network-based information, Lynch predicted. Current signs of this include preprint centers and initiatives by some professional societies, such as the Association for Computing Machinery (ACM). Lynch speculated that network-based communication may become a higher-level channel for peer recognition.

Developments in mass market publishing, such as popular magazines and newspapers now going up on America Online and other networks, are worth following, Lynch said. These can provide further useful experience with technical and economic models, which may or may not be applicable to scholarly publishing. Also, mass market publications feed into research and collections and so must be addressed by information providers.

Key issues accompanying transformation will be security and integrity of information. Privacy will also be challenged, in ways that many users may not appreciate fully. It is easy for computers to count and record transactions exhaustively; that information can then be used by whoever owns it. Library policies may protect user privacy, but publisher policies may not; and users accessing publisher services through library facilities may not realize with whom they are dealing. Libraries may acquire duties, probably as educators and possibly as advocates for protecting privacy rights of users.

The international flow and control of networked information is emerging as a similarly problematic area. The Internet really is international and fast-growing, Lynch observed. In the United States, other countries, and global policy organizations, there are current proposals to consider taxing or otherwise regulating international data transfers. Proponents claim to be interested primarily in commercial or mass market publications, but implications for scholarly communication are serious, also. At what point such regulation becomes censorship of the Internet is highly arguable, especially since different national cultures have different standards for what is acceptable discourse. What Americans consider allowable "scholarly communication" may be offensive in other countries.

Serialists should be actively interested in aggregation and standards, Lynch said, because it is not certain that publishers will deliver all the serials libraries want in a uniform manner. He asked system operators to consider problems they have now handling small numbers of electronic publications with different individual technical specifications and then to imagine the same demands extended to the majority of serials acquired for their libraries. The prospect is frightening; yet that, he said, is a plausible projection from the status quo in electronic publishing. One solution may lie in organizations that aggregate heterogeneous networked serials and supply them to clients in a single, standard stream. Lynch called these services true added value, but doubted that aggregation services' coverage can be complete.

Consequently, hopes to deal with residual problems also depend on development of standards. Progress is currently being made in this area. Noteworthy examples include new Serial Item and Contribution Identifier (SICI) codes and an infrastructure of uniform resource identifiers in development, represented by the present Uniform Resource Locators (URLs) and the proposed Uniform Resource Name (URN), Uniform Resource Characteristics (URC), etc. Increasing adoption of Standard Generalized Markup Language (SGML) is also promising but not a cure-all. SGML is really a standard for writing other standards, Document Type Definitions (DTDs), and admits enough differences in those to cause problems. For example, different publishers have adopted different SGML standards for handling mathematical equations.

Lynch envisioned a pivotal role for professional and scholarly societies in bridging the vectors of innovation and transformation. Some are already engaged in innovation initiatives. He cited ACM's new publishing plan as an excellent example. These societies have defined promoting scholarship, not primarily publishing, as their missions; so they are natural agents for transformation of the scholarly communication process. For example, Lynch reported that the ACM's announced interim copyright policies may be motivating other scientific publishers to make their own policies more author-friendly in order to stay competitive with ACM. Lynch encouraged

NASIG members to promote these issues in professional societies to which they belong.

"Follow the money" was Lynch's closing advice for gauging the speed with which transformation is overtaking innovation. Libraries now expend relatively little of their capital on electronic resources. Time studies of how fast and how strongly their profile grows within acquisition budgets may serve as an indicator of change in scholarly communication generally. Lynch suggested this would be a worthwhile area for NASIG research.

CONCURRENT SET I: ELECTRONIC PUBLISHING– HOT PROJECTS IN PROGRESS

PROJECTS SESSION 1

SCAN:
Scholarship from California on the Net

Rebecca Simon

SUMMARY. SCAN is a pilot project to facilitate broad scholarly access to humanities journals and monographs by publication on the Internet. A collaboration among the University of California Press, the University Libraries at Berkeley, Irvine, and Los Angeles, and the Division of Library Automation of the Office of the President, SCAN represents an early experiment to develop an economically viable publishing model for humanities scholarship that integrates electronic publishing, library access, and scholarly use. *[Article copies available from The Haworth Document Delivery Service: 1-800-342-9678.]*

WHAT IS PROJECT SCAN?

SCAN, which stands for Scholarship from California on the Net, is a pilot project to facilitate broad scholarly access to humanities

---

Rebecca Simon is Manager of the Journals Division, University of California Press, Berkeley, CA.

© 1996 by the North American Serials Interest Group, Inc. All rights reserved.

[Haworth co-indexing entry note]: "SCAN: Scholarship from California on the Net." Simon, Rebecca. Co-published simultaneously in *The Serials Librarian* (The Haworth Press, Inc.) Vol. 28, No. 1/2, 1996, pp. 123-128; and *Serials to the Tenth Power: Tradition, Technology, and Transformation* (ed: Mary Ann Sheble, and Beth Holley) The Haworth Press, Inc., 1996, pp. 123-128. Single or multiple copies of this article are available from The Haworth Document Delivery Service [1-800-342-9678, 9:00 a.m. - 5:00 p.m. (EST)].

journals and monographs by publication on the Internet. The project is a collaboration among the University of California Press, the University Libraries at Berkeley, Irvine, and Los Angeles, and the Division of Library Automation of the Office of the President. Through this collaboration, SCAN hopes to draw together the resources of the University of California community to harness electronic technologies in support of new methods of scholarly communication in teaching, learning, and research. We hope the end result will be a viable electronic publishing and research model.

WHAT ARE THE GOALS?

SCAN, which is funded in part by the Mellon Foundation and has been designated a Coalition for Networked Information (CNI) Initiative, has four major aims over the next five years:

- It will mount on the Internet a base of electronic humanities journals and monographs in literary studies, classics, and history. This base will ultimately form the core of a database from which pieces can be combined and repackaged by individual users to meet a variety of specialized needs.
- In order to achieve the general goal of creating a large, coherent database, the SCAN partners will develop and implement a suite of consistent Standard Generalized Markup Language (SGML) document type definitions (DTDs) for these materials by using and modifying existing DTDs as necessary. We chose SGML because it is the emerging international standard for encoding and exchanging text. We will be using the DTD prepared by the American Association of Publishers for publishers, authors, and editors that has been revised and adopted as an ISO standard.
- The project will conduct user studies among faculty and students to evaluate the use of SGML-based authoring tools, end-server systems for sophisticated searching and navigation, and the most appropriate content and access structures for such on-line information.

- Finally, cost recovery experiments will monitor and document both costs and ways for publishers to charge for access to electronic journals, monographs, and databases.

WHY ARE WE DOING IT?

SCAN was developed in response to several perceived needs in the academic community that scholarly publishing serves. First, of course, we are responding to economic pressures. Like research libraries throughout the country, the University of California Libraries are faced with declining ability to acquire the results of scholarly inquiry for faculty and students. This reduction in buying power that is being faced by all academic research libraries stands in stark contrast to the sheet volume of publications available. As one grave example, at the University of California Berkeley Library, the total number of volumes acquired each year has been halved while the number of serial subscriptions has been reduced by 14 percent. With these kinds of reductions, the Press finds it increasingly difficult to publish scholarly monographs on a break even basis. Publishing on the Internet offers the promise of a cost effective means of dissemination for this type of scholarship.

The SCAN project also allows an opportunity to employ new technologies in publishing. Electronic technologies offer possibilities for improving the delivery of and access to scholarly information, reducing the cost to libraries and end-users, protecting the contribution of the monograph, and sustaining the economic viability of university presses. For the library, such technologies offer the potential of developing an SGML coding structure for finding aids that will serve as navigational tools to access archives and other primary research materials in the humanities.

The third goal of the SCAN project is to serve scholars in the humanities. While much attention has been devoted to electronic publishing in science and math, relatively little attention has been paid to creating a critical mass of materials in electronic form for the humanities. Ultimately, the database created by the SCAN project will provide simultaneous electronic access to scholarly publications and primary research resources such as archives and manuscript collection in ways that are likely to transform the way scholars and students conduct their work.

Finally, the SCAN project will explore the changing roles for librarians and publishers. In the electronic world, the roles of author, publisher, librarian, and user of scholarly texts will probably begin to merge. SCAN allows the Press and Library to work together closely on the technical, methodological, training, and monitoring issues involved in electronic publishing. In the Library, the SCAN project will proceed in concert with other efforts to digitize special collections. Once such collections are online, students and researchers will be able to peruse electronic journals and monographs from the Press in conjunction with related primary source materials from the Library, using a single search process. Thus, by its completion, the SCAN project, in conjunction with these others materials, will begin to mirror the traditional library of print and place with a viable digital library of the future.

We believe the SCAN project has the following strengths:

- integration of journals and monographs, allowing for easy and integrated searching
- the creation of an accessible mass of materials in concentrated fields
- it transfers current value-added practices of the Press in peer review and editing/design work into the electronic environment
- creation of a searchable database, accessible from office, library, and home that will provide easy electronic identification of scholarly resources
- provision of a formatted version of those resources that can be downloaded and printed by a wide variety of hardware and software tools
- provision of a multi-campus environment for testing, in which faculty and students from several distinct academic programs will form user groups to provide input as the project is designed
- and finally, collaboration between the Library and Press in establishing, mounting, and archiving the materials and in facilitating, testing, and evaluating end-user systems.

In the remaining time, I'd like to talk about where we are now with the project. In its five-year pilot phase, SCAN will move through a series of stages as we develop an economically viable publishing model for humanities scholarship that integrates electronic publishing, library access, and scholarly use.

During the first year of the project, we have created a prototype electronic edition of an existing print journal, *Nineteenth-Century Literature* to test networked access from remote and local workstations, ease of use, searching tools, and cost recovery mechanisms. NCL-E, as we refer to this electronic version, has been online at the University of California Berkeley Library for the past eight months, mounted on a gopher server, with ASCII search hits and full-text files in Rich-Text Format (RTF) available for printing. We are in the midst of developing a World Wide Web (WWW or Web) version which we hope to mount at the Library by mid-summer. The University of California Library has begun baseline use studies of the print versions of the journals intended to be put online so that we can conduct comparable use studies with the online versions. Beta testing by user groups is underway. Plans for user groups drawn from subscriber lists and from other scholars located on the University of California campuses will begin soon. To encourage widespread use and feedback, the current and recent back issues of NCL-E are available free of charge on the gopher server and soon, on the Web server.

We are now entering phase two, and are currently in the planning stages of mounting our classics and history journals, this time in a multi-tiered format which will be accessed through WWW as well as gopher clients. The final format tier will be SGML-encoded files formatted for use with an SGML viewer.

The Press will begin offering site licenses to the wider library community for these journals in fall, 1995 for calendar year 1996 site access. The license will be valid for a calendar year, offering access to the full database of the current volume and five years back volumes, including tables of contents, abstracts, and full-text. The database will be searchable and linked to related primary source materials. This will be a domain license, which provides access to all authorized Internet Protocol (IP) addresses within the domain, defined geographically, of the institute. The license will not include multi-campus consortia or interlibrary loan, although we are willing to negotiate a license that would take these arrangements into account.

Archiving will take place at the University of California Berkeley Library and at another site outside the California power grid. The pricing structure we envision will offer the combined print and electronic version of the journal for 120 percent of the print price and offer an electronic version only for 80 percent of the print price.

The libraries will begin to work intensively with scholars to assist in the design and evaluation of the database navigational tools being developed. Over the course of the project, numerous high-end workstations will be installed in the libraries and department offices to facilitate use by scholars and students. In addition, the Teaching Library at the University of California Berkeley will begin to introduce the online journal database in bibliographic instruction so that students can incorporate online publications in their course-related study. As the project progresses, SCAN will expand to include additional journals, monographs, and primary source materials in literary studies, classics, and history.

We envision SCAN, ultimately, as a sustainable model for the creation, dissemination, and utilization of humanities scholarship that will offer an economically viable transition to electronic communication which, at the same time, supports the University's mission of providing widespread public access to the research results achieved by its scholars.

Resources for Mathematicians: The Evolution of e-MATH

Ralph Youngen

SUMMARY. Mathematicians have a history of devising electronic solutions to problems of production and dissemination of information. Thus, mathematics is a natural area for development of fully featured full-text databases. The AMS has responded by providing a communications network, e-MATH, on the World Wide Web. Currently the network serves as the home to an umbrella preprint server, the e-journal, *Electronic Research Announcements of the AMS*, and a variety of member services. In 1996, e-MATH will offer on-line access to AMS's flagship publication, *Mathematical Reviews*, with links from published reviews to complete papers available in on-line versions of AMS journals. *[Article copies available from The Haworth Document Delivery Service: 1-800-342-9678.]*

e-MATH: INFRASTRUCTURE FOR AMS ELECTRONIC PUBLISHING

The e-MATH Internet delivery system constitutes the core of the American Mathematical Society's (AMS) electronic publishing program. Partially funded through a National Science Foundation (NSF) grant, e-MATH was developed in 1990 as an Internet information

---

Ralph Youngen is Assistant Director of Electronic Products and Services for the American Mathematical Society, Providence, RI.

© 1996 by the North American Serials Interest Group, Inc. All rights reserved.

[Haworth co-indexing entry note]: "Resources for Mathematicians: The Evolution of e-MATH." Youngen, Ralph. Co-published simultaneously in *The Serials Librarian* (The Haworth Press, Inc.) Vol. 28, No. 1/2, 1996, pp. 129-134; and *Serials to the Tenth Power: Tradition, Technology, and Transformation* (ed: Mary Ann Sheble, and Beth Holley) The Haworth Press, Inc., 1996, pp. 129-134. Single or multiple copies of this article are available from The Haworth Document Delivery Service [1-800-342-9678, 9:00 a.m. - 5:00 p.m. (EST)].

service for the worldwide mathematical community. E-MATH has since evolved into the delivery mechanism for all AMS electronic products and services on the Internet, including: Member Services, Electronic Journals, and MathSci Products.

E-MATH has evolved significantly from its initial release in terms of how it can be accessed over the Internet. In 1990, the e-MATH Telnet offering provided a simple menu interface to access member services. Since 1990 pre-dated the existence of a common Internet interface, such as Gopher, the e-MATH Telnet menu system was written from scratch by AMS staff. Telnet access is still supported on e-MATH; however, most services will be phased out as those services become available on the current World Wide Web (WWW) option. (To support users without local World Wide Web capabilities, the AMS has added, and will continue to support, a LYNX option on the Telnet menu. LYNX provides limited access to the World Wide Web for users unable to do so another way.) To Telnet to e-MATH:

telnet e-math.ams.org

or telnet 130.44.1.100

(login and password are "e-math" (lowercase))

In 1990, e-MATH also offered file transfer protocol (FTP) access. e-MATH users could (and still can) conduct simple file transfers of TeX macros and fonts, preprints, and other information items. (Instructions for FTPing information from e-MATH can be obtained on the e-MATH Home Page on the WWW or from the main menu using Telnet.)

The first major evolutionary step for e-MATH occurred in 1992 when e-MATH became a Gopher server. The e-MATH Gopher was a mirror of the e-MATH Telnet interface, providing access to many of the same services accessible via Telnet with additional pointers to many other Gopher servers maintained outside of the AMS. This was the first time that mathematicians could use e-MATH to access not only AMS information, but worldwide information of interest. As with Telnet, the e-MATH Gopher server is still accessible, but will be phased out as services move to the WWW. To Gopher to e-MATH:

gopher e-math.ams.org

or gopher 130.44.1.100

In January 1995, the AMS announced the release of e-MATH on the World Wide Web, the second major step in the evolution of e-MATH. With the new e-MATH WWW offering came a completely revamped user interface. Taking advantage of the technology of the Web, users could use hypertext linking and Internet search tools to access mathematical information of interest.

At this time, all e-MATH Telnet and Gopher services are being migrated to the Web, making the e-MATH WWW site the access method of choice. New services are also regularly added to the e-MATH home page. To access e-MATH on the WWW:

http://www.ams.org/

or http://e-math.ams.org/

e-MATH PRODUCTS AND SERVICES

E-MATH has become the delivery mechanism for all AMS electronic products and services on the Internet, including Member Services, Electronic Journals, and MathSci Products.

MEMBER SERVICES

Member Services have been the basic building block on the e-MATH system. Member services presently feature the AMS Preprint Server and links to other mathematical preprint servers; employment listings in the mathematical sciences; mathematical meetings information; a TeX resource information page; and a searchable version of the Combined Membership List of the AMS, the Mathematical Association of America, and the Society for Industrial and Applied Mathematics. New services are continually posted to the e-MATH home page.

AMS MATHEMATICAL PREPRINT SERVER ON e-MATH

One of the most prominent member services featured on e-MATH is the AMS Preprint Server. The AMS Preprint Server is an umbrella for all mathematical preprints on the Internet. Preprints may be stored on e-MATH, on the author's personal machine, or on another mathematical preprint server; e-MATH contains bibliographic information about the preprint, an abstract, and a pointer to the actual text. This allows e-MATH to serve as a clearinghouse for all mathematical preprints on the Internet.

As with other preprint servers, copyright for preprint submissions remains with the author. Once a paper is published, an author must withdraw preprints upon request from publisher; however, the withdrawal may leave pointer to final work.

The e-MATH system offers several methods for viewing preprints. Preprints may be viewed by date received (100 most recent), by Math Subject Classification, or by keyword searches. Access the AMS Preprint Server from the e-MATH home page or at the URL:

http://www.ams.org/web/preprints/

ELECTRONIC JOURNALS

In January 1995, the first electronic journals were posted to the e-MATH WWW service: *Notices of the AMS* and *Bulletin of the AMS*. The *Notices of the AMS* is the Society's journal of record; the *Bulletin of the AMS* features expository articles and book reviews. Both electronic versions are free. These two primary journals marked the AMS's initial venture into the electronic publishing arena.

In July 1995, the AMS's first specialty electronic-only journal was released: *Electronic Research Announcements of the AMS* (ERA-AMS). ERA-AMS reports research announcements of significant advances in all branches of mathematics. ERA-AMS is a free journal.

The AMS believes that research journals in electronic form will play a significant role in mathematics research for years to come. In 1996, the AMS intends to offer both print and electronic versions of all primary AMS Journals. These include *Bulletin of the AMS, Journal of the AMS, Proceedings of the AMS, Transactions of the AMS, Mathematics of Computation,* and *Notices of the AMS*. In addition, several new electronic-only specialty journals are planned (topics have yet to be determined).

AMS electronic journal offerings can be accessed from the e-MATH home page or via the URL:

http://www.ams.org/web/publications/

The AMS has experimented with various pricing models for dual print/electronic journals. These models consider the cost of maintaining the information source from which these journals are prepared (the most costly component), as well as the actual product production costs. For 1996, AMS electronic journals are priced as follows: Paper only: 100%; electronic only: 90%; both paper and electronic: 115% electronic-only specialty journals library price: $125; individual price: $50.

MATHSCI PRODUCTS

MathSci is the electronically searchable bibliographic database composed of Mathematical Reviews (MR) and Current Mathematical Publications (CMP). From the MathSci database, the AMS generates a number of products including: Mathematical Reviews (print), MathSci Disc (CD), MathSci Online (Dialog, CompuServe), and, to be released in 1996, MathSciNet (Internet).

MATHSCINET:
MATHEMATICAL REVIEWS ON e-MATH

MathSciNet is the new Internet accessible version of the MathSci database being developed by the AMS. MathSciNet is scheduled for release in January 1996.

MathSciNet covers MR and CMP from 1940 onward, providing bibliographic information from 1940 until the present and full review text from 1980. MathSciNet features daily updates, making MathSciNet the most up-to-date version of the MathSci database available.

As with other WWW services, MathSciNet features hypertext links to relevant mathematical information including: reviews cited in on-screen review, journal names and publisher information, journal tables of contents, author address information, and much more.

In addition, MathSciNet stands alone as the only MathSci product capable of producing on-screen mathematics, allowing users to view fully-formatted mathematical notation by downloading a DVI, PostScript, or PDF files.

A limited demo of the MathSciNet is available on the e-MATH home page or via the URL:

>   http://www.ams.org/mathscinet/

MathSciNet will be incorporated into the pricing structure for Mathematical Reviews products. To subscribe to MathSciNet, an institution will pay an annual Data Access Fee and the MathSciNet Product Delivery Fee. In addition, discounts will be available to subscribers of both MathSci Disc and MathSciNet.

Pricing for MathSciNet in 1996 is as follows:

DATA ACCESS FEE (for Sites)	
List Price	$4,950
Institutional/Corporate Member	$3,960
PRODUCT DELIVERY FEE	
MathSciNet only	$1,775
MathSciNet plus current subscription to MathSci Disc	$2,600

For more information about any of the electronic products and services described above, contact the AMS Electronic Products and Services department:

e-mail: eps@ams.org

PROJECTS SESSION 2

Electronic Journal Update: CJTCS

Janet H. Fisher

SUMMARY. The *Chicago Journal of Theoretical Computer Science* is an experimental electronic journal from MIT Press begun in an effort to establish an economic model for pure electronic journals from standard publishers. The journal is published article-by-article to speed the time from acceptance to publication, with articles available in LaTeX source and PostScript forms. Arrangements with the MIT Libraries and Information Systems Department ensure archiving in several forms. I will update the status of the journal, its costs, subscription level, and feedback from users and contributors, and MIT Press's future plans. *[Article copies available from The Haworth Document Delivery Service: 1-800-342-9678.]*

I am happy to be here today to give you an update on the status of our electronic journal *Chicago Journal of Theoretical Computer*

Janet H. Fisher is Associate Director for Journals Publishing, MIT Press, Cambridge, MA.

© 1996 by the North American Serials Interest Group, Inc. All rights reserved.

[Haworth co-indexing entry note]: "Electronic Journal Update: CJTCS." Fisher, Janet H. Co-published simultaneously in *The Serials Librarian* (The Haworth Press, Inc.) Vol. 28, No. 1/2, 1996, pp. 135-138; and *Serials to the Tenth Power: Tradition, Technology, and Transformation* (ed: Mary Ann Sheble, and Beth Holley) The Haworth Press, Inc., 1996, pp. 135-138. Single or multiple copies of this article are available from The Haworth Document Delivery Service [1-800-342-9678, 9:00 a.m. - 5:00 p.m. (EST)].

Science (CJTCS). I will start with a description of how the journal was developed, and then follow with information about its costs and status at the present time.

The idea for the journal began as a response to several internal needs in addition to the needs of the scholarly community for quicker publication in the field of computer science:

- to establish a paying model for an electronically distributed journal
- to retool our internal publishing process in order to handle proposals for electronic journals in the future
- to respond to the library community's urging for electronic journals.

Our reputation and strong list in computer science, contacts with the academic community who would be readers of, and authors for, the journal, the author community's familiarity with LaTeX, and the readiness of the market made us respond favorably to the idea for an electronic journal in the field of theoretical computer science.

The journal is published article-by-article, with articles numbered sequentially in the calendar year. Publication is defined by deposit of LaTeX source and PostScript forms of the article on Massachusetts Institute of Technology (MIT) Press's fileserver. Subscribers receive a message informing them of availability of an article, its relevant statistics (title, author, number, abstract), and where it may be retrieved. CJTCS is available by annual subscription of $125 for institutions and $30 for individuals. Paper copies of individual articles are available to nonsubscribers through MIT Libraries Document Services Division, and electronic copies of individual articles are available to nonsubscribers through the MIT Press Journals Department.

Library subscribers are allowed to:

- Store the journal on any fileserver under its control, and make it available online to the local community to print or download copies.
- Print out individual articles and other items for inclusion in its periodical collection.

- Place the journal on its campus network for access by local users or post article listings and notices on the network to inform its users of what is available.
- Print out individual articles and other items from the journal for the personal scholarly use of readers.
- Print out articles and other items if requested by a professor, student, or staff member of the university.
- Share print or electronic copy of the articles with other libraries under standard interlibrary loan procedures.
- Convert articles from the journal to another medium (i.e., microfilm/fiche/CD) for storage.

We have arranged for permanent archiving of the journal by MIT Libraries and Information Systems. The specifics of this arrangement are:

- MIT Press will store the articles on its fileserver for as long as there is demand for on-line delivery, after which articles will be removed to off-line storage.
- Information Systems will store the LaTeX source files on magnetic tape, with plans to refresh the files every five years.
- MIT Libraries Document Services will store the PostScript files and will use them to supply paper copies of articles for interlibrary loan and for non-subscribing individuals.
- At the end of each year, MIT Libraries will receive Linotronic output of all articles published that year and will make archival microfiche.
- Back-up archives exist at the Computer Science Department at University of Chicago and the Scholarly Communication Project at Virginia Polytechnic Institute.

We issued a call for papers in July 1994 (which was revised and issued again in September 1994). To date, the editors have received twenty articles for review and have rejected ten. Four have been accepted, with the remaining six still under review. The first article is in production now and is expected to be out by the end of June, with the other accepted papers following shortly thereafter.

Financially there are several differences from print journals. First, we expect production costs to be $13-$15 per page, rather than the $40-$90 per page we experience with our print journals. Second, we project the journal will run a deficit for at least three years, at which time it will hopefully cover its direct costs and contribute to the Press's overhead costs for maintaining it. CJTCS will cover its direct costs of publication (i.e., production, marketing, editorial) when it has two hundred library subscribers, and will break-even with three hundred library subscribers (assuming publication of fifteen articles in a calendar year).

What future plans does MIT Press have regarding electronic publication? We have accepted two other electronic journals, *Journal of Functional and Logic Programming* and *Contemporary Neurology*, and will be announcing another one shortly. In the Book Division, our first online book is now available, *City of Bits* by William Mitchell. You can access it from the Press's World Wide Web catalog at http://www-mitpress.mit.edu/. We believe there will be increasing demand for standard publishers to be involved with electronic journals and books in the future, and we believe projects like CJTCS will help us work through the new processes and systems they will require.

Developing an Electronic Journal: A John Wiley & Sons Project

Gregory St. John

Workshop Presenter

Melissa Nasea

Recorder

SUMMARY. Technology has leapt ahead to the point where what was impossible to imagine a year ago is feasible today. But technology is only one component of the publishing revolution. Developing an electronic journal for Internet delivery presents challenges on every front. It is nothing less than reinventing the business of publishing. The story of the development of the *Journal of Image Guided Surgery* illustrates the challenges, the pitfalls, and the excitement of this new medium. *[Article copies available from The Haworth Document Delivery Service: 1-800-342-9678.]*

Gregory St. John is the director of STM New Media Development at John Wiley & Sons. In his presentation he stated that the *Journal of Image Guided Surgery* (*JIGS*), an electronically peer-reviewed journal, is just one of the electronic initiatives at Wiley. Mr. St. John then described several other electronic initiatives.

Melissa Nasea is Serials Librarian at the Health Sciences Library, East Carolina University, Greenville, NC.

© 1996 by the North American Serials Interest Group, Inc. All rights reserved.

[Haworth co-indexing entry note]: "Developing an Electronic Journal: A John Wiley & Sons Project." Nasea, Melissa. Co-published simultaneously in *The Serials Librarian* (The Haworth Press, Inc.) Vol. 28, No. 1/2, 1996, pp. 139-141; and *Serials to the Tenth Power: Tradition, Technology, and Transformation* (ed: Mary Ann Sheble, and Beth Holley) The Haworth Press, Inc., 1996, pp. 139-141. Single or multiple copies of this article are available from The Haworth Document Delivery Service [1-800-342-9678, 9:00 a.m. - 5:00 p.m. (EST)].

Several years ago in a strategic partnership with CARL UnCover, Wiley conducted a successful pilot project on electronic document delivery, faxing articles directly to the user. They conducted this project in an experimental research and development environment. Wiley also participated in the Red Sage project where they mounted many journals at a university site. Another project in which they participated was the University of Illinois-Urbana Champaign's digital library initiative. They converted documents from HyperText Markup Language (HTML) to Standard Generalized Markup Language (SGML) which resulted in a much richer search capability and allowed Wiley to control the final look. They created documents in SGML to distribute on the World Wide Web (WWW) so libraries would not have to mount large numbers of journals themselves.

Wiley also plans to test the prepublication delivery of tables of contents. They will deliver the table of contents of fifteen genetics journals via e-mail every two weeks. Subscribers will receive the tables of contents about twelve weeks before the publication of the print issues. Wiley is expecting that World Wide Web information centers will be developed. These will be subject clusters with a variety of information on the subject area.

Mr. St. John then stated that Wiley's original plan was to produce a print version of the *Journal of Image Guided Surgery*. However, they found several visionary editors in St. Louis interested in producing an electronic journal. *JIGS* has both a print and an electronic component with six print issues planned for this year. Wiley already had the infrastructure for producing print journals, and print journals automatically provide an archival copy. Since doing something different is difficult, Wiley wanted to make their first electronic journal as close as possible to their current print journals.

On the receipt of the author's manuscript for *JIGS*, Wiley converts it to an electronic format. They send it over the Internet to the peer reviewers who send it back electronically. The production process begins with word processed files set in PageMaker and converted to PostScript and HTML. Preprints, which may lack the mathematics and images, are mounted online within twenty-four hours of acceptance by the editors. The finished article later replaces the preprint.

The electronic *JIGS* includes much information about the journal itself with links to the editorial board members and to Wiley, subscription information, instructions to contributors, and copyright information. At the beginning of each article is a list of the sections to which the reader can jump. There are internal links from the article's body to the references and to Web sites. Wiley could put more illustrations in the electronic version than in the print one, but they have not done this yet. There were six ads in the first issue; none of them had electronic capability.

Previewing the *Journal of Image Guided Surgery* is currently possible. The Internet address is http://www.igs.wiley.com/. Both guest and subscriber registration are possible. Guests cannot access the actual contents, while subscribers get user IDs and passwords.

A journal subscription includes both the print issues and the WWW access. An individual subscription to *JIGS* costs $98. The subscriber can access the journal from any computer he or she wishes but only from one computer at a time. Institutional subscriptions cost $245 and entitle the institution to up to five concurrent users with unlimited registration on campus.

Mr. St. John stated that Wiley found the electronic journal development process to be harder than it first looked. It was a case of making order out of chaos. About thirty-five people from Wiley plus outside developers were involved in developing *JIGS*. Wiley management was very supportive of the process. They developed the journal over a compressed time line with the editors first being contacted in Spring 1994.

The developers sometimes spent days working on something before deciding that it did not look right. They then had to take it apart and start all over. This was an ongoing process. Print journals have to be perfect when published, but this is not as true in the electronic environment.

Print journals have a history of hundreds of years, but electronic journals are new. Electronic journal screens differ from print journal pages. The *JIGS* developers considered how to use the screen effectively, wanting to avoid what would confuse the journal's readers. Development is an ongoing process, and the journal has changed drastically in the six weeks it has been online. Mr. St. John concluded by showing a video clip of a rotating spinal column with arrows showing where to insert the surgical pins.

PROJECTS SESSION 3

Carnegie Mellon University and University Microfilms International "Virtual Library Project"

Charles B. Lowry
Denise A. Troll

SUMMARY. Carnegie Mellon University and University Microforms International (UMI) are collaborating on a three and one-half year development project for a virtual library. More than 650 bit-mapped journal titles from UMI will be available through the University's Library Information System to Carnegie Mellon University students and faculty over the campus fiber optic network. The paper provides an overview of the project and discusses how journal information is presented to users. An overview of the economics of full-text journals online is also provided. *[Article copies available from The Haworth Document Delivery Service: 1-800-342-9678.]*

Charles B. Lowry is University Librarian, and Denise A. Troll is Head of Research and Development for Library Information Technology, Carnegie Mellon University.

© 1996 by the North American Serials Interest Group, Inc. All rights reserved.

[Haworth co-indexing entry note]: "Carnegie Mellon University and University Microfilms International 'Virtual Library Project.'" Lowry, Charles B., and Denise A. Troll. Co-published simultaneously in *The Serials Librarian* (The Haworth Press, Inc.) Vol. 28, No. 1/2, 1996, pp. 143-169; and *Serials to the Tenth Power: Tradition, Technology, and Transformation* (ed: Mary Ann Sheble, and Beth Holley) The Haworth Press, Inc., 1996, pp. 143-169. Single or multiple copies of this article are available from The Haworth Document Delivery Service [1-800-342-9678, 9:00 a.m. - 5:00 p.m. (EST)].

FOUNDATIONS–
MERCURY/LIS, UMI/E-JADS SERVICE AND TULIP

Carnegie Mellon Libraries have had some special opportunities to implement information technology which will characterize the virtual library paradigm.[1] During the Andrew project (1983-1991) the University, assisted by major computing partners like IBM and Digital Equipment Corporation (DEC), developed and implemented a distributed computing architecture facilitated by high-speed, robust telecommunications. All buildings on the campus, including dormitories, are wired for Ethernet using the IBM cabling system. The buildings are connnected to the campus backbone using 10 MBT per second copper or fiber cable. The campus network is connected to the ANS backbone using 10 MBT per second fiber links. The University will incrementally upgrade to 100 MBT per second, starting with the backbone followed by academic, administrative and residential buildings. The Andrew system exploits the client-server design and distributed file systems working in an environment characterized by literally thousands of servers and workstations.

Given the opportunity presented by this infrastructure, it is not surprising that the library was successful in securing funding from the Pew Charitable Trust, DEC, Apple, Online Computer Library Center (OCLC), and other partners to initiate the Mercury Project (1989-1992). Mercury resulted in the successful development of a distributed public access service called the Library Information System (LIS), which is running today at Carnegie Mellon.[2] LIS has a graphical user interface and terminal emulation interface (both true clients), which allow users to retrieve library information residing on numerous servers, including the online catalog, and other local databases, several periodical indexes, and full-text information in both ASCII and bitmapped image format. The graphical user interface provides the user with a number of powerful tools for managing retrieval, as well as the capacity to routinely connect with other sites on the Internet, selected by the library because of the premium services they provide to users. These include the members of the local Pittsburgh Oakland Library Consortium (OLC), the Center for Research Libraries (CRL), Colorado Alliance for Research Libraries (CARL), and OCLC's FirstSearch. It is very important to note that these clients present the user a single point of entry to library services, so that all of these distributed resources are available seamlessly and easily, fulfilling the goal of "one-stop shopping."[3]

Among the key goals of the Mercury LIS project was the provision of not only traditional bibliographic access, but also full-text access. The first successes in this regard were ASCII-based text managed with the OCLC Newton Engine (today available as "Site Search") and retrieved using keyword Boolean strategies. These included the Grolier Academic American Encyclopedia, the American Heritage Dictionary, and Business Dateline, a collection of regional economics and business journals from University Microfilms. In addition, with the implementation of LIS in 1991, the Libraries had already developed the basic infrastructure for retrieving bitmapped images and had experimented with retrieval of journal pages. Over 20,000 pages of artificial intelligence journals from Elsevier and IEEE were scanned as a testbed in preparation for the Elsevier TULIP (The University LIcensing Program) project, which began in 1992.[4] TULIP was an excellent opportunity to learn the problems of managing TIFF images, and to that extent was an important prelude to the more demanding and large-scale work with UMI. Hence, it will be discussed later in the context of the UMI implementation.

Carnegie Mellon had developed a close working relationship with University Microfilms during the Mercury Project. As mentioned, Business Dateline was mounted on LIS as were ABI/INFORM and the Periodical Abstracts. LIS alerted users of these periodical indexes to the availability of journal articles which could be printed from the ProQuest Power Pages System™ through the Enhanced-Journal Article Delivery Service (E-JADS) which will be discussed later, as well.

E-JADS was envisioned as a preliminary step to the provision of full display access to Power Pages journals in LIS. In 1992 and early 1993, negotiations began with UMI leading to the Virtual Library Project, which had several significant goals:

- Image server and index server–the implementation of new information technology applications built on the work of the Mercury Project and on UMI's ProQuest Power Pages™.
- Cache manager–the primary new technology to be developed is an image server and cache manager with appropriate algo-

rithms to facilitate the ability to display articles from the UMI collections at a remote workstation.
- Jukebox manager–the development of a UNIX jukebox driver to enable the exchange of information between the ProQuest jukeboxes and the cache manager (this objective was added halfway through the project);
- User research–the gathering of detailed information concerning user behaviors in a large-scale test of a virtual library environment.

The Virtual Library Project illustrates the opportunities for successful collaboration between libraries and library vendors. It also indicates the long-standing tradition of University Microfilms to work closely and successfully with libraries to build opportunities for better information services to patrons. Carnegie Mellon's partnership with UMI has brought mutual benefits to both publishers and libraries by pushing the envelope of the development of digital libraries. Carnegie Mellon has a considerable investment in the LIS environment and in the work of the Virtual Library Project. UMI has contributed significant funding to this three-year project, recently extending it to the end of 1996, as well as strong technical support and, most importantly, the journal information necessary to undertake the project. UMI is tracking usage as part of the project and paying publishers royalty whenever a document is printed.

ARCHITECTURE AND USER INTERFACE

The Current Implementation of the Indexes and Images

The current implementation of LIS includes four retrieval servers that house twelve ASCII databases (many of them replicated on multiple servers), one image server (for TULIP images), and two UNIX clients (Motif and VT100). An additional image server will be added in 1995-1996 for the UMI images. The retrieval and image servers locate and return information requested by library patrons using LIS clients. Retrieval servers also sort information. The user interface client submits requests and handles the display of requested information. The information the client needs to request and display results is passed dynamically from a reference server when a user begins an LIS session. Four reference servers run simultaneously to handle the load. LIS uses Kerberos authentication, developed at MIT, and access control software developed by the University Libraries to meet licensing agreements, that is, to ensure that only Carnegie Mellon students, faculty and staff have networked access to the data licensed for mounting on local servers. Guest IDs are issued to visitors to provide access to these resources, but function only on workstations located in the Libraries and "time out" after 24 hours. LIS usage is monitored at the client and the server.

The current implementation, released to campus in December 1992, enables users to search two UMI databases, ABI/INFORM and Periodical Abstracts, and order laser prints of selected journal articles stored in page image (TIFF) format on CD ROM. When a retrieved bibliographic record has images associated with it, in ProQuest PowerPages™ Business Periodicals Ondisc (BPO) and General Periodicals Ondisc (GPO) respectively, an Order Article button is activated at the bottom of the LIS Records window (see Figure 1). The LIS client determines whether to activate the button based on the contents of the "Article Reference Number" (ARN) field in the displayed record.

When users click the Order Article button, an Order Form appears, prompting them to select a payment and delivery method (see Figure 2). When they submit the Order Form, the LIS client sends an electronic mail message containing the Order Form information, the citation and ARN from the displayed record to library staff. Staff read the electronic mail and queue the laser prints of the articles from CD ROM. In the current implementation, users cannot display the pages (images) or print selected pages; they must print entire articles. The DOS-based PowerPages™ system, i.e., the print station, printer and six jukeboxes are not linked to the campus network. The service is called the Enhanced Journal Article Delivery Service (E-JADS) because it parallels the University Libraries' Journal Article Delivery Service (JADS) which delivers photocopies of journal articles to users in campus mail.

The Materials Science (TULIP) database and images were

released to campus in the Spring 1994. Similar to the UMI implementation, LIS users can search the Materials Science bibliographic database and follow links to the full text of articles (images) indexed by the records. Printing the TULIP images also involves the use of electronic mail and the mediation of library staff. However, because the TULIP images are stored on magnetic disks connected to the campus network, users can browse and display the Materials Science Journal (image) Collection. The image software currently used in LIS is a prototype developed in Project Mercury.

The Future Implementation of the Indexes and Images

With funding from UMI and Carnegie Mellon University, the University Libraries are developing an image system that will replace the Mercury prototype and facilitate rapid desktop delivery of the UMI images stored on CD ROM. Figure 3 shows the architecture of the system as it will be integrated into LIS.

The numbered steps in Figure 3 track the user from startup of the LIS client through retrieval of an image linked to a bibliographic record. The software components and transactions involved are:

1. When a user begins a session in LIS, the Retrieval Client contacts the Reference Server. The Reference Server provides access control (i.e., determines what databases the user may see) and returns the names, locations, and requisite database information (e.g., field and index names, display instructions, associated image collection names and keys).
2. The Retrieval Client connects to and queries a Retrieval Server. The Retrieval Server returns database records. When the user displays a database record, the Retrieval Client will enable or disable the Print Article and Display Article buttons appropriately, based on the presence or absence of the image key, e.g., the contents of the ARN field in the UMI databases.
3. When the user clicks the Display Article button, the Retrieval Client will submit the request to the Image Client (display window). If an Image Client is not already running, the Retrieval Client will start one. The request includes the name of the image collection and the image key.

4. The Image Client contacts the Image Index Server to determine the location of the image collection and the structure of the requested document. The Image Index Server provides the information needed to browse the image collections and navigate the documents, e.g., in the case of journal articles, to navigate by next or previous page, article, issue.
5. The Image Client then submits the request to the Image Server which then asks the Cache Manager for the image. If the image is in the cache (i.e., on magnetic disk), the Cache Manager returns the requested image to the Image Server and the Server returns it to the Image Client. If the requested image is not in the cache, the Cache Manager contacts the Jukebox Manager to copy it from CD ROM. The Cache Manager caches entire articles. When the article images are in the cache, the Cache Manager returns the requested image to the Image Server and the Server returns it to the Image Client.

The new Image Client, like the current Mercury prototype, will have two primary windows: a Document Display window for viewing and navigating page images, and a hierarchical Collection Browser window for viewing and navigating image collections. Work on this new design involves close cooperation with Carnegie Mellon's library management system vendor to ensure that the work fits into the SIRSI/Unicorn environment. Ultimately, this architecture will be implemented so that the SIRSI user interface clients work with Carnegie Mellon's retrieval and image servers maintaining consistent access for users to all online library resources through a single interface.

USERS–EXPERIENCES AND EXPECTATIONS

Online systems such as LIS have long offered the opportunity to investigate the "information behavior" of library users at the bibliographic retrieval level and there has been a large amount of publication based on logging in library systems. The study of user behaviors in a well-integrated virtual library environment, such as LIS, offers expanded opportunities to answer many important questions for the first time, including:

FIGURE 1. The LIS Records window displaying a bibliographic record from UMI's Periodical Abstracts database and an activated Order Article button.

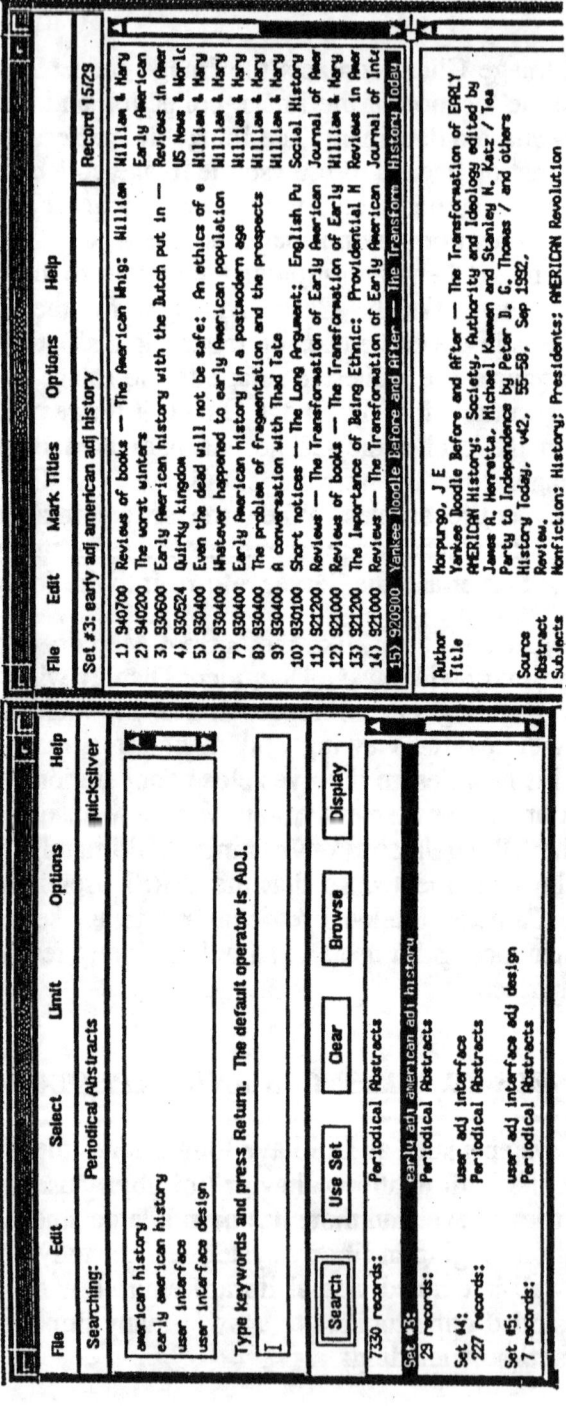

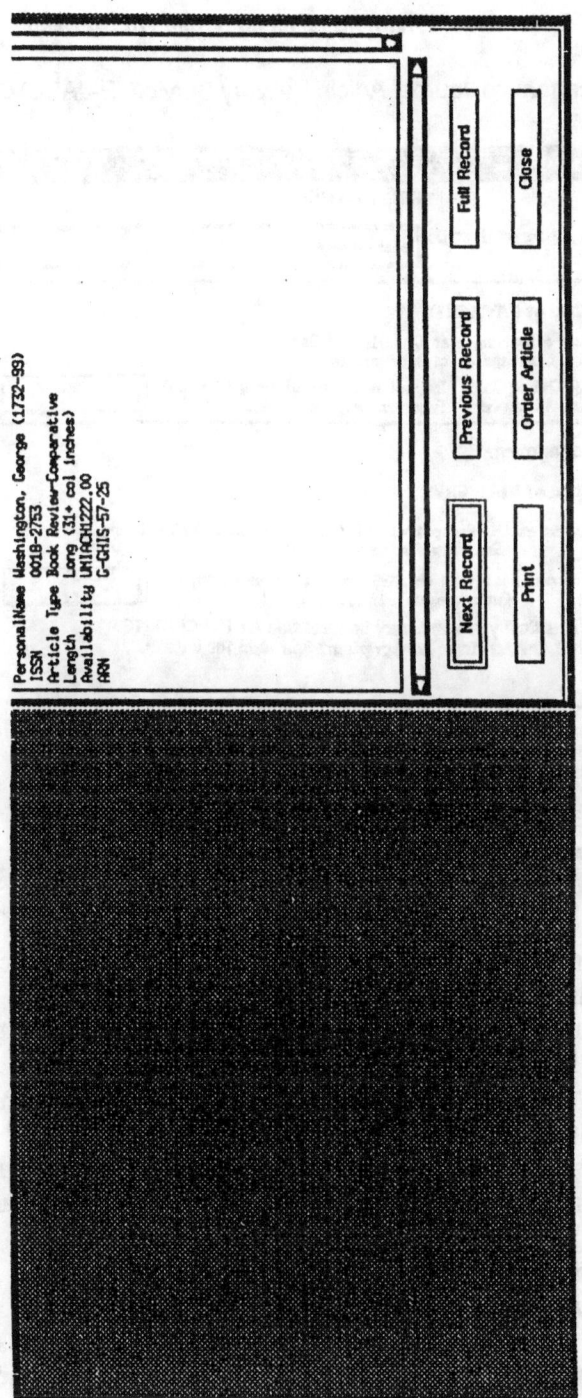

FIGURE 2. The Enhanced Journal Article Delivery Service (E-JADS) Order Form.

```
┌─────────────────────────────────────────────────────────┐
│                       E-JADS                            │
│                    PRINT ARTICLE                        │
│   Enter Your Name or UserID: [shakespeare]              │
│                                                         │
│  Select one method of PAYMENT:                          │
│  ◆ Pay by Copicard (purchase at Circulation Desk.)     │
│     Present Copicard at time of pickup.                 │
│  ◇ Charge to my CMU or JADS (Journal Article Delivery  │
│     Service) account number. Enter number (not SSN): [ ]│
│                                                         │
│  Allow 2 hours for printing.                            │
│                                                         │
│  Select one method of DELIVERY:                         │
│  ◆ Pickup articles at the Periodicals Office, 3rd Floor,│
│     Hunt Library. See Help for service hours.           │
│  ◇ Deliver in campus mail (CMU or JADS account         │
│     payments only). Enter campus address:          [ ]  │
│                                                         │
│  REMEMBER, the article you want may be available AT NO  │
│  CHARGE if CMU has a print or microform subscription.   │
│  See Help for details.                                  │
│                                                         │
│  DISCLAIMER:                                            │
│  When necessary, we will issue reprints but not refunds.│
│  Articles may NOT be returned because content is not as │
│  expected. However, users will not be charged for errors│
│  in the database (i.e. improperly scanned articles,     │
│  etc.).                                                 │
│                                                         │
│     [ PRINT ARTICLE ]    [ CANCEL ]    [ HELP ]         │
└─────────────────────────────────────────────────────────┘
```

- What information do people read online? What sequence of pages do they typically read online?
- Does online viewing/reading or printing differ from patterns of citation studies?
- How often do people print the articles they view? How many pages do they view before they print?
- How often do people view/read articles without printing them?
- How often do people print articles without viewing/reading them?
- Do they print entire articles or selected pages?
- How long are people willing to wait for a page or article?
- How long does it take to deliver a page or article across the campus network from a local cache? Across the Internet from a

central repository such as UMI's ProQuest Power Pages Direct? How greatly does it vary with time of day, day of week, month of year?
- How important is a local cache? What information should be cached?
- Do answers to these questions vary across user groups (e.g., students, faculty) or across departments (e.g., English, Architecture, Chemistry, Math)?
- How do answers to these questions vary over time, as people become accustomed to reading online and as more information is available online?

Answering such questions at a very granular level is feasible because of innovations in logging that are possible with the client/server architecture, and also because of Kerberos authentication which permits measurement of online activity at the level of the individual user. Privacy implications have been a major concern, and the libraries have been "religious" in observing the rules about the use of human subjects. Most importantly, information about who a user is will not be retained in the logs. In addition, the data is managed on a secure machine. Information about users' status (e.g., faculty, graduate student, undergraduate, staff) and affiliation (e.g., department, college, center) is not logged at run time, but plans are to determine this information through post-processing of the transaction logs when monthly reports are run.

Until February 1995, LIS logged only server-side transactions. With the February release, client-side monitoring of save, mail and print requests began. LIS now logs all of the usage data required by the UMI and TULIP projects, except the time when the image is displayed at the client. Logs have been maintained since the beginning of the Tulip implementation in April 1994, but the software to manage them routinely and create reports is not yet complete, so that only preliminary data and analysis can be reported at this time. The remaining work on logging includes combining the usage data from LIS clients, retrieval servers and image servers: building the affiliation table to convert system-supplied unique user numbers to user department and status; and writing the scripts to analyze the data and convert the results into a useable format. This work should be completed in the Summer of 1995.

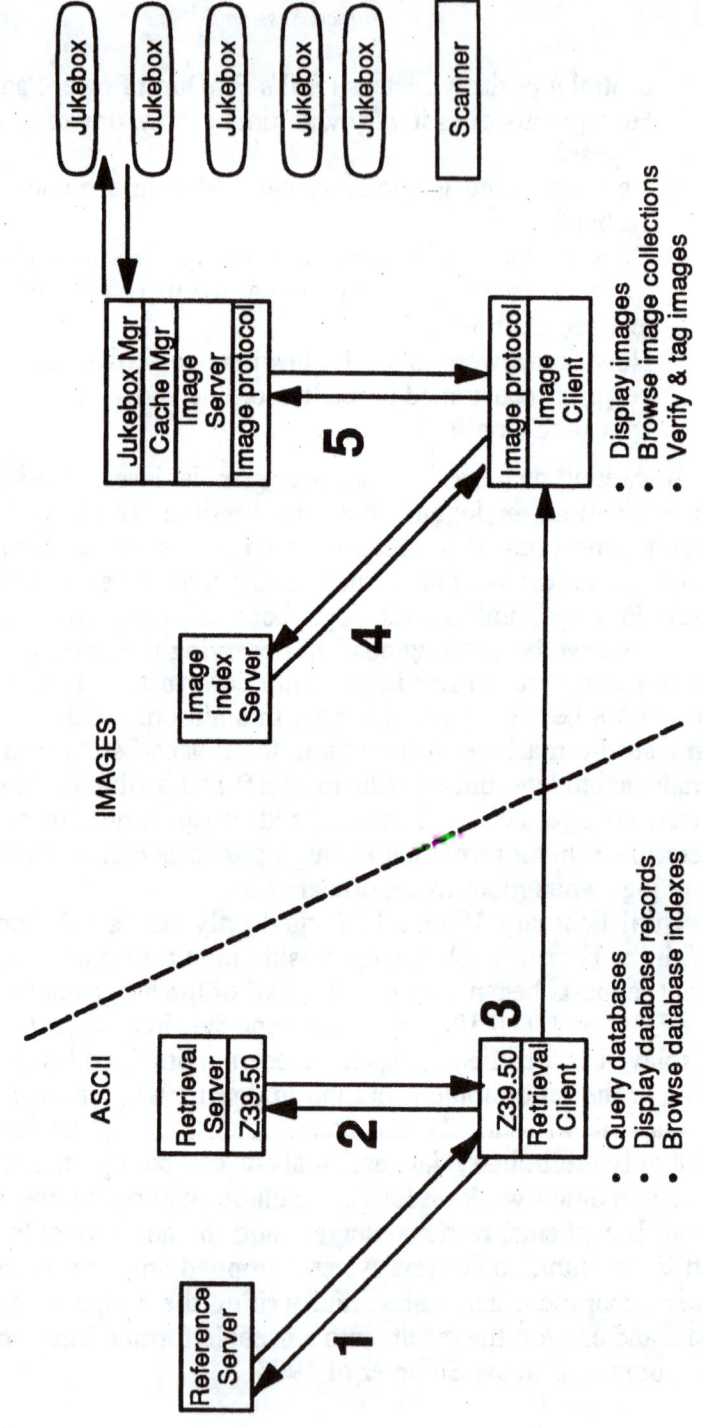

FIGURE 3. The architecture of the LIS retrieval and image systems.

Table 1 provides the first glimpse at the nature of use when full text material is integrated into the library's online environment. The use and retrieval from UMI's ABI/INFORM and Periodical Abstracts is much greater than with the smaller TULIP Materials Science database during this time period, but comparisons are possible. The over 105,000 searches submitted to the UMI databases represent together over 10% of the total searching done on all LIS services. TULIP searches are less than 1%, but since they have full-text images they allow us to infer usage to the larger UMI collections. Users displayed 2,067 bibliographic records from Materials Science and in turn displayed over 10,765 page images. Thus, for every record displayed they viewed or read 5.2 pages on average. However, this statistic understates the actual use ratio of bibliographic to full-text information. There are 43 titles indexed in the Material Science bibliographic database, and Carnegie Mellon subscribes to 29 of these so that the actual ratio of bibliographic records to full text is 27/43 or 63%. This means that for the 2,067 records retrieved by library users, only 1,302 had corresponding full text, and that increases the estimates of the average number of pages read/viewed significantly–from 5.2 pages to 8.2 pages per record. What has not yet been established is the proportion of this reading that resulted from retrieval through bibliographic search versus the image browser–i.e., the user looked at the journal title directly online and displayed/viewed the article. Nevertheless, the inference one may make is that a significant amount of reading of journals online is happening with TULIP for a small set of journals with a fairly narrow disciplinary focus. As a predictor of user behavior, this does not necessarily mean that full-text access for journals will have equivalent large scale online use, because print-

TABLE 1. Library Information System (LIS) Statistics for Fiscal Year 1994–1995 (July 1 through April 30)

Database	Searches Submitted	% Total Submitted	Records Retrieved	% Total Retrieved	Bib Records Displayed	% Total Bib Displayed	Images Displayed
Periodical Abstracts	80,497	7%	100,777,326	22%	43,027	7%	NA
ABI/Inform	24,754	2%	13,883,218	3%	15,098	3%	NA
Materials Science (TULIP)	4,646	<1%	973,512	<1%	2,067	<1%	10,765

ing is not effectively supported at this time in the TULIP project. If it were, perhaps there would be less online reading and a great deal of printing. To date there has been no patron printing of TULIP articles, probably because of the difficulty of doing so. When an article is viewed, users must cut/paste/mail the citation to staff for later printing. Directions on how to do this are hidden in the help functions, not displayed automatically like the E-JADS form. The Virtual Library Project will help determine the answer to this question.

When the online display feature is implemented in the fall of 1995 for the UMI databases a larger amount of viewing/reading might occur for several reasons. In the first place, unlike TULIP these scholarly and popular journals cover a much larger array of subject disciplines–business, management, company information, and general and scholarly journals in the areas of social sciences, arts, humanities, general sciences and current affairs–which means that a greater number of students and faculty will use them. In addition, the sheer size of the UMI project dwarfs efforts with TULIP. ABI/INFORM adds about 150,000 citations a year for over 750 periodical titles, and there are currently over 1.5 million records online. Periodical Abstracts is even larger–400,000 citations per year totaling nearly 4.5 million records in the database. Image storage is also dramatically larger for UMI than TULIP. Both projects use TIFF with compression. UMI now occupies nearly 850 GB of storage and TULIP around 27 GB.

The ratios of titles indexed to those with full-text images is 403/1000 or 40% for Periodical Abstracts and its ProQuest equivalent GPO. Similarly, the ratio is 485/750 or 65% for ABI and its ProQuest equivalent BPO. Of the 403 GPO titles and 485 BPO titles that are scanned cover to cover, 52 titles overlap. If the TULIP experience holds (8.2 pages viewed/read per citation displayed), then the number of pages displayed for a year from these UMI databases will be in the range of 350, 000. That is a great deal of online demand for reading/viewing full text. On the other hand, the facility of printing (not present with TULIP) could well encourage a surge of printing, once users review the full text and make a decision regarding its utility for their individual needs.

Needless to say, the implications for printing are a cause for concern, but TULIP does not allow for any inferential conclusions because E-JADS type printing has not been implemented for this database. However, the E-JADS experience with UMI's BPO and GPO may give some benchmarks for what to expect when full text is available. Figure 4 shows that the number of requests for (staff mediated) copies from E-JADS fluctuates between a low of 50 per month in August 1994 to a high of 336 in November 1994.

The average number of pages printed for BPO and GPO combined is 9.2 for title consulted during each "Time Period" (see Table 2). More precisely, for the 836 titles in Power Pages, the average printed is 21 per title from July 27, 1993 to May 17, 1995. Thus during a busy month, around 1,700 pages are printed per month based on the E-JADS experience, or in the vicinity of 10,500 a year. However, it is probable that the numbers will be much higher since users will be able to view/read larger portions of articles online and will have more information on which to base a decision to pay for hardcopy. The experience with print journals is informative. Users print readily from library collections articles which they have a chance to consult fully. For instance, in 1993-94 users printed over 1.4 million copies in the Carnegie Mellon Libraries. If only half, around 700,000, of those represented journal copying, then the ratio to the 3,834 titles in the print journal collection was 183 pages printed for every title, compared to the UMI E-JADS ratio of 21 per title. A similar phenomenon with full text online seems likely. This would result in annual printing from the 836 BPO and GPO titles of at least 152,634 pages as opposed to the current 10,500 pages using E-JADS. This is 15 times more printing from BPO and GPO than is currently the experience with the staff-mediated E-JADS service based on a very conservative estimate of photocopy ratios from the print collection. A more liberal estimate that 1,000,000 pages of the copying was from journals would result in a printing average of 261 pages per journal title. An equivalent from BPO and GPO would be 218,196 pages per year.

Patterns of use for the full text GPO and BPO present some interesting contrasts when compared to the equivalent bibliographic databases–Periodical Abstracts and ABI/INFORM respectively. For instance, although Periodical Abstracts represents (see Table 1) nearly three times more searching in LIS than ABI, the resultant use

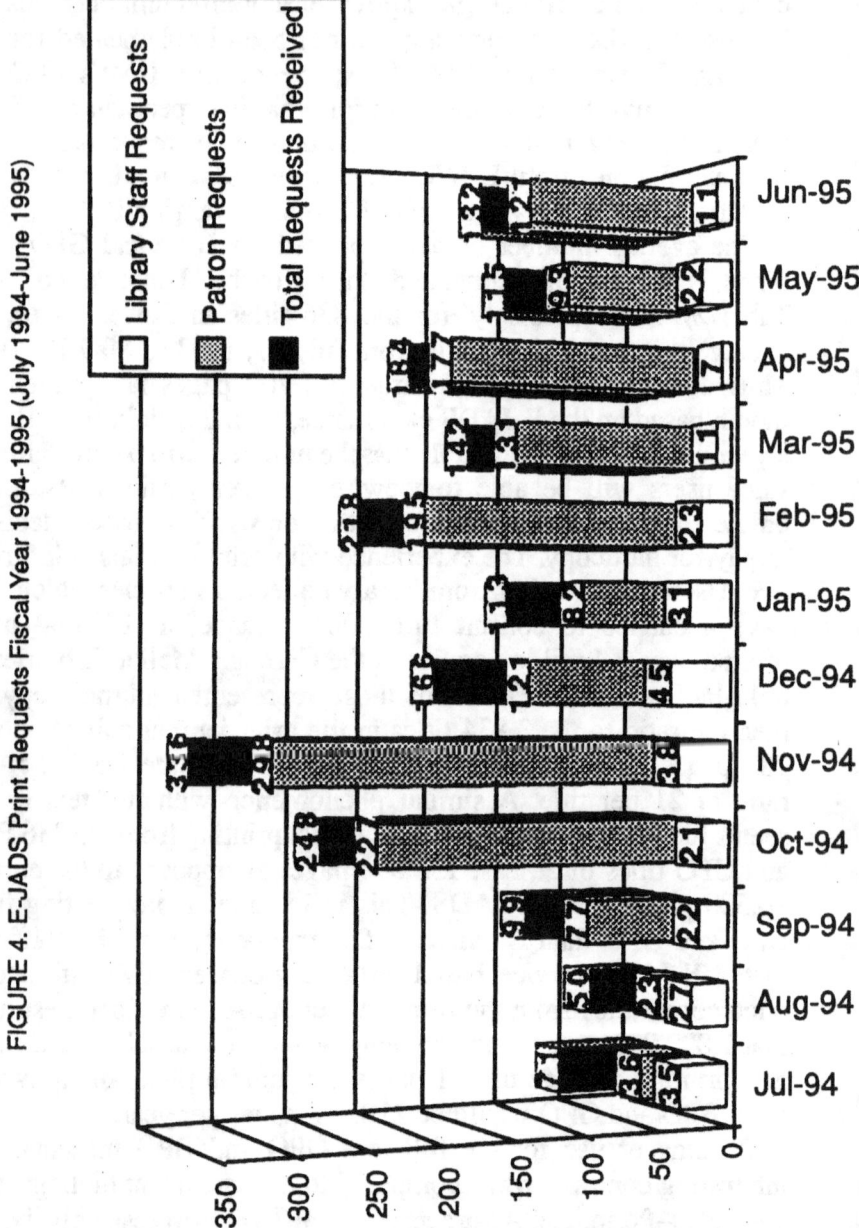

TABLE 2. ProQuest/Power Pages
Database Retrieval and Printing

Time Period	Database	Titles Consulted**	Pages Printed	Average Printed
7/27/93-11/15/93	BP	202	2160	10.7
	GP	122	1451	11.9
11/11/93-2/25/94	BP	130	1751	13.5
	GP	144	1321	9.2
2/25/94-3/17/94	BP	52	647	12.4
	GP	74	566	7.6
3/17/94-5/17/94		NO DATA AVAILABLE		
5/17/94-6/21/94	BP	56	505	9.0
	GP	36	209	5.8
6/21/94-9/19/94	BP	78	1488	19.1
	GP	44	207	4.7
9/12/94-10/27/94	BP	56	748	13.4
	GP	76	420	5.5
10/27/94-12/05/94	BP*	*	*	*
	GP	85	839	9.9
12/05/94-1/17/95	BP	67	701	10.5
	GP	48	214	4.5
1/17/95-2/27/95	BP	85	1677	19.7
	GP	77	436	5.7
2/27/95-5/17/95	BP	276	1130	4.1
	GP	202	1115	5.5
TOTALS	BP	1002	10807	10.8
	GP	908	6778	7.5
Grand Totals	**ALL**	**1910**	**17585**	**9.2**

* BP Data not available for this period.

**The "Titles Consulted" expresses the total unique titles for the "Time Period" covered. There are 836 unique titles in GPO and BPO.

of hardcopy is the reverse. During 21 months for which there is data (see Table 2), 10,807 pages were printed from BPO and 6,778 from GPO although users consulted about an equal number of periodical titles (1,002 vs. 908, note that these numbers represent the sum of titles consulted for each "Time Period," and so exceed the total number of 836 titles in the database) in both databases. What does this mean? One might conclude that the more focussed BPO database with a high proportion of discipline-oriented titles generates greater interest and propensity to print and use the articles.

It is also interesting to observe the distribution of use of materials based on their date of publication. The UMI bibliographic databases begin in 1986 and the ProQuest full text in 1987, so that there is a fair amount of comparability. On the other hand, users have tended to consult and print more from recent issues (see Table 3). Nearly 54% of the printing with E-JADS is for the most recent three years of the eight years of data and the most recent year 1994 is partial. This is a phenomenon that should be closely observed in the future as the size and timespan of the databases grow. In one respect this result is unexpected. Automation of catalogs and better access to holdings has traditionally resulted in better use of older materials than the Trueswell distribution predicts. It will be surprising if this trend is reversed when online full text becomes a dominant form. One explanation may be that the predominant printing of current materials should be expected from business disciplines where currency is an important consideration.

ECONOMICS OF DIGITAL LIBRARIES– PRINT vs. ELECTRONIC

Too often, work on digital libraries, not to mention much theoretical discussion, proceeds without a thorough grounding in the realities of cost. There are certain assumptions which precede this state of affairs, among them the notion that digital libraries somehow will be cheaper than print libraries, perhaps even free. One suspects that this arises from the misplaced hope that digital libraries will liberate

TABLE 3. ProQuest/Power Pages

Issues Consulted and Pages Printed by Year of Publication

Source Publication Year	Issues Consulted	% of Total Consulted	Total Pages Printed	% of Total Pages	Average Printed
1987	36	1.14%	307	1.75%	8.5
1988	282	8.90%	1534	8.72%	5.4
1989	282	8.90%	1776	10.10%	6.3
1990	307	9.68%	2468	14.03%	8.0
1991	377	11.89%	2197	12.49%	5.8
1992	522	16.47%	3068	17.45%	5.9
1993	918	28.96%	4178	23.76%	4.6
1994	446	14.07%	2057	11.70%	4.6
Total	3170		17585		5.5

us from the difficult cost dynamics of print libraries. There is also a presumption that electronic access will mean added value to library patrons, but it begs the question if the access is at a cost patrons are unwilling to pay. Recently, a neuroscientist stated in a library journal "I want all these [library] services to be affordable, and by 'affordable' I mean free."[5] So, exploring the underlying economics of the development of digital libraries is a critical feature of this work.

In the first place, it seems clear that libraries will not have large amounts of new funding with which to purchase electronic materials, although it is not a zero-sum game. It follows that publishers may not expect to have large sources of new profits from the sales of electronic products that represent the scholarly information published today in books and journals. The economics of scholarly book and journal publishing, in short, how to make a profit from them, are well understood.[6] The profit largely arises from transactions with libraries in the form of subscriptions and book orders, not from sales to end users. The magnitude of the undertaking before publishers is no less daunting than that facing libraries. A few publishing statistics illustrate the point graphically.

Journals have been the format which has received most attention from publishers in attempts to begin providing refereed scholarly information in electronic form. A few publishers have begun converting existing print files into electronic formats using principally scanning or re-keying to ASCII, the former providing access to the images but no indexable text, and the latter providing indexable text but no access to the graphical materials. In addition to University Microfilms, Inc., other projects have been undertaken by the few publishers or vendors who are working closely with publishers. These include Elsevier's TULIP project, IEEE's journal project, Institute for Scientific Information's recently announced biomedical journal project, and Information Access Corporation's ongoing ASCII project for full text. Among various full-text efforts, there is a fair amount of duplication of conversion for key titles, and a reasonable estimate is that the total number of titles available in electronic form is not more than 2,500. The 1994-95 edition of *Ulrich's International Periodical Directory* indicates that there are "more than 147,000 serials published throughout the world."[7] Over

11,500 new titles were added during this period, and 9,532 ceased publication. The striking statistic is that less than 2% of the serials published world-wide are currently available in electronic format. These few are largely being digitized by the retrograde process of scanning or re-keying from the print.

Thus, serial publishers are faced with the large and complex task of moving to electronic publication, which means completely reorganizing their technology and workflow process to take advantage of electronic publishing. To make things more difficult, they will for some time have to produce both electronic and print formats, because they are publishing in an international market, which will require multiple formats. They will not be able to move away from print publication any faster than subscribers worldwide can build the infrastructure to receive electronic publication.

This does not even take into consideration the serious obstacles to converting books into electronic formats. It seems unlikely that books will be adapted to the needs of the digital library as quickly or easily as journals may be. The nature of monograph publication and use militates against this prospect. So do the numbers. "American book title output reached a peak in 1987, with a grand total of 52,027; three successive years of falling figures bottomed out in 1990, when the total output stood at only 46,743."[8] Data from the *Bowker Annual* indicates that 49,000 new titles were published for 1993. If one uses scholarly books as the primary target for digital publication, then the total for the same period (1993-1994) as reported by *Blackwell North America* is a smaller 33,630 titles.[9] With the exception of CD-ROM formats for reference materials, almost nothing has been done to test electronic media for the purposes of publishing scholarly monographic materials. Thus far the work on the "electronic book"–e.g., Bellcore's "Super Book," Sony's "DataDiscman," and Megaword's "Smart Book Text Pact"–has not transformed book publishing. Even if a breakthrough technology appeared tomorrow, diffusion and general adoption would take ten years or more if the cycles for TVs and VCRs are any guide.

Three years into the UMI and TULIP projects, it is possible to begin making estimates of the infrastructure costs to the library for managing print versus electronic text. Some extrapolation is necessary in order to make legitimate comparisons of costs. Using the TULIP project as a basis, Carnegie Mellon subscribes to 29 of the 43 journals in materials science which are part of the project and, for these titles 85 volumes a year are bound. Tables 4-6 illustrate the comparative costs for print, magnetic, and CD jukebox storage of journals. The key costs for print storage (see Table 4) are binding and the capital for library buildings and shelving. The cost for storing the print volumes from these 29 titles is $914 and the net cost for the 3.5 years is $3,199. The magnetic storage costs (see Table 3) include a DEC Alpha 200 configured with five 9.1 GB Seagate disk drives, a 45.5 GB capacity. Only 30.1 GB is actually required to hold the 29 journal titles in compressed Group Fax IV TIFF images that conform to the 29 titles in the project for 3.5 years. The prorated cost for server and magnetic storage of TULIP journals is $16,891. Table 6 illustrates jukebox storage. The current cost for a 240-slot CD jukebox of the type used with UMI's Power-Pages is $15,500. Each CD holds approximately 640 MB, and the entire jukebox full is 154 GB. At these capacities, the jukebox storage would cost $3,928 to store the equivalent information from the TULIP project. Thus, the CD format using jukeboxes presents a much more cost-efficient medium for local storage than does the magnetic, but it is still 23% more expensive than print.

Several observations should be made about this costing method. It is striking that the annual maintenance for the floor space required for all three storage methods is relatively close: $19.37 for print, and $24 for either magnetic or jukebox storage (see Table 7). These cost figures do not include any of the expense of stack maintenance by library staff, cost for computing staff, or cost for the necessary computing and telecommunications infrastructure to actually exploit electronic digital journals. Nor do they reflect the expense of the subscriptions to the journals. Perhaps it can be assumed that the maintenance of the print collection by the library staff or the electronic collection by computing staff is equivalent. It might also be assumed that the telecommunications infrastructure will ultimately be available on most campuses, and that students will routinely have small, inexpensive but powerful workstations at their disposal to access such information. Finally, it might be assumed that publishers will charge no more (perhaps less) for a

TABLE 4. Print Storage Cost

Element	Explanation	TULIP cost
Library Binding	85 volumes per year @ $7.10 each	$604.00
Compact Shelving	69 volumes per sq. ft. @ $52/sq. ft.*	$64.00
Library Building	Construction $200 per sq. ft.*	$246.00
Annual Cost	Subtotal	$914.00
Project Cost	3.5 Years	$3,199.00

TABLE 5. Magnetic Storage Cost

Element	Explanation	TULIP cost
Server	DEC Alpha 200 $7400	$4,895.00
Disk Space	Seagate 9.1 GB @ $3400 × 5 = $17,000	$11,246.00
Computer Room	Construction $250 per sq. ft.**	$500.00
Project Cost	3.5 Years	$16,641.00

TABLE 6. Jukebox Storage Cost

Element	Explanation	TULIP cost
Juke Box	Kinotronics 240 CD Capacity	$15,500.00
Computer Room	Construction $250 per sq. ft.**	$1,000.00
Subtotal	Cost for 154 GB Box	$16,500.00
Project Cost	36.4 GB Utilized	$3,928.00

TABLE 7. Annual Building Maintenance

Element	Explanation	Cost
Library	4.3 sq. ft. × $4.50 sq. ft.	$19.37
Computer Room	4 sq. ft. × $6.00 sq. ft.	$24.00

*Storage for 85 TULIP volumes will require 1.23 sq. ft.

** Floor space for either magnetic or CD storage requires approximately 4 sq. ft., but racks will allow stacking thus reducing real requirements for space.

subscription to the electronic version of the journal than to the print version. If these assumptions prove incorrect, then electronic text will be even more expensive to support than print.

On the other hand, magnetic storage has dropped dramatically in price. For instance, in 1985 a mainframe 260MB disk was $11,340 with a 40% educational discount. If prices had not dropped, the inflation-adjusted price of this disk would be $15,876 in 1994 dollars and 1 GB would have been over $60,000. But, today better storage may be purchased for a fraction of the cost–1 GB at about $374. In addition, storage costs for both TULIP and UMI are the result of the storage of inefficient TIFF images. There will be alternatives as publishers begin to exploit SGML and HTML, which are all "logical" descriptions of the page. These formats can be arbitrarily complex and refer to enormous images just like TIFF files. However, if you just want to record the text, with minimal markup, the space required is probably 5-10 KB per page. A TIFF file for the UMI project will be somewhere between 60 KB and 125 KB. Thus, standards like SGML are about one-tenth the size, and that means one-tenth the storage cost. But no publishers are yet capable of supplying marked-up, formatted journals on a scale which would make this advantage useful. Moreover, the planning estimates used by Elsevier indicate that SGML may in the last analysis provide no real savings in storage capacity, only improved information retrieval.

As the tables clearly show, the current cost for magnetic storage is 5.3 times greater than print, and jukebox storage on CDs is 1.2 times greater. It is also worth considering that the typical book stack will last well over 30 years, but not the information technology. The $16,891 server and magnetic storage will have to be replaced at least every eight to ten years, and this is stretching the point. Based on a ten-year replacement cycle, digital storage and access will cost academic libraries 16 times as much as print to store locally. It seems unlikely that a persuasive case can be made for the added value of electronic access and retrieval without a dramatic change in the ownership concept. From firsthand experience, it is clear that jukeboxes are not nearly so robust and the replacement cycle on this technology will be every three to five years. It is also questionable that jukebox technology will continue to be available since it does not have a large number of applications, and is not widely used and manufactured. One final note on comparative capital expense: the cost of building will continue to increase at something like the CPI, and (if recent past is a guide) the cost of servers and storage will continue to fall at a more rapid rate. The problem is guessing correctly when these trend lines will cross and make digital storage cheaper than print.

PRELIMINARY CONCLUSIONS

As much as any, Carnegie Mellon Libraries have participated vigorously in the work of digital libraries, and the authors have enthusiastically supported this work. It seems certain that within two decades we will reach a state of development in which electronic networked access to scholarly information is the norm. That does not free us from critical analysis of the facts which may lead to better understanding of the problems and realistic decisions about what should be done to support libraries and scholarly information in the meantime. While there is cause for much optimism about the future of digital libraries, there is no cause for us to be "cockeyed optimists." These conclusions, based as they are on the facts of our experience, are offered to temper optimism with reality.

However the rate of publication for serials and books is estimated, the plain fact is that electronic publication, which will be required to support the virtual library, is in its infancy. There are many inhibitors, both technical and human, to the process of converting to electronic publication. Thus, the answer to the question, "Should we build more library space in the next 15 years?" is "you bet." In addition, to fully understand the dynamics of cost, one must make comparisons between the various forms of storage, both print and electronic.

The current publishing environment and the cost analysis of the work at Carnegie Mellon do not support the notion that digital libraries are about to happen. The world of publishing is anything but monolithic, and the comprehensive adoption of SGML-type editors in the near future (five to ten years) is not highly likely, although it is essential if the digital library is to emerge as the dominant paradigm. It is also critical if we are to have the text available for indexing and the application of advanced information retrieval technologies like natural language processing.[10] In addition, the necessity to repeat capital expenditures on servers and storage will not encourage the development of digital libraries, even though hardware is becoming more like a commodity than ever, and storage cost may be trivial in the not-too-distant future.

Moreover, there are serious local information technology issues which must be resolved. The high-capacity telecommunications network at Carnegie Mellon enables the transmission of large image files, with little cost to the user in time waiting for a response. This is not the case on most campuses or, for that matter, on the Internet. In addition, the Library Information System supports efforts like the Virtual Library Project within the context of basic library access, rather than a stand-alone demonstration. These conditions must be prevalent on campuses everywhere for it to be an inducement to publishers to provide electronic information. These conditions are currently emerging as library vendors begin to incorporate state-of-the-art technologies into their systems; as colleges and universities improve their telecommunications networks (a necessary element in their educational effort); and as Internet capacity is improved. Ten years ago, Carnegie Mellon's telecommunications network was considered state-of-the-art and almost unique, but that is hardly the case today. Similarly, library automation vendors are moving vigorously to exploit the client-server distributed computing architecture. For instance, Carnege Mellon Libraries work closely with SIRSI Corporation in order to ensure the likelihood that development efforts are not lost to the library community as a whole. These advanced infrastructure capabilities must be available "off-the-shelf" at affordable prices in supported product offerings.

One final telling conclusion may be drawn from the economic analysis. The traditional model of local ownership, which has dominated the vision of library organization and collection development for a century must change. The access model which is emerging will mean the libraries may subscribe or license access to information formerly packaged as a book or a journal, but it is not likely that they will store much of it on the local campus network. It only makes sense to share information technology resources among libraries and the cost of shared access to databases. Emerging networks like OhioLink are good examples of the opportunities which are presented. Smaller consortia like the Oakland Library Consortium may equally take opportunities for sharing such efforts. It also seems likely that the library vendor and publishing community will provide some forms of access. For instance, University Microfilms has already begun experimenting with ProQuest Power Pages Direct, a server which will provide access to the same information now provided on CD. Similarly, a large publisher such as Elsevier has opportunities to provide its own servers or even distributed servers to give good access to journal information. OCLC is also working on this problem. However, these are all new relationships. They mean that the nature of ownership must be carefully redefined and this will take time and it may not be very easy to accomplish. Publishers will want to know that their materials are being used appropriately. They will expect that access is for the campus community, that ILL and reserve reading conform to "fair use" and that authentication and authorization prevent the significant access to information for those who have not paid for it. Libraries will want to know that a subscription to a title gives them permanent access to the contents over time, that the server on which it is found will be consistently available, that the technology will be robust and stable, and that if the supplier (e.g., consortium, publisher, network) ever withdraws the service, then there is a plan for giving them the data they paid for. If such relationships are properly worked out, we may expect opportunities for new types of subscribed access. For instance, a library may subscribe to a "block" of pages for electronic access to journals not in "core" collecting areas, but which faculty and students may need occasionally.

Whatever the model for shared access, the needs of the user for seamless, easy access must be given high priority. This means that the local library systems must be interoperable with remote servers. For instance, as previously noted, the cache manager being developed for the Virtual Library Project will be modular, so that with minimal work, images can be retrieved, not only from our local TULIP server and the UMI jukeboxes, but also from the Power Pages Direct server in Ann Arbor, Michigan. It is library users who will, in the end, play the key role in deciding how digital libraries are implemented. Systems which are not an improvement over current print organization, give inadequate information, or cost exorbitantly will not be used. Therefore, it is the user studies beginning in the fall of 1995 that will establish the best insights into the future and the clearest idea of the way to shape digital libraries.

NOTES

1. Charles B. Lowry, "Catching the Second Wave of Library Automation, Information Technology and Transformation," chapter in Mel Collier and Kathryn Arnold (eds.), *ASIS, Proceedings of the First International ELVIRA Conference* (1994), Milton-Keynes, UK (May 3-5, 1995): 13-28.
2. Denise A. Troll, Project Mercury & the Development of the Library Information System, Mercury Technical Report Series, Number 7. Pittsburgh, Pennsylvania: Carnegie Mellon University, 1993.
3. Charles B. Lowry and Barbara Richards, "Courting Discovery, Managing Transition to the Virtual Library," *Library Hi Tech Journal*, 12, no. 4 (1994): 7-14.
4. Denise A. Troll, Charles B. Lowry and Barbara Richards, "TULIP at Carnegie Mellon," *Library Hi Tech Journal*, forthcoming, 1995.
5. Charles B. Lowry (ed.), "Managing Technology." Feature by Edward M. Stricker, "Managing the Information Revolution," *Journal of Academic Librarianship* 20, no. 5/6 (November 1994): 315-16.
6. Herbert White, "Scholarly Publication, Academic Libraries, and the Assumption That These Processes are Really under Management Control." *College and Research Libraries* 54, no. 4 (July 1993): 293-301.
7. Judith Salk (exec. ed.), 33rd Edition *Ulrich's International Periodicals Directory, 1994-95*, The Bowker International Serials Database (New Providence, New Jersey: R. R. Bowker, A reed Reference Publishing Company, 1994): p. vii.
8. Catherine Barr (ed.), *The Bowker Annual, Library and Book Trade Almanac*, (New Providence, New Jersey: R. R. Bowker, A reed Reference Publishing Company, 1994): p. 532.
9. *Blackwell North America, Approval Program Coverage and Cost Study* (Blackwood, N. J.: Blackwell North America, Inc., 1993): p. 10.
10. Lowry, "Catching the Second Wave ... " pp. 20-24.

Recent Steps Toward Full-Text Electronic Delivery at Elsevier Science

John Tagler

SUMMARY. Elsevier Science has been active in development efforts to move the technology of full-text electronic journal delivery forward. This presentation will focus on several projects scheduled for implementation during the first half of 1995. Consideration will be given to the goals and planning process behind the projects. Three specific products–Immunology Today Online, Tetrahedron Information System, and the TULIP model for large scale full-text electronic delivery–will be explored. *[Article copies available from The Haworth Document Delivery Service: 1-800-342-9678.]*

When we talk about the electronic future for full-text journal delivery and begin to contemplate the many options available, I think it is important to clarify the two worlds involved–both the world we know and the world we envision. First is a fairly predictable scenario, basically a standardized series of steps leading to the traditional delivery of information in print format, with everyone subscribing to a journal essentially receiving the same product or item (i.e., a printed journal issue).

John Tagler is Director of Corporate Communications, Elsevier Science, New York, NY.

© 1996 by the North American Serials Interest Group, Inc. All rights reserved.

[Haworth co-indexing entry note]: "Recent Steps Toward Full-Text Electronic Delivery at Elsevier Science." Tagler, John. Co-published simultaneously in *The Serials Librarian* (The Haworth Press, Inc.) Vol. 28, No. 1/2, 1996, pp. 171-179; and *Serials to the Tenth Power: Tradition, Technology, and Transformation* (ed: Mary Ann Sheble, and Beth Holley) The Haworth Press, Inc., 1996, pp. 171-179. Single or multiple copies of this article are available from The Haworth Document Delivery Service [1-800-342-9678, 9:00 a.m. - 5:00 p.m. (EST)].

Contrast this with the scenario of the future and information delivery becomes something very different. We are moving from an environment of limited functionalities to one of open possibilities and flexibility. In the electronic future, there is the prospect of delivering information in a variety of different formats to different audience sectors. But just as the channels of delivery will vary, so too will the types of products and product enhancements that are being developed to meet a variety of end-user needs. If we are no longer limited to the functionalities of the print page, we can begin to adapt and enhance the traditional journal format into something that meets the unique needs of individual audience groups.

Today I want to discuss three distinctly different types of electronic journal development that have recently been launched within Elsevier Science:

- Elsevier Electronic Subscriptions (EES)
- *Immunology Today Online (ITO)*
- *GENE-COMBIS*

Each of these products represents a response to a different audience group and supplies a different type of information delivery.

The most notable development within Elsevier Science since the beginning of this year is the announcement of Elsevier Electronic Subscriptions (EES). This is a commitment by Elsevier Science to make its entire list of journals available in electronic versions; this involves over 1100 titles totalling over 1.5 million journal pages in all. This is an important move forward in assembling electronic primary information for the digital library, and following upon the experiences of the TULIP Project, EES is the logical next step in a series of steps toward providing information for electronic libraries.

The core product to be delivered to EES customers is a dataset of full article and bibliographic files:

- Bit-mapped FULL text/FULL page files for each page in a journal issue at TIFF/FAX Group IV 300 dpi resolution.
- Standard Generalized Markup Language (SGML) tagged bibliographic information (title, author, abstract) for each editorial item.

- Optical character recognition (OCR)-generated ASCII representation (i.e., dirty ASCII) of full text.
- File system control files to enable different storage strategies for files.

The electronic editions include not only full-length scientific articles but all editorial material including product reviews, correspondence, editorial notes, etc.

EES enables customers to start developing a baseline system which provides sufficient functionality and content to form the foundation of a truly electronic library. This program represents an important step in the logical transformation of the fundamental ways in which information is acquired, used and shared within the scientific research community. There are significant enhancements of EES over paper format:

- Requirements can be defined by or redefined through program implementation.
- Products are adapted to serve requirements of end-users, information specialists, and librarians.
- It offers multiuser simultaneous access and access from desktop.
- Browsing and searching are possible using navigational and retrieval tools.
- Alerting, profiling, and remote access options are offered.
- Librarians able to monitor journal use.

Depending upon the implementation, page images can be displayed on the end-user's desktop using image viewer software with capabilities such as zooming, panning, and paging. Page images can also be printed on most standard laser printers, allowing for printing at the user's office as well as on high-volume production laser printers located centrally in the library or computer center.

EES offers three retrieval techniques:

- Searching all or any combination of structured bibliographic data fields and/or the full text (i.e., raw ASCII files).
- Browsing the article plus such features as tables of contents, journal cover representations, statements of aims and scope, and additional classification features for each journal title.

- Profiling of individual users' interests for automatic notification about new articles of potential interest.

I think it is important to emphasize that EES is available in 1995 on a pilot program basis only. We envision this first year's implementation as being an evolutionary period. In light of the diversity of requirements and close working relationship between Elsevier Science and participating institutions to get successful implementation in place, customization is necessary and this is currently possible with a limited number of participants.

One of the challenges to both library and publisher is to develop a pricing and licensing model that is reasonable and acceptable to both sides. As we develop licensing agreements and the associated pricing models for EES, we find that they are influenced on the level of implementation and functionality desired by each customer organization.

Among the important factors in licensing and pricing are the following:

- Electronic versions are available in addition to or in lieu of paper subscriptions.
- Electronic versions may be searched, browsed, displayed, downloaded and printed.
- Lower subscription fees are offered in exchange for per-use fee for downloading or printing.
- Institutions may have single or multiple sites as well as simultaneous access.
- User community is defined.
- Unlimited access within defined user community.
- No downloading or prints for distribution outside defined user community without document delivery fee structure built into license.

There are important technology requirements, at both the institutional and end-user level, for organizations involved in a large-scale electronic delivery operation like EES:

- *Software*: EES is intended to be implemented with either a library's own or third-party software. Librarians may choose OCLC's Site Search® and Guidon® graphical user interface.

In addition, Elsevier is in negotiations with other technology providers to offer libraries a broad scope of possibilities. But the decision on the software to store, organize, retrieve, display, and print the files rests with the subscribing institution. The technology basis for EES is a genuinely open architecture, allowing libraries to extend and modify the service in the future. Customers are encouraged to work with existing software packages rather than build from scratch, thus increasing speed of implementation and satisfaction with the end result.

- *Hardware*: the requirements are considerable. Without getting into too great detail, let us look at some rough statistics. If an institution subscribed to electronic versions of 200 journals (a substantial but not comprehensive part of its Elsevier Science list of journals holdings), these journals would be delivered in approximately 2500 issues. Assuming these journals averaged 160 pages per issue, the yearly storage capacity requirements would be around 34 Gigabytes per year. This is not a trivial capacity to add to already existing hardware systems.

We recognize that some institutions do not want to store the entire files locally, and we are working on a number of systems for remote storage or a combination local and remote file storage.

- *Printing*: electronic files cannot be printed well on all printers and can be slow in an ill-configured system. Print speed and quality are very much a factor of investment in equipment, often at the end-user level, and maintaining equipment standards for high-end workstations across a large network of users can carry a substantial price tag.
- *Delivery*: at least initially delivery will be via either CD-ROM or magnetic tape. Delivery would be weekly or biweekly depending on the customer's profile of holdings. Our experiences with TULIP have proven that the capacity of the Internet to transmit files of this size is simply not viable in the near term.
- *User training and feedback*: these must be done on a continuous basis. A commitment on the part of the librarians, computing center and end-user community are crucial to making implementation a success. The end goal is to encourage maxi-

mum use, to respond quickly to evolving needs and to measure use as unobtrusively as possible.
- *Collaboration*: close collaboration between the library and the publisher, on both a technological and contractual level, is essential particularly during the development and early implementation stages. It is going to be a very different scenario from the paper environment where every subscriber receives the same material in a standard format. Electronic subscriptions will require an in-depth planning process to determine what is delivered, in what format, at what price and accessible to whom.

If we move on to another type of electronic subscription, *Immunology Today Online* (ITO) represents a very different approach to electronic full-text delivery. Launched in January 1995 in a collaboration between Elsevier Science and OCLC, *ITO* represents a much more integrative process, a step beyond the traditional conversion of paper into electronic format. It offers hypertext links that enable users to move between related articles and access additional information not carried in the paper journal. In accessing *ITO*, the end-user, while reading any one article in the journal, will find hypertext links that open up access beyond the information contained in a single article or even a single issue, but rather relevant information in the entire *ITO* database. This is especially important when you consider the importance of using links to connect articles with letters to the editor, comments and addenda.

But I think it is important to emphasize the differences right up front. In the case of EES, we are talking about a massive conversion of potentially 1.5 million pages of text. By way of contrast, *ITO* is something very different; it is a monthly review magazine that publishes somewhere around 700 text pages per year. Also germane to the discussion is the nature of *ITO* and the role it fills, which is quite distinct from the traditional primary research journal.

Immunology Today is one the Elsevier Science family of "Trends" publications and, as such, it monitors advances in its field of coverage and brings together results in readable, topical, lucid review articles. In adapting this concept to an online environment, it was necessary to re-think how the information being delivered should be reconfigured to be of maximum usability in an electronic environment.

In its electronic version, *Immunology Today* offers everything it does in print, plus the following:

- Optimal searching – virtually every word in every article can be searched electronically by subject, title, author, keyword and date with a full range of Boolean and proximity operators.
- In a single search, the user can cover the entire collection of *ITO* from 1994 onward.
- Full hypertext functionality allowing users to move through related articles at the click of a button.
- Hypertext links to abstracts of cited papers from the *Excerpta Medica (EMBASE)* bibliographic database.
- Articles from *Immunology Today* are supplemented with news items and an online 'Product Finder' that enables users to access relevant product information.
- A 'Bookstore' provides information and ordering procedures for new books and journals.
- An online 'Job Trends' lists job opportunity for immunologists worldwide.

In order to implement this scenario, we carry on our traditional publishing operations which are augmented by the following steps:

- Editorial coordination to create indexes, identify hypertext links, etc.
- SGML tagging of files.
- Integration of *EMBASE* files.
- Preparation for OCLC processing and delivery.

So, *ITO* is everything *Immunology Today* is ... and more. *ITO* is a free-standing product that is widely available on a commercial basis at the following price schedule:

Pricing: 1995

	Individuals	Institutions
Immunology Today	$ 115 (100%)	$ 514 (100%)
Immunology Today Online	$ 132 (115%)	$ 642 (125%)
Combined subscription	$ 138 (120%)	$ 694 (135%)

As with EES, we have made *ITO* available in print alone (as *Immunology Today*), in electronic alone and in a combined subscription.

In a departure from the notion of delivery full-text of an existing journal, we have *GENE-COMBIS*. COMBIS, which stands for The *C*omputing for *M*olecular *B*iology *I*nformation *S*ervice), can be viewed as a new section of our long-established journal *Gene*. Instead of adding a new paper section to the journal, as publishers have done so many times in the past, Elsevier is offering electronic functionalities for a group of papers, to be published within the *Gene* umbrella, that take these particular articles beyond the traditional bounds of the print journal. In this instance, it is not the existing papers that appear in *Gene* that will be available electronically but rather a new group of papers dealing with analytical information and molecular biology techniques.

GENE-COMBIS is a joint undertaking between Elsevier Science and the European Bioinformatics Institute (EBI). The service will be available on the WorldWide Web, starting July 1st, 1995.

As with *ITO*, a bit of background is in order. Molecular biology, the study of molecular structures and events underlying biological processes, is the fastest growing area of research in the life sciences. In recent years, a vast amount of data on gene and genome mapping and protein sequencing has been published. The launch of *GENE-COMBIS* responds to the demands for a medium to discuss and disseminate, at unprecedented speed and with enhanced searching functionalities, information concerning the analysis of this ever-increasing amount of data.

GENE-COMBIS offers:

- Electronic submission of manuscripts = electronic peer review for computational microbiology papers.
- Upon acceptance, electronic tagging or linking of gene sequences or protein structures to genetic databases (EBI, GenBank, DDBJ).
- Upon acceptance, electronic submission of new sequences.
- Accepted papers available online with hypertext links to gene sequences or protein structures.
- Sophisticated search facilities per above.
- Online access to genetic databases.
- Online access to references in *EMBASE* database.

GENE-COMBIS is available on a subscription basis (@ $75.00) to molecular biologists and researchers affiliated with institutions that subscribe to the journal *Gene*. For institutions currently subscribing to *Gene*, we will be offering the remainder of 1995 to researchers on a free trial basis.

Rather than work within the conventional strictures of offering the existing print papers from *Gene* in electronic format, Elsevier is offering an electronic enhancement that extends the value of a journal package in a way that responds to the needs and work patterns of the research community that the journal serves.

But in returning to my opening comparison of the present and future delivery formats, the notion of flexibility and service is very much in keeping with the future that we envision. There is not going to be–there cannot be–a single format for all users.

The realization of the scenario for the electronic future now seems to have acquired a momentum of its own. We are not there yet, but important strides are being made as the technology continues to develop, as the user community continues to explore and articulate how it wants the information customized and delivered, and as the publishers and producers continue to blend the emerging technologies with market demands.

PROJECTS SESSION 4

Springer-Verlag's Electronic Projects

Robert C. Badger

Workshop Presenter

Beatrice L. McKay

Recorder

SUMMARY. Since mid-1992, Springer-Verlag, AT&T Bell Laboratories, and the University of California San Francisco have been cooperating on Red Sage, an experimental project to bring scientists and researchers electronic access to medical journals. Robert Badger, Director of Electronic Projects for Springer-Verlag, discussed the development of the project, the difficulties it has encountered, its successes, preliminary conclusions drawn from the project, and possible future directions. *[Article copies available from The Haworth Document Delivery Service: 1-800-342-9678.]*

In 1992, Springer-Verlag, AT&T Bell Laboratories and the University of California-San Francisco (UCSF) began a project called

---

Beatrice L. McKay is Serials Cataloger for Trinity University, San Antonio, TX.

© 1996 by the North American Serials Interest Group, Inc. All rights reserved.

[Haworth co-indexing entry note]: "Springer-Verlag's Electronic Projects." McKay, Beatrice L. Co-published simultaneously in *The Serials Librarian* (The Haworth Press, Inc.) Vol. 28, No. 1/2, 1996, pp. 181-184; and *Serials to the Tenth Power: Tradition, Technology, and Transformation* (ed: Mary Ann Sheble, and Beth Holley) The Haworth Press, Inc., 1996, pp. 181-184. Single or multiple copies of this article are available from The Haworth Document Delivery Service [1-800-342-9678, 9:00 a.m. - 5:00 p.m. (EST)].

Red Sage. Each partner provides a particular benefit: UCSF brings its strength in the medical field; Bell Labs contributes its RightPages software; and Springer-Verlag provides its publishing experience. The project partners have now brought together 21 publishers to provide access to 70 journals in radiology, molecular biology and general medicine. The purpose of Red Sage is to explore ways to create and manage a large database of full-image electronic versions of journals and to bring them to scientists' desktop computers. An equally important goal of the project is to understand how scientists will use such databases. The UCSF Knowledge Management Center has a special interest in this aspect, one of its purposes being to understand how scholars manage their work and accomplish their writing. During the three-year development and testing phase, access is being offered free to approximately 1,100 UCSF scientists in the San Francisco Bay Area.

The project began in November 1992 with an informal agreement among the 3 participants. In early 1993, other publishers were invited to join. *The New England Journal of Medicine* was the first and others quickly followed. The database grew through 1994 and in January 1995 was made available to UCSF users.

AT&T Bell Laboratories' RightPages software serves several functions. First of all, it presents scientists with a familiar-looking version of the print journal they are accustomed to using. RightPages maintains as much of the look and feel of print as possible. (For additional description of the software and of the project in general, see Thomas J. DeLoughry's "Effort to Provide Scholarly Journals by Computer Tries to Retain the Look and Feel of Printed Publications," in *The Chronicle of Higher Education*, Apr. 7, 1993, pp. A19-21.) A second important role played by RightPages is its "alerting" service. This service helps scientists manage their information flow by alerting them by means of an e-mail message when new issues of titles they have "subscribed to" become available. If the scientist has completed a user profile, RightPages will also notify them when "non-subscribed" titles containing articles that match their interest profiles become available. Finally, the software provides a search engine which allows users to identify and retrieve articles at will from the database.

The software is able to measure use, and tracks the number of articles that are viewed and printed. The rate of use at UCSF has grown from accessing 1,158 articles through 432 searches in January 1995 to accessing over 3,000 articles in April 1995. It also tracks activity by category of user: faculty, graduate students, staff or librarians. Librarians were the heaviest early users, but the teaching faculty have now overtaken them. As to currency, the electronic version of a journal may be available as much as a week before the print version.

Managing the material flow, such as claiming missing issues electronically from the various publishers, is an important challenge for the project. Another challenge is the storage requirement for such large amounts of material. As of July 1995, University of California-Los Angeles (UCLA) is supplying additional computer storage space as space at UCSF becomes filled. Fractile compression is also being investigated as a way to compress half-tone graphic images to be stored separately then combined on command.

Because many publishers are involved in the project, agreement on standards is essential. All 21 publishers create their files in Acrobat. All use the same base level DTD (Document Type Definition). Because of the standardization among the files in Red Sage, the National Library of Medicine (NLM) has become interested in carrying out an indexing experiment based on Red Sage's journal database. NLM wants to accelerate its indexing, and access to electronic files could enable such improvement. However, the lack of standardization among different publishers who use different DTDs and tagging conventions make such indexing from the electronic file difficult. Because all publishers in Red Sage use the same formatting and definitions, NLM may be able easily to experiment using the Red Sage database.

AT&T is currently developing versions of the RightPages software, originally written for UNIX, for Apple MacIntosh and IBM. Future developments include a World Wide Web implementation.

Preliminary conclusions drawn thus far from the project suggest that, first of all, the collection of journals is important. It must be large enough and complete enough to serve the purposes of its intended users. Second, links with other databases and projects will be important; for instance, a link between Medline and the Red Sage database would allow the user to search Medline, find a citation and abstract, then retrieve the actual document from his desktop. Links with other projects such as the Visible Human Project also need to be considered. Finally, it is clear to the project participants that in such projects, an integrator is needed. The integrator in the Red Sage project is AT&T Bell Laboratories. They act to integrate the work of the various participating publishers so that the database is consistent and conforms to project-wide standards.

The Red Sage Project is scheduled to end after 1996. Springer-Verlag is beginning to discuss how it will implement a commercial version of the database to begin tentatively in 1997.

CONCURRENT SET II: SERIALS AND SERIALISTS ON THE MOVE: ISSUES AND CHALLENGES IN THE ELECTRONIC AGE

SESSION 1:
ROLES IN TRANSITION

The Alarmists versus the Equilibrists: Reexamining the Role of the Serials Professional in the Information Age

Thomas W. Leonhardt

SUMMARY. The Alarmists say that librarians will soon be replaced by commercial publishers, icons, and the Information Superhighway. Equilibrists take the view that librarianship and librarians will maintain the status quo in spite of environmental change. The truth may lie somewhere in between the two extremes, neither of which may be a realistic approach to take in a world that has always been changing if perhaps never at such a fast rate and with such uncertain results. The serials professional must learn from the past, not for nos-

---

Thomas W. Leonhardt is Director of Library Technical Services and Head of Collection Development, University of Oklahoma Libraries, Norman, OK.

© 1996 by the North American Serials Interest Group, Inc. All rights reserved.

[Haworth co-indexing entry note]: "The Alarmists versus the Equilibrists: Reexamining the role of the Serials Professional in the Information Age." Leonhardt, Thomas W. Co-published simultaneously in *The Serials Librarian* (The Haworth Press, Inc.) Vol. 28, No. 3/4, 1996, pp. 187-195; and *Serials to the Tenth Power: Tradition, Technology, and Transformation* (ed: Mary Ann Sheble, and Beth Holley) The Haworth Press, Inc., 1996, pp. 187-195. Single or multiple copies of this article are available from The Haworth Document Delivery Service [1-800-342-9678, 9:00 a.m. - 5:00 p.m. (EST)].

talgic reassurances but for ascertaining patterns, issues, and strategies. While microforms and facsimile issues are not completely parallel to the electronic journal, there are similarities that may provide some important lessons. Serials professionals can analyze current trends, study the issues, and take steps that will solidify their positions in libraries without trying to guess what will happen to the publishing world by the year 2000 or any other year. Complacency has no room in librarianship but neither does a sense of despair and panic. Solutions abound. The trick is to find the right ones.

The theme for this year's NASIG conference, "Serials to the Tenth Power: Tradition, Technology, and Transformation," is apt and timely, not just because this is NASIG's tenth anniversary conference, but because tradition, technology, and transformation figure heavily in current discussions about the future of libraries, librarians, and librarianship. The title of this paper was inspired by an editorial in *College & Research Libraries*, in which the editor divided the debaters on the future of libraries into two camps, the Alarmists and the Equilibrists.[1]

The Alarmists are defined as those who "predict that the needs of primary academic library users will eventually be met either by specialty scholarly publisher [sic] *or* by libraries." Equilibrists are those "who believe that the status quo can be maintained in spite of environmental changes."[2] This is, of course, a grossly oversimplified statement of the issues we face, and librarianship is so narrowly defined as to be almost unrecognizable, even if we limit the discussion to academic libraries, which we do not. The issues facing our profession transcend type of library.

In *The Crisis of the Self in the Age of Information*, Raymond Barglow postulates, "As cars represent the values of industrial culture, so computers represent those of post-industrialism, defined as a social order in which the leading economic sector is the production, distribution, and processing of information."[3] This definition mirrors Peter Drucker's assessment of our "age of social transformation," an economic order in which knowledge, not labor or raw material or capital, is the key resource." This new order is embodied by the "knowledge worker," a phrase coined by Drucker in his 1959 book, *Landmarks of Tomorrow*.[4] These knowledge workers, according to Drucker, will work in jobs that "require a good deal of formal education and the ability to acquire and to apply theoretical and analytical knowledge. They require a different approach to work and a different mind-set. Above all, they require a habit of continuous learning."[5]

"In the knowledge society, clearly, more and more knowledge, and especially advanced knowledge, will be acquired well past the age of formal schooling and increasingly, perhaps, through educational processes that do not center on the traditional school. Increasingly, an educated person will be somebody who has learned how to learn, and who continues learning, especially by formal education, throughout his or her lifetime."[6]

Charles W. Anderson, in his *Prescribing the Life of the Mind*, also sees the need for university educated persons who continue to learn but who start out with what he calls practical reason. "The aim of practical reason is the improvement of practice. Creativity is the aspect of thought which leads to the proposals of better ways of doing things. This means that a program of education which would cultivate practical reason must *aim at* creative effort as its culminating objective."[7]

Librarians have always been knowledge workers and have always valued continuing education, formal and informal, and have focussed, as practitioners should, on practical reason, on finding better ways of doing things. Librarians have always embraced technology, eagerly and creatively, to help us do things better, but we have not let technology lead us where we have not seen fit to go. That is until recently. The coming millennium seems to have robbed us of our practical reason, if we are to judge by the glut of articles that have been written about information technology, the information superhighway, and the future of libraries and librarians, most of which include some version of the end of the book, the virtual library, and the end of the world as we great unwashed, technology-threatened librarians know it. Change our way or perish!

Librarians, at least since Melvil Dewey's days, have speculated about what the library of the future will be like. This gazing into the future is a human foible that at one level is merely harmless, at another level somewhat helpful in dealing with current problems, and at a third level, dangerous in its tendency to abandon reality, reason, and responsibility. Futuristic navel gazing can sometimes be a good tactic, but for good strategy, we must also look to the past, our tradition, and not simply extend the present into the future, presuming that we know what the future holds. Such extensions are often colored by fear, wishful thinking, and just plain guessing about what might happen. Such guessing, however, is even less certain than picking the final four for the NCAA basketball championship before the regional pairings are even announced.

In 1926, Melvil Dewey looked ahead fifty years and in doing so may have been the first librarian to incorrectly predict that the book would become obsolete. He guessed that it would happen by 1976.[8] In 1993, Fred Kilgour, another librarian visionary, also predicted the end of the book, this time by the year 2005.[9] He is wrong, too, but he is in good company. Why is he wrong?

The book and the year 2005 are not really the questions we ought to be considering. Crawford and Gorman explain, "The debate about the future of print is really not about print-on-paper versus electronic technology (after all most print-on-paper is the result of computer technology). It is about reading and the best means to read."[10] This book versus computer issue is just one of several false dichotomies thrown at us by technojunkies and shows how we can lose our practical reason and buy into a false information-age future that is predicted by people who are so closely associated with new technology that they become arrogant and overly optimistic about outcomes, usually failing to see that possibility and probability are words with different meanings. The observation that certain kinds of publishing serve us better electronically than on a printed page is then extended to include all printed material despite evidence to the contrary, for example, the strong growth of the print industry, reading, and book ownership. Evidence that does not support the arguments at hand is ignored and not pursued, is misinterpreted and not fully understood. Perhaps it is the fear of seeming ignorant that makes us accept these predictions meekly and without a murmur, with no critical response, even when we know they are wrong.

Recently, however, there have been some thoughtful, scholarly replies to the millennial hysteria about the future of libraries and librarians, beginning in 1992 with Roma Harris's book, *Librarianship: The Erosion of a Woman's Profession*,[11] followed in 1994 by *The Myth of the Electronic Library: Librarianship and Social Change in America*, by William F. Birdsall,[12] and now, in 1995, *Future Libraries: Dreams, Madness, and Reality,* by Walt Crawford and Michael Gorman.[13]

The latter work is especially pointed in its responses to the virtual library, the future of the book, and the role of libraries in general. There is a strong philosophical base to each of these books but their real value lies in their use of practical reason and hard facts brought to bear on heretofore unchallenged pronouncements and unsubstantiated, often silly claims.

Birdsall takes the reader from the myth of the library as place through the myth of the electronic library and into the present information society. He reminds us of statements and predictions made by Lancaster, Giuliano, Dowlin, and others, while putting those electronic visions into a context that shows them to be incomplete visions, visions false to the spirit of librarianship.[14]

Harris argues that in a search for status and validation of status from others, librarians may have lost their collective soul and most certainly have put it in mortal danger. We are what we are, and by trying to be something else, we stand to lose the very status, power, community standing, and dignity that is ours.[15]

By definition and education, librarians are neither lawyers nor doctors, and should not behave as such. Birdsall writes,

> There is much in the myth of the electronic library to appeal to librarians and others concerned with libraries. It appears to be in tune with the social and technological changes identified by social scientists and futurists. It is identified with a powerful, awe-inspiring technology—the computer. It offers concise goals for the "library" and precise roles for librarians. It promises enhanced professional prestige and the possibility of greater material compensation. And there is an inevitability about it all. But does it represent a new epoch in librarianship, the chance at last to attain the high professional status (and its material rewards) so longed for by librarians for over a century? Before we rush onto the electronic highway, do we need to stop and look in all directions before we put the pedal to the floor? Some think not.[16]

What does all of this have to do with NASIG and serials librarians? Everything. Serials librarians, serialists to be more inclusive, work in a tradition-bound profession but one that has dealt with and is dealing with change admirably. I am not convinced, however, that the changes we have dealt with, even automation and online serials systems, have been life-threatening and fundamental. Henry David Thoreau once observed, "All change is a miracle to contemplate; but it is a miracle which is taking place every instant." He goes on to quote Confucius, "To know that we know what we know, and that we do not know what we do not know, that is true knowledge."[17]

What do you know as a serialist? A lot. What do you know about the future? Nothing. And even what you know about serials changes with each mail delivery. What a bleak world it would be without the worst serials title change of the year and a sense of humor to help deal with it!

In our not-so-distant past, those halcyon days when money flowed like water and seemed to go as far, university libraries invested heavily in microform sets and facsimile reprints of books that were not acquired when they first came out or that had found their way into *Books for College Libraries,* second edition.

One of the great debates of the time—heated, passionate, learned debates—was about how to catalogue those microforms and other facsimiles. How to serve the public by showing that the text was identical to the original but that the format was different. We had tradition, reason, and the welfare of the library user to guide us. Those were librarians debating library service issues and not information specialists concerned only with access to raw data.

AACR2 came along a few years later and made us re-examine the way we cataloged serials. Which was better and for whom, latest entry or successive entry? Again, the debate was knowledgeable and passionate, as it should have been. And again, the commitment to service and the welfare of the library patron were at the forefront of the debate.

What do the terms "equilibrist" and "alarmist" mean to serials librarianship? I hope that they are just words that spur discussion and that they are not representative of most librarians who are better characterized by the term realist. A realist is a librarian armed with practical reason who

> can and should unite reason and imagination and, with their aid, create future libraries that will continue to serve and enrich individuals and the society in which they live.[18]

Future libraries will be open to any and all suggestions about how to do things better and will be flexible enough to adopt new ways and new technologies when they are appropriate. It takes insight to distinguish between, on the one hand, the need to accept change in methods and, on the other hand, the need to preserve constancy of purpose and mission.[19]

As examples, I offer the Kardex and automated systems. I remind you of the heated debate, even vitriolic at times, over what appeared to many to be a senseless abandonment of the tried and true Kardex, for automated systems that did not save time, staff, or money and that seemed to create as many problems as they solved. There are some who would still argue that the Kardex is superior to a computerized system, and who could point to some reasonable evidence to back up the argument. Part of this attitude exists because, while automated systems, overall, may be superior to the Kardex, the basic mission and even the routines have remained essentially the same.

Are you worried about electronic journals? Are they fundamentally different from print journals? How so? Is your mission to represent those titles fundamentally different from representing serials on paper, audio cassette, video cassette? When I worked in the University of California Berkeley's Rare Books and Special Collections from 1970 to 1973, we received a box of matzoh wafers–concrete poetry. We also acquired a poetry magazine with a name that would raise eyebrows even today, but twenty-five years ago the title was unutterable by the rare-book librarian who would refer to it rather obliquely, whenever it was necessary to mention it at all. That was change. That was radical–concrete poetry, obscene titles. But cataloging the matzoh crackers and the poetry magazine was not. A title is a title is a title even when it is a four-letter word or something to eat.

How are electronic journals different? Electronic journals represent change and present challenges to you, but to represent those changes and challenges as threats to your existence seems a stretch.

Anderson tells us that ". . . practical reason requires an 'insider's' perspective. The participant is not spectator but protagonist. The point of analysis is not simply to find causes for a pattern of action but to grasp its rationale, to see what commends it as a way of doing things. Practical reason necessarily means to advocate one plan against alternatives. There is nothing 'value neutral' about it. Criticism is not simply interpretation, but the effort to rethink assumptions, to consider improvements in style and method. And note, in practical reason one is neither objective nor detached, but *committed* to the endeavor in question."[20]

We must re-examine, constantly as it turns out, how we do things. We must question why we do things. We must and do change, constantly. The very nature of serials work is change–detailed and constant change. But re-invention? Re-tooling? We have downsized and right-sized, not out of greed, as have many of our giant corporations, but out of budgetary necessity. It is nothing short of self-delusion to think that suddenly we know exactly how many staff and librarians we really need just when money is short, serials inflation is high, and library percentages of funding-agency budgets are constantly shrinking. Suddenly, we discover that we have too many library employees.

Gorman and Crawford, quotidian by necessity in much of what they write about, close their book in elegance. I would like to close, too, with that paragraph, and leave you with something to guide you– you knowledge workers, armed with practical reason, continuing education, and creative minds–as you come to work each day in a real library with walls and colleagues and patrons who are eager to use *all* of the resources that you are providing:

> Librarians should never be afraid to defend the eternal mission of libraries–to collect, preserve, organize, and disseminate the records of the knowledge and information of humankind and to provide human services based on those records. Moreover, they should never be ashamed to defend and to show by example the core values–community, literacy, learning, service, reason, democracy, and intellectual freedom–upon which the culture of libraries is built.[21]

NOTES

1. Gloriana St. Clair, "Editorial: Choosing to Choose," *College & Research Libraries*, 55 (May 1994): 194.

2. Ibid., 194.

3. Raymond Barglow, *The Crisis of Self in the Age of Information: Computers, Dolphins, and Dreams* (London and New York: Routledge, 1994), 1.

4. Peter Drucker, "The Age of Social Transformation," *The Atlantic Monthly* 274 (November 1994): 62.

5. Ibid., 62.

6. Ibid., 66-67.

7. Charles W. Anderson, *Prescribing the Life of the Mind: An Essay on the Purpose of the University, the Aims of Liberal Education, the Competence of Citizens, and the Cultivation of Practical Reason* (Madison, Wis.: The University of Wisconsin Press, 1993), 113.

8. Melvil Dewey, "Our Next Half-Century," *Library Journal*, 51(15 Oct. 1926): 888 in Klaus Musmann, *Technological Innovations in Libraries, 1860-1960: An Anecdotal History*, Contributions in Librarianship and Information Science, No. 73 (Westport, CT: Greenwood Press, 1993), 17-18.

9. Frederick Kilgour, "Looking Forward: The Next 25 Years in Library and Information Technology," unpublished paper delivered at the LITA President's Program, American Library Association Annual Conference, New Orleans, Louisiana, June 28, 1993.

10. Walt Crawford and Michael Gorman, *Future Libraries: Dreams, Madness, and Reality* (Chicago and London: American Library Association, 1995), 13.

11. Roma M. Harris, *Librarianship: The Erosion of a Woman's Profession*, (Norwood, N.J.: Ablex Publishing Corporation, 1992).

12. William F. Birdsall, *The Myth of the Electronic Library: Librarianship and Social Change in America*, Contributions in Librarianship and Information Science, Number 82 (Westport, CT: Greenwood Press, 1994).

13. See note 9 above.

14. See note 11 above.

15. See note 10 above.

16. Birdsall, 43.

17. Henry David Thoreau, *Walden*, (New York: Illustrated Modern Library, 1946), 13.

18. Crawford & Gorman, 183.

19. Ibid., 183.

20. Anderson, 35.

21. Crawford & Gorman, 183.

What If They Started Talking? New Roles for Staff in Change Management– A Case Study

David S. Goble
Kathleen Brown

SUMMARY. Commercial enterprises with a bottom-line-driven discipline and rapidly evolving competitive markets have learned much about change management. As the environment faced by academic libraries becomes less stable, much can be learned from the for-profit sector. Central to successful change efforts is the understanding that change is about people not technology, that our problem is not change but continuous change, and that defining the purpose of change is vital. A case study demonstrates the level of achievement that can be obtained when these lessons are applied. *[Article copies available from The Haworth Document Delivery Service: 1-800-342-9678.]*

The inspiration for this paper stems from a question following a presentation dealing with the benefits of utilizing support staff in workflow design. "What if they started talking?" asked a member of the audience. "They might change something, and how would you

---

David S. Goble is Resource Delivery Manager and Dr. Kathleen Brown is Head of Acquisitions at North Carolina State University Libraries, Raleigh, NC.
© 1996 by the North American Serials Interest Group, Inc. All rights reserved.

[Haworth co-indexing entry note]: "What If They Started Talking? New Roles for Staff in Change Management–A Case Study." Goble, David S., and Kathleen Brown. Co-published simultaneously in *The Serials Librarian* (The Haworth Press, Inc.) Vol. 28, No. 3/4, 1996, pp. 197-207; and *Serials to the Tenth Power: Tradition, Technology, and Transformation* (ed: Mary Ann Sheble, and Beth Holley) The Haworth Press, Inc., 1996, pp. 197-207. Single or multiple copies of this article are available from The Haworth Document Delivery Service [1-800-342-9678, 9:00 a.m. - 5:00 p.m. (EST)].

know what they changed?" The question so missed the point of the presentation that an acceptable answer was difficult to construct. This paper attempts to provide a more satisfactory answer by exploring roles for support staff in the context of change management. It represents the personal views of two managers–one who has worked in libraries over twenty years, and one who has recently entered the field after eighteen years in commercial banking. Most of those eighteen years were spent in what librarians would call technical services (bank operations/processing), with assignments over the last ten of those years as a project or operations manager dealing with the effects of bank mergers and acquisitions.

The case study reported in this paper focuses on a major change management effort that occurred in the technical services division of the North Carolina State University Libraries during the second half of the fiscal year 1993/94. Since the authors were directly involved in the events, the perspective is undoubtedly tinged by subjectivity. In retrospect, at the start of the process we were somewhat naive about the breadth and depth of the changes involved. As the process unfolded, we engaged in numerous discussions about the similarities and differences of managing change in the profit and non-profit sectors. These discussions, which often included a cross section of the staff, served as a springboard for exploring theoretical and pragmatic concerns.

CHANGE MANAGEMENT IN THE PROFIT AND NON-PROFIT SECTORS

Change management is as difficult for business as it is for libraries. It is probably less daunting for business, because the environment demands it. Commercial enterprises operate in competitive markets in which innovation is basic to survival. They are supported by investors who require a return on capital, which in turn requires uninterrupted revenue streams. To insure those streams, the enterprise must dynamically change to meet the ebb and flow of consumer needs and desires. It is understood that change involves risk, and that risk must be rewarded. The reward system provides incentive for risk and, hence, for change.

Academic libraries, on the other hand, have traditionally operated in stable environments with essentially a captive clientele of students and faculty. The system provides few tangible rewards to encourage risk-taking, and little discretionary money to support bold new initiatives. In recent years the environment we have faced as librarians has become less stable as a result of decreases in funding, the proliferation of information sources, and increases in user expectations. In a world in which change is the prevailing factor, librarians can draw upon the experience of the business sector for guidance. In the following paragraphs, three relevant lessons from the business sector are presented. How these lessons applied to the change efforts in the technical services division at North Carolina State University Libraries will be explored in the case study.

First, business has learned that change management is not about technology: it is about people, process, and communication. People have to be involved and the involvement has to be managed. In *The Change Masters*, Rosabeth Moss Kanter states:

> Employees can be energized–engaged in problem solving and mobilized for change–by their involvement in a participative structure that permits them to venture beyond their normal work roles to tackle meaningful issues. They gain an experience of the *communitas* of teamwork on a special project–to use Victor Turner's term for dramas of high involvement–which lifts them out of the humdrum, repetitive routines of their place in the ongoing structure.[1]

Librarians must consider the "participative structure" that enables all levels of staff to engage in the evolution of change. This will require the sharing of power, active listening, encouragement, and, at times, conflict resolution. It will be challenging to many and terrifying to others. Managing the process will require equal measures of confrontation and sensitivity. Librarians are often short on the first and long on the second.

Second, business is well aware that managing change is not enough; the challenge is managing continuous change. Peter Drucker, an astute observer of both profit and non-profit organizations, believes that higher education will no longer be characterized as a stable environment:

> [I]t is a safe prediction that in the next 50 years, schools and universities will change more and more drastically than they have since they assumed their present form more than 300 years ago when they reorganized themselves around the printed book.[2]

If Drucker is correct, then academic libraries, often touted as the heart of the university, can anticipate a rate of change similar to that of their parent institutions. The rate will be even faster if libraries intend to lead the way in the field of information technology. Some librarians already understand this lesson, and others are coming to understand it. All who wish to flourish in the new environment will learn to embrace this principle. Librarians must become attuned to the fact that there will never be one right way of doing anything ever again.

Third, business has discovered that in the midst of continuous change, it is vital to define the purpose of the organization or effort. Drucker observes that: "Only a clear definition of the mission and purpose of the business makes possible clear and realistic business objectives. It is the foundation for priorities, strategies, plans, and work assignments."[3] We will be most successful if we define our purpose in terms of our clients' information needs. The simple act of defining a library's purpose will have a profound effect on its future. There is a world of difference, for example, between a gateway to information and an information delivery system.

Coming to grips with these three lessons will not be enough. The organizational structure of most libraries serves as a barrier to implementing change. Hierarchical organizations with functional alignments will not provide the level of success desired or needed. The dynamics are all wrong. The decision-making authority tends to be focused at the top of the organization, and this can stifle innovation at the operating levels. The division of effort between public services and technical services often blocks communication. In too many instances these areas fail to understand, or appreciate, the issues faced by the other and how these issues affect service to the client. Stratification of work within the hierarchy can devalue the contributions of support staff, who play a crucial role in service delivery throughout the organization. The case study which follows presents one approach to overcoming the limitations of the formal structure and leveraging the value contained in the three lessons.

CASE STUDY

The events outlined in this case study began in 1994, when North Carolina State University's Acquisitions Department started planning for a switch from a manual to an automated environment. The staff, which had been anticipating this transition for several years, was enthusiastic about the advantages that automation would offer and apprehensive about the additional effort the implementation would impose on its regular workload.

In terms of the regular workload, the staff had cause for concern. The rhythm of the ordering cycles during fiscal year 1993/94 had been pulsating rather than steady, and in early March expenditures were not as high as the department would have liked. The final ordering push resulted in 8,000 items that had to be paid and processed manually against fiscal year 1993/94, and 4,000 items that would be processed online and charged to 1994/95 funds. Of vital importance was the need to process the items quickly in order to implement a smooth workflow and to prevent the potential development of a forbidding cycle of processing bulges. The automated system would provide much-needed management information but few gains in productivity. Large swings in processing volumes would be problematic for the system, and, of greater consequence, would erode staff morale.

It was apparent to everyone that implementing the new system represented an effort far greater than teaching twenty people how to manipulate a software package. Virtually every process had to be examined and analyzed. While Acquisitions faced tremendous change, the system also had dramatic implications for change at the divisional level. Bibliographic records would be downloaded in Acquisitions at the front end of the process rather than in Cataloging at the end of the workflow. Catalogers would be working in real time on the system and would see their work immediately in the online catalog. On-order information that had previously been available only on paper in staff areas would be accessible online to the public.

The workload in conjunction with the new system and the other issues faced by the division looked like a blueprint for disaster. The strategy adopted to handle this formidable situation was of prime importance to the ultimate success of the change effort. Throughout the winter and spring the administrative level of the division, which consisted of the Associate Director for Technical Services and Collection Management and the heads and assistant heads of Acquisitions, Cataloging, and Collection Management, considered the various implications of the implementation project and its overall workload demands. The group decided to live with the stress presented by the immediate issues and to focus on the desired end result. In essence, the administrative team determined the purpose of the change process.

Management's initial position paper included a discussion of how the change process would occur and what criteria would be used to determine priorities. Central to the document was a description of what the final process would look like. At the heart of the vision was a desire to improve responsiveness to user needs by enhancing access and responding effectively to individual requests. Any divisional workflow should be even and inclusive, should deal with all items in all formats, and should result in timely, effective processing with no backlogging of currently received items and no forwarding of uncataloged items to housing locations. The process should be sensitive to staff interests and should enable staff to participate in maintaining an enriched work environment, individual effectiveness, and outstanding services to patrons.

These principles clearly represented the ideal. Four primary criteria were selected for evaluating proposed workflows:

1. Would it improve service or information to the user?
2. Would it improve quality, in terms of importance to the patron, compliance with standards, or accuracy?
3. Would it improve efficiencies, in terms of timeliness, cost, or reduction of redundancy?
4. Would it improve workload levels, in terms of balancing the load among staff or meeting ergonomic concerns?

After the guiding principles had been delineated, the administrative level assembled a cross-divisional team and asked it to develop solutions to the issues facing the division in a way that would meet the requirements of the purpose defined for the overall change-management effort. The team called itself the Workflow Planning Group and became known as the WPG for short. It consisted of six support staff chosen from Acquisitions, Cataloging, and Collection Management, and a facilitator. Members were equivalent in rank and had primary responsibilities for maintaining the processing flow through the division.

The Workflow Planning Group serves as an excellent example that people and process are more important than technology in managing change. The members of the team were exceptionally strong individuals with years of experience in the library. All had the potential to succeed on the basis of their technical competence, their knowledge of the organization, and their interpersonal skills. They were committed to the organization's goals, and they were willing to take the broad view of what needed to be done. Of particular importance to what was ultimately accomplished by the team, the members had a stake in the outcome. The team members had the opportunity to participate in determining and controlling their work environment and responsibilities, as well as that of their co-workers.

The facilitator, a library school intern, contributed some unexpected value to the chemistry of the mix. The WPG perceived the intern as being neutral, so they were able to explore thorny issues without feeling uncomfortable about confronting existing biases. The intern had been attending the administrative team's meetings, so he understood their goals and could provide constant feedback in both directions. As a student in search of employment, he also had a stake in the outcome of the WPG and the project. Not having substantial library experience, he could not bring solutions to the table. He could, however, draw upon extensive project experience in the commercial sector to raise questions and guide the process. The process was fairly simple: help the team form a common understanding of the goal to be met; help them focus on the goal; document progress; keep the administrative team aware of progress, issues, and concerns; and provide feedback to the team.

The WPG was extremely successful. They were not directly responsible for all that was done, because many people throughout the library contributed to the project. But in any examination of the division's achievements, the efforts of the WPG are apparent. The WPG analyzed the situation and communicated peer to peer across divisional lines. Their discussions rippled beyond the group itself and led everyone to a better understanding of the processing problems facing the division. The WPG identified the overhead associated with card production and recommended the elimination of shelflist cards. After receiving the green light, they devised an interim workflow that stripped processing steps to the bare minimum and mounted a divisional project to process 8,000 monographs in a fifty-day time frame. In this environment other staff came forward with streamlining suggestions. One staff member contacted other libraries and worked with the Systems Department to program barcode readers to search OCLC records by the International Standard Book Number. While staff learned the new acquisitions system, the WPG outlined another workflow and organized a second divisional project—this one to receive, pay, and catalog 4,000 monographs entirely online.

The results achieved by the WPG were dramatic. In retrospect, two factors in their success seem obvious. First, managers were able to remove obstacles very quickly and effectively due to improved communications. Second, and just as important, the WPG created energy and synergy as it experienced success. Staff and librarians throughout the division supported the group as they realized they had the opportunity to be actively involved in developing the workflow.

The achievements of this temporary group were so compelling that the WPG has been made a permanent aspect of the technical services organization. The group has added members as appropriate and has been a driving force in several initiatives over the past year, including an automated process for generating spine labels, the elimination of all card production for monographs in the main library and the branches, and an examination of methods to save staff time and real dollars associated with the use of OCLC. The library school intern has moved on to a full-time position elsewhere in the organization, and facilitation is now being shared on a rotating basis by the department heads and the Associate Director for Technical Services and Collection Management. While this arrangement means a certain loss of neutrality, it assures an open line of communication between the WPG and the administrative level.

The impact of the Workflow Planning Group has gone beyond its product of a more effective and efficient processing flow. The group can be justifiably proud of what it has accomplished, and its visibility has spread the concept of active involvement. The WPG has been disciplined in presenting, researching, and testing its ideas. They have assumed responsibility for serving as proponents of ideas and have held themselves accountable for implementation. Long-term employees in the group have described the experience as the most meaningful thing that they have done in the course of their careers. Other staff members–including professional staff–have asked how they can join the group. The organization has shown that it is receptive to new ideas, and that individuals can shape the direction of change.

The Workflow Planning Group's approach has in turn created certain organizational imperatives. Management is obligated to listen to the group's ideas and to be equally disciplined and accountable in responding quickly. The administrative team must demonstrate a conscious effort to develop and maintain a comfortable working relationship with the WPG. One of the administrative team's key roles now consists of removing barriers so ideas can move forward.

The division is still grappling with various aspects of the acquisitions implementation project, as well as with numerous other initiatives. In an attempt to expand upon the lessons learned from the WPG and to involve more staff in shaping the future, Technical Services has established a new group called the Ideas Group. This group initially consisted of four support staff and two librarians, and was authorized to design a system that would capture, acknowledge, and consider ideas. The system has been designed and is in the early stages of implementation. Anyone in the division can submit an idea, which is acknowledged and entered into a log. A filter group reviews the idea and attempts to make sure that all submissions receive equal footing in terms of presentation and data. Once equalized, the idea is publicly posted and circulated for discussion, reaction, and feedback. The Filter Group gathers any comments and prepares a package of information for the WPG. The

Workflow Planning Group is not responsible for implementation, but insures that the idea receives due consideration by the appropriate people.

The evolution of the system shares certain similarities with the evolution of the Workflow Planning Group. Management authorized the group to proceed within certain parameters. The requirements of the system were explored and delineated: why the system was needed, what needed to be accomplished, and what users were expressing for their expectations of the system. The team kept management apprised of its progress as design work progressed, and presented the design to the Workflow Planning Group to make sure that they were comfortable with its concepts. The team unveiled the system in presentations at the divisional and the departmental levels and provided opportunities for discussions.

As with the Workflow Planning Group, all parties have to exhibit commitment and responsibility. The suggester has to give some thought to the feasibility of the idea in terms of patron benefit, workflow impact, morale benefit, costs, and savings. Because ideas are posted publicly both initially and throughout the process, management has to follow through in removing barriers or in implementing the suggestions. The Ideas Group serves as another channel to enhance communication within the division, and it is a forum where staff can see action that results from their initiative. It is too early to tell how this experiment will fare, but a number of ideas have been submitted and are traveling through the system.

CONCLUSION

The Workflow Planning Group and the Ideas Group constitute one philosophical approach to managing continuous change. The groups point out the importance of people, process, and communication in working with change. People need to know what the vision is and to be given room to make decisions in bringing that vision to fruition. They need a process to focus the efforts of teams and to organize innovation. They need communication across departments and divisions and up and down the organizational structure. This case study illustrates the vital role and value of staff contributions. It also demonstrates that success has a way of becoming its own engine, and that good ideas have a way of becoming contagious. The central question for management is not "What if they started talking?" The real question is "What will happen if they don't?"

NOTES

1. Rosabeth Moss Kanter, *The Change Masters* (New York: Simon and Schuster, 1983), 203.
2. Peter F. Drucker, "The New Society of Organizations," in *The Learning Imperative: Managing People for Continuous Innovation*, ed. Robert Howard (Boston: Harvard Business Review), 5.
3. Peter F. Drucker, *Management: Tasks, Responsibilities, Practices* (New York: Harper & Row, 1974; Perennial Library, 1985), 75.

SESSION 2:
CONVERSATIONS WITH E-EDITORS

The Rhetoric of Serials at the Present Time

Eyal Amiran

SUMMARY. The rhetoric of serials promotes invisibility, timelessness, and order, and prevents us from being able to think what we might want from serial publications, or whether we want serials at all. Serial rhetoric makes us cling to our ideas of what serials publishing should be and think of any publishing in terms of traditional print paradigms. These limitations corroborate, on the one hand, a fin-de-siècle rhetoric associated with electronic text (discussed in the essay), and tie in on the other with the publishing world's attempts to think of new ventures in term of established practices. *Postmodern Culture* has offered new models for pricing serials which attempt to rethink what we want from published work. These have not met with success partly because of another rhetoric, that of experimental

---

Eyal Amiran is Assistant Professor of English, and Co-Editor of *Postmodern Culture* in the Department of English, North Carolina State University, Raleigh, NC.
© 1996 by the North American Serials Interest Group, Inc. All rights reserved.

[Haworth co-indexing entry note]: "The Rhetoric of Serials at the Present Time." Amiran, Eyal. Co-published simultaneously in *The Serials Librarian* (The Haworth Press, Inc.) Vol. 28, No. 3/4, 1996, pp. 209-221; and *Serials to the Tenth Power: Tradition, Technology, and Transformation* (ed: Mary Ann Sheble, and Beth Holley) The Haworth Press, Inc., 1996, pp. 209-221. Single or multiple copies of this article are available from The Haworth Document Delivery Service [1-800-342-9678, 9:00 a.m. - 5:00 p.m. (EST)].

media. This rhetoric is in some ways like the rhetoric of serials, so that when the two combine they doubly screen us from our alternatives. This essay explicates the paradigms that govern our perception of serials and calls for some sane measures for the immediate future. *[Article copies available from The Haworth Document Delivery Service: 1-800-342-9678.]*

For a long time, I used to go to bed early in the morning, wondering why it's so hard to say what we really want from electronic serials. The medium's utopian element is one reason which I will discuss in a bit. As Martin Spinelli has argued in a recent paper, this utopian thinking, which characterizes the reception of emergent media like the radio (a better equivalent to the Internet than the ubiquitous automobile and its borrowed highway,[1] though that too produced its share of technological utopia), actually makes it harder to consider real issues in electronic serial publishing.[2] "You can't have art without resistance in the materials," as William Morris says, and the material resistance of electronic publishing is, in part, its fabulousness, its mythical time, its ethereal order–its apparent lack of resistance. Another reason lies in the rhetoric of seriality. By "rhetoric" I mean simply the argument articulated implicitly by something–by the way it is presented or perceived. So, to give a literary example, because Faulkner's writing is convoluted and arcane, it produces the idea that the world is cryptic and convolute, and that the coherence we find in it lies in the consciousness that recognizes this cryptic convolution.[3] Faulkner's rhetoric produces complication, whatever else he might be writing about.

What then is the rhetoric of seriality? Two of the serial's rhetorical moves concern me here. First, and most obviously, it produces a particular model of order, that of serial succession. The series is one of the most pervasive of Western metaphysical orders. Whether with the family tree, the hours and the days, the houses of the sun, or the apostolic generations, Western culture has organized time and phenomena in succession. Serials extend this vocabulary. In serials, issues are numbered and appear in volumes–in this they replicate the library itself. And the uniformity of articles and features produces the idea that valuable information is ordered; its greatest information is order itself. So the function of serials is not only to determine what counts, but also to count. Second, the serial connects history with timelessness. It appears in time (and sometimes on time), with an exaggerated dramatization of this timeliness; at the same time it is an open form, like a diary, and has no closure or end. It is always not-yet, gesturing toward what Wordsworth calls in "The Prelude" "something evermore about to be." This open gesture toward a receding future connects the present of the serial with its timelessness.[4] Furthermore, the work published in each issue is supposed to belong there by virtue of an intellectual affinity that relates to the journal's identity over time. This belonging, itself a rhetorical function of the genre, is not a reading of the work in its historical context but a claim made on it that is implicitly larger than that, a classification and affiliation that unites the work with what is past, and passing, and to come, in that serial. Where this seriality is entirely arbitrary, as in the daily newspaper, it loses its ability to signify order. Newspapers appear serially and in time, but they do not produce the timelessness of serials.

These rhetorical functions of the serial, order and timelessness, are in some ways at odds, suggesting a temporal formality that exists beyond time, or an order that is atemporal. I'd like to suggest an interesting parallel to this contradictory relation in the serial poetic form of the sonnet sequence. Poetry in general is, like a serial, about counting. "Counting," writes Elaine Scarry,

> has its own cadence; cadence imposes the constraint of counting. So does lineation. Thus the names of poetic forms are persistently numerical—couplets, quatrains, terza rima, octave, sestet, sestina, ottava rima, iambic pentameter, hexameter, triolet—because the poetic voice seldom ceases to count.[5]

Poetry, as Scarry puts it, "has in common with the calendar the unceasing act of numerical counting. In any sonnet, in other words, regardless of the decade, the iambs, the pentameter line, the octave and the sestet establish at its interior a calendric sequence of moments and hours."[6] This concern with counting in poetry counts doubly in the sonnet sequence, a kind of serial in itself.[7] There was a craze in England for the sonnet sequence in the 1580s and 1590s; that craze, at the end of that century, and the genre itself, are, as Margaret de Grazia argues, about exhaustion and ending:

these runs of English sonnets represent what cannot be perfected, perfected in the Renaissance sense of brought to completion. Their content is chronic discontent. The form repeats itself because the desire it articulates, be it erotic, political, artistic, can never be satisfied.[8]

Our strictly defined yet open-ended serial repeats the sonnet sequence, and its repetition reproduces rhetorically, in part, the sonnet sequence's obsession with the end. That end, I hasten to add, is apocalyptic–not a dead-end but a transformative one. The contradictory rhetorical functions of the serial are reconciled, or elevated, in apocalyptic time. In apocalyptic vision, time has a structure: in phase one our ancestors lived–it's hard to say how long–in a timeless, deathless Eden; in phase two they ate from a tree and fell into a world of time and base materialism, which is where we are today; and in phase three, which is coming any time now, we will be translated from phase two into a spiritual world, saved or damned at the end of the days. Counting, both for the serial and for the poetic sequence, leads inevitably to anniversaries, centuries, millennia.[9] It leads to the fin-de-siècle, a heightened awareness of the end that assumes a naturalness, an air of inevitability. If we had started to count from a different point in time–say, the *death* of Jesus–then the first world war, for instance, and literary modernism, would have been in our 19th century.[10] The cataloguing and placing function we associate with our counting system lends weight to and naturalizes the arbitrary turning of the serial dial. "2000 zero party's over we're out of time," says Prince, "But tonight we're gonna party like it's 1999." Why would we be "out of time" in the year 2000? Why the repetition of the double zero? By "out of time" Prince also means the end of the days, when we would be *outside* of time, in a world where, as he writes in "Purple Rain," "you can always see the sun, day or night."[11] It's this apocalyptic vision of time that structures our understanding of the serial's contradiction, its double time. The serial is conscious of its death not because the great librarian in the sky will cancel her subscription but because it is always near the end of a volume year, and on the brink of a new one.

That the traditional cardboard serial should be, in fact, nearing its end near this end of the millennium turns out to be especially significant because of current discussion of the death of print culture, and of the birth of its ghost, the electronic publication. The book, as Sven Birkerts has said in a nostalgic eulogy, "spatializes knowledge," and its materiality "represents the claim it will make *upon our time* and attention [emphasis added]."[12] Electronic text, in contrast, is disembodied and exists outside of time. The electronic serial brings with it the promise of that everlasting world where you can always see the electron, and therefore also by necessity the threat of apocalypse. The electronic serial fulfills the utopian promise of the serial form because it is itself (like other emergent media) utopian, heralding an era of equality of information and access.[13] At the end of the print days, everything will fit in the eye of a needle, or at least a communications closet. If the serial form ties time with timelessness in a manner both utopian and threatening, so does the electronic medium. The two do not contradict each other, as we're often told, but uncannily reinforce one another, so that the danger that the rhetoric of electronic text would prevent us from finding out what we want from publishing is in some ways the same one we encounter with the serial form itself.[14] Like the serial form, electronic text powerfully masks its production process in favor of a hypostatic product; as Greg Ulmer has argued,

> The same drive of realism that led in cinema to the "invisible style" of Hollywood narrative films, and to the occulation of the production process in favor of a consumption of the product as if it were "natural," is at work again in computing.[15]

I have been arguing that the rhetoric of serials is in part the rhetoric of electronic text itself, and that its discrepant logic is explained in apocalyptic time, the very millennial time in which electronic serials find themselves today. This powerful alignment, I want to argue, structures current positions in the serials pricing debate. Pricing, among other issues, reflects the reception whose production I have been elaborating. Many publishers, like the public, fear the advent of electronicity and the consequent decline of civilization (or else—that electronicity is the symptom of a dying society); if they want to publish electronically, it is not, at least today, because they want to further an electronic future, but because they're afraid that people will get what they want for free and without their permission. Recently I argued informally at the University of Michigan that we should not become complacent about the success of electronic publishing, only to find that audience members were far from ready to take electronic journals for granted–in fact they nodded most vigorously when I listed some concerns about electronic text, like copyright and credibility issues, that, I then went on to say, were no longer the overriding issues.[16] Some publishers are, in effect, getting into electronic text today to curb and control it, not to develop it. They treat electronic text much as they do print media, due to management and pricing considerations, though this is shortsighted policy for which there is no compelling rationale. It is no wonder that CD-ROM is popular with electronic publishing, and will continue to be in the intermediate future: it is a cheap, hard product that can be managed traditionally. But consider this startling instance: recently the novel *Uprisings in Libertyville, USA* (1995), by Peter Seulund, was produced in 500 numbered and autographed copies on 1.44 diskette by the publisher (Serendipity Systems of Big Sur, California and Spitin' Image Publications of Neillsville, Wisconsin).[17] Surely the practice of numbering electronic text and underscoring its authorship and authority is contradictory, and reveals the ordering impulse behind such electronic publishing. Similarly, a recent article in *Lingua Franca* celebrates Jerome McGann's electronic Rossetti Archive project at the University of Virginia because it "repossesses" the materiality of Rossetti's poetry.[18] In fact, the desire to be practical and realistic on the subject leads even sophisticated interpreters of electronic text to rearticulate the rhetoric of traditional serial forms. So in an article titled "Landlords and Tenants: Who Owns Information, Who Pays for It, and How?" Anita Lowry considers "the shift in libraries from 'ownership' to 'access,' from 'landlord' to 'tenant'" and concludes that "Utopian dreams notwithstanding, *somebody* is going to own and control the rights to the most desirable information published in electronic form."[19] The cladistic model of electronic publishing–the family hierarchy of information and its ownership–is said to thwart the utopian rhetoric of electronic text.

But the two rhetorics, as I have argued, are not separate. For this reason, Jim O'Donnell, the co-editor of *Bryn Mawr Classical Review*, argues in an essay subtitled "The Tree of Knowledge and

How It Grows" that the electronic medium fulfills the possibilities inherent in the codex.[20] "Ever since the time of Cassiodorus," he writes, invoking the model of serial descent or succession, "we have been at work in Latin and post-Latin culture building a common tree of knowledge, an invisible but powerful structure by which we agree together to organize what we know and to make it accessible." As French philosophers Deleuze and Guattari have put it, "the tree has dominated Western reality and all of Western thought":[21]

> All of tree logic is a logic of tracing and reproduction. In linguistics as in psychoanalysis, its object is an unconscious that is itself representative, crystallized within a syntagmatic structure. Its goal is to describe a de facto state, to maintain balance in intersubjective relations, or to explore an unconscious that is already there from the start, lurking in the dark recesses of memory and language. It consists of tracing, on the basis of an overcoding structure or supporting axis, something that comes ready-made.[22]

The serial and arboreal (or tree-like) structure suggests a codified structure bound up–in the case of serial publications–in paper products. It is predetermined, fixed, and grows in set directions. O'Donnell's arboreal model, which I take here as paradigmatic, is the one that determines our thought as it did, for instance, when I gave the talk in Ann Arbor. The journal article is, on this arboreal model, fixed, a product and not a process, a becoming, or a possibility. It is something you can catalog and price rather easily. It's for this reason, then, and not because of a logical necessity, that we think of the electronic text in terms of print culture. What compels this way of thinking, for publishers, is serial order itself; as Freud puts it in *Civilization and its Discontents*,

> Order is a kind of compulsion to repeat which, when a regulation has been laid down once and for all, decides when, where and how a thing shall be done, so that in every similar circumstance one is spared hesitation and indecision.[23]

Publishing practice is linked to this idea of the product, to which we have become habituated by the serial form.

Let me illustrate my point with the example of the electronic journal *Postmodern Culture* (PMC) and its publisher, Oxford University Journals. Under their publishing contract, Oxford and PMC are supposed to agree on a pricing model that would enable Oxford to publish PMC electronically. Currently Oxford pays for some advertizing and office supplies, and produces disk and fiche versions of PMC, but it does not produce or distribute the journal in its listserv or World Wide Web versions. Oxford's preference is to charge for the journal, which is currently free on the Web and through listserv, in order to be able to produce the journal. PMC's editors want to keep the journal as free and accessible as possible, but Oxford Journals dismissed with some puzzlement the notion that one should give anything away if one could charge for it. Now, *Postmodern Culture* has over 4,000 listserv subscribers, and receives about 100,000 hits (or requests for text) on the Web each month. Preliminary statistics on the use of the journal show that the ratio of reader requests for files from back issues to the current issue is two to one; for instance, from 5/8/95 to 5/20/95, there were 6,147 hits on the current issue (then vol. 5 no. 2), and 13,886 hits on the back issues.[24] Oxford has suggested that PMC charge for electronic text what it asks for the disk and fiche versions, but PMC feels that if it were to charge even a nominal fee today for the journal, it would lose many of its readers–most, probably, if it tried to cover the real expenses incurred in production with these revenues. Thus it could not experiment with traditional pricing models in the current environment without jeopardizing its vital interests and the interests of its authors and readers. Instead PMC suggested an alternative model that would not consider the journal as a traditional serial product. On this model, PMC would provide the current issue free of charge, and would charge a nominal fee for back issues. In an access-restricted back-issue collection, Oxford would mark up the old issues (both the plain ASCII and the Hypertext Markup Language versions), and would make available searching tools, such as Pat, that would take advantage of that markup. Libraries could collect each issue in text-only format and make that available. In other words, Oxford would be selling access to a richer version of the journal (to markup, illustrations, etc.) and access to better searching tools to use on that version.

I am not convinced that this proposal is the best solution available to cost-recovery in electronic serials, and there are clearly complex technical and financial issues involved that would require another discussion altogether, but it is an interesting direction to consider. Oxford Journals believes that electronic journals should be priced as print journals are, and that it would cost as much to produce electronic text as paper text.[25] They have, therefore, in absence of hard numbers on user patterns and inclinations, rejected PMC's preliminary cost-recovery proposal. The problem of pricing and circulation illustrates the problem of paperthink in electronic serials, but other issues serve equally well–copyright, for instance, where the old model is destructive and inapplicable. It does, however, seem clear that printed academic serials will not be viable for much longer–indeed, that the costs of print and the possibilities opened up by new media will close the book on traditional publishing.

What, then, is for breakfast? What should we do to develop new models for serial publication? I make two related suggestions, one for institutional action, the other regarding the serial form. First, we do not need to make utopian claims for the new media–not because their aims aren't true but because they close off the possibility of change. Utopian rhetorics about the electron reinforce arboreal visions of serial publishing and prevent experimentation, rather than (as they would themselves have it) enabling it: utopian rhetorics invoke apocalyptic visions that, because they are foreign and seem impractical, remain fantasies that do not invite action. We need not think with Kantian imperatives, so that whatever we propose must obtain for all libraries all the time. We need instead an experimental virtual library–for instance–sponsored by the Association for Research Libraries (an early and active advocate of sensible thought in the new environment), where ideas about new librarianship can be explored, and where serials models and cost-recovery models can develop. To have this experimentation, we need to put off sweeping decisions for a while longer. Second, we need to rethink our attitudes toward serial publications and to distinguish our needs from the ones produced by the genre. It is into that trap that many over-cautious discussions of electronic publishing fall. A model I think may help us in this was articulated by the Russian scholar Mikhail Bakhtin in the 1930s. According to Bakhtin, the homogeneity of a fixed genre (in Michael Holquist's paraphrase) "corresponds to ideas about the privileged status of a unitary, centripetalizing language shared by its practitioners on the one hand and its students on the other."[26] The novel, instead, is not a fixed genre, and offers a different relation to language:

> "novel" is the name Bakhtin gives to whatever force is at work within a given literary system to reveal the limits, the artificial constraints of that system. . . . "novelization" is fundamentally anticanonical. It will not permit generic monologue. Always it will insist on the dialogue between what a given system will admit as literature and those texts that are otherwise excluded from such a definition of literature. What is more conventionally thought of as the novel is simply the most complex and distilled expression of this impulse.[27]

This interpretation of novelization, says Bakhtin, has been obscured by the "tree diagrams" borrowed from the analysis of formulaic genres like folktales and detective fiction.[28] The parallel with electronic serials is striking, I think. They offer the dialogic potential of novelization, but have yet to push the envelope of paper serials. What I propose, then, is the novelization of the serial, an approach that would lead to open-ended forms that could include interactive phenomena hitherto excluded from the series. These new forms could raise as many difficulties for tenure and promotion committees as they would for librarians organizing catalogues, but the change need not be abrupt. Serial publishing should begin to take these challenges seriously: if it does not, it will soon be out of time, in its own promised land of a timeless afterlife. I say we stay here in the wilderness, and build a living, and a dying, culture.

NOTES

1. Max Frankel (to cite but one recyclable comment) argues that just as most would reaffirm the early-century's enthusiasm for the automobile today, despite its various sins, so we should not fear the chip as the end of judgement. See "Horseless in Cyberspace," *The New York Times Magazine*, May 28, 1995, p. 18.

2. "An emergent medium," writes Spinelli in a recent paper, "represents a structural change in communications technology around which social change is

promised. . . . the rhetoric of these promises prevents any real understanding of the material place of the emergent medium in our lives." Martin Spinelli, "The Ideology of Emergent Media: Radio Lessons for the Internet," March 24, 1995, SUNY-Buffalo, NY. See gopher://wings.buffalo.edu/hh/internet/library/e-journals/ub/rift/documents/conversations.

3. For this discussion, see Stanley Fish, *Is There a Text in This Class?: The Authority of Interpretive Communities* (Cambridge, MA: Harvard UP, 1980). I use the example of Faulkner because he is given as the example of "The Author" in the NCSU library electronic search menu (au=faulkner william).

4. I thank Professor Rei Terada of the University of Michigan, who brought a cheesecake just at the moment I was composing this part of the text, and made it possible for me to continue.

5. Elaine Scarry, "Counting at Dusk (Why Poetry Matters when the Century Ends," Scarry, ed. *Fins de Siècle: English Poetry in 1590, 1690, 1790, 1890, 1990* (Baltimore: Johns Hopkins UP, 1995), p. 3.

6. Ibid, pp. 3-4.

7. Some examples of sonnet sequences in English are Petrarch's "Sonnets," Sir Philip Sidney's "Astrophel and Stella" (considered the first English sonnet cycle), William Shakespeare's "Sonnets," Edmund Spenser's "Amoretti," Elizabeth Barrett Browning's "Sonnets from the Portuguese," George Meredith's "Modern Love," Rainer Maria Rilke's "Sonnets to Orpheus," and Robert Lowell's "History." Two dozen sonnet cycles survive from the 1580s and 90s alone; the spell was broken by John Donne, who opposed Petrarchanism and its influence in the early 1600s.

8. Margareta De Grazia, "*Fin-de-Siècle* Renaissance England," *Fins de Siècle: English Poetry in 1590, 1690, 1790, 1890, 1990*, Ed. Elaine Scarry (Baltimore: Johns Hopkins UP, 1995), p. 42. In fact, the word "century" was originally bibliographical, and only came to refer to years beginning with 00 in the sixteenth century, according to De Grazia (pp. 44-6).

9. The word "century," writes De Grazia, was first "a bibliographical rather than a temporal unit"; only in the mid 16th century was it applied to years beginning with 00 in the common era, and only in the 18th century did it become a temporal unit exclusively. See her "*Fin-de-Siècle* Renaissance England," pp. 44-45.

10. As De Grazia notes. The western custom of counting time beginning with the Nativity became standard only in the 8th century (De Grazia, p. 46).

11. Prince, *Purple Rain* (NY: Warner Communications Co., 1984).

12. "The book spatializes knowledge, puts a roof over its head, as it were. And the reflex of the reader is to project attributes upon it. The material substance of a book represents the claim it will make upon our time and attention. Its three-dimensionality testifies to the palpability of its subject, the merit of its claims. . . . It establishes the material status of a thought." Sven Birkerts, "The Book as Emblem: The Besieged Stronghold?" *Journal of Scholarly Publishing*, vol. 26, no. 1 (October, 1994), 3-7: 5.

It is worth noting that print also aims to produce, rhetorically, the idea of timelessness. Of museum catalog style, for instance (and museums are about time especially), Julia Henshaw writes that "The look is often referred to as 'timeless good taste'," "timeless good taste which seems to have been established in the 1920s, when American museums were in their heyday." Julia Henshaw, "Design Considerations in Museum Publications," *Journal of Scholarly Publishing*, vol. 26, no. 2 (January, 1995), 121-128: 121, 122.

13. Jean-François Lyotard has popularized the notion that electronic information which will lead to profound political democratization in *The Postmodern Condition: A Report on Knowledge*, trans. Geoff Bennington, and Brian Massumi (Minneapolis: Minnesota UP [1979], 1984).

The notion has been embraced by both sides of mainstream USA political culture. See The White House, *The National Information Infrastructure: Agenda for Action* (Washington, D.C.: The White House, 1993), and Newt Gingrich, "Newt's Brave New World," *Forbes* (February 27, 1995), p. 93.

14. On the rhetoric of electronic publishing, and for an argument against the notion that reading electronic text leads to perdition, see Eyal Amiran, John Unsworth, and Carole Chaski, "Networked Academic Publishing and the Rhetorics of its Reception," *The Centennial Review* v.36, n.1 (Winter 1992), 43-58.

15. Greg Ulmer, "Grammatology Hypermedia," *Postmodern Culture* vol. 1 no. 2 (January, 1991); get ULMER.191 from listserv@listserv.ncsu.edu or point to URL http://jefferson.village.virginia.edu/pmc/contents.all.html.

For an interesting discussion of the relation between anonymity and proliferation (or invisibility and normativity) in the Internet see Christopher Pound, "Imagining In-Formation: The Complex Disconnections of Computer Networks," in George E. Marcus, ed., *Technoscientific Imaginaries: Conversations, Profiles, and Memoirs* (Chicago: Chicago UP, 1995), 527-547.

It's remarkable how transparent technology is, and how transparent the process of its becoming-transparent is. In *The Ego and the Id* Freud writes about secondary repression, the repression that allows us to forget that we are repressing information. For if we remembered about something that it had to be repressed, we'd not be able to repress anything. There may be a small problem with this model, actually, because it's hard to explain how we repress secondary repression without invoking a regression of repression mechanisms. But this kind of repression is relevant to our reaction to electronic publishing, where the new technology becomes invisible so readily: we forget our own happy assimilation of technology into old models of academic work that are themselves left unquestioned, grounded as they are on print-based models of writing, dissemination, and institutional legitimation.

16. The talk was "The Ego and the Bit: Electronic Professionalism and the Profession of Electronicity," SILS, Univ. of Michigan Libraries, December 6, 1994.

17. This publishing event recalls F. T. Marinetti's attempt to revolutionize publishing:

Marinetti was opposed to the rare and precious volume, printed in a limited quantity of numbered copies and destined to a wealthy public, for bibliophiles or art collectors, and instead he viewed the book as a militant product aimed at wide usage.

But to do this he published elaborate, exaggeratedly physical products, like "litho-tin" books made of tin, with color serigraphs. See Claudia Salaris, "Marketing Modernism: Marinetti as Publisher," trans. Lawrence Rainey, *Modernism/modernity* vol. 1, no. 3 (September 1994), pp. 121-2.

18. Steven Johnson, "Repossession: An Electronic Romance," *Lingua Franca* vol. 5 no. 4 (May/June 1995), 24-33. The article is blurbed in the Table of Contents as "One Man's effort to digitize the humanities" (1).

On this point, Stuart Moulthrop has written in a recent discussion on the electronic Pynchon discussion group: "Copyright–as we know it–is a corrupt, unworkable, and perverse institution that serves the rights of publishers, not authors. The same can be said for the publishing industry–as we know it–(though fortunately it is doomed). Good, reasonable alternatives exist for both publishing and copyright, but so far there seems little interest in these alternatives, particularly among intellectuals. If you doubt this, have a look at the latest *Lingua Franca*, whose cover story is all about 'repossessing' electronic media for the Book." Message-Id <01HR4575I2FM00HJR8@UBmail.ubalt.edu> to owner-pynchon-l@sfu.ca, May 30, 1995.

19. Anita Lowry, "Landlords and Tenants: Who Owns Information, Who Pays for It, and How?" *The Serials Librarian* vol. 23 no. 314 (1993), 61-71.

20. James J. O'Donnell, "St. Augustine to NREN: The Tree of Knowledge and How It Grows," *The Serials Librarian* vol. 23 no. 314 (1993), p.33.

21. Gilles Deleuze and Félix Guattari, *A Thousand Plateaus: Capitalism and Schizophrenia*, trans. Brian Massumi (Minneapolis: Minnesota UP, 1987), p. 18.

22. *Ibid*, p. 12.

23. Sigmund Freud, *Civilization and its Discontents*, trans. James Strachey (NY: Norton, 1961), p. 40.

24. Those issue-based statistics can be found at: http://jefferson.village.virginia.edu/iath/treestats.html. See also the user surveys done by the Graphic, Visualization, and Usability Center at Georgia Tech, available on the World-Wide Web at http://www.cc.gatech.edu/gvu/user_surveys/User_Survey_Home.html.

25. This seems to have been an assumption at the ACRL Journal Costs in Academic Libraries Discussion Group at ALA Midwinter, February 4, 1995. See *Newsletter on Serials Pricing Issues* no. 132 (February 19, 1995). This seems wrong to me, based on my experience producing PMC: it would cost us about $6000 more to print each issue. Also, factors cited as contributing most significantly to price increases are paper and postage costs. White, non-recycled paper is in limited supply. Overall, serials are projected to rise about 10.5% while inflation is calculated only at a projected 2.5%. See Marcia Tuttle's "From the Editor," *Newsletter on Serials Pricing Issues* no. 133 (February 20, 1995).

26. Michael Holquist, "Introduction," M. M. Bakhtin, *The Dialogic Imagination*, trans. Caryl Emerson and Michael Holquist (Austin: Texas UP, 1981), p. xxx.

27. Holquist, p. xxxi.

28. Page xx. Novelization has been misunderstood by its students because they "continue to view the novel through the optic of a traditional stylistic that has proved so successful with other text types, but is quite inappropriate to novels" (Holquist xxx).

Five Years of *Bryn Mawr Classical Review*

James J. O'Donnell

SUMMARY. *Bryn Mawr Classical Review* will be five years old in the fall of 1995. What have we learned? Where are we going? Are we old-fashioned yet? Are we a classic? Are we obsolete? If we go on giving it away, will people think it is only worth what they paid for it? *[Article copies available from The Haworth Document Delivery Service: 1-800-342-9678.]*

When I addressed the North American Serials Interest Group (NASIG) meetings in Chicago in 1992, I spoke of the remote past and the immediate future: as a classicist practicing the craft of editing an electronic journal, those were the things I knew about. It is a sign of our time now that I am here today to speak about the 'history' of the electronic journal. Something surely has changed when an entity so novel to so many imaginations already has a history. What I wish to do here is summarize briefly where we have been, then draw a few lessons that may be useful for those reading what we produce or thinking about how to cope with such artifacts.

Bryn Mawr Classical Review (BMCR) began in 1990 with a first-rate idea that arose with my colleague Richard Hamilton, who

---

James J. O'Donnell is Professor of Classical Studies at the University of Pennsylvania, Philadelphia, PA.

© 1996 by the North American Serials Interest Group, Inc. All rights reserved.

[Haworth co-indexing entry note]: "Five Years of *Bryn Mawr Classical Review*." O'Donnell, James J. Co-published simultaneously in *The Serials Librarian* (The Haworth Press, Inc.) Vol. 28, No. 3/4, 1996, pp. 223-228; and *Serials to the Tenth Power: Tradition, Technology, and Transformation* (ed: Mary Ann Sheble, and Beth Holley) The Haworth Press, Inc., 1996, pp. 223-228. Single or multiple copies of this article are available from The Haworth Document Delivery Service [1-800-342-9678, 9:00 a.m. - 5:00 p.m. (EST)].

holds the Paul Shorey Professor of Greek endowed chair at Byrn Mawr College. Hamilton saw that there was a need for a book review journal in classics that would give concise, timely reports of new work, in a field where reviews were often so long delayed that they appeared after the book had slouched off to the remainder tables. There was nothing electronic about his idea. It seemed feasible for several reasons.

First, he had led for a decade, at that point, a textbook-publishing project, "Bryn Mawr Commentaries," which had produced dozens of intermediate texts of Greek and Latin classics for use in university classrooms. The cadre of colleagues who had come together in writing and editing these (I was one of them) formed a group of mostly thirty-somethings and forty-somethings whose ability to do good work within specified limits on a short deadline had already been tested and a kind of *esprit de corps* formed.

Second, computer technology had both facilitated that series and been proven in it. Bryn Mawr Commentaries did desktop publishing when nobody else had heard the word, hence Hamilton knew well how to use cheap technology efficiently to produce an economical product. A paper journal was what he had in mind.

Third, the availability of electronic mail meant that a great deal of the correspondence in producing the journal could be done more swiftly and cheaply than ever in the world of paper. It remains true that, even if we published *only* in paper, we could not do what we do without computers and the Internet, if only for the way they facilitate and reduce costs for the production side of the operation.

The first good idea was Hamilton's; I was lucky enough to have the second. A year or so earlier, I had taken to the networked waves at first because of a specific database I could consult no other way, and then was hooked by the emerging culture of that period best embodied by Willard McCarty's fabled years as editor of *Humanist*. So my suggestion was that we experiment with distribution of the journal by e-mail. We settled on a plan to sell the four issues per year of the journal cheaply ($10)–in fact today we distribute about 7 issues per year for $15–and to give it away on the Internet. In November 1990, we printed our first edition and shipped its e-version on the network.

If any of you heard unusual loud noises about that time, it was the sound of e-mail boxes around the world crashing to a halt under the weight of a 250K file, BMCR 1.1, slamming into them. For the first two or three issues we repeated this assault on the integrity of the network until it dawned on the present writer—who is sometimes slow but not entirely stupid—that the electronic journal did not have to be merely a clone of the paper version and that indeed a book review journal was an ideal vehicle for fragmented distribution, one review at a time. From that time on, we have followed that practice.

Our list of subscribers to the listserv-variant distribution list began to grow. New subscribers would ask for "back issues" and I would tell them to clear the decks for incoming fire and launch the Internet bulk-packs of preceding "issues" (still bundled together in retrospect to resemble the paper version). As the number of new subscribers grew and the number of back issues grew apace, this task grew increasingly wearisome. I was rescued in 1992 when the first small but perky gopher poked its head above the Minnesota tundra. Within a few months we had an arrangement with the University of Virginia Libraries to archive our back issues there as individual review files and make them available with Wide Area Information Server (WAIS)-indexing over the Internet. The Virginia site was one of the first and remains one of the most distinguished scholarly resources on the Internet. It is a pleasure to praise and thank John Price-Wilkin (now of the University of Michigan) and Kendon Stubbs for their support over the years at Virginia.

The success of *BMCR* was remarkable. Publishers paid us the homage of sending us their books and of quoting our reviews out of context in their blurbs. Classics is a relatively homogeneous field in America, in that those who practice it generally have wide interests in the field and know at least a little of current work across a broad range. This creates a community of readers and writers with excellent word-of-mouth potential. I think it fair to say that we are now one of the standard resources for American classicists.

By 1993, our success had attracted attention and emulation. With the collaboration of Eugene Vance (whose turn it was to have the initial idea) and Paul Remley, both of the University of Washington, we founded *Bryn Mawr Medieval Review* (BMMR), created in the image of the original. The first reviews for that journal shipped in the summer of 1993 and it has now reached a level of stability and consistency that compares favorably with *BMCR*. We also created a separate purely notional rubric "Bryn Mawr Reviews" for those who wished to subscribe to both journals and receive no overlap (for some items are indeed shipped to both lists, e.g., a book on Vergilian influence on medieval poetry). The number of subscribers accelerated its growth in that year, partly because of the new journal and partly because the general population of the academic Internet was growing explosively itself. By 1993 we had about 800 *BMCR* subscribers; we now have about 2500 subscribers for the three journals and see constant growth. We will shortly ship our 1,000th review and a typical year will now see publication of approximately 250 items.

It is past time to let our gophers burrow back down into the prairie and move on to the arachnid metaworld of the World Wide Web (WWW). A welcome grant from the Andrew W. Mellon Foundation is allowing us to do a thorough job of reconsidering our practices for the long term and we hope to have improved distribution and archiving by 1996. A particular problem for us has been the transmission of Greek alphabetical characters and diacritics, essential for classicists' discourse, on the network. We hope to solve that as a subset of what we are doing and in so doing make things easier for electronic publishing for classicists of every kind in a variety of forms.

Our lessons from this exercise have been many and rewarding. First, I would insist on the fact that our point of departure was not a zeal to experiment with computers; it was precisely a good old-fashioned editorial idea about something that people would want to write and to read. That explains our success more than anything else.

Second, that relatively homogeneous community of classicists and in particular our cadre of longtime companions in unindicted coconspiracy gave the enterprise a center of gravity at the outset. (The medieval review has been slower aborning both because the fields covered by "medieval studies" are more diverse and dispersed and because we had no such well-organized cadre of colleagues in place at the outset.)

Third, the networked nature of the publication makes many differences. Chief among them is the diversity of our audience, embracing many people who do not define themselves as professional classicists. This can only be good for a discipline like ours, which runs the risk of becoming a hermetic club for experts, dwindling over the years, if we do not find ways to address a wider public with our best work. *BMCR* has subscribers on six continents from every kind of networked address and we know from correspondence that many of our subscribers are indeed "The Enlightened General Reader," just as many more are indeed professors of classics.

Fourth, an accidental innovation has enriched us in a particular way. One month while publishing our list of *Books Received*, Hamilton had the further good idea of marking with a star those not yet placed for review and soliciting qualified volunteers to identify themselves. This is now a regular ritual and we brace ourselves for the flood of e-volunteers. We will give any credible claimant a trial and we find that the results include the excellent, the ordinary, and the awful in proportions that resemble closely (uncomfortably closely!) those that obtain among reviews written by carefully chosen friends and colleagues of the editors. The value of this practice, however, is that it not only increases our coverage of the hard-to-place book, but it draws the community of those who read the journal and those who write it closer together. Hamilton and I teach at privileged institutions on the east coast and our network of friends and relations includes a high percentage of people like ourselves. That is a formula that too often in the past has produced mandarin classes telling the rest of the world what to think. With *BMCR/BMMR*, the rest of the world more easily becomes part of the conversation.

Fifth, with our journals, the review only begins the conversation. We have guaranteed right of reply to authors and published many. This has taught us what we did not specially want to know but perhaps already did, that few scholars respond with grace and highmindedness to a bad book review, but it also means that reviewers write in a different tone, knowing that their censures are themselves open to censure.

Sixth, we have paid close attention very recently and will continue to study the behavior of those readers who come to consult our archives. Conclusions can only be preliminary but one is tantalizing. We are a general interest book review journal, covering many topics in the broad chronological regions of our interests. But if you have a special interest in some way orthogonal to our purposes, the ease of e-access and e-searching means that you can make of us a specialized journal for your own purposes. We noticed, for example, a period when there was a particular run on any and all of our items having to do with issues of gender and sexuality in antiquity. We have no measure of the ideological or scholarly affiliation of our readers, but we make some surmises and imagine people who would not pause to leaf through a five year run of a general interest journal in search of two or three items per issue, but who quite happily ask a couple of questions of a WAIS-index and get, with instant efficiency, just the items most likely to suit their interests. This reduces the need for specialized journals precisely because one large umbrella can function as a specialized journal for those who want it. The theoretical and practical implications of this insight, if valid, are far from obvious but deserve exploration.

The conclusion of greatest general applicability, however, is the most general and should be the most obvious. The success of specific enterprises in electronic publishing in academia will be most closely correlated to their intellectual and organic coherence with the interests and practices of scholars and scientists. We are past the time when we can press e-experiments merely for the sake of adventure and entering, I believe, a time in which it makes increasing sense for more and more journals to consider e-distribution, not because a zealot or a tyrant claims that this should or must be done in response to the inexorable law of the future, but simply because it makes good practical sense. I said at the outset that it was striking to be speaking now of a piece of the 'history' of the e-journal. What we can now look forward to is a time when we can stop thinking about the future of e-journals for the good reason that we will have all gone to live in it.

SESSION 3:
CATALOGING ON THE EDGE:
PROVIDING ACCESS
TO REMOTE RESOURCES

Mr. Serials Revisits Cataloging: Cataloging Electronic Serials and Internet Resources

Eric Lease Morgan

SUMMARY. This text describes the Alcuin Project, an informal project whose goal is to discover methods for effectively cataloging electronic serials and Internet resources at the North Carolina State University Libraries. The Project builds upon previous work including the Mr. Serials Process, DRA/World Wide Web gateway scripts, the Alex database, the Alcuin database, and cumulating in Son of SID. Each of these projects is briefly outlined and future directions are presented.

Eric Lease Morgan is Systems Librarian for North Carolina State University Libraries, Raleigh, NC.

© 1996 by the North American Serials Interest Group, Inc. All rights reserved.

[Haworth co-indexing entry note]: "Mr. Serials Revisits Cataloging: Cataloging Electronic Serials and Internet Resources." Morgan, Eric Lease. Co-published simultaneously in *The Serials Librarian* (The Haworth Press, Inc.) Vol. 28, No. 3/4, 1996, pp. 229-238; and *Serials to the Tenth Power: Tradition, Technology, and Transformation* (ed: Mary Ann Sheble, and Beth Holley) The Haworth Press, Inc., 1996, pp. 229-238. Single or multiple copies of this article are available from The Haworth Document Delivery Service [1-800-342-9678, 9:00 a.m. - 5:00 p.m. (EST)].

STARTING AT THE END

The ultimate goal (or end) of the Alcuin Project is to create a systematic method for cataloging and classifying electronic serials and Internet resources.[1,2] At the North Carolina State University (NCSU) Libraries we believe we have successfully outlined the work flow of such a method. It does not differ very much from traditional acquisition strategies. This is how it will work: the collection management department, in conjunction with "subject teams" will select resources for inclusion into a database of relevant items:

- The Universal Resource Locator (URL) describing the resource is passed on to our cataloging department that analyzes the resource in terms of its author, title, notes, subjects, etc.
- The results of this analysis are used to update a database program.
- Reports based on the content of the database are then generated updating our dissemination tools, namely, an online catalog and our World Wide Web (WWW) server.
- The balance of this essay describes the process we have gone through and are going through to accomplish this goal.

MR. SERIALS VISITS CATALOGING

At the 1994 NASIG conference there was much discussion concerning the newly approved MARC 856 field. This field is designed to accommodate descriptive information concerning electronic materials such as URLs, location descriptors of Internet resources. As an experiment, the NCSU Libraries updated its catalog with two records containing URLs in the 856 fields. Using scripts written by Tim Kambitsch, access to these records was provided through WWW client and server software. A description of this demonstration is available in an essay entitled "Mr. Serials Visits Cataloging."[3] With the addition of 856 fields in our online public access catalog (OPAC) database and Kambitsch's scripts, we believe we have at least one dissemination tool at our disposal.

ALEX: A CATALOG OF INTERNET RESOURCES

About the same time the NCSU Libraries began mirroring the Alex database.[4] The Alex database, originally created by Hunter Monroe, is a catalog of electronic texts found on the Internet. Working with Monroe, we learned he was maintaining his collection through the use of a database application. Each record in his application contained fields describing each Internet resource in terms of title, author, date, location, and (eventually) subjects. At the outset, the Alex database was made available through a gopher server. To this end, Monroe used his database application to automatically create gopher link files, the substance of gopher servers. With just a bit of encouragement, Monroe was able to modify his database application and create hypertext markup language (HTML) documents as well. The Alex database has proven to be a model for the rest of our development work.

SIMPLE INTERNET DATABASE (SID)

In an effort to mirror Hunter Monroe's ideas, we created a database of our own. We called this database the "Simple Internet Database" or SID for short. The application was written in HyperTalk, the language of HyperCard. Each record in the database contains a field for title, author, date, URL, abstract, major subjects, and minor subjects (see Figure 1).

Internet resources were added to the database after being evaluated in terms of their identifying elements. Most of the database's records were completed in a straightforward manner; it is usually not too difficult to determine the title, author, and URL of Internet resources. Abstracts were included to facilitate future keyword searching. They were copied, when available, directly from the Internet resources themselves and pasted into the records.

The database was designed to accommodate as many major and minor subject entries as needed. Since, at the present time, the breadth and quality of Internet resources does not match the breadth and quality of our printed resources, and since the controlled vocabulary of our traditional database applications (OPACs) does not

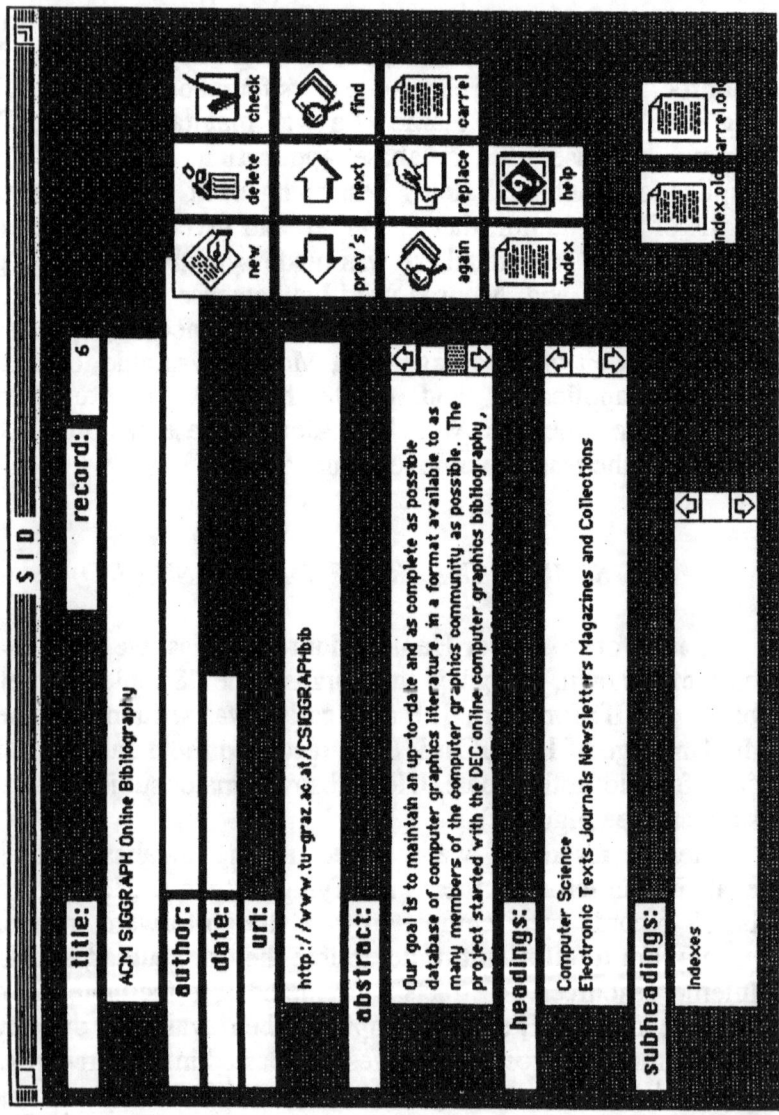

FIGURE 1. Simple Internet Database (SID) is a rudimentary database program, written in HyperCard, used to manage a collection of Internet resources.

seem to fully satisfy the needs of our clientele, we began creating our own controlled vocabulary. This controlled vocabulary was not created systematically. Rather, when a "critical mass" of Internet resources presented themselves that seemed pertinent to the educational and research needs of our clientele, a new, major and/or minor subject term was created. Presently, the controlled vocabulary contains about two dozen terms. Minor subjects usually represent the form of Internet resources or sub-subjects. We have created quite a number of minor subject terms.

Learning from our experiences taken from Hunter Monroe, reports can be created based on the contents of the database. At the present time, these reports are HTML documents. Each document contains all the records matching sets of major subject/minor subject pairs. After the documents have been created they are saved in a directory of the library's WWW server. These files form the bulk of our server. Access to these documents is then provided via browsing as well as a searchable, keyword index. Field searching is not supported.

ALEX MEETS ALCUIN

Our experience with the addition of URLs in 856 fields of MARC records taught us the difficulty of creating original cataloging records within our OPAC software. First, the interface is not graphical, making it difficult to move the cursor around the screen. Second, since much of the information that would be making up the new records already existed in electronic form, it makes sense to try to copy and paste that information from one window into another, thus eliminating data-entry error as well as speeding up the process. Unfortunately, dumb terminals do not accommodate copy and paste functions very well. To say the least, creating original MARC records on our system is a "user hostile" experience.

Since one of our goals is to create MARC records, we created a MARC record-writing program. This Microsoft Windows-based program, written in VisualBasic, allows end-users to copy and paste text into an editable field and then click a button creating a USMARC record. As new records are created they are appended to previously created records.

To accommodate these records, a new database was created using our OPAC software. The database was named Alcuin after the Medieval librarian and advisor to Charlemagne. Then, the USMARC records were copied to the same computer hosting the OPAC and imported into Alcuin. Alcuin was indexed and made available through slightly modified DRA/WWW gateway scripts mentioned above.

Realizing that our Windows-based program, dubbed Alcuin's Little Helper, could be modified to import specially formatted text files and output USMARC records, we asked Hunter Monroe to create yet another type of report from his database. He accommodated us; Alcuin's Little Helper was modified; and consequently we created USMARC records from the Alex database. These records were then uploaded into the Alcuin database and made available to the Internet. Furthermore, the original USMARC records were made available via File Transfer Protocol (FTP). For more-detailed information concerning these aspects of the Alcuin Project you are invited to read "Alex Meets Alcuin."[5]

SON OF SID

The original SID program did what it was designed to do, create HTML documents; it did not create MARC records. Alcuin's Little Helper did what it was supposed to do, create MARC records, but it was not a database application. Neither of the prototypes were platform independent; SID only runs on a Macintosh and Alcuin's Little Helper only runs on a Windows-based computer. Thus enters our newest but incomplete solution, Son of SID.

Son of SID works on the client/server model of computing. In brief, this means there is one application (the client) handling the user interface, and there is another application (the server) processing requests. One of the greatest advantages of this sort of computing is the wide range of dissimilar computers that can participate in a single computing task. The WWW works upon such a model and provides the framework for Son of SID.

The client side of Son of SID is only a specialized HTML document called a FORM. FORMs supply software developers with rudimentary data-input features like fields, pop-up menus, check boxes, and radio buttons. These data-input features can make up the skeleton of MARC records and provide the means for data entry (see Figure 2).

The server side of the equation includes a WWW server, a number of common gateway interface (CGI) scripts, and a database application. In this particular case, the WWW server is MacHTTP, a server for Macintosh computers. Our particular CGI scripts are programs interacting with the database application providing functions for adding, finding, editing, and deleting records. Soon it will include functions for HTML and MARC record generation.

This is how it all will work. First, catalogers receive a URL and

FIGURE 2. Son of SID represents the beginnings of a client/server-based database application used to manage collections of Internet resources.

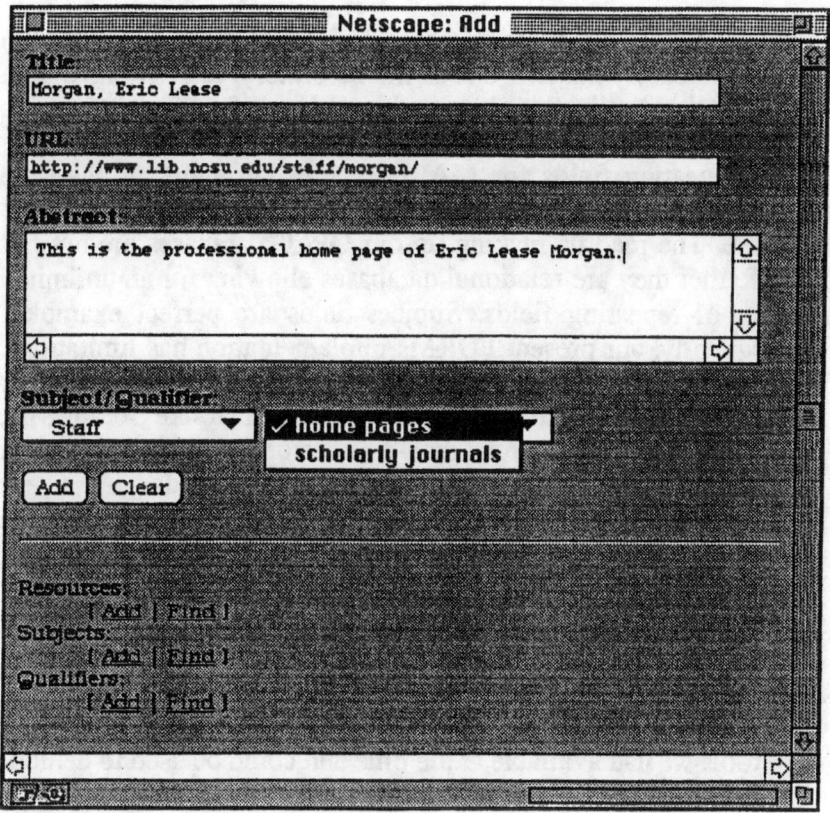

they use their various Internet applications to evaluate it in terms of its identifying elements. Second, they use their favorite WWW browser to connect to the Alcuin Project WWW server. Once connected, they will have the options of modifying the database or creating reports. Modifying the database will entail copying and pasting information from one screen into the FORM and selecting menu options. HTML and MARC record generation will be accomplished by simply answering a few questions. Next, after the reports have been created they will be "automatically" FTP'ed to their respective servers (another WWW server and the Alcuin database, respectively) where the new data will be reindexed and made available to the public.

DISCUSSION AND FUTURE DIRECTIONS

Son of SID is not being extensively used at the present time. In fact, it has barely made it out of the laboratory yet! We have high hopes for this application, but it will not be perfect. To begin with, the HTML FORMS are static entities providing a maximum number of repeating fields for MARC records. In short, as they are implemented in Son of SID, they represent the records of a flat file database. The records making up our OPAC databases are not flat files. Rather they are relational databases allowing for an unlimited number of repeating fields. Subject fields are perfect examples. Consequently, our present FORMs implementation has limitations. One possible solution to this problem is to create a client/server version of Alcuin's Little Helper that works much like Son of SID, but this can lead to numerous data-entry errors and requires a much better understanding of the structure of MARC records.

Another limitation of Son of SID may be its robustness and scalability. The underlining database application is FileMaker Pro. While FileMaker Pro works, it does not have the reputation for speed like other database applications. Additionally, the CGI scripts are written in a scripting language called AppleScript. Again, AppleScript is not as responsive as other programming languages. On the other hand, the two tools (FileMaker Pro and AppleScript) were tools we had available at the time and could be used to demonstrate our concepts. Furthermore, they are popular tools and more likely to be readily available in other institutions and thus supported by a wider audience, specifically the Internet community. Last, it is doubtful FileMaker Pro will be able to handle thousands of records.

In the future we plan to make available all of the software we have developed as well as the MARC records created from the process. Additionally, we may open up the entire system to librarians outside NCSU. For example, we may create a second set of databases. This second set will be maintained by any number of librarians who want to make contributions. The librarians will have the opportunity to add records to the database much like we will be doing inside NCSU. Once a record is created, a MARC record representing their data will be returned. The librarians can then add that data to their own OPAC. NCSU may then add the contributed records in our own database. Last, all these records will be made available via FTP to whoever wants them.

ACKNOWLEDGMENTS ALONG THE PATH OF DISCOVERY

The process leading us to our method of cataloging electronic materials has been analytic, synthetic, and creative, but not necessarily systematic. It is a process fraught with dead ends and inspirational discoveries. More importantly, it is a process building upon the successes and suggestions of others. For example, Marilyn Geller first lead me to the 1994 NASIG conference and there I learned about the 856 field. Tim Kambitsch demonstrated how to access DRA databases through a WWW server. Hunter Monroe illustrated the flexibility of database applications which ultimately led to SID and Son of SID. Doris Sigl of the NCSU Libraries explored and shared the procedures for creating DRA-based databases which lead to the Alcuin database. David Williamson of the Library of Congress inspired Alcuin's Little Helper. Walt Crawford de-mystified and pointed the way to the creation of valid USMARC records. Without the input from these people as well as the support of the administration of the NCSU Libraries, none of this would have been possible.

The age in which we live is changing at a rate unseen in previous times. This change, in my opinion, is being driven by computers and new communications technologies. Some people throw their arms up in frustration with the advent of this change. For me it is stimulating. I believe it can be stimulating for you, too. Go back to your workplaces. Pause and reflect on the things you have picked up at the conference. Ask yourself how the things you were exposed to can be applied in your own situation. Then play with and explore those possibilities. If enough of us librarians can discover ways to improve and refine what we do, then librarianship can continue to provide useful and beneficial services for generations, if not centuries, to come.

NOTES

1. http://www.lib.ncsu.edu/staff/morgan/alcuin/alcuin-visits-nasig.html
2. http://www.lib.ncsu.edu/staff/morgan
3. http://www.lib.ncsu.edu/staff/morgan/mr-serials-and-cataloging.html
4. http://www.lib.ncsu.edu/stacks/alex-index.html
5. http://www.lib.ncsu.edu/staff/morgan/alcuin/alex-meets-alcuin.html

U-R-Stars: Standards for Controlling Internet Resources

Priscilla Caplan

SUMMARY. The library and internet communities have been working on standards for identifying and referencing electronic resources. This is a report on recent library efforts, including work to record URL and URN (Uniform Resource Locator and Uniform Resource Number) information in USMARC records, and collaboration with the IETF to define a Uniform Resource Citation for electronic publications. *[Article copies available from The Haworth Document Delivery Service: 1-800-342-9678.]*

It is a real pleasure to be invited back to NASIG. Two years ago I spoke at the 8th annual conference in Providence in a session on cataloging electronic serials. At that time I reported on the OCLC Internet Resources Project and two of the products to come out of that effort: a draft set of guidelines for cataloging Internet resources, and a number of proposed changes to the USMARC format. My talk ended with the observation that "although things are happening, not much has actually happened to this point in time. The 856 field has been defined, but it has not been implemented on any local

---

Priscilla Caplan is Assistant Director for Library Systems at University of Chicago Library, Chicago, IL.

© 1996 by the North American Serials Interest Group, Inc. All rights reserved.

[Haworth co-indexing entry note]: "U-R-Stars: Standards for Controlling Internet Resources." Caplan, Priscilla. Co-published simultaneously in *The Serials Librarian* (The Haworth Press, Inc.) Vol. 28, No. 3/4, 1996, pp. 239-246; and *Serials to the Tenth Power: Tradition, Technology, and Transformation* (ed: Mary Ann Sheble, and Beth Holley) The Haworth Press, Inc., 1996, pp. 239-246. Single or multiple copies of this article are available from The Haworth Document Delivery Service [1-800-342-9678, 9:00 a.m. - 5:00 p.m. (EST)].

system or bibliographic utility, and neither the guidelines nor the recommended changes to [AACR2] Chapter 9 have been approved."[1]

What a difference two years can make! Now I am probably the only person in this room who has never actually cataloged an e-journal. The 856 field for electronic locations has been implemented in OCLC and any number of local systems, and in March the Library of Congress published a set of guidelines for its use.[2] The draft cataloging guidelines from the Internet Resources project were published last winter as Nancy Olson's "Cataloging Internet Resources: A Manual and Practical Guide."[3] OCLC followed the Internet Resources Project with its current project called "Building a Catalog of Internet Resources," and I believe that project has reached its goal of 135 participating libraries. I do not think I even know anyone who is not subscribed to the INTERCAT discussion list[4] for those involved in cataloging Internet resources.[4]

It has been very gratifying to see the level of discourse rise from "why would anyone want to catalog this stuff?" to whether or not the 300 field is appropriate for recording the number of pages in an original electronic text. Of course, at the same time this means that I personally, as a non-cataloger, am less and less competent to participate in the discussion, or even to follow it. So I would not presume to talk about that kind of cataloging today. What I did want to do was talk briefly about some related initiatives coming out of the Library and Internet communities that I think will be equally important in the effort to gain bibliographic control of Internet-accessible resources.[5]

I am assuming you are all familiar with the URL, or Uniform Resource Locator. That is the string you see most often in World Wide Web documents, which usually looks something like this: http://www.oclc.org/oclc/man/catproj/catcall.htm (the home page for the Internet Cataloging project). The URL standard is a syntax for locating an object using various existing Internet protocols. The beginning of the string, before the first colon-slash, specifies the protocol, for example "http" for the Web or "ftp" for file transfer, and the rest of the string specifies the document you are citing or requesting in an appropriate syntax for that protocol.

The URL was defined by the Uniform Resource Identifier (URI) Working Group of the Internet Engineering Task Force (IETF).

Working documents of the IETF working groups are called "Internet-Drafts," and proposed standards are published as "RFCs" or Request-for-Comments documents. The URL itself is defined in RFC 1738.

The URL is the most common way of providing access to an Internet resource; it is used as the anchor or hypertext link in Web documents, and we have provided a place for it in USMARC in the subfield $u of the 856 field. In this respect it serves a function somewhat analogous to that of the call number for an in-library resource: it tells you where to find it. Unfortunately, once we put something on the shelf in the library it usually stays there, but electronic documents are notoriously peripatetic. They just love to be moved from server to server or copied exactly or with just the teeniest difference, and the second this happens the URL no longer works.

As an attempt to get around this problem, the URI Working Group is working on a standard for something called the Uniform Resource Name, or URN. The URN is just a text string that unambiguously identifies an Internet resource, much as an ISSN unambiguously identifies a serial. There are several competing proposals now for the URN syntax. Under one model a URN could look something like this: urn:x-dns2:library.bigstate.edu:aj17-mcc.[6] The initial "urn" would identify this as a URN, the next segment after the colon would identify the naming scheme in use, and the last segment would be the name according to that naming scheme. In this example, the naming scheme "x-dns2" requires a two-part name, where the first part designates the naming authority (here, "library.bigstate.edu"). The second part, called the "request id," gives the name of the object being referenced ("aj17-mcc"). I have not seen it explicitly addressed, but I do not see any reason why for a published journal article, either paper or electronic, the SICI could not be incorporated into a URN scheme.

The URN actually has a number of problems that need to be resolved before it will achieve any sort of widespread acceptance like that of the URL. However, most of the people who are working on the URN agree that it is not intended to be an end in itself, but rather something used as part of a resolution service. The primary function of a resolution service is to accept a URN and return one or more URLs that can be used in retrieving the resource. A secondary function of the service could be returning information about the resource. So, where our current model is to get some kind of software, for example a Web browser, and hand it a URL, and have it go out and fetch the resource, under the new model we would pass our software a URN instead. The program would go to a resolution service (presumably that referenced as the naming authority in the URN) to find out the locations known to store that resource and perhaps some additional information about the resource. Then the program would either go fetch the resource or display the information to us so we could decide what we wanted to do about it. The important point is that we would not have to store or maintain URLs in MARC records anymore, only the unchanging URNs.

This leads me to the URC, or Uniform Resource Characteristic. (This used to be called the Uniform Resource Citation, but the name was changed to encourage people to think about it more generally.) The URC is intended to associate a URN with one or more URLs for the purpose of resolution. It can also provide a description of the resource for the purpose of discovery and/or utilization.

Now all these UR* things may be sounding a little abstract, but the URC is actually relatively familiar stuff; you would not be frightened if you bumped into one on a dark street. To provide URN to URL resolution, of course, the URC ought to contain a URN and at least one URL. It will probably have fields for recording restrictions on access and a signature for electronic verification. In addition, the URC will contain what is essentially bibliographic information like author, title, subject, and publisher.

The latest draft of the URC specification is based on the "Dublin Core," a set of data elements first proposed at the March 1995 OCLC/NCSA Metadata Workshop.[7] The premise behind the Dublin Core is that there needs to be a simple, relatively small, commonly understood set of data elements that can be used to describe most textual resources (called "document-like objects" in Dublin Core parlance) on the Internet. If small enough and simple enough, information providers like authors and publishers would be encouraged to start supplying such information for their own resources. Developers of authoring tools could incorporate templates for this metadata in their software, and developers of locator services could use this metadata for discovery and retrieval. Librarians and other specialists could use the metadata supplied with the resource as a leg-up in creating more complex and complete descriptions, like catalog records or TEI headers.

All of these proposed standards are moving targets, of course, but at this time the Dublin Core consists of a dozen data elements in addition to an identifier like the URN: subject, title, author, publisher, other agent, date, object type, form, relation, source, language, and coverage. Most of these are self-explanatory, which is precisely the intent. "OtherAgent" is used for parties having some responsibility for the intellectual content of the object other than authors, so this would include translators, illustrators, and editors. The "Source" is the object from which the resource was derived (e.g., the print version of a scanned page-image) and "Relation" is a work related to the resource in some capacity other than as its source.

A very simple example of the Dublin Core in operation is shown below, taken with some modifications from the workshop report:

Title	– On the Pulse of the Morning.
Author	– Angelou, Maya.
Publisher	– University of Virginia Library Electronic Text Center
OtherAgent	– Transcribed by the University of Virginia Electronic Text Center.
Source	– Newspaper stories and oral performance of text at the inauguration of President Clinton
Date	– 1993
ObjectType	– Poem
Form	– 1 ascii file
Language	– English

As noted above, the Dublin Core is likely to be incorporated into the RFC for the URC. A scenario that I would love to see would be authors including Dublin Core metadata with their works; publishers including URNs when they make these resources available on the net; and resolution services automatically incorporating the metadata in the URCs used to resolve URNs into URLs.

I want to end with just a word on how this all relates to library cataloging and bibliographic databases. I have already mentioned that one possible use of Dublin Core data provided with a resource would be as an aid to library staff in cataloging the resource. It is also possible that some machine-conversion to USMARC could be done. The Dublin Core element set is syntax independent, which means it does not specify how elements should be encoded. The description in the Maya Angelou example could theoretically be represented in SGML (Standard Generalized Mark-up Language), in USMARC, or in any other standard syntax that can handle bibliographic data. In practice, however, it will not always be easy or even possible to create a valid MARC record from Dublin Core metadata, and it could be even harder to create good AACR2 cataloging.

For example, the MARC bibliographic formats require you to know any number of things to properly encode an author: whether it is a main or added entry (which only makes sense in reference to certain cataloging rules); whether it is a personal, corporate or conference name; and details about the form of name. A human cataloger looking at the metadata example above would probably build a good 100 field for Maya Angelou, but a computer program would lack the information required to automatically map the author element correctly. There are at least two possible approaches to a solution.

One is to add information to the Dublin Core description to make machine mapping possible. The rules for the Dublin Core state that any data element can be qualified with a variety of qualifiers. The qualifier "scheme" applies to most data elements and is used to specify the scheme or authority used for the content of the element. For example, we might say:

Language (scheme = USMARC Code List For Languages)–eng

Other qualifiers include "role" (e.g., the role of the OtherAgent here could be "transcriber") and "type" (e.g., the type of Author could be "personal"). By taking advantage of this facility, it would be possible to include enough information to map any Dublin Dozen element to its appropriate USMARC representation. (Note, however, that it will not necessarily be possible to guarantee the appropriate choice of entry, authorized form of name, or other things that relate to data quality.) Under some circumstances, this may be desirable. The downside, of course, is that this necessitates greater intellectual effort in creating the original metadata, and may militate against having the metadata created at all.

A different course would be to simplify MARC, or at least allow simplified content designation under certain circumstances. It would be possible, for example, to add a new field defined simply as "author" to the bibliographic formats and map all Author elements to it. This would allow a far wider range of data to be mapped automatically to USMARC with the advantage it could be used in our MARC-based bibliographic systems. The concomitant disadvantage is that in many cases there is good reason for the complexity of our cataloging and encoding rules, and that oversimplification will be reflected in poorer displays and less effective retrieval.

Two discussion papers related to the Dublin Core will come before MARBI (Machine Readable Bibliographic Information) and the USMARC Advisory Group at this summer's ALA–"DP86: Mapping the Dublin Core data elements to USMARC," and "DP88: Defining a generic author field in USMARC." MARBI meetings are open to observers and the discussion ought to be lively so if you are going to Chicago and interested in these issues you should think about attending.

In conclusion, I would like to say I think there is tremendous potential in the Dublin Core, but there is tremendous inertia also. For authors to provide metadata it has to be easy to supply, and there has to be obvious utility to having it. To make it easy to supply there must be software applications that will not be developed unless there is demand for the metadata. For the utility to be evident there must be locator services and URC resolution services that will not be developed unless the metadata exists. The library community will have to play a major role in encouraging the adoption of this or some similar metadata standard if it is to succeed, and not only in the obvious way of providing mapping to USMARC. We will have to work with University publishers and with the faculty and departments on our campuses who are mounting papers and images on departmental servers and show them how and why to provide metadata. To do this, we will have to believe that this effort is complementary to, not in competition or conflict with, other library efforts at bibliographic control of Internet resources. I personally think this is the case, and I am glad to have had the opportunity to talk to you about it today.

NOTES

1. Priscilla Caplan, "Controlling E-Journals: The Internet Resources Project, Cataloging Guidelines, and USMARC," In *New Scholarship: New Serials: Proceedings of the North American Serials Interest Group, Inc.* ed. Gail McMillan and Marilyn L. Norstedt (New York: The Haworth Press, Inc., 1994): 103-111.

2. *Guidelines for the Use of Field 856* (Washington, DC: Library of Congress Network Development and MARC Standards Office, 1995). Available by sending e-mail to listproc@loc.gov with the message: get usmarc 856_guidelines.

3. Nancy B. Olson, ed., *Cataloging Internet Resources: A Manual and Practical Guide* (Dublin, OH: OCLC Online Computer Library Center, Inc., 1995). Available at URL:ftp://ftp.rsch.oclc.org/pub/internet_cataloging_project/Manua1.txt

4. INTERCAT@oclc.org, the listserv for the OCLC Internet Cataloging project.

5. Special thanks to Ron Daniel, Jr., of the IETF URI Working Group for reviewing and correcting excerpts from this paper. Errors are still all my own.

6. This example taken from "x-dsn-2 URN scheme" by Paul Hoffman and Ron Daniel, Jr., an Internet-draft available at
   URL:ftp://ds.unternic.net/internet-drafts/draft-ietf-uri-urn-x-dns-2-00.txt.

7. The full report of the workshop, "OCLC/NCSA Metadata Workshop Report," by Stuart Weibel, Jean Godby, Eric Miller, Ron Daniel Jr., is available through the Workshop's home page at
   URL:http://www.oclc.org:5046/conferences/metadata/metadata.html.

NASIG WORKSHOPS

WORKSHOP SET I

Trading Back Issues on the Internet

Marilyn Geller
Janice Lange

Workshop Leaders

Joseph P. Hinger

Recorder

SUMMARY. The BACKSERV and DEU-L electronic projects are some of the first resources available on the Internet that deal solely with offering and requesting back issues and other print materials. *[Article copies available from The Haworth Document Delivery Service: 1-800-342-9678.]*

In this workshop, Marilyn Geller, Internet Product Specialist at Readmore Inc., and Janice Lange, head of Collections and Technical Services at Sam Houston State University (SHSU), reported on

---

Joseph P. Hinger is Associate Librarian for Technical Services and Automation, Detroit College of Law Library, Detroit, MI

© 1996 by the North American Serials Interest Group, Inc. All rights reserved.

[Haworth co-indexing entry note]: "Trading Back Issues on the Internet." Hinger, Joseph P. Co-published simultaneously in *The Serials Librarian* (The Haworth Press, Inc.) Vol. 28, No. 3/4, 1996, pp. 249-255; and *Serials to the Tenth Power: Tradition, Technology, and Transformation* (ed: Mary Ann Sheble, and Beth Holley) The Haworth Press, Inc., 1996, pp. 249-255. Single or multiple copies of this article are available from The Haworth Document Delivery Service [1-800-342-9678, 9:00 a.m. - 5:00 p.m. (EST)].

two recent electronic projects that address trading back issues on the Internet. Several resources on the Internet can now be used to resolve back-issues problems that previously could only be dealt with by telephone or correspondence ("snail mail").

Geller began the workshop by summarizing the back-issues problem, if it is a problem. The first aspect of this problem is that a need exists for specific serial issues. Possible reasons for this need are: the back issues were never received, they cannot be claimed or claimed in time, they were destroyed either accidentally or maliciously, and/or they were lost. Another aspect to the back-issues problem is the need to eliminate title runs and excess volumes brought about by space concerns, title cancellations, receipt of duplicate issues, and/or receipt of gifts. Both Geller and Lange also humorously stated that librarians would rather find good homes for things by recycling, trading, or giving them away, instead of discarding them. The last aspect is that back-issues dealers need to replenish their stock, as well as fill requests from their customers.

Before the advent of lists and groups on the Internet, librarians utilized several methods to acquire specific back issues. The primary method was by being a member of a library exchange program, such as the Medical Library Association Exchange Group. Another method was by corresponding with the publisher. The problem here is that publishers do not keep much back stock, and many times could not supply the requested issues. Other methods included acquiring the specific back issues from back-issues dealers, or from subscription agents.

The Internet continued to develop and more and more subject oriented lists were being created. Librarians' interest in the Internet also continued to develop. Suddenly, other places to look for and to offer back issues were being created. MEDLIB-L, an electronic forum for ideas, questions, announcements, and concerns specific to health sciences libraries, and Art Libraries Society E-conference (ARLIS-L), as well as many other lists, had frequent posts of back issues either needed or being offered. Serials in Libraries Discussion Forum (SERIALST) accepted posts of back issues needs and offers when it began; but due to the high volume of messages each day, the policy for posting changed to exclude messages requesting or offering back issues. Similarly, Library Gifts and Exchange (GIF-

TEX-L), an electronic forum for ideas, questions, announcements, and concerns specific to gifts and exchanges, created in early 1995, does not accept posts that request or offer back issues. One of the first creations of an electronic list solely for requesting and offering back issues was by the American Society of Electrical Engineering, Engineering Library Division (ASEE/ELD). Librarians continued to manually create their library exchange lists, and sent them to ASEE/ELD. ASEE/ELD staff collated the lists, entered the data online, and electronically distributed the lists to its members.

Lange discussed the evolution of dealing with back issues at SHSU, and the birth of the Association for Library Collections and Technical Services (ALCTS) Duplicate Exchange Union (DEU) electronic project. Prior to any electronic means for trading back issues, SHSU discarded any duplicate issues or sent them to back-issues dealers. Staff time to deal with trading back issues on exchange lists was minimal. Several years ago, the computer center at SHSU wrote a computer program based on an old serials holdings database, that allowed the library staff to enter data for material available on exchange lists. Data entry was easy since the program prompted the staff member for the specific information to be entered. SHSU printed these lists and sent them to the ALCTS DEU paper project. This project promotes the free exchange of excess library materials among libraries, and includes both monographs and serials. Any institution can become a member of the DEU paper project by registering with the office, sending at least one exchange list per year, and reimbursing any postage over one dollar. Currently there are approximately 400 libraries of all types that are members of this project.

In January 1994, talk began about automating components of the DEU, in order to take advantage of computer power to make the exchange of back issues easier and more efficient. A pro-library Internet expert on the SHSU campus was consulted, and work on the ALCTS DEU electronic project (DEU-L) began. By May 1994, everything was ready for the DEU-L listserv[1] and the DEU-L gopher[2] to operate.

The main purpose for the DEU-L listserv is to serve as a communication medium for all subscribers to the electronic project. The DEU-L listserv, an unmoderated list, initially served as a forum for discussion of members on how the listserv would be operated. Its function evolved to become a communication method, primarily to notify members that exchange lists have been received and posted. The features and defaults of the DEU-L listserv are the same as many other listservs on the Internet.

The DEU-L gopher, which is the majority of the DEU electronic project, has three major features. The first major feature is that several information files are contained in the DEU-L gopher. Examples of these information files are the DEU-L archives, addresses and DEU codes of participating institutions, duplicate exchange listings, information about searching, and information about the DEU file format. Another feature is the ability to search the exchange lists and the addresses of contributors. The lists and addresses are searched using Boolean searching logic (AND, OR, and NOT). Wildcard searches (*), multiple word searches, keyword searching, and browse capabilities are all supported. The third feature of the DEU-L gopher is the ability to retrieve an exchange list and to request back issues. Some ways that exchange lists can be retrieved are by sending the list to your e-mail address, downloading the list to a diskette, saving the list to a file, or printing the list on paper. File transfer protocol (FTP) is also supported.

Contributing an exchange list of monographs or serials to DEU-L is relatively easy. The first step is to fill out an address template, which is simply a form that prompts the user for the specific lines of an address. The second step is to enter the data about the back issues being offered on the exchange list. This data can be entered in any format. The only requirement is to separate each entry with 80 equal (=) signs. The equal signs are mandatory for proper indexing. The final step is to get the information to SHSU for posting to DEU-L. The information can be transmitted electronically to SHSU via e-mail or FTP, or it can be sent on a diskette. The length of the document for posting is not important. The longer the document, the more powerful the searching capabilities will be.

The DEU electronic project has proven well since its inception, and ways are now being looked at to enhance both the DEU listserv and gopher. The most recent development to DEU-L is access to it via the World Wide Web (WWW).[3] A Frequently Asked Questions (FAQ) file on the gopher is also a coming attraction.

Geller continued this session by describing how and why The Back Issues and Duplicate Exchange Service (BACKSERV[4]) began.

She stated, "Librarians use the Internet daily, they need to fill in back issues of runs, and they would rather trade or recycle usable material rather than discard it; therefore, we knew that there was a need for a free and easy electronic medium for trading back issues on the Internet." She also stated that this electronic medium, soon to be created, should have as few rules as possible.

Phase one of BACKSERV's creation entailed defining the list features. Such features included producing an automatic copy of a message to the person posting the message, being able to reply to the originator of the message automatically, and allowing access to the list by non-subscribers. Once these features were programmed into the computer, BACKSERV was born on September 29, 1994.

Two common questions from librarians are whether one has to be a Readmore client in order to access BACKSERV, and how much BACK- SERV costs. One does NOT have to be a Readmore client to be a subscriber to BACKSERV. It is available to anyone that wants to subscribe. It is also absolutely free. The only charge incurred in subscribing to BACKSERV is the staff time used to read, reply, and post to the list. Another frequently asked question is whether dealers may subscribe to the list. Dealers are allowed to subscribe to the list, but may not post any messages. They may also contact subscribers privately about any backissues requests or offers that have been posted.

The only guidelines that exist for posting to the BACKSERV are common sense guidelines, and participant-created ones. An example of the latter is to include in the subject line of the message either the word WANTED or AVAILABLE, plus the subject area of the material wanted or being offered. With so many posts from different types of libraries, librarians can use the subject line to discriminate whether they need to read a message or not. Examples of common sense guidelines are to always include complete contact and reimbursement information in the body of the message.

As the months passed, BACKSERV began to grow. The number of subscribers quickly grew to more than 550, and the number of posts distributed each day averaged between ten and twenty. Librarians began asking whether posts for duplicate books were appropriate for this list. An informal survey of BACKSERV subscribers yielded the result that any print material can be posted to the list. Subscribers also began to post messages that dealt with guidelines. Some topics discussed were the length of posts, and ways to reimburse a library for postage costs incurred from sending back issues. Informal guidelines have never been distributed to the subscribers, yet everybody is considerate when making posts to BACKSERV, and when reimbursing postage for material received. Most subscribers rarely place more than ten items per post. If a post does contain a long list of items, subscribers are usually alerted by a short message in the subject line. Conflicts about the method or nonreceipt of postage reimbursement are resolved by private e-mail conversation between the two parties that carried out the transaction.

BACKSERV continued to grow and it became necessary for the listowners to add and enhance some list features. Phase two of the BACKSERV project initially began by providing gopher access to the list.[5] Another enhancement was the addition of Wide Area Information Server (WAIS) indexing searching capabilities, which allow subscribers to search the list archives using Boolean logic. Also in Phase two, the listowners added back-issue dealers' catalogs and resources to the BACKSERV gopher menu. To date, three back-issue dealers have their catalogs mounted on the BACKSERV gopher. All the catalogs are browsable and searchable, and provide order templates for online ordering of back issues. Another feature of the back-issues dealers' catalogs is a menu option to print a text copy of an order form. Once printed, the form can be filled out and forwarded to the appropriate library department to order.

Phase three of the BACKSERV project began in early 1995, and is still in progress. The main enhancement for this phase was to provide access via the WWW. To date, all functions that can be done on the BACKSERV gopher can also be performed on the WWW,[6] with the exception of searching the back-issues dealers' catalogs. Enhanced searching capabilities of the back-issues dealers' catalogs via the WWW will be operable in mid 1995.

As the subscriber list and the use of BACKSERV grow, more and more enhancements to the electronic project will be required. Geller stated, "The number of enhancement phases to come is unknown. The different phases are generated according to the needs of the participants." Some future enhancements to BACKSERV include adding more back-issues dealers' catalogs, being able to search combined dealers' catalogs, providing better list searching for the archives (i.e., displaying subject line of a message on a retrieved list), copying selected searches to order forms, and creating complete access via the WWW. Some questions raised about the future of BACKSERV include: (1) Should BACKSERV be split into lists by subject? (2) Should ways be found for more back-issues dealer participation on BACKSERV? (3) Should the back-issues dealers have their own list? The listowners hope to resolve these matters in future phases of the BACKSERV project.

A member of the audience questioned how often the back-issues dealers' catalogs were updated on the BACKSERV project. Geller responded that since the three catalogs have been mounted, none have been updated; however, all the catalogs are less than six months old. She proceeded that all the catalogs can be updated whenever the listowners are sent updated versions either on a diskette or via FTP.

This session closed with the speakers responding to an audience member's question on hit rate for items being requested or offered on the electronic projects. Both Geller and Lange responded that to date no formal studies have been made regarding hit rate since both projects are relatively young. Geller stated that occasional messages posted accidentally to BACKSERV instead of to an individual e-mail account indicates that people are meeting and transactions for back issues are being made. Both speakers anticipate studies to determine what the hit rate is for back-issues trading on BACKSERV and DEU-L.

NOTES

1. To subscribe to the DEU-L listserv, send a message to LISTSERV@SHSU.EDU that reads: SUBSCRIBE DEU-L "your real name in quotes".

2. To access the DEU-L gopher, point your gopher to Niord.SHSU.Edu and select DEU Library Prototype Demonstration Area from the menu.

3. To access the DEU-L WWW home page, point your web browser to HTTP://WWW.SHSU.EDU and select DEU under Project NIMO.

4. To subscribe to BACKSERV, send a message to listserv@sun.readmore.com that reads: subscribe backserv [your name].

5. To access the BACKSERV gopher, point your gopher to gopher.readmore.com and select BACKSERV from the menu.

6. To access the BACKSERV WWW home page, point your web browser to http://www.readmore.com/electron/backserv.html.

New Technology and Traditional Sources

Karen B. Nichols
Emerita Cuesta

Workshop Leaders

Sandy Gurshman

Recorder

SUMMARY. Financial constraints have caused many libraries to reevaluate their collection development policies, while new electronic resources are changing the needs and expectations of library patrons. The effect that the interaction of financial contraction and electronic expansion has had on library collections and the suggestions and possibilities offered by new technologies are examined. *[Article copies available from The Haworth Document Delivery Service: 1-800-342-9678.]*

Karen B. Nichols, Electronic Services Librarian at Lamar University, and Emerita Cuesta, head of Access Services at Hofstra University, examined the effects of these forces in two different environments. The two presenters illustrated the difference between cancellation projects imposed by severe budget constraints, and collection shifts supported by adequate funding. The ability to provide a variety of databases at Lamar enabled Nichols to conduct studies and make evaluations of their usefulness to the library patrons.

Sandra J. Gurshman is Manager of Publisher Services at Readmore, Inc., New York, NY.

© 1996 by the North American Serials Interest Group, Inc. All rights reserved.

[Haworth co-indexing entry note]: "New Technology and Traditional Sources." Gurshman, Sandy. Co-published simultaneously in *The Serials Librarian* (The Haworth Press, Inc.) Vol. 28, No. 3/4, 1996, pp. 257-262; and *Serials to the Tenth Power: Tradition, Technology, and Transformation* (ed: Mary Ann Sheble, and Beth Holley) The Haworth Press, Inc., 1996, pp. 257-262. Single or multiple copies of this article are available from The Haworth Document Delivery Service [1-800-342-9678, 9:00 a.m. - 5:00 p.m. (EST)].

Cuesta, on the other hand, needed to work within a narrower framework to bring costs under control. Innovation and transformation will proceed more deliberately under these circumstances. The similarities are not to be overlooked: regardless of circumstances, collection goals must be identified and met, and patrons must be satisfied.

Nichols, in a presentation co-authored by Sarah Tusa, Serials Acquisitions Librarian at Lamar, first outlined the situation at the University. Lamar is a state-supported commuter campus of approximately 9000 students; many of the students are older than the typical college student, and have no previous college experience.

During the past decade or so, the library experienced the usual fiscal woes: severely declining budgets coupled with rising serials prices. However, in 1994 the library initiated a student use fee of $3.00 per credit hour (most students pay the maximum $30.00), and found itself with a bonus of $540,000, which presented a special challenge: how to spend the money wisely for both the present and future needs of the library's patrons. The fee created a "double bind" since it is difficult to impose extra charges for such things as printing documents when the students have already paid a fee.

The University consists of two two-year campuses, a four-year campus, an institute of technology, and advanced degree programs. For the two-year campuses, $135,000 of the student use fees provided ProQuest: software, hardware (three single-use stations), and full-text business and social science databases. In two months, these stations generated 41,000 printed pages (8200 articles).

ProQuest is not the only article-access service. FirstSearch is offered free on the OPAC (the library picks up the $0.50 charge per search). UMI full-text is provided on three workstations and offers Periodical Abstracts Research II, ABI Inform Global, and Social Science Index. UNCOVER has been available since its inception, although it is expensive, and the library pays for document delivery.

Students want access and they want it immediately. These nontraditional students, many of whom have limited time on-campus, are not satisfied with ILL. The reference department needs to have material that is quickly, easily, and readily available to meet their needs. The serials department needs to know the cost, use, access, and format of the information sources selected.

Nichols stressed the importance of knowing the products, as well as the patrons and their needs, in order to make good decisions. She pointed out that when trading ownership for access it is vital to know what journals are covered by the databases, and what percentage of these journals have been subscribed to by the library.

To test coverage and overlap among the various services, she selected six topics each in business and general topics from each of two sources: *Reader's Guide* and *Business Periodicals Index*. She then searched ABI Global, Periodical Abstracts II, and UNCOVER for overlap and uniqueness. In the business topics, she found only eight titles common to both ABI and UNCOVER. The library owned many of the journals retrieved in the searches of ABI Inform and Periodical Abstracts, but few of those retrieved from UNCOVER. Subscriptions to all titles the library did not own would have totalled $25,000. The cost of document delivery from UNCOVER for those articles was $5000.

However, many of the selected areas had upwards of 100 hits, and Nichols raised a few questions about these cost comparisons: How many students would actually use more than fifty citations on these subjects? What is the best service money can buy? Is a subscription the best use for funds? What happens to journals the library subscribes to if patrons use ProQuest or other online services instead?

Other approaches are also being pursued. The Library is adding ARIEL in ILL to reduce the time lag. TEXSHARE, a statewide group, will provide additional access to databases.

Nichols drew the following conclusions from her study: (1) Communication among technical services, public services, vendors, and publishers is essential; (2) There is no one best product or service; a variety of products is necessary to serve the needs of the patrons; and the mix of subscription products and access products needs to be constantly re-evaluated.

When Cuesta's studies began, the library at Hofstra was facing simultaneous crises: in personnel, the serials librarian was retiring and the assistant dean for public services had left for another job; a space crunch was emerging; and $50,000 was requested from the serials budget for the purchase of monographs. Complicating the picture further was the generally conservative atmosphere which considered books to be the core of the library, and a drive to build the book collection to 1,000,000 volumes. Something had to be done. The often painful and prolonged cancellation project taught some valuable lessons. Lesson One was "keep your Rolodex handy" and ask for advice from people who "have been there."

The closed periodical stacks, which include the microforms, had provided an opportunity to collect extensive usage statistics. (Samples were provided in handouts.) Between 800 and 1000 requests for material are received each day. Counting every slip over the past six years, staff had created lists of use patterns for both completed and ongoing titles. Recommendations to the Dean were to weed out completed journals with no usage, and convert to microfilm the following categories: completed with little use, current subscriptions with no use, and current subscriptions with some use.

Lesson Number Two was "keep an eye on the faculty" to get their support and avert obstruction. The Hofstra faculty rejected the usage statistics as not meaningful for their use patterns because they did have browsing privileges and were therefore not filling out slips. To counter this perceived lack of relevant statistics, the staff requested that faculty not reshelve, but place the volumes they had used in a "drop." After a year of counting these volumes, only two titles were moved from the "no use" to "some use" category; no titles were moved to the "heavy use" list.

Faculty also felt that microfilm would not meet their needs, because they could not borrow it to use in their offices. Without a reader in the stacks, browsing was impossible; and, they would have to wait to make copies. A reader was therefore installed in the faculty reading room.

Lesson Number Three taught Cuesta to "find an advantage in a necessity" (make lemonade out of lemons). She was able to locate a vendor who would exchange print runs for microfilm on a one-for-one basis and give credit for weeded volumes. This credit was then promoted to faculty as a way to purchase back runs and replace missing issues of heavily-used titles.

Faced with shortfalls in the periodicals budget, the library began cancellation projects. The Assistant Dean for Technical Services drew up a list of proposed cancellations based on the "current subscription, no use" category of titles, and presented this list to the faculty, along with a memo detailing the financial problems. However, the faculty was unaccustomed to being told that materials were to be unavailable, and returned the lists with fewer approved cuts than were necessary to meet the budgetary crunch.

At this juncture, a serials librarian was hired, and Lesson Number Four was learned: "listen to your experts." The serials librarian recommended that lists of proposed cancellations include prices and the history of price increases, and that meetings be held with faculty to discuss the cancellation project. Regrettably, both recommendations were rejected, and the process stagnated.

The Serials Librarian and Access Services Librarian then began a project to relate periodicals to curriculum by assigning each journal to a department. To facilitate this they used vendor-supplied lists of the journals broken by LC class. They immediately discovered grey areas, such as interdisciplinary journals, or journals assigned to one discipline but used heavily by another department; these journals needed to be submitted to several departments before being canceled.

The Collection Development Committee prepared a periodicals policy that required any department wishing to add a title to agree to drop the dollar value in existing subscriptions. This policy was accepted, but journal replacement in the interdisciplinary areas is still being negotiated.

Other approaches are also being explored. "E-journals" are being reviewed for their usefulness. Hofstra defines these as those that appear ONLY in electronic form. There must be either LAN or DRA access. And the collection development policy of "add one-drop one" applies to e-journals as well as print. The selection of e-journals is in its early stages.

The Fifth Lesson brought loud agreement from the audience, "You will do this again." The evaluation project is now an ongoing process at Hofstra. Lists of journals will be circulated for ranking purposes, and librarians will meet regularly with department chairs to keep them informed about price increases and the ways the library is meeting these challenges.

Workshop participants volunteered their experiences with cancellation projects and noted changes in usage patterns and library acquisitions. Traditional statistics continue to drop as usage of e-journals and online services rises; this will increase the number of journals considered as candidates for cancellation. One library is now being asked to prepare course packets and clear copyright on their contents; this will cut into available funds for subscriptions.

Document delivery services, such as UNCOVER, are being substituted for print subscriptions. One librarian reported that when free document delivery was offered on any canceled journal that the faculty insisted was needed, no requests were made.

There was general agreement with the proposition that, if differing usage patterns by students and faculty suggest different courses of action, the students needs should take precedence, since the faculty would have other options; however, there was equally general skepticism that the students would, in fact, prevail.

Cataloging Electronic Journals: The University of Virginia Experience

Allison Mook Sleeman

Workshop Leader

Mary Ellen Soper

Recorder

SUMMARY. Serial catalogers at the University of Virginia selectively catalog electronic journals and make them available on the local campuswide information system and/or the World Wide Web. How to handle titles on both the local OPAC and the WWW and how to catalog serials such as *WILS* and *Current Contents* are explained through examples. *[Article copies available from The Haworth Document Delivery Service: 1-800-342-9678.]*

The workshop was presented by Allison Mook Sleeman, cataloger at Alderman Library, University of Virginia (UVA) since 1989. She is responsible for coordinating serials cataloging, with specific attention to cataloging electronic journals. The two presentations of the workshop were attended primarily by catalogers, some of whom already had experience cataloging electronic journals (e-journals). There were approximately 80 attendees at the first session, and 25 at the repeat session.

Mary Ellen Soper is Assistant Professor at the Graduate School of Library and Information Science, University of Washington, Seattle, WA.

© 1996 by the North American Serials Interest Group, Inc. All rights reserved.

[Haworth co-indexing entry note]: "Cataloging Electronic Journals: The University of Virginia Experience." Soper, Mary Ellen. Co-published simultaneously in *The Serials Librarian* (The Haworth Press, Inc.) Vol. 28, No. 3/4, 1996, pp. 263-267; and *Serials to the Tenth Power: Tradition, Technology, and Transformation* (ed: Mary Ann Sheble, and Beth Holley) The Haworth Press, Inc., 1996, pp. 263-267. Single or multiple copies of this article are available from The Haworth Document Delivery Service [1-800-342-9678, 9:00 a.m. - 5:00 p.m. (EST)].

UVA began cataloging electronic journals a year ago. Only those titles selected by the collection development selectors are cataloged, and so far they have been slow to select items. But during the past year, new developments have occurred that are designed to meet the needs of librarians and their users as this kind of material has become more prevalent. Standards are evolving, and more librarians are becoming familiar with the routines of organizing electronic serials for use in their own libraries.

The OCLC Internet Cataloging Project[1] began recently, and quickly signed up the number of participants for which it was aiming. The goal of the Project is to have a variety of libraries actually catalog resources available through the Internet in order to discover how the present cataloging standards work, and how they need to be changed. One of the early artifacts of the Project is Nancy B. Olson's *Cataloging Internet Resources: A Manual and Practical Guide*.[2] The Association for Library Collections & Technical Services (ALCTS) Institute entitled Serials Cataloging in the Age of Format Integration, offered in Atlanta in April, 1995, also covered the cataloging of direct access and remote access computer files.[3] The *CONSER Cataloging Manual* will issue in print form *Module 31: Remote Access Computer File Serials* sometime this summer.[4] It is already available on CONSER's Web server. An example of local practice is included in the UVA Cataloging Services Department's *Cataloging Procedures Manual, Chapter 12: Computer Files Cataloging, Part D: Serials: Remote Access*.[5]

Sleeman had many illustrations that covered various aspects of UVA's procedures. Initially UVA planned to catalog and report to OCLC only e-journals it planned to maintain, but has now decided to report e-journals it does not own nor maintain to OCLC. Though few e-journals have been cataloged so far, there is increasing interest and discussion concerning their selection. The organization of these materials can cause various problems. E-journals can be published as complete issues, making up volumes, the way print journals are commonly published, or article by article, with release when the individual article is ready. All of the e-journals are available on the Internet, but UVA access is provided in various ways. A gopher client has been established on the GWIS (Grounds-Wide Information System), the UVA campus wide information system.

At the time of the workshop 18 titles were listed on the gopher. A World Wide Web (WWW) server has also been established.

Maintaining the collection of e-journals and their cataloging records will be an ongoing chore, but this is also true of print serials collections. The links to the location on the Internet need to be checked periodically, as do the journals themselves to detect such things as title changes. The question of maintaining holdings for this material is an interesting one. Since the material is not physically in the library, but instead exists somewhere in e-space, should the library try to show what issues or articles are accessible? UVA has decided that when it catalogs an e-journal it owns, it will show holdings through a volume holdings record. Examples were also shown of e-journals not owned nor maintained by UVA for which a note is added to the copy holdings record asking users to check the gopher or World Wide Web for holdings. An example of a bib record created prior to May, 1995, was shown, along with how it had been revised to reflect format integration and to add the new 856 field (Electronic Location and Access). Previous to adoption of format integration the 590 field (Local Notes) was used to show a Uniform Resource Locator (URL) or other Internet address.

NOTIS, used by UVA, cannot yet handle the editing and display of certain fields authorized for serial records by format integration. Since UVA uses the serials format for all e-journals this affects how the bib record is displayed. The 856 field does not show, but the 590 field does, and it contains the URL. When the record is reported to OCLC it has to be edited to conform to national standards. An example of an e-journal accessible through the Web server was shown, and it contained all the necessary tags and subfield codes.

Sleeman also discussed some of the specific problems that must be considered when cataloging e-journals. A 130 field (Uniform Title, Main Entry) will be necessary for all these serials if there is also a print version. Until multiple versions treatment is available it will continue to be necessary to create separate bib records for print, microform, and electronic versions of the same title. UVA will use (Online) as the qualifier in the 130 field for e-journals. A 500 field (General Note) with the source of the title is required for all e-journals, with no exceptions, as this is a greater problem than with print serials. The order of preference for selection of source of the title information is:

file of a complete issue, files containing introductory information, home page (WWW serial), README files, and other files.

The 516 field (File Characteristics) will usually be necessary to display such information as journal availability in ASCII, postscript, hypertext, etc. The 538 field (Systems Details) will contain the system requirements and mode of access to the title. The URL or other specific address in Internet is not given here by UVA catalogers, but is in the 856 field. UVA will use '7' as the first indicator in the 856 field, then subfield 'u' for URL information and subfield '2' for access method. The 099 field (Local Free-Text Call Number) is used by UVA to show the title is an electronic journal, but does not contain a classification number. All 6XX fields use 'Periodicals' as a form sub-division after the subject headings.

Sleeman's presentation was very well-organized. The transparencies she used, which were also copied and distributed to the audience, emphasized the various points she made about the cataloging of e-journals in a large academic research library. The audience was enthusiastic and a lively discussion followed the formal presentation. One question concerned the failure to assign a subject classification number to this material. At present, access to these titles is alphabetically by journal title; in the future, classification may play a much more important role, and providing numbers now would make it unnecessary to add them later. The audience also questioned why NOTIS could not handle all the fields; the answer apparently is that it has not yet reprogrammed for format integration, though there has been a long lead time for this change. The multiple versions problem was also discussed, as it seems uneconomical to have separate records for both print and electronic formats if the electronic format is an exact copy. But so far, this is the way UVA does it.

The 856 field is apparently still new to many catalogers. Not many are using it yet, but the OCLC Internet Cataloging Project may change this. UVA is a member of this Project. The exact meaning of maintained and nonmaintained serials at UVA was also queried: if the title is on the UVA gopher it is considered that the Library has control over it, and it is maintained. If not maintained, only a URL is given to the distant location where the file is maintained. A question was asked about whether different formats needed different ISSNs. A representative from the ISSN office, present in the audience, explained that different physical formats get different ISSNs; this is the international agreement. But there is not a different ISSN for different electronic versions (gopher vs. hypertext markup language (HTML), etc.). Whether there should be is presently being discussed on the international level. For a couple of weeks, UVA put a qualifier (Print) after the ISSN for a print version when this is recorded in the 022 field in a bib record for an e-journal until it found out at the workshop from the ISSN representative this was not permissible. The audience got diverted to various ISSN questions because of the ISSN representative.

Obviously there are many questions about specific aspects of cataloging remote access e-materials, and no doubt there will be many more as more catalogers start organizing this material. Sleeman's workshop was a useful introduction to many of these problems, with very helpful examples of how a specific, large academic library is solving them. She did not pretend to have all the answers, but UVA had made a good start, and the audience should find its experiences of great use as they face similar problems in their own libraries. It was also useful to be advised of some of the important publications now available in this area, and to get audience feed-back. This is an area of great concern and of lively interest. Sleeman's workshop should help ease some of these concerns by showing that solutions are possible, and are based on traditional, standard cataloging practices.

NOTES

1. To subscribe to Intercat, the public e-mail list dedicated to facilitating communication about the OCLC Internet Cataloging Project, send a message to LISTSERV@oclc.org. In the body of the message enter: subscribe intercat (your name)

2. Nancy B. Olson, ed. *Cataloging Internet Resources: A Manual and Practical Guide*. 1995. URL: ftp://ftp.rsch.oclc.org/pub/internet_cataloging_project/Manual.txt.

3. Regina R. Reynolds, *Cataloging Electronic Serials (Remote Access)*. (Atlanta: ALCTS Serials Cataloging in the Age of Format Integration (Institute), Atlanta, Georgia, April 7-8, 1995.)

4. *Module 31: Remote Access Computer File Serials*. Prepared by Melissa Beck, with the assistance of Bill Anderson, Les Hawkins, and Regina Reynolds. 1995. URL: http://www.library.Vanderbilt.edu/serials.html. To be issued in print as Update 3 of *CONSER Cataloging Manual.*

5. University of Virginia Library. Cataloging Services Department, *Cataloging Procedures Manual. Chapter 12: Computer Files Cataloging, Part D: Serials: Remote Access:* URL: http://www.lib.virginia.edu/cataloging/manual/chapxiid.html.

Optimizing Serials Access in the Online Catalog

Paula Sullenger
Ruth H. Makinen

Workshop Leaders

Patricia M. Wallace

Recorder

SUMMARY. Searching for serials in the online catalog is not easy and patrons need all the help they can get! Catalogers devote considerable time and resources to provide access to serials. How much of that effort results in increased access? A serials cataloger analyzes a transaction log to examine patron behavior, and a medical librarian describes several techniques to enhance access to serial records. *[Article copies available from The Haworth Document Delivery Service: 1-800-342-9678.]*

Searching for serials in online catalogs is becoming both easier and more difficult. Format integration allows serials catalogers greater options for enhancing records and improving access. The development of computer programs which permit greater sophistication in search strategies has added both flexibility and complexity to searching. Yet, has this ever-increasing capability been matched

---

Patricia M. Wallace is Head of the Serials Department at the University of Colorado Libraries, Boulder, CO.

© 1996 by the North American Serials Interest Group, Inc. All rights reserved.

[Haworth co-indexing entry note]: "Optimizing Serials Access in the Online Catalog." Wallace, Patricia M. Co-published simultaneously in *The Serials Librarian* (The Haworth Press, Inc.) Vol. 28, No. 3/4, 1996, pp. 269-273; and *Serials to the Tenth Power: Tradition, Technology, and Transformation* (ed: Mary Ann Sheble, and Beth Holley) The Haworth Press, Inc., 1996, pp. 269-273. Single or multiple copies of this article are available from The Haworth Document Delivery Service [1-800-342-9678, 9:00 a.m. - 5:00 p.m. (EST)].

with serial records that can be retrieved successfully, and with patrons who know how to search successfully for serials? Two serialists have undertaken this challenge in varying ways and reported their results in a workshop replete with practical examples.

Paula Sullenger, Serials Cataloger at Auburn University, began the workshop by describing the results of a transaction log taken for twelve days in October 1994 at eight Auburn University public access terminals. Many transaction log analyses have been done in recent years to examine users' success in searching online catalogs, but until Sullenger's study none focused exclusively on searching for serials. She began by describing the study's venue and various data elements common to most transaction logs. Auburn University uses the NOTIS system, so it was also necessary for Sullenger to describe the search conventions and other features of that system which affected the log's display. For example, all search statements in NOTIS must begin with the key letter of that search and a blank space or =. Examples are k=congress or t moby dick. Any search which did not begin with this convention automatically got a "0" (zero) for the number of records (hits) retrieved.

Sullenger found that serials did not seem to be a very popular search request. Out of 105,897 lines of search commands, only 1,078 appeared to be requests for serial titles. It was difficult at times to know whether a t-search was for a serial, so 1,078 was not a definitive number. Short of reconstructing every title search, Sullenger relied on selected researching of suspected serial titles and she had to rule out searches for such common titles as "science" and "nature" in cases where it was not obvious from nearby searches that the patron was looking for journals. Patrons made extremely low use of keyword or subject searches for serials, only 105 out of the 1,078, and in most cases it seemed obvious to Sullenger that they should have used a title search.

Zero hits were a significant problem for patrons searching serial titles. The NOTIS system is unforgiving and requires exact data entry, so there was a high percentage (28.57%) of serial title searches which resulted in zero hits. Fortunately, patrons discovered their error 22.4% of the time and were able to self-correct. Sullenger researched the remaining zero hits by correcting search strategy or spelling and netted another 17.2% hits.

Sullenger detected several types of errors patrons made in serial title searching that can be corrected through enhancing bibliographic records by adding 246 fields. While her library already has a lot of 246s in the catalog, which patrons searched, she noticed they also searched for titles they could have found if the cataloger had thought to put in a 246 for that variant. The majority of variant title searching problems involved the dilemma of searching "*and*" or "&," and this is easily resolved by adding a 246 for the alternate form. Also, two-word titles such as "value line" frequently are mis-searched as one word; adding a 246 field to the record is a viable enhancement when it's possible patrons may search the title as one word or two words. Serials catalogers may find it profitable to look occasionally at transaction logs from their institutions and examine failed title searches to find instances where they need to add some 246 fields. Knowing when to add the 'right' 246s is a vexing problem for serials catalogers.

This was Sullenger's first venture in working with transaction logs, and her high expectations were mollified somewhat as she realized the analyses would not be as sophisticated as she wanted. What she ended up with was a very straightforward transaction log analysis, just a printout of what users typed into the system. Her original intent was to analyze patron serial searches to find ways to improve serials cataloging, and she found only a couple of minor areas that could be addressed. For example, she discovered patrons were getting zero hits on titles the library really does own. By routine examination of zero hits on logs, catalogers could discover when patrons were searching a conceivable version of a journal title and add that variant in a 246 field on the bibliographic record. Of course, this would not include misspellings. Another enhancement serials catalogers could make would be to add the abbreviated titles commonly found in indexes and abstracts. Sullenger occasionally noticed patrons searching these abbreviations, and this addition would save searchers' having to return to the index or abstract to look up the full serial title.

In Sullenger's closing, she noted that a transaction log by itself is too limited and could be a more useful study tool when combined with patron surveys or interviews. There were just too many places in the log where she wished she could ask the searcher, "What are you really looking for?" or "Is this what you wanted or expected when you began your search?"

The second presentation in this workshop focused on a variety of ways serials catalogers could enhance serial records to increase access in the online catalog. Ruth H. Makinen, Head of Technical Services at the Biomedical Library, University of Minnesota, displayed examples of MARC-tagged serial records to illustrate a variety of possible enhancements. She began by emphasizing her presentation's 'low-tech/nitty-gritty' approach and that these were solutions their library had devised to help users increase access to serials. Makinen stressed throughout her presentation that any enhancements should adhere to national standards. For example, if the library is a Name Authority Cooperative Project (NACO) participant, any enhancements to authority records must be reviewed by the local NACO coordinator.

Makinen's first examples were of enhancements which would improve keyword searching. Monographic series records can be enhanced with 520 notes fields, which add unique terms not present in titles and subject words elsewhere in the record. Now that format integration has become a reality, contents notes (505 field) also may be added to serial records. However, with both summary and contents notes, it often is necessary to update these fields as new editions or volumes are received and there are changes in the content and emphasis. Once the library begins to enhance a record in this fashion, it must commit to continued enhancements as new volumes or editions are added.

Authority records may be modified to help users navigate through title changes in the online index. Using the title *NM, Journal of Nuclear Medicine*, Makinen illustrated how the 530 field, with the "w" control subfield and the "a" and "b" indicator positions, will guide the user to earlier and later titles in the online index. She has found this to be useful with straightforward title changes.

Makinen displayed several examples of journal bibliographic records which were enhanced with journal index abbreviations in the 246 field to provide access via the abbreviation. This enhancement was also seen to be useful by Sullenger in her transaction log study, as library users can type in the abbreviation for title access rather than having to look up the full title and then search for it in the online catalog.

Whether to analyze irregular serials issues/volumes which do not warrant full cataloging is a perennial problem for serials catalogers. Minimal level records are acceptable by national standards, so Makinen's library has enhanced their online catalog by providing minimal analytic records in these instances. Although no notes or subject headings are added to minimal level records, searchers can simplify retrieval by combining keywords from individual titles and series titles and volumes.

Makinen's library also has added stack numbers to the call number field for unclassed serials to save time retrieving volumes from the shelves. Patrons in libraries which do not classify their journals would undoubtedly find this to be a very useful enhancement to the record, but Makinen acknowledged that when stacks are shifted, staff need to update this field during the shift process.

Makinen closed her presentation with comments about the time involved in making enhancements to serial records. A key issue with any enhancement is weighing the additional staff time required against the overall benefit to users. Makinen found value in having serials staff work at the reference desk: they know the collection, understand how to use the catalog records for retrieval, and through interaction with patrons they can learn new ideas to improve access. In closing, she stated that "all library work is public service."

Most of the questions at the end of the workshop were to elicit from the presenters additional information about their respective library settings. In response to one question, there was acknowledgement that keyword enhancements will add some 'noise' to searches. Both presentations were oriented toward practicality rather than theory, thus enabling the workshop attendees to reflect upon how transaction log analyses and enhancements to bibliographic records might provide increased patron access to serials in their own institutions.

Truck and High-Tech: Document Delivery in the '90s

Robert Bland
LeiLani Freund
Martha Whittaker

Workshop Leaders

Gail Julian

Recorder

SUMMARY. While access continues to displace ownership as the key focus of libraries, the question of document delivery takes on an increased urgency. This workshop evaluates and compares a variety of document delivery methods, including (1) van service, (2) traditional interlibrary loan, and (3) commercial on-demand services. Comparing costs and developing guidelines to determine when and where the various methods are most efficient and effective are emphasized. *[Article copies available from The Haworth Document Delivery Service: 1-800-342-9678.]*

Networking and document delivery services are no longer peripheral issues to the ownership of materials. In the 1990s, document delivery is an integral part of all collection development activ-

---

Gail Julian is Serial Acquisitions Librarian at Thomas Cooper Library at the University of South Carolina, Columbia, SC.

© 1996 by the North American Serials Interest Group, Inc. All rights reserved.

[Haworth co-indexing entry note]: "Truck and High-Tech: Document Delivery in the '90s." Julian, Gail. Co-published simultaneously in *The Serials Librarian* (The Haworth Press, Inc.) Vol. 28, No. 3/4, 1996, pp. 275-281; and *Serials to the Tenth Power: Tradition, Technology, and Transformation* (ed: Mary Ann Sheble, and Beth Holley) The Haworth Press, Inc., 1996, pp. 275-281. Single or multiple copies of this article are available from The Haworth Document Delivery Service [1-800-342-9678, 9:00 a.m. - 5:00 p.m. (EST)].

ities. Document delivery as defined by Robert Bland is "the movement or transferring [of materials] from one library to another or to an individual." Four methods of document delivery were set forth by Bland with each of three presenters, in turn, concentrating on one or more of these methods. The methods as listed on page one of a handout distributed by Bland at the workshop are

1. Local or regional courier services.
   Local or regional physical movement of books, journals, photocopies.
2. Wide-area courier, mail, and parcel delivery.
   Nation-wide physical movement of books, journals, photocopies.
3. Facsimile transmission.
   Faxes, scanned documents, photocopies moved electronically or by conventional means.
4. Online electronic services.
   Online full-text, images, moved electronically.

Robert Bland, Associate University Librarian for Technical and Automated Services, University of North Carolina, Ashville, discussed local or regional courier services. Secondly, LeiLani Freund, Head, Interlibrary Loan, University of Florida, concentrated on traditional interlibrary loan services and, thus, covered methods two and three on Bland's list—wide-area courier, mail, and parcel delivery and facsimile transmission. Thirdly, Martha Whittaker, General Manager, The UnCover Company, discussed methods three and four—facsimile transmission and online electronic services. The methods of document delivery were compared throughout the presentation. Emphases were placed on cost comparisons, the complementary relationship of the methods, and the development of criteria to determine the best method to use under specific circumstances. Bland's presentation focused on the "truck" component of the document delivery process. Three university libraries in Western North Carolina have formed a network which shares an integrated library system and extensive resource sharing/document delivery endeavors. A van service, called ABC Express, is used to transport documents among the three institutions. The van runs three times per week with a goal of a 48 hour average turnaround for the delivery of materials. A unique feature of this service is the delivery of the original document to the requestor as opposed to the delivery of a reproduction. Audio-visual materials are currently excluded from the service. However, books, bound periodicals, single periodical issues, and microforms are routinely supplied through the service with only minimal damage or loss of materials. Staff and equipment costs are reduced because any photocopying is done by the end-user. The ABC Express service itself is provided at no charge to the user. Statistics provided by Bland for the ABC Express service indicated that borrowing was expected to more than double from 1992 to 1995. This increase was attributed to a combination of factors including "word of mouth," advertising, implementation of a new online catalog shared by the three institutions, and, in 1995, the ability of the end-user to request materials directly through the online catalog without the use of an intermediary.

The direct costs of the service were totaled for 1994 and divided by the total and filled transactions for 1994 giving a cost per total transaction of $5.74 and a cost per filled transaction of $6.34. The direct costs computed did not include overhead, building costs, integrated library system costs, and the costs of the materials themselves. The ABC cost of $6.34 per filled transaction represented a savings when compared to an average $12.42 per CARL UnCover document and an average cost of $24.51 for traditional ILL document services. Further, a small sample of citations, excluding citations for materials held locally, revealed the expected. ABC Express was able to provide 87% of citations located in InfoTrac, thereby, providing materials supporting undergraduate instruction. ABC Express fared less well in comparison to CARL UnCover in providing documents when citations were located through *Science Citation Index* and *Social Sciences Citation Index*. UnCover was able to provide 72% of those documents assumed to be requested by faculty and graduate students as opposed to 33% provided through ABC Express. The cost analyses and the availability comparisons demonstrate the complementary nature of document delivery services and the need to develop criteria to be used in selecting among the available options.

LeiLani Freund focused on traditional interlibrary loan services defined as the transfer of materials, both photocopies and originals, from one library to another. These libraries mainly depend upon reciprocal agreements. Although fees are sometimes charged, traditional interlibrary loan is not operated on a "for-profit" or "cost-recovery" basis. Requests are usually made through a bibliographic utility (OCLC/RLIN) or by use of a printed form. According to Freund, "1993/94 ARL statistics show a 99% increase in borrowing activity between 1986 and 1994." This trend can be expected to continue as access and document delivery supplant ownership as a means of acquiring information. The continued "proliferation of information," budget cuts or flat budgets that cannot cover journal inflation, thus, necessitating cancellations, and increased electronic access to information about what is being published, all indicate the continuance and acceleration of this trend. According to Freund, "electronic access makes it easier for clients to identify and locate items and makes it much easier for ILL to borrow needed materials."

The success of document delivery seems to rely on the expediency with which users' requests can be filled. Traditional methods of delivery, the U.S. mail service in particular, are often seen as being too slow by users. Interlibrary loan departments, thus, are investigating electronic means of document transmission. These electronic means will serve to provide the user with the information in a more timely fashion, but will result in the need for increased library staff hours. ARIEL workstations offer one avenue of investigation for electronic transmission. ARIEL workstations seem to have several advantages over fax machines for document delivery but have some disadvantages as well. ARIEL allows scanning from the original document, bypassing the photocopy step; however, scanning can require an average of 18 seconds for each page. The scanning process, thus, can be quite labor intensive. ARIEL does provide high resolution copy and highly compressed data which can be transmitted via the Internet. A major drawback of ARIEL workstations, at this time, is that the machine at the other end of the transmission must also be an ARIEL workstation and must be operational at the time of transmission.

Other means to improve turnaround time, and thus, increase user satisfaction with interlibrary loan service were put forth by Freund. These means include the need for

> an all purpose, uniform ILL system that interfaces with all bibliographic utilities;

delivery directly to users;

strengthening regional reciprocal networks and cooperative collection management;

online end-user requesting; [and]

use of commercial/document suppliers.

Freund provided a comparison of commercial document delivery suppliers with traditional interlibrary loan services. This comparison indicates pluses and minuses for both commercial document suppliers and traditional ILL. As expected, commercial document suppliers provided easy ordering and a short one to two day turnaround time for delivery of information. Conversely, the average cost of $12.50 per article could be prohibitive. Also, copyright fees must be paid on every order; whereas, with traditional interlibrary loan, there is no copyright fee within CONTU guidelines. Commercial suppliers have a limited number of journal titles and limited coverage for those titles. Therefore, traditional ILL services would still be required for titles not available locally or through commercial sources. Freund's experiences at the University of Florida with mediated use of commercial document delivery services indicate a substantial savings using access over ownership for expensive journal titles with low use statistics. In order to expedite requests, commercial document delivery is sometimes used as a first resort at the University of Florida. Freund also quoted ARL statistics as indicating an increase of 13% in the use of commercial document delivery services over the last two years.

Freund's comparison of document suppliers with traditional ILL services and her experiences with electronic transmission of documents again serve to illustrate the complementary nature of these services and the importance of knowing which service to use to provide the user with an acceptable turnaround time while maintaining acceptable library staff costs.

Martha Whittaker, General Manager, The UnCover Company, described document delivery as being an "important complement to traditional library service." Whittaker described the four basic approaches to commercial document delivery and listed advantages associated with each approach. These four approaches are listed below.

Subsidized Unmediated Ordering: End-users may search the database and request articles that are not blocked. The costs of these articles could then be charged to a library-funded deposit account. Blocks can be placed based upon library holdings, cost, copyright royalty fees, etc. Advantages to this approach include reducing staff requirements in ILL and assuring monies are used only for items not in the library's collection.

Third-Party E-mail: Users may select citations from an online database and send those selections to their e-mail account or to their ILL Department. These citations can then be used to create bibliographies or to provide a list of items to be ordered. The user may also switch to document delivery functions within the system and place orders directly.

Electronic Mail Alert Services: Selective Dissemination of Information/SDI): These alert services provide tables of contents for selected journal titles or article titles based on subject search criteria directly to the user's e-mail account via the Internet. The user's profile provides the basis for the service which "can be linked to ordering." Per Whittaker, this alert service is "less labor-intensive than paper-based alerting services."

Image Delivery as Document Delivery: Image files would be supplied on a transaction basis to a requestor's workstation.

Following Whittaker's remarks, the presenters entertained questions from the audience. Several questions were directed toward Robert Bland concerning the concept of loaning the original material via ABC Express. Bland elaborated on his earlier remarks by explaining that few users from the loaning institution complain when materials are borrowed by the others in the network. Loan periods using ABC Express are three weeks for books and from "one van delivery to the next" for journals. Bland further explained the limited need for bibliographic verification pertaining to orders placed through ABC Express since the bibliographic record in the shared online catalog provides the basis for the request. As a result, interlibrary loan handles the more difficult requests.

In response to a query concerning ARIEL, Martha Whittaker indicated that UnCover would be using ARIEL beginning Fall 1995; However, she pointed out that UnCover documents supplied through

ARIEL would appear slightly different than usual ARIEL documents.

In response to a question concerning time spent on bibliographic verification, verification of interlibrary loan requests was found to be extremely labor intensive while both ABC Express and UnCover options required little bibliographic verification since the bibliographic record and article citation were used, respectively, for ordering.

Questions asked by the audience indicated an earnest interest in all aspects of the presentation. Their questions evoked additional commentary and explanation on some key points. Handouts by Bland and Whittaker served to emphasize cost analyses and commercial document delivery options.

RECOMMENDED RESOURCES

Higginbotham, Barbra Buckner. *Access Versus Assets: A Comprehensive Guide to Resource Sharing for Academic Librarians.* Chicago : American Library Association, 1993.

Journal of Interlibrary Loan, Document Delivery & Information Supply. Binghamton, N.Y. : The Haworth Press, Inc., 1993.

ILL-L Policies, Procedures, Problems, etc. for Interlibrary Loan. LISTSERV@UVMVM (Bitnet). LISTSERV@UVMVM.UVM.EDU (Internet).

Serials Interfaces: Planning and Implementation

Amira Aaron
Alan Nordman

Workshop Leaders

Roger L. Presley

Recorder

SUMMARY. This workshop provided an overview of serials interfaces available today in the library industry. Topics included Electronic Data Interchange (EDI), the work of the industry standards organizations, and what is actually involved in the implementation of an EDI standard by the library, ILS vendor, and agent. The presenters suggested how to enlist the support of library trading partners to develop EDI interfaces and address the items that an ILS vendor must consider before undertaking an interface project. *[Article copies available from The Haworth Document Delivery Service: 1-800-342-9678.]*

With over 80 in attendance, Amira Aaron, Academic Automation Specialist, Readmore, Inc., and Alan Nordman, Dawson Subscription Service, gave an excellent presentation covering serial interfaces. Aaron's part of the workshop concentrated on library/ILS vendor interfaces, although she mentioned publisher interfaces. Nordman covered EDI interfaces specifically.

Roger Presley is Head of the Acquisitions Department at Georgia State University, Atlanta, GA.

© 1996 by the North American Serials Interest Group, Inc. All rights reserved.

[Haworth co-indexing entry note]: "Serials Interfaces: Planning and Implementation." Presley, Roger L. Co-published simultaneously in *The Serials Librarian* (The Haworth Press, Inc.) Vol. 28, No. 3/4, 1996, pp. 283-290; and *Serials to the Tenth Power: Tradition, Technology, and Transformation* (ed: Mary Ann Sheble, and Beth Holley) The Haworth Press, Inc., 1996, pp. 283-290. Single or multiple copies of this article are available from The Haworth Document Delivery Service [1-800-342-9678, 9:00 a.m. - 5:00 p.m. (EST)].

The main reasons for the development of interfaces are to save time, money, and re-keying of data. The interface is a partnership which provides mutual benefits for the library and its trading partner. It is also important to work towards standardized versus customized interfaces. Customized interfaces are expensive to set-up, and they only work between the originating developers. You will have to start over if you change trading partners.

TYPES OF INTERFACES– FUNCTIONS AND TECHNOLOGIES

Aaron discussed numerous interface functions, including: initial transfer of records; claims and responses; invoice data; holdings and pattern data; check-in data and functions; and collection development/management data.

The technologies presently available that permit interfacing to take place are the use of disks, cartridges, tapes, and CD-ROM's. The different ways to load and transfer data are:

- Barcodes (various uses);
- FTP (File Transfer Protocol);
- EDI (Electronic Data Interchange).

There are many different types of barcodes. For example, there are serials management barcodes and invoice barcodes. The SISAC Item Identifier Barcode is now on the cover of several scholarly journals. Its primary use is to aid in the check-in of the serial into a library's ILS serials module. Aaron stressed that we need to urge our ILS vendors and publishers to implement the SISAC barcode. Barcodes are dependent on scanner and terminal type, not the system.

After reviewing these detailed components of the various types of serial interfaces, Aaron discussed the practical aspects of implementing them. One of the most important points she made was *PLAN AHEAD*. Think carefully about what local data will need to be kept in the vendor's system and how to get it there. It is usually easiest if you can get this data on the vendor's system during the initial transfer. Make sure that the vendor has in its system unique numbers that are in your local system on which you can match for reports and statistics. Check on the consistency and accuracy of the data before it is transmitted.

You should be as generic as possible at the local level with your data, and do not customize. Avoid, whenever possible, free-text fields and use fixed fields whenever possible. If you must use a free-text field, be sure to use standardized codes, spellings, and consistent locations. Don't get creative with fields in your local system, and use them in the way they were meant to be used.

CHOOSING A SYSTEM OR A VENDOR

Aaron said that one of the most important things is to "Get It In Writing!" You need to be specific as to what you want. For example, what do you mean by EDI capabilities? There are, after all, many different opinions as to what it is and is not. If the vendor says it has interface capabilities, ask for references for those using its services. Many interfaces will require that there be a local translation software and these are often expensive. These translation software also need "programmer" type staff to set them up, which may require additional training costs to the library.

When working with a vendor on a serials interface, always get the interface specifications and terms in writing. Both sides should sign the actual specifications as agreed to. If there are optional selections, they need to be defined in writing. Get samples of data and reports, rather than a verbal description of them. Always work with test data first before transmitting actual, live data.

However, Aaron warned that we need to be practical. If the interface you are setting up takes 100 hours of expensive programming and set-up time, and you can change the data manually in 300 hours, then it is obviously more cost-effective to key it manually. On the other hand if the interface will be used repeatedly, it may be worth developing. Remember that interfaces require testing and that there is a very good chance that it is not going to work the first time or that there will be changes. Aaron said that you should expect and accept a 20 percent fallout and clean-up. Lastly, be practical about who should pay for interfaces. If the interface is not part of the service you have agreed to, you need to pay for what it is worth to you. If you are willing to be a guinea pig in testing the interface, you should negotiate for a discount on the product.

BE ASSERTIVE

Aaron said that librarians should be assertive. If the information you get does not seem appropriate, do not accept it at face value! Do not take no for an answer easily and ask to speak to the person in the vendor's organization who is responsible for interfaces. Aaron said that often, you, as a librarian, may even have to speak to the programmer. If not satisfied, complain to a salesperson or manager. Do not accept a run-around situation. Insist that the vendors or parties involved talk to each other if there is a problem!

BE CREATIVE

When thinking about your interface needs or fantasies, ask, even if it seems like a wild idea. Do not be afraid to brainstorm about what can be done using technology rather than always doing it manually. Use the vendors' experience and expertise. They can be a consultant for your operations and share with you what is going on at other sites that might be useful for you. Network with your colleagues and counterparts, and find out what has been done or what are they trying to do.

BE INVOLVED

As a serial librarian you need to be proactive. So much is now going on in the way of serial interfaces and the technology that permits them, that you need to be on top of things. You need to go to technical sessions and get involved with the creation of standards. These standards will ultimately determine how interfacing will work for you. Aaron cited SISAC (Serials Industry Systems Advisory Committee, CSISAC (Canadian Serials Industry Systems Advisory Committee), and ICEDIS (International Committee for the Electronic Data Interchange of Serials), as organizations that can keep you abreast of developments. All of these groups have subcommittees and task forces with which you can get involved.

INTERFACES IN GENERAL

Aaron concluded by stating that libraries have to demand the development of interfaces from their vendors and their ILS systems.

They must insist that the ILS user groups and their library directors put these developments high on their list of priorities for funding and development. Unfortunately, technical services interfaces often are given lower priority than public services interfaces, not only for development, but also for funding. Systems vendors presently are only developing EDI interfaces, but requests for other interfaces from clients are becoming more frequent.

EDI (ELECTRONIC DATA INTERCHANGE)

Following Aaron, Alan Norman began his discussion by giving DISA's (Data Interchange Standards Association–the Secretariat of ASC X12), definition of EDI. Nordman stated that Electronic Data Interchange is:

> The transmission, in a standard syntax, of unambiguous information of business or strategic significance between computers of independent organizations ... The user must translate this information to go from his own computer system, but this translation software has to be prepared only once.

Nordman said that by using this definition, we trace the first known ASC X12 EDI transactions for the Serials Industry back to June of 1990 when the Faxon Company completed transactions with several publishers. This was then followed by library transmissions in January of 1991 from the PALS Minnesota consortia of libraries. Thus, the overall development of EDI for users with the serials industry is a relatively new process. A true EDI transaction is one whereby data is clearly defined and transmitted in such a way that no human intervention or interpretation is required. This needs to be done in a way that the translation software needs to be created once to handle all trading partners.

Nordman gave a report on the status of current standards being developed. He stated that the following transactions have been approved by SISAC, CSISAC and ICEDIS:

- Invoice (Agent to Publisher)
- Claim (Library to Agent/Agent to Publisher)
- Claim Response (Publisher to Agent/Agent to Library)

- Dispatch Data (Publisher to Agent).

The transactions that are currently in "live" testing are:

- Purchase Orders (Combined Subscription/Book Orders)
- Price/Sales Catalog (Publisher to Agent).

And, the transactions currently in development are:

- Purchase Order Acknowledgment (All parties)
- Purchase Order Change (All parties)
- Cancellations (Agent to publisher)
- Invoices (Publisher to agent).

Nordman said that most parties, agents, ILS vendors, publishers, and libraries desire structured data streams. Most agents and libraries are ready to try to proceed with EDI. Publishers seem to have either limited resources or desire, and ILS vendor's various modules are lacking in required data elements.

Nordman said that the interface, as it relates to "true" EDI, is the most abused and misused term, from a technical perspective, in the serials industry today. Most vendors will tell you that they can do EDI, but it usually is not true EDI. At best they mean that they have proprietary formats for invoice loading, electronic receipt of claims transmissions, and electronic receipt of order transmissions. However, these order transmissions are usually a "free-format" text. Nordman said that he could count on one hand the number of EDI ILS vendors. He said that the agents were at the mercy of the ILS vendor. He said that the ILS vendor must be able to accept or send the appropriate data.

Nordman then discussed the pros and cons of using a commercial vs. a "Home Grown" X12 translation. He gave us the following information.

COMMERCIAL TRANSLATOR

Positive	*Negative*
X12 Rules Change Yearly	Initial & Maintenance Cost
Rapid Interface Start-ups	Software Learning Curve
"Non-Technical" Human Resources	Requires a VAN for communications

Commercial Support Desk
Trading Partners can provide initial configuration

"HOME GROWN" TRANSLATOR

Positive	Negative
No licensing fee	No different than proprietary transfers
No Software Learning Curve	Requires Technical staff to create
No VAN	Requires Technical staff to receive
	Slow to develop
	No external support
	Expensive to maintain
	Difficult to realize VAN Advantages

Nordman then discussed the advantages and disadvantages of using a VAN (Value Added Network), as opposed to using the Internet for EDI transactions. He gave us the following chart for these two scenarios.

VALUE ADDED NETWORK

Positive	Negative
Performs data integrity verification	On-going costs
Tracks messages to box	
Allows for automatic functional acknowledgment	
Send/Receive multiple transmissions to multiple trading partners in a single transmission	
Restricted Access–Private Network	

THE INTERNET

Positive	Negative
No on-going costs	Not everyone has "free"

> access
> Difficult to use in conjunction with a commercial translator–therefore all "Home Grown" translator negatives apply
> No Data Integrity Verification
> No ability to find "lost" data
> Public Access Network
> No Automatic Acknowledgment

It was pointed out that there is a task force working on standards for using the Internet for EDI transmissions. Nordman also conceded that some of the negatives on the Internet side can be overcome by money. He said that the only "REAL" issues are costs. Nordman then gave the workshop participants some estimated costs related to EDI. For instance, a PC based commercial translator will cost between $500 to $5000 initially and will require an annual maintenance fee. A VAN could have an annual cost of $150, a monthly fee of $9, and message fee of $.20 cents, and an average character fee of $.05 cents per 1000 characters. In addition there is a message gateway fee of approximately $3.00. Thus, the cost of the VAN is not exorbitant. Nordman said that Dawson was charged approximately $41 for currently sending/receiving 810,000 characters.

Following the two presentations, several questions were raised, and there was considerable discussion about how to set-up a request for proposal (RFP) for EDI services with your vendors. After several suggestions for possible inclusions on such an RFP, it was announced that SISAC would be submitting shortly a statement and guidelines for writing an RFP for EDI services. The workshop was definitely a success and provided its attendees with much needed information and advice.

Preparing Tomorrow's Serial Leaders: Creating New Alliances Among Library Schools, Libraries, and Serial Professionals

Linda Golian
Ellen Leadem
Workshop Presenters

Katy Ginanni
Recorder

SUMMARY. Mentoring and internships are two effective learning methods that can be used for developing tomorrow's serial leaders. Discussion includes practical advice on establishing these programs in the library for the beginning professional and for librarians seeking career changes. The workshop shows how all serial librarians can build new learning alliances with local library schools, for increased educational opportunities for tomorrow's serial leaders. *[Article copies available from The Haworth Document Delivery Service: 1-800-342-9678.]*

A small audience, composed of mostly librarians, with a couple of vendors and at least one library and information science educator, provided some of the intimacy which Linda Golian believes is

---

Katy Ginanni is Account Services Manager at EBSCO Subscription Services, Birmingham, AL.

© 1996 by the North American Serials Interest Group, Inc. All rights reserved.

[Haworth co-indexing entry note]: "Preparing Tomorrow's Serial Leaders: Creating New Alliances Among Library Schools, Libraries, and Serial Professionals." Ginanni, Katy. Co-published simultaneously in *The Serials Librarian* (The Haworth Press, Inc.) Vol. 28, No. 3/4, 1996, pp. 291-295; and *Serials to the Tenth Power: Tradition, Technology, and Transformation* (ed: Mary Ann Sheble, and Beth Holley) The Haworth Press, Inc., 1996, pp. 291-295. Single or multiple copies of this article are available from The Haworth Document Delivery Service [1-800-342-9678, 9:00 a.m. - 5:00 p.m. (EST)].

necessary for any good, productive mentoring relationship. Education of serials librarians and mentoring were the primary topics on which Golian, Serials Department Head at Florida Atlantic University, focused. Her presentation began with the background on how she came to develop a course in serials management for the library science program at the University of South Florida (USF).

In 1992, USF asked Golian to be a guest lecturer for several of their library science classes. Some of the topics she addressed were looseleaf services, serials cataloging, collection development of serials and binding. As a self-described "person of many hats," Golian also happens to be a doctoral student in Educational Leadership, with a specialization in adult higher education. Shortly after Golian joined USF as an adjunct faculty member, she received an assignment in her doctoral program to develop a sixteen-week, graduate level course that would identify and fill a gap in a specific school's curriculum. After conducting a needs assessment of the courses offered in library science at USF, she determined that a gap existed in serials education. While some courses, such as cataloging, collection development, and technical services management, touched on serials issues, there was no course that integrated all information about serials into one comprehensive overview. By conducting a quick review of some graduate school handbooks and talking with members from ALISE (Association for Library and Information Science Education), Golian further determined that there appears to be a gap in serials education in many library school curricula in the United States. With the encouragement of Kathleen De La Pena McCook, dean of the USF School of Library Science, Golian began to design a course in serials management.

At this point in her presentation, Golian stopped and conducted a quick, informal survey of the audience. Among the questions she asked were: How many people in the audience had a course in library school devoted to serials management? How many people in the audience had a course that touched on or included the subject in library school? How many people just kind of fell into serials librarianship? How many people believe that their current knowledge of serials librarianship is the result of their personal dedication and professional development in the field? Although the sample group was small, it was interesting to note that the quick survey here supported the findings of a similar study conducted by Lois N. Upham in the late 1980s. One of the trends Upham noted is the increasing variety of continuing education opportunities for serials librarians. These opportunities are especially important when one considers the lack of formal education for serials management in the United States. As Upham did several years earlier, Golian has concluded that serials librarians who are successful in their jobs have become so through their own professional development efforts and through formal or informal mentoring.

As Golian designed the course in serials management, she was faced with several obstacles. One was that there were few library educators with backgrounds in serials with whom she could network. Interestingly, another problem is that there seems to be confusion within the profession about what, exactly, is a serial. The biggest problem she faced was the absence of an all-inclusive text about serials. Some technical services texts include information about serials, and some texts include serials information from a public service point of view. It is surprising to learn that no text exists that covers the many different aspects of serials management, such as acquisitions, budgeting, cataloging, contract negotiations, personnel administration, patron assistance, and collection development. When one considers how much of a library's materials budget is spent on serials, this does seem to be a glaring omission in the field. At this point in the presentation, audience members suggested to Golian that she write such a text!

After developing the serials course, Golian became interested in how she could assist the beginning serials professional, or a professional who might be considering a move into serials librarianship. Some of the educational tools that she learned about in her doctoral program were continuing education programs and conferences (such as ALA and NASIG), internships, mentoring, and networking. Mentoring was a subject in which she was especially interested, having had some personal experiences that were beneficial to her professional development. She presented several definitions of mentoring, and noted some themes that appear in many of the definitions. Mentoring: Is a process within a contextual setting; involves a relationship of a more knowledgeable individual with a less experienced individual; is a developmental mechanism; is a social and reciprocal relationship; provides an identity transformation for both mentor and protege. Research usually classifies mentoring into (1) formal (or sponsored) and (2) informal. While Golian feels that formal mentoring can be beneficial, she believes that the most effective mentoring occurs in informal relationships. She then outlined some of the benefits of mentoring for the mentor, protege, library organization, and the library profession, all of which were included in her handout. She strongly believes that mentoring is a process that can help in the recruitment and retention of new professionals to the field of serials librarianship.

The next presentation was given by Ellen Leadem of the National Institute of Environmental Health Sciences (NIEHS), a branch of the Environmental Protection Agency (EPA) in Research Triangle Park, North Carolina. The EPA and the library school at University of North Carolina-Chapel Hill have a contractual arrangement that provides for twelve internship positions; three of those are in the NIEHS library. Leadem repeated the notion that many serialists simply "fall into" the profession. She argues that on-the-job training through internships increases the possibility of bringing people into serials librarianship. To be eligible for internships at the EPA, the students must have completed one year of graduate study, must be enrolled full time and are required to go through an interview process. When an intern is hired, he or she is expected to work twenty hours per week. The interns are paid as employees of the EPA, and the term of employment is usually fifteen to twenty months. Every NIEHS intern goes through three rotations, including serials, cataloging, and reference. The NIEHS staff assumes all training for the students, and they try to emphasize how each rotation fits into the library's workflow and information flow. The librarians remain very visible and approachable during an intern's tenure.

The first rotation for the interns is done in serials. One reason for this is that in special libraries, speed and service are critical. Ultimately, no technical service task has validity unless it improves service to the public. This can be seen especially when dealing with questions about serials. The serialist intern becomes the first and primary contact for patrons with questions about the serials collection. Leadem believes that this gives the interns a keener sense of service, which is beneficial to both the library users and the interns.

The intern is responsible for the daily receipt, check-in, routing, binding, and some vendor contact. They are expected to leave the rotation with a mastery of all aspects of serials management.

Leadem provided some advice and cautions to librarians who may be developing internships in their own libraries. She stated that a training structure is critical to assure a productive experience for both the intern and the library. The handout outlined some of the factors to be considered when developing a training schedule for an intern. Some of those include a needs analysis, workflow components, training method, training schedule, feedback, and performance evaluation. She also provided suggestions about some of the skills that should be developed or nurtured in an intern. Some interns may not even be aware of having certain skills; in those situations, it is the librarian's job to help bring them out. When asked by an audience member how many of the interns have gone on to careers in serials, Leadem replied that it has not been many. However, she firmly believes that their experience in serials management at the NIEHS library arms them with knowledge, helps create empathy for serialists, and helps them give better reference service to library users. She does believe that the internships are a successful method of encouraging budding professionals by giving them practical, hands-on experience.

The conversation following the two presentations was animated. The audience asked questions of the speakers and shared their own experiences, and the speakers asked questions of the audience and of each other. A number of provocative ideas were raised about education of, mentoring of, and internships for new serialists. Each speaker provided fine examples and suggestions of ways that we can all help encourage serialists in our professional lives.

Change and the Impact on Serials Staff

Gene Sullivan
Karen Darling
Bill Kara

Workshop Leaders

Jay Harris

Recorder

SUMMARY. What are the consequences of change in serials departments, the training and classification of staff, and planning for the future? During the last decade, while automating operations and increasing the processing of serials in varied elctronic media, serials staff have had to develop new skills. This workshop examines the changes in three serials operations, emphasizing staffing issues. *[Article copies available from The Haworth Document Delivery Service: 1-800-342-9678.]*

The workshop was attended by a variety of serials librarians who have dealt with or will be dealing with changes in their serials units. Three papers were presented outlining the impact of changes on the serials staff of three distinct libraries.

Gene Sullivan began the presentations with a historical overview of serials. He described the work of William Frederick Poole, who worked at Yale University in the 1840s. In 1848, Mr. Poole com-

---

Jay Harris is Head of Collection Development at Lister Hill Library of the Health Sciences, University of Alabama at Birmingham, Birmingham, AL.

© 1996 by the North American Serials Interest Group, Inc. All rights reserved.

[Haworth co-indexing entry note]: "Change and the Impact on Serials Staff." Harris, Jay. Co-published simultaneously in *The Serials Librarian* (The Haworth Press, Inc.) Vol. 28, No. 3/4, 1996, pp. 297-304; and *Serials to the Tenth Power: Tradition, Technology, and Transformation* (ed: Mary Ann Sheble, and Beth Holley) The Haworth Press, Inc., 1996, pp. 297-304. Single or multiple copies of this article are available from The Haworth Document Delivery Service [1-800-342-9678, 9:00 a.m. - 5:00 p.m. (EST)].

piled a treasure trove of information from personally-gathered sources to create "Poole's Index." This was the first periodical index and he pioneered periodical access. Moving ahead to 1927 was the beginning of more modern-day indexing as the American Library Association and H. W. Wilson Company worked to create the Union List of Serials with over 200 libraries contributing. Now, almost seventy years again ahead into the future, serials librarianship is discussing issues such as automation, document delivery and Access vs. Ownership. Thus, the history of serials has been how the serial has impacted itself.

Mr. Sullivan is from the University of South Alabama, located in Mobile, Alabama. The university's main campus library supports 12,500 students and maintains a current subscription base of 2,600 serial titles. During a strategic planning session held in 1994, they combined Technical and Public Services into one unit. The staff in each unit was involved little in the planning of this combination.

With the onset of automation in the workplace, the employee's world has been changing. Early in library work, the job skill needed to complete most tasks was manual dexterity, placing an "X" on the Kardex was all that was required to check in a periodical issue. Around 1975, punch cards began to replace Kardexes and these were used to generate lists of serials. Then in 1982, the University received it's first integrated library system with NOTIS. This transition from manual to punch cards to automation placed new challenges on the staff and they worked well as a team. The realization coming from all this was that jobs will change as units move from manual to automation, regardless of whether a staff is static or not.

Mr. Sullivan feels that a sub-profession has developed from clerical to highly skilled technicians. Personnel departments have problems with upgrading job descriptions to compensate. Librarians must provide increased educational opportunities for their staff to grow with the changing job market. Additionally, serials staff should be instructed in using Internet as a resource and have other skills-training in order to compete in a more computerized marketplace.

Karen Darling is Head of the Serials Department at Knight Library of the University of Oregon in Eugene. The university has 18,000 students. A serials staff of 10 provides the "care and feeding of all serials, but not ordering." The history of its catalogs and database indicates that the library used a manual style of check-in for serials. In 1984, the library began its automation activities with InnoVacq and in 1989 the library migrated to InnoPac. Its catalog continues to expand and offers several indexes in addition to its main catalog.

During the time of pre-automation, serial staff who checked in using the Kardex method were not required to know typing. All that was needed was a high school education and a pencil. The staff did not need to know what was going on in the rest of the library. Nor did they need to know where the periodical issue went once it left the processing unit. It was believed that there was time to do everything. The onset of automation has changed all that. If one looks at a "before" picture, they will see an electric eraser, typewriter, and cards. The "after" picture now contains personal computers, MAchine-Readable Cataloging (MARC), CD-ROM, wrist splints, wands, barcodes, etc.

Integrated library systems have made the requirements different for what serials staff members need in order to perform their duties. Today's workers need a better understanding of English, since a larger number of staff actually see the bibliographic records. Although foreign language skills have always been useful, they are still in demand given the large amount of accompanying materials. More emphasis is placed today on keyboarding skills. Twenty years ago, a high school education was sufficient, yet today, more education is needed to pick up the skills necessary to compete in the serials workplace. The older serials staff workers do not have many of the skills their employers now require of entry level workers.

In terms of equipment, early automation efforts relied on dumb terminals which today may not be good enough or useful for today's library systems. In some libraries there exists a mix of PCs and dumb terminals, depending on the job function required. The University of Oregon is no exception. They have a mix of older dumb terminals and PCs. Some staff have felt this is unfair, but the university could not wait until it had the money to purchase PCs for everyone. The training involved in using these terminals has become more difficult.

The outside world is moving faster than the inside world of many universities' serials units. There is more stuff, more formats and everything tends to be more difficult. Serials is "not the same job that it used to be." Tasks such as e-mail and electronic invoices mean a greater need for staff training. More is being published than ever before and the need to be a filtering agent places greater demands on the serials staff.

Serials check-in is not the same job it used to be. Libraries still receive all the same things they used to and now receive even more, in a wider variety of formats. Staff must deal with coding of automated records. There are more details to learn and remember such as MARC standards. Staff have more and more duties being classed as "regular duties" which require more training and increased skills.

The serials arena is more complex than ever before. There are many more accompanying materials which are arriving in many different formats. It is not unusual to have a print serial issue accompanied by a diskette or a video supplement. Some serial titles have made these kinds of supplements a standard part of their regular subscriptions. Now that the public has access to the bibliographic records in integrated library systems, a different approach is required from serials staffers. The information in these records needs to be readable. The timeliness of the information being placed in the information system is more critical than ever before. People want access to be more complete, more timely, and more accurate.

The solution is all about training. It is always ongoing and it is never all done. Where is a serials manager to find the staff and expertise to do the training required for today's serials worker? Many serials managers cannot stay one step ahead of their staff nowadays. They must rely on others to share the work. Today's department head relies on others to go off, learn and bring the information back to train others in new routines. Routines can become so complex that they cannot be written down. One method has been to use a team approach to training in absence of official trainers. Someone on the staff will become proficient in a task and return to teach others.

Breaking down a difficult task into smaller segments and training the staff by concentrating on these smaller units is one way to approach training. This may be useful when training a reticent staff. Using this method may help staff by giving them a small amount of new knowledge to absorb at a time and then adding to it incrementally. Thus, people who are learning at a slower pace can repeat some training as needed without going all the way back to square one.

Training helps to foster interest in a serials staff. By focusing on particular functions, staff is made to understand why certain things are important and, where possible, allows workers to do the things they like. For certain employees who appear too reticent, telling them that they have to keep up may be enough of an incentive for them to do so. Another way is through the use of peer pressure. Other staff who feel that they can no longer perform those revised functions may have to be relocated to other departments.

There will always be older staff for which none of the aforementioned methods will work. Many staff who have worked in the library for many years are simply not as qualified to take on these duties. Many may feel intimated by staff who catch on quickly and are better prepared. One solution may be to move staff to jobs with less impact. Older staff may be better at searching OCLC rather than paying electronic invoices, as an example.

Another area in demand is cross-training. Having a staff member from technical services work with a staff member from public services may help them understand what information the record displays. It may also assist them in knowing what is important to the general library user. The time for cross-training may be in short supply given the amount of processing work to be done in the unit. Managers cannot let their work get too behind because so much is interdependent, and bibliographic records along with their item level or summary information are visible to the public. Cross-training is important for public services staff as well. They need to understand what information a bibliographic record in their library system conveys: what information the serials staff has included and why it is important to be displayed.

The University of Oregon's serials staff began including short reminder lessons as part of its department meetings. As problems are returned from other units, these questions are being used to facilitate on-going training. Recently a union strike forced the unit head to perform serials check-in for the first time in years. It reminded her of what is needed to know how to do the work.

Bill Kara was unable to attend the NASIG Conference. His paper was read aloud to the workshop participants by Gene Sullivan. Mr.

Kara's paper was entitled "Changes in the Serials Unit: New Responsibilities–New Skills." He is Acquisitions Librarian at the Albert R. Mann Library at Cornell University. The acquisitions unit is comprised of 7 staff, 4 for serials, 2 for acquisitions and the acquisitions librarian. The library subscribes to 9,300 titles, mostly in print formats, although there exists an increasing number of electronic publications. Some of these exist in a tangible form while others are available only in electronic form. These formats have impacted library staff significantly and call for changes in the way staff are hired and trained.

Electronic resources received in a tangible form (CD-ROM, floppy discs) have been easier to add to existing work flows. While the physical piece itself is different, the staff has become comfortable with its handling. Many more details are necessary to watch out for when handling these accompanying pieces. Serials staff have become used to the unexpected and take the handling of these materials in stride.

Electronic resources require different handling since they may be received differently, need different information recorded about them for both the bibliographic record and the holdings record. As with any new format, there are new questions to ask, more notes to make on the routing slip and more new information to interpret.

The major tasks involved with checking-in these alternative format products may not differ greatly from those for traditional print materials. All are checked in and sent off to their respective shelving locations.

Since December 1993, the nature of processing done by serials staff has changed remarkably. Staff are now asked to handle a variety of materials not previously received. These include datasets received by the library on floppy discs. These datasets are uploaded by the serials staff onto a locally-maintained gopher. In order to do this, staff needed training in utilizing UNIX, DOS, and other telecommunication skills. These types of titles now number 160.

Full-text reports arrive via e-mail or by using file transfer protocol (FTP). As with the datasets, the knowledge required to work with these electronic files includes a working knowledge of the file structure of the materials, as well as the directory structure of the gopher-server on which they are loaded. These full-text reports are growing in number and may double within the next year. While alternative in format, this information is still received in traditional intervals (i.e., weekly, quarterly, monthly, annually); although, some of the titles involved are received as often as 10-20 times a week.

Internet-accessible resources make up another component of Mann Library's non-traditional acquisitions. These have been selected but are not archived locally. Acquisitions records are created in their public catalog then catalogers provide links or pointers to that information. Some electronic journals selected for archiving require unique handling. Mann's electronic journal system allows use of hypertext markup language (HTML) for easy retrieval and access to this material. Since many publishers use different formats for their titles, each must be dealt with on an individual basis.

The staff at Mann Library has needed to maintain a high level of skill to process these non-traditional materials. Many of these electronic resources are more heavily used than print sources. To adapt and develop the skills needed, the staff had to become flexible and willing to be involved. Increased staff training, planning, and preparation was required. Support for these changes has been strong as many tasks were developed, reorganized or re-evaluated.

The growing number of materials received in non-print formats is large enough for Mann Library to begin making choices about handling. Materials may either still be handled through the acquisitions department or be handled by computer technicians. The Acquisitions Department for now has developed necessary computer skills through its use of and enhancements to its library system. Various business and management reports are now done online. The staff has embraced new technology as a way for their tasks to be made easier to accomplish, and thereby their work flow made more efficient.

Staff development courses have helped others to learn about new and interesting work being done throughout the library. Particular staff members learn about a new or innovative procedure. Working in small teams, these individuals then review this new topic with others in the Unit. Topics have included e-mail tips, using and creating macros, and basic DOS commands. These informal training sessions led to having the individual write up a short procedure and then demonstrate the topic in a 15-20 minute presentation to others. By having staff involved in all aspects of this work, their enthusiasm for learning and participating has been maintained at a high level.

In the Unit, computer skills were advanced simply by the hiring of new personnel. More and more, workers are being hired with higher levels of computer skills requisite for positions throughout the library. No longer are these requirements considered specialized; they have become prerequisites to many of the traditional library positions. Utilizing the training by regular use is the best way to ensure that training does not lose its meaning.

Most libraries have undergone an evolution of sorts in the last few years. Many of the job descriptions for library positions have been rewritten. Since computer skills are now expected for most library positions, promotions may not be forthcoming simply due to having to use a computer. In the past this may have been the case. Computers are a tool to be utilized rather than a specialized skill to be coveted. Only a short time has transpired where the computer has gone from being a special skill demanding a higher salary to being a prerequisite required for most entry level positions.

All three speakers presented a picture of their library in the midst of change and these changes are mirrored in libraries across the nation. Academic and public libraries are being pressured by their users to bring about changes in the ways they access information. By the incorporation of computers into the everyday lives of millions of individuals, their wanting more and better access to information is a natural by-product. Libraries will have to continue to change with the changing times. Their roles in disseminating information may increase and their abilities to process vast amounts of information must increase with the increasing demand.

Serials staff are people who never get caught up with their work. While a public services unit may get fewer calls during a semester break, the flow of incoming mail to the serials unit does not stop, and processing that information for storage and retrieval never ends. Change is inevitable in ways none of us dreamed about even 15 years ago. The serials staffs at these institutions have demonstrated that they are willing to keep growing and learning in order to change with the changing times.

CONSER Live:
A Conversation
with CONSER Coordinator

Jean Hirons

Workshop Leader

Sally Sorensen

Recorder

SUMMARY. Developments and new initiatives in the CONSER (Cooperative Online Serials) Program are discussed. Participants learn about how they can contribute to and benefit from the work of CONSER, covering access of serials, emerging cataloging guidelines for remote access serials, and possible revisions to serial rules and rule interpretations. Policy issues are also addressed. *[Article copies available from The Haworth Document Delivery Service: 1-800-342-9678.]*

INTRODUCTION

Jean Hirons, Acting CONSER Coordinator, Library of Congress, began this informal workshop by remarking on the extraordinary amount of change currently underway involving serials. Serials themselves are changing as more and more appear in electronic

---

Sally Sorensen is Head of Special Formats Cataloging at Texas Christian University, Fort Worth, TX.

© 1996 by the North American Serials Interest Group, Inc. All rights reserved.

[Haworth co-indexing entry note]: "CONSER Live: A Conversation with CONSER Coordinator." Sorensen, Sally. Co-published simultaneously in *The Serials Librarian* (The Haworth Press, Inc.) Vol. 28, No. 3/4, 1996, pp. 305-310; and *Serials to the Tenth Power: Tradition, Technology, and Transformation* (ed: Mary Ann Sheble, and Beth Holley) The Haworth Press, Inc., 1996, pp. 305-310. Single or multiple copies of this article are available from The Haworth Document Delivery Service [1-800-342-9678, 9:00 a.m. - 5:00 p.m. (EST)].

form; format integration is resulting in changes to the way we tag our records; changes are being considered to *Library of Congress Rule Interpretations* (LCRIs) and *Anglo-American Cataloging Rules, Second Edition* (AACR2); the serial core record may change the amount of information given in a CONSER record, and, finally, CONSER itself is considering changes to its management and governance structures. Hirons divided the workshop into five areas of interest, commenting on and inviting discussion of each topic in turn.

FORMAT INTEGRATION

Hirons summarized the recently implemented first phase (variable fields) of format integration, commenting that it has had relatively little impact on serials catalogers. The major changes are in the title added entry fields (246, 730, and 740). Field 246 subfield $i, which allows catalogers to supply introductory words to create a note, generated a brief discussion regarding its use in local systems. Hirons suggested that placing subfield $a, which contains the title, before subfield $i would be an acceptable solution for systems that cannot index subfield $a when it is in the middle of a field. CONSER definitions of the 730 and 740 fields were also provided.

The second phase (fixed fields) is still being refined. The biggest change for serials will be for non-print serials where the 008 field will describe the physical format of the material and a new 006 field will describe its seriality. (At present, all CONSER records must be input using the serial 008 in order for the records to be identified and distributed as CONSER records. Other catalogers can use the computer file 008 field. Once format integration is complete, all cataloging will be done in the same manner and there will no longer be discrepancies between CONSER and non-CONSER records.) OCLC is adapting its display to accommodate these changes; LC and local systems are also in various stages of preparation, hoping to be ready in 1996. Hirons stressed that phase two will require the cataloger to determine what is being cataloged in order to properly code fixed fields. But it will also provide new options and possibilities, e.g., a loose-leaf publication can be coded as "Bib lvl=m," with the seriality of the updates being coded in an 006 to enable check-in through local systems.

Hirons stressed that format integration is intended to be a simplification, especially for catalogers of more than one format, and that changes to existing records do not need to be made, at least for phase one. Old and new records will co-exist for a long time. Changes to fixed fields may, however, be required once format integration is complete.

REMOTE SERIALS

Module 31 of the CONSER Cataloging Manual (CCM), Remote Access Computer File Serials, will soon be available from the Cataloging Distribution Service and is currently available through an FTP site. The module was prepared by Melissa Beck (University of California, Los Angeles), with assistance from the cataloging staff at LC. Highlights of the module noted by Hirons included what is/is not a serial; file formats and use of one record; file characteristics, type of computer file; system details, mode of access; linking notes and fields; 856 guidance and examples; and subject heading subdivision.

Discussion centered on the use of one record for multiple file formats, and the use or non-use of fields 256, 516, and 538. The use of the general material designation (GMD) "computer file" and other descriptive terms, e.g., electronic journal, was briefly discussed. Some questions regarding the 856 field were also raised but have not yet been resolved. How many 856 fields should be included on a record? Who will maintain them--OCLC, CONSER, the cataloging agency?

Recommendations made by the CONSER Electronic Resources Task Force have been addressed in Module 31. The task force is now looking at putting some of the recommendations into "law" through rule interpretations and rule changes. Also needing further attention is the concept of monograph vs. serial, with the possibility of defining a third category of "dynamic" publications to incorporate looseleaf publications, directories, and other such items which are not issued in individual issues, but which are continually changing.

CHANGES TO LC RULE INTERPRETATIONS

The Program for Cooperative Cataloging (PCC) has made a recommendation to greatly reduce the number of LCRIs. A task force is currently working on proposals to simplify, clarify, and eliminate LCRIs, as well as recommending some changes to AACR2. Review of Chapter 12 LCRIs took place this spring, aided by suggestions from LC serial and CONSER catalogers. Hirons pointed out that many of the serial LCRIs are necessary because the information is not adequately covered in the rules, and these RIs will be retained until such time as the information is added to AACR2. The task force proposals will be distributed for comment this summer and will likely undergo revision before final publication.

Hirons discussed two LCRIs in particular: LCRI 12.0B1 and LCRI 12.3. The proposed addition to LCRI 12.0B1 of guidelines concerning the use of "sample," "preview," or "introductory" issues as the earliest issue arose from the realization that guidelines for treatment were included in CCM but had never been addressed in the rules. Another proposed change to LCRI 12.0B1, which Hirons considers a highlight of the recommendations, would allow the use of a page other than the title page, such as the cover, to be used as the chief source for retrospective cataloging in cases where a title page is added or dropped, and the use of the cover would avoid needless title changes. A third proposed policy change is the revision of LCRI 12.3 which would allow transcription of issue designations which include both number and date as long as either is sufficient to identify the issue, e.g., "Vol. 1 (May 1990)-" or "Vol. 1, no. 1 (1990)-." The designation becomes a complete statement consisting of enumeration and chronology, rather than a statement made up of two separate elements. The source of the designation has also been simplified by removing the prescribed list of sources and saying that the designation may be recorded from the most complete source. This raised a question: If the cover says 1:1 and inside it says vol. 1, no. 1, which should be used? Hirons's answer: Probably 1:1, but it would be up to the cataloger.

A question was asked by a publisher in the audience: What should the publisher be doing to help the cataloger to catalog publications properly? Hirons suggested that one thing would be to supply complete dates on issues. The publisher replied that they have actually started doing that this year. This was not done before because if a journal was coming out "late" it looked bad for an issue to have April on the cover when it was delivered in May.

CONSER CORE RECORD

The CONSER core record for serials was finalized last January. The core record for monographs had been previously defined by the Program for Cooperative Cataloging. CONSER catalogers now have three levels at which records can be created: full, core, and minimal.

The serial core record includes fields that are essential to describe and provide adequate access to the serial, as well as authoritative headings. It differs from minimal in that headings are authoritative, and subject headings are present when applicable. It differs from full in that less emphasis is placed on notes and links, there are possibly fewer subject headings, and the 041, 043, 300, and 310 fields are optional.

Machine Readable Bibliographic Information (MARBI) has approved a new encoding level for core level; however, it will be some time before OCLC can make it available. Until that time, CONSER core records will be identified by the word "core" in subfield $e of field 040; the encoding level will be coded as "blank." At present, only program participants can create core records. The core record will be defined in Update 1 of the *CONSER Editing Guide* (CEG). Work will begin this summer on defining core records for commonly encountered non-print serials and other types of serials, such as microforms.

CONSER TASK FORCES AND INITIATIVES

A Conference Task Force, consisting of serial and monograph catalogers, has been charged with examining the complicated nature of conference proceedings. They will look at whether these should be cataloged as serials or monographs, or both, as well as choice of title and title changes. An interim report is due mid-winter and the final report at the CONSER operations meeting next May. In the meantime, the task force will probably be conducting a survey which would appear on several listservs to obtain both monograph and serials input.

The CONSER Maintenance Project has over the past two years enabled a small group of non-CONSER institutions to make changes to a record when the title changes or dies. During the first phase, project participants worked with Bill Anderson at the Library of Congress. The project is now in the second phase, in which project participants are working with CONSER representatives. The CONSER Policy Committee will consider the usefulness of this activity and whether it should be built into the membership structure.

The existing manual for cataloging newspapers has become dated and a new CCM module is being developed as well as a new chapter of the CEG. These will hopefully be finished in the spring of 1996.

The CONSER Policy Committee will meet this fall to consider its strategies for dealing with electronic resources. They will also review membership levels and criteria for membership, as well as possible changes to governance, including CONSER's relationship to the Program for Cooperative Cataloging.

CONCLUSION

Hirons concluded the workshop by encouraging further questions from the audience which, at the first workshop, consisted of about thirteen individuals, most of whom were catalogers and OCLC users. The questions centered primarily on individual practical problems. There was some discussion of handling analytics in a different fashion to provide fuller access, perhaps by creating a full serial record with a brief, linked analytic record, or by using the series authority record as a means to "collect" serial-like items. Hirons mentioned that the Conference Task Force is considering the practicality of using the conference name as title; one audience member suggested that this is how patrons search for a conference anyway, unaware that the conference name is actually an author. Workshop participants were most interested in resolving recurring conflicts among CONSER policy, idiosyncrasies of local systems, publishing peculiarities, and local requests for access, particularly from public service areas. Hirons provided practical advice and a positive outlook for the future.

Making the Most of Electronic Journals–Library and Secondary Publisher Perspectives

Beth Jane Toren
Isabel Czech

Workshop Leaders

Judy Luther

Recorder

SUMMARY. As the number of electronic journals increases, so does the number of decisions libraries and publishers must make to incorporate this new medium into existing structures. The workshop evaluates theses decisions from two standpoints–the library and the secondary publisher. *[Article copies available from The Haworth Document Delivery Service: 1-800-342-9678.]*

The dual perspective on considering and selecting electronic journals was presented from the consumer perspective by Beth Jane Toren, Serials Librarian at West Virginia University (WVU) followed with the business perspective by Isabel Czech from the Institute for Scientific Information (ISI), a secondary publisher. Toren

---

Judy Luther is Director of North American Sales for the Institute for Scientific Information.

© 1996 by the North American Serials Interest Group, Inc. All rights reserved.

[Haworth co-indexing entry note]: "Making the Most of Electronic Journals–Library and Secondary Publisher Perspectives." Luther, Judy. Co-published simultaneously in *The Serials Librarian* (The Haworth Press, Inc.) Vol. 28, No. 3/4, 1996, pp. 311-316; and *Serials to the Tenth Power: Tradition, Technology, and Transformation* (ed: Mary Ann Sheble, and Beth Holley) The Haworth Press, Inc., 1996, pp. 311-316. Single or multiple copies of this article are available from The Haworth Document Delivery Service [1-800-342-9678, 9:00 a.m. - 5:00 p.m. (EST)].

addressed the attributes of electronic journals, focusing on e-journal options and how to determine which is best, illustrated with a description of the process at WVU. Czech presented guidelines used by ISI for inclusion of e-journals in their published indexes and solicited input on points of concern such as how and when citations on electronic references should be included.

A group of 65 librarians and publishers participated in the presentation and discussion on electronic journals. Today journals frequently comprise 90 percent of a library's materials expenditures and are evolving from print to electronic. To provide a perspective on the evolution of journals, Toren presented page copies of the title page to volume one of *Philosophical Transactions* from The Royal Society, the first scholarly journal published in English. It has very good illustrations and has been published continuously since 1665. Many electronic journals, such as *Mental Workload*, which began in 1980 and did not have notable illustrations, are no longer being published.

Print journals serve as a current awareness tool and also provide a permanent scholarly record that adds a measure of quality and credibility to the work being presented. They are valued for their reliability and portability. Electronic journals, in addition to being a current awareness tool, can serve as an interactive scholarly record, are available prior to the print and therefore are valued for speed and accessibility. In the future, we can anticipate multimedia functions including sound, motion, and increased interaction.

Expected advantages of electronic journals are several. Time between acceptance of a paper and its publication would be shorter than for conventional journals and long papers could more easily be published without the page restrictions imposed by printing and mailing expense. Costs related to print distribution would be eliminated once the transition to electronic has been accomplished completely, and this will result in the additional benefit of conserving paper.

In an electronic environment, the scholar submits work to the publisher/editor on a disk or over the network and the publisher releases the scholar's work on disk or in an electronic file. The reader retrieves a citation for the work from a database, views the full text on-line, selects the work to download, and prints it if necessary. This is in dramatic contrast to the predominantly print environment where the work is submitted and published on paper, only to sit on the shelf and deteriorate as the audience finds the citation in a paper index, searches for the physical volume in the library, views the full text, selects the work, and photocopies it if necessary.

In the future, researchers will be able to perform searches from their office/home and be connected directly to a full multimedia version of the work with sound, images, and interactive ability. Databases, at this point, become knowledge bases. Bibliometric analysis of article citations permits presentation of hierarchies and ranking of relevant material. National databanks serve to archive journals. The library has become the icon on a screen somewhere and the library building functions as a book warehouse.

Currently periodicals are available in a combination of formats from paper only, paper with an electronic counterpart, digital including audiovisual, electronic with paper or microfilm counterpart to electronic with full text delivered or only the table of contents delivered. Periodicals include: magazines, newsletters, newspapers, journals which are/are not refereed, monographic serials, and the newer 'zines.

Electronic journals can be refereed or not refereed, but still monitored by an editor or moderator. Some electronic journals are free of charge in ASCII text only or have a subscription fee which includes special software to support images such as *The On-line Journal of Current Clinical Trials.*

Three things are needed for the electronic journal to become a fully integrated library format: bibliographic records, patron access, and indexing by services such as ISI. As more electronic journals become available, libraries will need to assess their need for the journal and their readiness to provide access to it in their environment.

When considering introducing electronic journals to a library's collection, it is necessary to evaluate the infrastructure within the institution in terms of the level it can support. Look at the hardware/software—do all users have PC access? Is there widespread Internet access? Has the necessary wiring been done? What is the level of connectivity?

On the human side—what is the level of demand for journals in electronic form? What is the level of expertise of the end users? How prepared are people for training? What level of support is available from the decision-making bodies? It is necessary to balance the benefits of speed, performance, dependability, accessibility, and ease of use with the cost of computer systems, work time needed to implement, and the level of staff readiness for training.

In the state of West Virginia, academic libraries in the northern part use NOTIS. Academic libraries in the southern part, as well as public and school libraries throughout the state, use VTLS. Statewide access is hindered by disparate library systems and occasional lack of port availability affecting network interconnectivity. The solution chosen is a standard Z39.50 approach through a client/server model.

To implement this, the West Virginia Library Commission, West Virginia University and the State Department of Education jointly applied for a matching $2.5 million dollar grant. WVNET (West Virginia Network for Educational Technology) wrote the successful proposal securing a total of $5 million to update the library systems in the state. Bell Atlantic is providing some cable, WVU is providing the systems positions for developing Internet services in the library, and the public libraries will provide MOSAIC for each library.

Czech's presentation addressed the fact that indexing services also face a series of questions about the selection process for considering electronic journals. ISI has had a committee studying this effort for two years to answer the questions: What's out there? What formats are available? What should be done with them physically?

ISI requires that three issues of a journal are published as an indicator of its survival and quality before it is considered to be indexed. Over 200 electronic journals were evaluated, some in e-journal format only, some on the Web, and many with print counterparts. A list of sixteen journals currently under review at ISI was distributed. In September 1994, ISI announced the first e-journal to be covered: *The Online Journal of Knowledge Synthesis for Nursing* from Sigma Theta Tau International, Honor Society of Nursing, which is available through OCLC's electronic journal on-line service.

There are five other criteria that are core requirements. There must be a need for the journal and it must be peer reviewed. Affiliations of authors and the editorial board are considered and citations used as a tool in that process. Grant funding is a plus and the journal must be published on time.

ISI has developed a form for Electronic Journal Review Guidelines, which were discussed covering presentation of the journal (aims, editorial board, subscription information), contents (articles/issue), article level (author's affiliation, abstracts, page numbers) and data format (ASCII, HTML, SGML). The distribution method is also captured, whether it is available on e-mail, listserv, FTP, gopher, WWW, OCLC.

Czech asked for feedback on the topic of criteria for journals to be indexed and this resulted in a lively discussion between librarians and publishers. One of the developing areas involves the citation of an electronic work, as authors are prone to cite the most recent reference rather than the original author. A plea was made to clearly credit the original author and to properly cite others involved.

Questions revolved around aspects of an electronic journal related to its stability, accessibility, integrity, and a formal published version which could be annotated with conversations monitored by an on-line editor. According to a representative from Wiley publishers, the electronic journal opens the door for added features such as color illustrations, not available in black and white format.

Cataloging problems parallel citation problems when dealing with an electronic work in the evolutionary process. Electronic files are not published until the file is sent to the printer to insure consistency with both editions. According to one publisher, studies have shown that readers look at citations to see if they are cited, then the illustrations, and then download the electronic article to read it.

Some readers/publishers are moving ahead to take advantage of the SGML format, using Acrobat. Initial electronic publications more closely resemble the print although the evolutionary process will result in more dramatic changes. Comments were made that, after working on a terminal all day, there is less of a desire to relax with one.

Pricing is complicated in the electronic world. One model offers the e-journal at a percentage increase over the print format. Another model offers a free subscription to the e-journal if a print subscription is purchased.

Archiving is another issue to be addressed. Bit-mapped images take up sufficient space that it is not practical to store copies of all issues locally, so systems resort to pointers to other files. This is true of the Electronic Library Project initiated by ISI to test new technology (such as cache management) which means only those articles in high demand are stored.

To learn more about different perspectives, Isabel offered three references to current articles on electronic publishing which further address the issues raised in the question/answer period.

SUGGESTED READING

Clement, Gail, "Evolution of a Species: Science Journals Published on the Internet," Database 17 #5 (October/November 1994): 44-45.

Gold, Jon D., "An Electronic Publishing Mode for Academic Publishers," JASIS 45 #10 (December 1994): 760-764.

Collins, Mauri and Zane Berge, "IPCT Journal: A Case Study of an Electronic Journal on the Internet," JASIS 45 #10 (December 1994): 771-776.

WORKSHOP SET II

What's in It for Us?
Internet Use in Technical Services

Betty Landesman
Steve Oberg

Workshop Presenters

Lauren Noel

Recorder

SUMMARY. The importance of Internet resources in public services work is a frequently discussed topic. But access to and effective use of Internet resources is crucial to current and future work of technical services personnel. The workshop examines commonly used Internet procedures and explores Internet tools available for acquisitions and cataloging personnel. *[Article copies available from The Haworth Document Delivery Service: 1-800-342-9678.]*

Lauren Noel is Foreign Newspaper Cataloger at the Center for Research Libraries, Chicago, IL.

© 1996 by the North American Serials Interest Group, Inc. All rights reserved.

[Haworth co-indexing entry note]: "What's in It for Us? Internet Use in Technical Services." Noel, Lauren. Co-published simultaneously in *The Serials Librarian* (The Haworth Press, Inc.) Vol. 28, No. 3/4, 1996, pp. 317-323; and *Serials to the Tenth Power: Tradition, Technology, and Transformation* (ed: Mary Ann Sheble, and Beth Holley) The Haworth Press, Inc., 1996, pp. 317-323. Single or multiple copies of this article are available from The Haworth Document Delivery Service [1-800-342-9678, 9:00 a.m. - 5:00 p.m. (EST)].

While there has been much discussion about the Internet's role in public and particularly reference services, little attention has been given to the Internet's potential uses in technical services. This workshop presented commonly used Internet terms and their applications, current uses of the Internet for technical services, and advocated involvement of technical services librarians in Internet development as it is crucial to current and future work in technical services.

DEMYSTIFICATION OF THE INTERNET: DEFINING AND APPLYING COMMON TERMS

Betty Landesman (Systems Planning, George Washington University) and Steve Oberg (Head of Bibliographic Control, University of Chicago) emphasized that this workshop was designed with the Internet novice in mind; it was specifically intended for people who may have heard about the Internet, but have yet to find in it practical applications to their work. With this in mind, Betty presented a glossary of Internet terms and provided an excellent handout of the same. She covered basic terms and concepts such as, e-mail, file transfer protocol (FTP), gopher, Telnet, and World Wide Web (WWW or Web), while including detailed explanations of each with accompanying examples. Betty expressed her hope that certain buzzwords, such as FTP, once understood, would cease to strike fear or apprehension in the mind of the user.

The first term covered was "e-mail" or electronic mail: a way to communicate with colleagues and vendors, or to subscribe to electronic conferences (lists) on subjects of interest to the user. Betty then focused on the concept of electronic conferences or discussion lists (the corresponding handout cited a broad range of discussion lists, as well as electronic journals, of interest to serialists and technical services librarians). These lists commonly contain a wealth of information, citations and guides to resources, and serve as a valuable tool for keeping abreast of current topics in the field. Betty pointed out that while most electronic lists are interactive, i.e., a subscriber may contribute messages to the list, some lists are not. She added that different lists use different software; one may see the term listserv, listproc or majordomo on a given list depending upon that list's software (specific instructions on how to subscribe to a list were included in the glossary handout under the term "e-mail").

Betty discussed the term "FTP" or "anonymous FTP." FTP is used to transfer files from one computer to another; areas are set aside on remote computers for users without accounts (hence the term "anonymous") to retrieve documents that are placed there to be publicly accessible. Betty maintained that the term FTP has an unreservedly nasty reputation, whereas she preferred to think of it as simply indicating that you can get a file. She mentioned that many files, once only available through FTP are now available on gophers, and WWW servers. Betty added, however, that she hoped once the procedure for FTP was clear, it would no longer seem daunting.

The term "gopher" was next in the glossary and is a way to access Internet resources organized in a hierarchical series of menus. A number of examples and sample menu screens were included in the handouts.

The next term covered was "Telnet:" a way to connect to a remote computer. Once connected to that computer, one's workstation essentially becomes a terminal on the remote computer system. Betty alluded to Telnet already being considered "old-fashioned" by much of the library world. However, since it is a method of connecting to a remote computer, i.e., it establishes a direct connection (unlike FTP or gopher) it is, in a sense, the world's biggest and fastest modem. Through the Telnet process many library catalogs and vendors may be accessed. Betty did caution that when one "Telnets" to a remote site one is using that system's commands; she stressed the importance of reading each and every screen's instructions, as it is especially annoying to have missed the EXIT command when one is ready to leave the site. Helpful hints were included for those situations when one is stuck at a remote site.

In contrast to the gopher with its hierarchical structure, WWW is another way to organize information in hypermedia links which can incorporate sound and graphics. WWW is a way to access Internet resources organized in a hypertext-based manner. Links are provided within a document that can take the user to another document or computer in a nonlinear fashion. Betty mentioned that in order to use a WWW site one needs a WWW browser (software that lets one navigate the Web). Text-based browsers, such as Lynx, use a

"TUI" (pronounced "too-ee"), or textual user interface; they do not require Windows and don't show graphic images. Graphical-based browsers, such as Netscape and Mosaic, use a "GUI" (pronounced "goo-ee"), or graphical user interface; they require Windows, a fast connection and provide access to graphics, sound, etc. Betty added that the text-based Lynx may be a useful alternative for those users who lack high-powered systems. Betty also touched on the term "home page" (the first screen of information one gets to at a WWW source, containing text as well as the links that take the user to the resources available), as well as the term "URL" or "Universal Resource Locator" (the address which gets the user to a resource). WWW URL's always begin with "http://" which stands for "hypertext transfer protocol."

CURRENT USES OF THE INTERNET FOR TECHNICAL SERVICES

Betty demonstrated three loosely related acquisitions resources, using gopher, Telnet and WWW systems. First, she showed how to access OCLC's FirstSearch through Telnet (this server requires a subscription; Betty emphasized that not everything on the Internet is free, it is merely a pike to information). Once in FirstSearch, Betty searched for a journal article and then demonstrated how to order it (article ordering is a feature of the FirstSearch software). A second example included searching a publisher's gopher, e.g., Readmore, Inc. Betty added that many sites are case sensitive. Finally, Betty used WWW to access AcqWeb through a WWW page at Vanderbilt University which points to a wealth of acquisitions resources, such as verification and collection development tools, home pages of professional associations, publishers and vendors, links to professional newsletters, journals, listserv archives, and various reference tools.

Continuing the topic of current uses of the Internet, Steve Oberg focused on the cataloging aspect of technical services. Steve presented several examples of how Internet use could facilitate cataloging. First, Steve mentioned searching other library catalogs (OPACS) on the Internet for cataloging information; he added that in 1991 the ability to view another library's OPAC was seen as a very important breakthrough for catalogers. Steve's first example involved a 1981/82 issue of a journal for which no descriptive information was present, nor did any authority work exist for this item. Steve was able to check for classification and subject headings by Telnetting to an Australian library's catalog which happened to have a record for the particular serial. Steve also mentioned a new procedure at the University of Chicago library whereby copy catalogers are trained to use Library of Congress' (LC) LOCIS to find full level records. A further example involved a puzzling monograph entitled *The Anthropology of Cyberspace*; after doing a keyword search in LOCIS on the term "cyberspace," Steve was able to see what LC had done with the term. Steve also mentioned that LC currently has a text transfer and capture protocol which is enormously helpful when chunks of material need to be cut and pasted from one system to another.

Steve moved on to electronic discussion lists and their role in cataloging. He stressed that one of the merits of discussion lists is the announcements of articles and resources. Recently discussion lists have been especially helpful in providing up to the minute information on current practice in cataloging electronic journals, with catalogers inputting their records to lists, such as INTERCAT, for comments. In addition, Steve mentioned a few WWW sites with outstanding access to reference sources, including encyclopedias (e.g., Brittanica Online) and dictionaries. He added that catalogers at various institutions have developed excellent technical services home pages with links to valuable information, such as Ann Ercelawn's "Tools for Serials Catalogers" (http://www.library.vanderbilt.edu/serials.html), "The Catalogers's Toolbox" developed at the Memorial University of Newfoundland (http://buddy.library.mun.ca/~char18P9/cathome.html) which includes USMARC documentation, Birdie MacLennan's "Serials in Cyberspace" (http://www.uvm.edu/~bmaclenn), and also a technical services Web page at the University of Virginia (http://www.lib.virginia.edu/cataloging/) which has mounted local documentation.

INVOLVEMENT IN INTERNET DEVELOPMENT

In the fourth section of the workshop, Steve emphasized that by involvement in Internet development he meant understanding applications and then getting involved. Steve described his own experience of getting a UNIX account and creating his own home page. At his home institution a committee, formed to manage the gopher-site, initially consisted of only public services and systems people, with technical services staff joining later; Steve expressed his concern that technical services librarians need to be involved in planning and management of Internet resources.

Steve asked the audience to describe their own experiences with the Internet. Some examples of current Internet use include the following: one acquisitions librarian echoed Betty's assertion that Internet access proved very helpful for obtaining current pricing information. A comment was made on the use of listservs such as AUTOCAT and SERIALST, where one can ask the advice of other catalogers, obtain reference information, and call on other librarians' language expertise. Another librarian said that every department in her library had been strongly encouraged and even instructed to set up its own home page. This raised the issue of time management and productivity. Members of the audience generally agreed on the importance of encouraging staff to learn how to navigate the Internet, yet concern was voiced as to whether all staff needed to be involved. While a comment was made that a great deal of experimentation (e.g., looking up weather reports) seemed to be taking place, this was similar to "the new toy" experience and would probably wear off after time.

Still another issue was raised concerning Internet use as an aid to cataloging and, in particular, whether this was an efficient use of time. Another librarian raised an interesting productivity issue. At his institution it is currently necessary to double-key all claims, i.e., claims are generated on their local system, then have to be re-keyed on the WWW to the vendor. While this may save time for the vendor, it was one glaring example of inefficiency and the need for the development of more and better interfaces.

The question of technical support was raised and it was generally agreed that technical services are not being given access to adequate equipment. Whereas terminals in public services often seemed to be of cutting edge caliber, computers in technical services are frequently out of date, do not contain sufficient memory, plus have to be shared among staff. It was also noted that, while most reference services librarians have their own workstations, few technical services librarians could say the same and most said that workstations are shared among staff. This dilemma seemed to be overwhelmingly prevalent as members of the audience compared situations at their home institutions.

Looking into the future, members of the audience voiced their hopes for a Hypertext Markup Language (HTML) version of AACR2R with links to the *Library of Congress Rule Interpretations* (LCRI), *Notes for Serial Catalogers*, and other cataloging tools. Steve commented that he hoped the Internet would eventually be fully integrated into the daily workflow in technical services. For this to happen, adequate training and access would have to be provided and time allotted to the above would be necessary as well. There was a general consensus that technical services staff need to get involved and most people spoke positively about the improvement in communication and speed of acquiring information that has so far occurred. In wrapping up the workshop, Steve recommended several articles on Internet related topics, and a bibliography of sources was included in the handouts.

Using the RFP Process to Select a Serials Vendor: A Work in Progress

Daniel H. Jones
Joan C. Griffith
Jane W. Maddox

Workshop Presenters

Bill Willmering

Recorder

SUMMARY. In this workshop, two librarians and a vendor described, and discussed the Request for Proposal (RFP) process to serials acquisitions librarians and vendor representatives. The format of the workshop followed the process of an actual RFP, beginning with the planning stage, the drafting of the request document, the submission to sources, the receipt by the solicited vendors, the preparation of a response, the evaluation, and the actual award.

The central theme of the workshop was the contrast between the formal Request for Proposal (RFP) and the informal RFP. The formal RFP is usually mandated by law or by institutional regulations and always involves a Purchasing Department or Contracting Office outside the library. The informal RFP is not required by institutional or governmental regulations and is administered totally within the library. *[Article copies available from The Haworth Document Delivery Service: 1-800-342-9678.]*

Bill Willmering is Head of the Serials Record Section, National Library of Medicine, Bethesda, MD.

[Haworth co-indexing entry note]: "Using the RFP Process to Select a Serials Vendor: A Work in Progress." Willmering, Bill. Co-published simultaneously in *The Serials Librarian* (The Haworth Press, Inc.) Vol. 28, No. 3/4, 1996, pp. 325-329; and *Serials to the Tenth Power: Tradition, Technology, and Transformation* (ed: Mary Ann Sheble, and Beth Holley) The Haworth Press, Inc., 1996, pp. 325-329. Single or multiple copies of this article are available from The Haworth Document Delivery Service [1-800-342-9678, 9:00 a.m. - 5:00 p.m. (EST)].

Daniel Jones (Assistant Library Director for Collection Development, Briscoe Library, University of Texas Health Science Center, San Antonio) began the workshop by describing the preparation and submission of an informal RFP, mandated not by law or institutional requirement, but by a desire to find the best vendor at the most reasonable price. In the case described by Jones, the RFP was used to select a new domestic subscription vendor when the incumbent vendor was sold.

Jones involved all levels of his staff in the preparation stage. Jones and his staff first prepared a timeline and decided who would be responsible for the various tasks of the process. After several iterations, they finalized a document with seven specific categories of requirements. Many of the requirements were prepared to elicit a yes/no response to facilitate preparation of a table with each vendor response in columnar form.

Joan Griffith (Director of Library Technology Development, University of New Mexico) described the formal RFP process, which is mandated by New Mexico state law. The law requires solicitation of proposals every eight years. In this case, the proposal was complex because it involved procurement of a large quantity of serials and continuations from a broad geographic area. In addition, the University purchasing department controlled portions of the process. The proposals were evaluated by a library-wide committee of ten members. All library staff were free to review the proposal.

In the University of New Mexico timeline, eleven vendors made presentations before the RFP was prepared. Following the presentations, the RFP was drafted and sent to vendors. As with the RFP prepared by Jones, that from the University of New Mexico had categories of requirements. Each of the factors was assigned a percent value for scoring.

Jane Maddox (Director of Library Services for North America, Otto Harrassowitz) continued the discussion by describing how a vendor processes an RFP. No two RFPs are the same, which means the vendor has to read through each page and paragraph to locate the specifications and requirements. If any mandated requirements are not currently in the vendor's services, the vendor has to assess the cost of bringing them into production and whether the award warrants such costs. An extremely expensive component of the vendor response is the preparation of an itemized quote based on a list of titles. Even when a quote of a library's detailed title list is not required, the vendor invests considerable resources to price the list to determine the service charge that will be proposed.

Maddox noted other difficulties, such as getting consent to list individuals and institutions as references, the many variations of procurement rules from institution to institution, the ineptitude of purchasing departments in both the dispatch and receipt of the documents (often within tight deadlines), the demands for excessive numbers of copies of the RFP response, the disallowance of a proposal for even slight omissions, and the lack of communication about the outcome of the proposal evaluation. The informal RFP process is still demanding, but provides for more open communication and avoids the excessive legal jargon or "official" purchasing and contracting texts that take so much time to analyze in the formal RFP process.

Jones and Griffith discussed the receipt and the evaluation of the vendor responses. Jones indicated most responses include some confidential information about the financial health and status of the offeror. In his case, there was a total of sixty specifications. There were fourteen specifications for which at least one vendor gave a response that differed from the other vendors. By careful analysis of these fourteen specifications, one vendor emerged as the best choice for the library's needs. Price was not the deciding factor in the award.

Griffith indicated that at her institution, the evaluation of the proposal was done by a Vendor Contract Review Committee. In this case, the proposal was tabulated and evaluated, with an actual score assigned for each factor, according to the percentage values stated in the RFP. Again, price was not the deciding factor in the award.

Both of the librarians summarized the pros and cons of their experience. Each reached a fairly positive conclusion. The RFP process provides an opportunity for the library to state what is wanted and can lay the foundation for a long-term relationship with a vendor. As described by Jones, the response to the RFP is the vendor's job description. As such, it makes concrete the requirements of the client and can make objective how the client will evaluate the vendor's performance.

Maddox was not so optimistic about the positive outcome of the RFP process. The mandating of the process by law has been around for some time. But in some cases, librarians have been able to convince their parent organizations that for serial subscriptions, it makes little sense to bid the product using mechanisms developed to select a vendor for commodities produced by multiple manufacturers.

Noting the extreme expense of processing proposals for one library, Maddox suggested working with a state-wide contract where every state institution can use the contract. Approved state lists of multiple vendors is even better as it preserves the library's option to select from different sources at different times.

Maddox indicated that "sole-source" was particularly damaging. By nature, purchasing agents prefer only one contract from one source because it reduces their work considerably. When this involves contracts for large amounts of money, it can be especially bad for both agents and libraries. The shifts mandated by changing vendors aggravate the peaks and valleys already experienced by agents and libraries in the normal cycles of serials business, where typically there is award and canceling from year to year. In the extreme, sole-source becomes a predatory situation which can result in monopoly.

For the library working with only one vendor, the advantage of interaction with a variety of organizations with varied outlooks is absent. Frequently, libraries working with only one vendor become myopic and may not be aware of new services offered by competitors. Sole-source does not provide flexibility, should the source vendor begin to decline in service.

Maddox concluded that for library serials procurement, the RFP process is a very simplistic solution to a very complex situation. With the excess verbiage, legal jargon, and proclivity to inhibit good communication, the formal RFP process can make a lot of work for both parties without corresponding benefits. A far better process would be ongoing evaluations and a continuous dialogue about performance expectations.

A question period followed the formal presentations. The lead-off comment was from a vendor who was not convinced of the value of the RFP process. Many of the comments from the audience underscored points made during the presentations of the three workshop leaders. For example, making documents available in electronic format can speed work for both the library and vendor. The need for a system which lends itself to better communication was repeated. For example, good post-award debriefing for unsuccessful offerors could lead to submission of better proposals during another round. Similarly, a contract can sometimes be strengthened by modification based on additional services offered in a proposal.

One vendor stated that the RFP places all the burden on the vendor without corresponding client obligations. Another participant suggested that arrangements between libraries and vendors might be better couched as trading partner agreements.

The workshop leaders prepared a bibliography and Maddox brought a looseleaf document on the preparation of RFPs for monograph purchasing, produced by librarians in Great Britain. The United Kingdom Serials Group has considered a similar document for preparation of agreements for serials but has now shifted toward a recommendation for a more service-level-type evaluation rather than the formal RFP process. This underscores the point made in the workshop subtitle. On both sides of the Atlantic, the RFP process is "a work in progress."

Cataloging Computer Files as Serials

Elizabeth Allerton

Workshop Leader

Cathy Kellum

Recorder

SUMMARY. Due to the nature of serials, cataloging machine-readable records that address the "serial" aspect of any material can be challenging as well as frustrating. The cataloging of computer files also presents unique difficulties. A serials cataloger discusses the advantages of treating computer files as serials for cataloging and processing purposes, and outlines methodologies for doing so. She examines general concerns and addresses issues pertaining to both direct and remote access to the materials. Giving hints from her own experience, she suggests tools and resources available that can assist both catalogers and non-catalogers in the interpretation of serial computer file records. *[Article copies available from The Haworth Document Delivery Service: 1-800-342-9678.]*

In a presentation that was informative and well received, Elizabeth Allerton, Serials Cataloger in the Resource Services Department at the University of Florida Library, addressed cataloging concerns of treating computer files as serials for both processing and access purposes. She began by defining the term "computer

---

Cathy Kellum is OCLC Services Coordinator at the Southeastern Library Network, Inc. (SOLINET), Atlanta, GA.

© 1996 by the North American Serials Interest Group, Inc. All rights reserved.

[Haworth co-indexing entry note]: "Cataloging Computer Files as Serials." Kellum, Cathy. Co-published simultaneously in *The Serials Librarian* (The Haworth Press, Inc.) Vol. 28, No. 3/4, 1996, pp. 331-335; and *Serials to the Tenth Power: Tradition, Technology, and Transformation* (ed: Mary Ann Sheble, and Beth Holley) The Haworth Press, Inc., 1996, pp. 331-335. Single or multiple copies of this article are available from The Haworth Document Delivery Service [1-800-342-9678, 9:00 a.m. - 5:00 p.m. (EST)].

file," and outlining the advantages for cataloging that type of material so as to address its seriality. She then identified three areas to be addressed in her treatment of those advantages: (1) acquisitions, (2) cataloging and additional technical issues, and (3) patron needs.

Acquisitions Needs. Allerton outlined the main points to consider for cataloging computer files as serials from the point of view of the Acquisitions Department.

1. One record created in the receiving database eliminates repetitive searching and verification to identify the correct item.
2. An open order record provides action dates for claims, accordingly saving staff time, with possibly an online claims function as an additional time-saver.
3. One record for receipt of items allows for consistent flow of notes and receipts. Problems with particular titles are easily identified, circumventing premature claims, etc., and allowing for the sharing of information among all with access to the records.
4. Licensing agreements can be fully outlined, ensuring consistency for access to the item from year to year.

Cataloging and Additional Technical Issues. From the cataloger's standpoint, Allerton listed additional technical issues to take into consideration.

1. Cataloging computer files as serials allows for less cataloging of items. Since each title will have only one open-ended record in the database, a holdings record is attached for each physical item upon receipt, thereby eliminating the necessity for re-cataloging each title over and over again.
2. Additions to the collection are quicker to process, getting the materials on the shelf in a more timely manner.
3. Serial records can provide an easy link to related titles, using cross-references and other database-specific tools.

Patron Needs. As with all library materials, the most important cataloging aspect to consider is its effect on patron access. Allerton stressed details in regard to patron needs when making the decision as to how to catalog particular items.

1. Since the cataloger is using a previously created cataloging record to attach an item record for holdings purposes, the pro-

cess takes less time; it is obvious that the less time it takes to process the item, the faster the patron will have access to it in the collection.
2. One record for all editions or items allows the patron a collective view of all available materials.

Allerton continued her presentation with a discussion of the concerns related to serials cataloging in general, and specifically how those rules affect the cataloging of computer files as serials. She began with the problem of discrepancies that exist among the title and its possible variants depending on the item and its relationship to the original cataloged title, citing computer games as one of the biggest problems in that respect.

Another concern with computer file serials is statement of responsibility, since the very nature of computer product manufacturers is fluid and mergers and collaborations in this arena are frequent and usually occur without warning or at least adequate notification. Edition statements may also be a troublesome area, as true "editions" of computer files may be an anomaly since computer programs are usually complete deviations from their previous forms. Accompanying material presents unique difficulties also; each subsequent release of the computer file may come with totally different notes, instructions, and accessories.

Anyone familiar with the dilemmas associated with serials has encountered the problem of nonsequential or non-standard enumeration and/or chronology. Publishers may not even understand the importance of this necessary piece of information fundamental to addressing the seriality of the material. Another important element of the serial computer file record is its links to print versions and other forms of the computer file. "Databases" as a form subheading may also be warranted.

System requirements are also an element essential to online descriptions of any computer file, not just those being addressed as serials. But those conditions themselves may present a problem for a serials cataloger. The medium for any computer file can be changed; backup files are sometimes kept in several different formats.

Methods of access to the computer file must also be stated clearly in its online cataloging record. Patrons may have direct access to computer file formats such as diskettes, compact disks, and disks as accompanying materials to regular print items. Remote access to computer files gets more complicated as the wealth of online informational databases grows. Today's libraries frequently allow remote access to their "card" catalogs as well as other electronic resources such as online retrieval databases on magnetic tape which have been loaded onto a mainframe computer, and may also provide Internet access through file transfer, gopher, or telnet capability, or World Wide Web sites.

Next Allerton guided workshop participants through exercises designed to highlight problems particular to online cataloging of serial computer files. Using "real life" instances from her own library environment, she illustrated specific examples of fields that should be addressed in the online representation. She also provided the attendees with a constant data record based on the OCLC-MARC record (Figure 1). This record, which is stored in the OCLC files of each individual library (not on the library's computer hard drive or mainframe computer), can be used as a template when cataloging computer file serials.

A lively discussion and debate ensued over the cataloging of Allerton's examples. The participants agreed that this was one area that should continue to be investigated, and standardization is necessary before the proliferation of computer files cataloged as serials causes the intrinsic problems that can be circumvented by adherence to guidelines. Format integration has helped the problems inherent to cataloging computer files as serials, with the validation of all variable fields in all formats of the MARC record.

Allerton concluded the session listing some tools and resources for use by serials catalogers, and described the merits and limitations of each. She explained common situations that occur in cataloging serials, and suggested the tools to use in each instance. Below is a list of those resources:

> CONSER Cataloging Manual, Module 30, Direct Access Computer File Serials
>
> CONSER Cataloging Manual, Module 31, Remote Access Computer File Serials

Cataloging Internet Resources : A Manual and Practical Guide

Guidelines for the Use of Field 856

NASIGNET's link to "Tools for Serials Catalogers"

The workshop participants were skillfully guided by Allerton through the somewhat unfamiliar territory of serial computer file cataloging. Members of the audience left the session feeling prepared for the inevitable: to begin the task of cataloging computer files as serials in the future online environment. Attendance at this workshop should enable the participants to feel comfortable with providing increased access to computer files in a more timely and efficient manner.

Training Aid in Cataloging Gopher Sites and Electronic Serials

John P. Blosser
Margaret Mering

Workshop Leaders

Beverley Geer

Recorder

SUMMARY. Data and information resources on the Internet are growing at a rapid rate. To identify and organize these resources is not only necessary but crucial to the Internet community. An interactive training tool developed and tested at Northwestern University Library instructs serials catalogers in cataloging electronic serials on the Internet. Alternatively, the University of Nebraska is using non-MARC formats to give access to gopher sites. *[Article copies available from The Haworth Document Delivery Service: 1-800-342-9678.]*

In a conference that presented many discussions of the value and problems presented by gophers, World Wide Web (WWW) sites, and electronic serials, this workshop provided catalogers with two practical and innovative approaches to cataloging electronic information.

John Blosser (Northwestern University) began with a description

---

Beverly Geer is Head Cataloger at Trinity University, Maddux Library, San Antonio, TX.

© 1996 by the North American Serials Interest Group, Inc. All rights reserved.

[Haworth co-indexing entry note]: "Training Aid in Cataloging Gopher Sites and Electronic Serials." Geer, Beverley. Co-published simultaneously in *The Serials Librarian* (The Haworth Press, Inc.) Vol. 28, No. 3/4, 1996, pp. 337-342; and *Serials to the Tenth Power: Tradition, Technology, and Transformation* (ed: Mary Ann Sheble, and Beth Holley) The Haworth Press, Inc., 1996, pp. 337-342. Single or multiple copies of this article are available from The Haworth Document Delivery Service [1-800-342-9678, 9:00 a.m. - 5:00 p.m. (EST)].

of the Interactive Electronic Serials Cataloging Aid (IESCA) developed at Northwestern University Library (http://www.library.nwu.edu/iesca). IESCA was designed by Blosser and Wei Zhang to provide aid to serials catalogers in creating bibliographic records for electronic serials located on the Internet. The tool resides on Northwestern's WWW and primarily provides ready access to cataloging rule guidelines and interpretations, examples of MARC bibliographic records in serial and computer file formats linked to instructional annotations, and a glossary of cataloging and computer terminology. Catalogers can move around in the training aid quickly and easily by clicking on links to documents, instructions and examples. The actual MARC bibliographic records reside on the library's online system.

IESCA is broken into three modules: bibliographic records and objects module, rules guidelines and local interpretations module, and a glossary module. The user is also provided with a comment form to provide feedback to the designers. Using an overhead display of the IESCA screens, Blosser demonstrated each module.

The first module contains examples of bibliographic records for serial and computer formats with examples of Internet objects for bulletins, digests, journals, and newsletters, and examples of hypothetical cases to handle multiple versions. The following is an example of how the page for this module appears.

>IESCA - Bibliographic Records and Objects Module
>
>Bibliographic Records and Objects Module
>
>Electronic Bulletin
>
>Electronic Digest
>
>Electronic Journal
>
>Electronic Newsletter
>
>Hypothetical Examples of Multiple Versions
>
>UPDATED: April 7, 1995
>
>IESCA Home Page
>
>RULES
>
>GLOSSARY

The user can click on any of the entries to see demonstrations of links from bibliographic records to Internet objects and to fixed and variable fields through authoritative documents, namely the USMARC documentation and OCLC Research Report Appendix B. Quick access to the rules and glossary is available from this page. Local practice notes are also included. Module 2 contains Library of Congress Rule Interpretations for AACR2 chapters 9, 12, and 25. Guidelines include *USMARC Concise Format for Bibliographic Data* broken into fixed fields, 0XX to 4XX, 5XX, 6XX to 8XX; links to various documentation to support new fields 256 and 856; MARBI proposals 94-9 and 95-1; OCLC Research Report Appendix B, and local practices. The third module provides definitions of terminology used in reference to computers, information handling, and the Internet; definitions of terminology used in the practice of cataloging; and an on-line dictionary of computer terms.

Margaret Mering (University of Nebraska, Lincoln) demonstrated non-MARC Internet resource catalog records entered in the University of Nebraska Lincoln (UNL) gopher (gopher://libfind.unl.edu:2000) and WWW site (http://libfind.unl.edu:2020/ home.html). The cataloging instructions, which were written by Karl Fattig and Julie Swann, are in paper form at this time, but there are plans for putting them on the WWW.

The UNL gopher's development began in 1993 and the WWW's development began in April, 1995. After some discussion, the library chose to create catalog records on the gopher and WWW rather than the library catalog. Mering indicated that there is support for not having the records in the regular catalog. The gopher and WWW were deemed more suitable because of the volatility of the Internet resources and the flexibility of the non-MARC cataloging procedures used.

The catalogers create records for whole databases as well as individual electronic texts. Individual electronic serials receive full MARC cataloging and their records are part of the Libraries' OPAC. The catalogers examine the electronic resource and provide the following information in each record:

- Access Number: an accession number supplied by the system office
- Subject: the broad subject matter of the Internet resource; this is not a Library of Congress Subject Heading (LCSH), but a

heading chosen from a list of subject areas in the local classified scheme used in Internet resource cataloging
- Menu heading: the name of the resource as the cataloger believes it will best be retrieved by the user
- Author: can include major contributors, maintainers, contact persons. The names are established in AACR2 form. Because there is no authority control, cross reference forms of the name may also be included
- Title: variant forms of title
- Keywords: the cataloger refers to the LCSH to establish keywords. The LCSH form is used, but the UF (used for) terms can also be used. The catalogers are instructed to use any words that apply to the resource. If LCSH does not contain a heading, the cataloger can establish one for the resource.
- Gopher/http server: the host name plus the port number
- Content note: any information that enhances access to the resource such as abstracts. The content note always contains menu headings from the various screens in the resource.

The following is an example of an Internet resource catalog record in the UNL Gopher:

ACCESS NUMBER: 375   SUBJECT: Art

MENU HEADING:

Artbase Bibliography of Arts Online

AUTHOR:

Gale, Bob

TITLE:

Artbase Connection List

KEYWORDS:

Art

Music

Performing Arts

Motion Pictures

Films

Electronic Bulletin Boards

BBS

Discussion Groups

Gophers

Listservers

Listservs

Internet Resources

GOPHER SERVER:

ucsbuxa.ucsb.edu 3001

CONTENT NOTES:

Describes gophers, BBS, discussion groups and other online resources for the arts, including information on how to contact them.

revised 2/24/95 lm

When the WWW site became accessible, the UNL library decided to catalog simultaneously for each site and so the above record also appears in the same format in the WWW site. The library has not retrospectively entered duplicate records in the WWW for the resources cataloged before the WWW site existed. The advantage of the WWW version over the Gopher version is that the WWW provides dynamic links to the item and the Gopher only points the user to the item. If the user is in the Gopher and wishes to see the item, the user must take note of the electronic address, leave the Internet resource catalog and connect to the Internet.

Mering pointed out that there is a fair amount of maintenance of the records in the area of the Gopher and WWW site addresses. Approximately 75 percent of the records required some kind of maintenance to keep the Gopher and WWW Internet resource catalog records current. The addresses are checked at regular intervals, the information is updated and a revision date is entered in the catalog record. If the site no longer exists, the record is deleted. Contents, subjects, and keywords are revised as needed. The maintenance effort takes five hours a week and is performed by two technical services staff members.

The workshop provided the participants with detailed accounts of two methods for creating records for Internet resources, one using MARC records that reside in the online catalog and another using non-MARC records that reside on a Gopher and WWW site. Both present practical and attainable approaches to organizing information that serials catalogers will find most useful and adaptable.

Transformation in the Library Bindery Through Increased Preservation Awareness

Fran Wilkinson
John R. Fairfield

Workshop Presenters

Marilyn P. Fletcher

Recorder

SUMMARY. Preservation and conservation have become vital issues in libraries. Two perspectives on these issues were presented at this workshop. Fran Wilkinson spoke about the new roles in function and staff training in the library bindery unit based on a survey of 108 ARL libraries. Jack Fairfield discussed the goals and objectives of commercial binders in the preservation of library materials. Each emphasized that libraries and commercial binders are becoming more aware of the importance of this critical step in conservation and preservation of books, serials, and other paper documents for future use by scholars. *[Article copies available from The Haworth Document Delivery Service: 1-800-342-9678.]*

If university and other institutional administrators frequently see the overall library budget as a "black hole," it is likely that the

---

Marilyn P. Fletcher is Project Coordinator for the New Mexico Newspaper Project at University of New Mexico General Library, Albuquerque, NM.

© 1996 by the North American Serials Interest Group, Inc. All rights reserved.

[Haworth co-indexing entry note]: "Transformation in the Library Bindery Through Increased Preservation Awareness." Fletcher, Marilyn P. Co-published simultaneously in *The Serials Librarian* (The Haworth Press, Inc.) Vol. 28, No. 3/4, 1996, pp. 343-348; and *Serials to the Tenth Power: Tradition, Technology, and Transformation* (ed: Mary Ann Sheble, and Beth Holley) The Haworth Press, Inc., 1996, pp. 343-348. Single or multiple copies of this article are available from The Haworth Document Delivery Service [1-800-342-9678, 9:00 a.m. - 5:00 p.m. (EST)].

library administrator has in the past seen the bindery budget as its own "black hole." You know, that place in the basement where books and journals go out loose and come back neatly bound. Patrons often complain vehemently when the journal they needed yesterday is at the bindery and will not be back for a month. These attitudes are changing as the importance of binding is recognized and better understood. Fran Wilkinson (Director of the Acquisitions and Serials Department at the University of New Mexico General Library) concentrated on the results of a survey of library binding units in ARL libraries. Jack Fairfield spoke from the commercial binder's perspective. Both emphasized the desirability of enhancing communication and understanding between the library as client and the binder as provider of the service. Preservation efforts must take place through consultation between libraries and binders. The two sessions of the workshop were attended by approximately fifty persons.

A few years ago, libraries around the country began to realize that their collections were perilously close to deterioration. Programs such as the "Brittle Books Project" were initiated. Though the use of acid paper was a primary reason for raising awareness about the condition of library materials, other simple yet dangerous practices also needed to be addressed, such as the use of rubber bands, paper clips, transparent tape, and most recently, post-it pads that often remove the print along with the note. Sometimes the procedures used in repair and mending actually did more harm than good. In-house library binding was not commonly linked to preservation. It was formerly a widely held belief that only rare books needed special treatment with acid-free pamphlet binders and archival tape. Yet it is in the bindery unit that preservation often begins.

Fran Wilkinson and her research partner, Rebekah Azen, recently completed a survey of ARL library bindery units and outlined the results of the survey. One hundred and eight library bindery units were sent survey questionnaires. The response rate was 60 percent (sixty-five libraries responded). The surveys were addressed to the Bindery Division Head with an individual's name if known. The purpose of the survey was to determine placement of the bindery unit within the library organization, involvement in library-wide preservation, education and training of bindery personnel, decision-making for preservation, and attitudes.

The library survey respondents indicated that 42 percent of bindery units are in the Preservation Department, 28 percent are in the Serials Department, and 30 percent are in various other departments. Staff education levels in ARL libraries vary from 37 percent with a high school diploma to only 2 per cent with an MLS degree. The highest number of staff (38 percent) have completed the bachelor's degree. The low percentage of MLS degrees is not surprising in view of the fact that 50 percent of bindery decisions are made in consultation with people trained in preservation whether it be the head of the Preservation Department, selectors, or bibliographers. Staffing levels indicate that ARL bindery sections have an average of 4.4 staff and .6 professionals, with nine to thirteen years of experience.

Of considerable interest was the response that 94 percent of library binding units surveyed have established training and procedures for identifying unique or valuable items to be relocated to a Special Collections area. Since this identification of "rare" and often valuable materials may occur only when a book or journal is in need of binding or re-binding, it is gratifying to see such a high percentage of libraries acknowledge the importance of recognizing such materials. Preservation training has occurred in 49 percent of bindery staff and the training may be one of the reasons for recognizing materials to be relocated or to receive special treatment. A large proportion of decision-making in the library binding unit is made by staff primarily in such areas as commercial binding options, simple repairs, and mending. The only area of decision-making that is done almost totally by professionals is the decision to microfilm if the material is extremely fragile and cannot be bound.

Overall, the responses to Wilkinson's survey were reasons for optimism for the future role of the increased awareness of preservation, the perception of the importance of the bindery within the library, and the need for more continuing education and training in preservation areas such as recognizing brittle paper, the importance of using "no-trim" options to conserve margins, the use of acid-free materials for boxes, tapes, and glues to prevent future deterioration, and the increased commitment of library administrations to preservation and conservation efforts. In addition to being Director of the Acquisitions and Serials Department, Wilkinson has served as the library's preservation officer for the past two years. During this time and in response to the survey, disaster preparedness plans have been conceived and documented, training has increased for bindery staff, and awareness of the preservation of library materials has proliferated throughout the library. In response to a question regarding the library's bindery software not being easily converted to the commercial binder's software and sometimes requiring rekeying, Wilkinson said that the survey did not address this question but would be included in a follow-up survey. Fairfield responded by stating that because the bindery component of OCLC and other library programs had been given a low priority, binders were forced to create their own software. He said that currently many binders are able to convert the information from the library software without rekeying.

Jack Fairfield opened his presentation with a comment made by one of his friends in the library community; the difference between commercial binders and terrorists is that one can negotiate with the terrorist. While perhaps true in the past, this is no longer the case and commercial binders are working in cooperation with libraries to ensure the proper and appropriate preservation of library materials. The commercial library bindery industry is composed of a relatively small number of businesses in the United States–thirty-five are members of the Library Binding Institute. There are small binderies around the country specializing in fine bindings and personal/vanity books and collections; however, most libraries deal with one of the thirty-five commercial binders. Fairfield displayed copies of books, articles, standards, and pamphlets relative to the binding process which the audience could request or order for their bindery collections. The three most important elements for a commercial binder to provide to libraries are volumes with openability, durability, and longevity of the volumes to be bound. Length of turn-around time is also important to libraries.

Fairfield stressed the acknowledgment of the necessity to change in the commercial bindery industry. Not only are library binding budgets going down due in part to subscription cancellations, but binding materials costs are increasing, and a successful binder must maintain and increase the quality of binding while supporting a profit margin to remain in business. Page attachments are one example of the change in binding preferences. Years ago, the most used page attachment method was oversewing. This process caused damage to books and journals as photocopying became so prolific. Students and faculty much prefer photocopying to taking handwritten notes. Today, oversewing is the third choice and has been surpassed by sewing through the fold as first choice, followed by double fan adhesive page attachments. Other improvements initiated by the bindery industry include the "new" buckram which is a woven 63/35 poly-cotton blend with an aqueous acrylic coating having no solvents or heavy metals, the use of polyvinyl acetate adhesive glues (a far cry from the animal glues used in the past), and the "no-trim" option which preserves margins even though it is less aesthetically pleasing. Of course, all the improvements do not address the quality of the paper used by publishers. As Fairfield observed, though many publishers are now committed to acid-free paper, many still unfortunately consider the book a "disposable" item. This perpetuates the future prospects for de-acidification projects in libraries and more brittle paper.

It was good to hear that commercial binders are a welcome industry in communities concerned with environmental impact. Binderies are not pollutants of the air nor of the water supply and are relatively quiet operations in this age of noise. Somehow this "quiet" aspect lends itself to a business whose major client base is libraries. One wonders if a "shhhh!" ever occurs inside a binding plant. Questions for Fairfield included a request for a description of the Library Binding Institute and the standards set for library binding by NISO. Fairfield and other commercial binders serve on standards committees and contribute to new standards and specifications. He commented that commercial binders were studying ways to expand their customer base in such ways as pre-binding for printers and publishers and scanning/digitalizing books and journals.

The two speakers presented contrasting perspectives on the views and objectives of the library bindery and the commercial binder. The views and objectives are becoming more similar as each understands the needs and procedures of the other. Discussions such as this encourage more communication and training of staff in both areas. Library bindery personnel need, perhaps, tours of commercial binderies in order to see the binding process in action and the reverse might also be helpful. It was agreed that a dissemination of information via newsletters and e-mail would also enhance the exchange of ideas. Both presenters expressed a commitment to opening more lines of communication and to the common goals of conservation and preservation of library materials.

Automating Journal Use Studies: A Tale of Two Libraries

Rick Ralston
Deborah Broadwater

Workshop Presenters

Karen Cargille

Recorder

SUMMARY. Fiscal managers, administrators, faculty, and staff demand scientific quantitative justification for serials budgets. Rising costs force librarians to examine current subscriptions closely to ensure that journals meet the needs of library patrons. This workshop presents the methodology used by two libraries to provide automated access to collection data and to analyze the data on the in-house use of journal collections. *[Article copies available from The Haworth Document Delivery Service: 1-800-342-9678.]*

The workshop presented two case studies on how to conduct automated journal use studies. The audience, which numbered about seventy-five, was composed largely of librarians. Both presenters agreed that the most important reason for conducting routine journal use studies is to provide clear, unbiased data on which to

---

Karen Cargille is Head of the Acquisitions Department for University of California, San Diego Libraries, San Diego, CA.

© 1996 by the North American Serials Interest Group, Inc. All rights reserved.

[Haworth co-indexing entry note]: "Automating Journal Use Studies: A Tale of Two Libraries." Cargille, Karen. Co-published simultaneously in *The Serials Librarian* (The Haworth Press, Inc.) Vol. 28, No. 3/4, 1996, pp. 349-353; and *Serials to the Tenth Power: Tradition, Technology, and Transformation* (ed: Mary Ann Sheble, and Beth Holley) The Haworth Press, Inc., 1996, pp. 349-353. Single or multiple copies of this article are available from The Haworth Document Delivery Service [1-800-342-9678, 9:00 a.m. - 5:00 p.m. (EST)].

base decisions. The libraries involved were medical libraries, the Ruth Lilly Medical Library at Indiana University School of Medicine, and the Eskind Biomedical Library at Vanderbilt University.

Rick Ralston of the Ruth Lilly Medical Library began by describing why it is useful to undertake a journal use study. Ralston stated that journal use studies are done to provide objective criteria based on data to make informed decisions about cancellations, retention, storage, binding, and to indicate when it might be advisable to migrate to an electronic format. In addition, he indicated that journal use studies are helpful in justifying those decisions to faculty members and to university administrators. Many libraries have done labor intensive manual use studies for many years. With the advent of hand-held barcode scanners and automated inventory control systems, it is logical to automate these studies.

The methodology used at Indiana University involved purchasing two portable barcode scanners which could be used in the stack areas of the library to gather data. To facilitate the process, the shelves, rather than the journal issues, were barcoded. Shelf labels with title and barcode were produced and linked to a Paradox database. The library made a decision to focus on title use information rather than specific volume and issue counts. Data were collected by having the shelver take the hand-held scanner to the shelf along with the items to be shelved. Titles were scanned as volumes and issues were shelved. Only the most recent three years of a publication were scanned, since library administrators are more concerned with use of current titles than retrospective use. At the Lily Library, most unbound titles are shelved in the periodicals stacks along with bound volumes. This arrangement allowed the inclusion of the majority of recent journal issues in the study.

Student shelvers were included in the data collection process design because they were directly involved in the collection process. This involvement helped to ensure that the new workflow was accepted by the student workers. Within two weeks of implementation, shelvers had adjusted to the new system and reported that they felt the new process was easier than the old manual marking process.

Once scanners were full (about once a week), use data were loaded into a file on a desktop computer. A delimited file was created and loaded into Paradox 4.02, a commercially available database management system. A download program provided by the scanner vendor was used. Data from the library's serials vendor were loaded to provide price, vendor, publisher, and subject information, and to enrich the possibilities of creating useful management reports. All files must have a common link, and in this case, the ISSN was used. When an ISSN was unavailable, the NOTIS system number followed by an X was used.

Reports were generated as needed. Three reports were produced regularly: cost/use index; use and cost by publisher list; and cost and use by subject list. The cost/use index lists ISSN, title, price, number of uses, and a gross cost/use index number. No attempt has been made to link cost/use to index periods so the figures do not represent a true cost per use. The index number is used as a standard basis of comparison and ranking for titles in the collection. Use and cost by publisher create a list of all publishers in the database, a total annual cost of titles, and the sum of use for publisher output. The cost and use by subject index collects subjects, total number of titles in that subject, total cost, total use, and use per title. If charts and graphs are required, the data can be loaded into a spreadsheet program, such as Quattro Pro.

Use data can also be considered by the library in decisions about which titles to bind in the face of bindery budget cut-backs. The data can assist in decisions about the number of issues to include in bound volumes and when to pull issues for binding. The library plans to move into collecting interlibrary loan data in the near future to track use for informing purchasing. Currently, data are collected continuously rather than by sampling.

Deborah Broadwater of the Eskind Biomedical Library described a similar library environment. Both the physical plant, with journal collections on two floors, and the automated library system in use, NOTIS, were the same as that of the Lilly Medical Library. The journal use study at Vanderbilt was described as a project in progress.

The motivation behind the Vanderbilt study was a desire on the part of library administrators to choose the "right" set of journals to collect. The medical library is in a new highly visible site on the campus. The library is experiencing an increase in use and an increase in requests for new journal titles. With limited materials budgets and limited time available to selectors, it is difficult to make informed choices. The library has a customer service orientation in support of users in the fields of medicine and nursing. However, the choices of new titles in support of these programs seem endless.

In the past, the library used quantitative measures to identify the "right" set of journals. These included expert lists such as the Brandon-Hill list and the ISI impact factors, as well as faculty/user recommendations, faculty/user questionnaires, and traditional manual use studies done by-hand with hash marks. These studies were useful, but were labor intensive and did not provide adequate insight into how well the holdings of the library matched the needs of patrons.

In 1992, Vanderbilt began to barcode bound periodicals and, in 1994, began barcoding single issues. This prepared the periodicals collection for an automated use study. Portable barcode readers were purchased. Initially one reader was purchased, but the library soon realized it needed one for each floor. In January 1995, an automated study of journal use began. All volumes and issues of journals were placed on a booktruck and scanned before shelving. The use data were downloaded into the NOTIS system about twice a week and monthly use reports were prepared. These reports provided a sense of collection use and tracked the items that were browsed. The reports have been used to inform decisions on weeding and the purchase of multiple copies.

A further method of analyzing use patterns was developed specifically for the Eskind Library, the Chisnell-Dunn-Sittig (CDS) Method. The method was devised by three librarians at Vanderbilt and bears their names. The method allows the library to monitor the use of journal databases within the library and to analyze the articles that were selected by patrons. The source data from these searches were used to produce lists of titles that the users identified. The lists were compared to the actual holdings to determine which titles users want to find in the library.

The CDS method is based on statistics from the library's OVID Technologies system which provides access to Medline, CINAHL, CancerLit, and the Health Reference Update. There are twenty-eight public workstations in the library with access to OVID as well as campus-wide networked access. Using the OVID statistics, the methodology was able to limit the user group to a desired subset of users, and then to rerun searches in an appropriate database. The "keep" statements generated by patrons were used to determine which articles patrons wanted to see. Source data were downloaded from the "kept" items and analyzed to provide lists and frequencies of occurrence.

Preliminary results are encouraging. One month of use statistics and one week of Medline analysis indicated an 80 percent overlap in titles identified by patrons versus by using the CDS method. Of the top 330 journals identified as "kept" by the CDS method, 10 percent were not held locally. The benefits of the system are particularly useful for collection development, in identifying titles for purchase and in identifying titles for cancellation. Because of the ability to limit analysis to a group of users, the library can better understand the needs of remote patrons versus in-house patrons. The method is patron centric, automatic, and quantitative. It shows great promise in helping the library understand the unique needs of its patrons.

The workshop presenters made the case for successful automated data collection for in-house journal use studies. The presenters concluded that members of their staff were much happier performing the new automated tasks than the former manual tasks. Hand-held barcode scanning technology was successfully used in both cases. Both speakers agreed that the most valuable outcome of the studies is to provide quantitative data to inform collection development decisions in support of library patrons.

A lively discussion concluded the workshop. Specific questions about how barcodes were generated, as well as more theoretical questions, were covered in the discussion.

Scholarly Journals at the Crossroads

Ann Schaffer
Neil Calkin

Workshop Presenters

Rita Echt

Recorder

SUMMARY. Scholarly journals have served the academic community well for almost 350 years. They are thoroughly embedded in the process of scholarly communication. These journals have developed their own genres and formats, supporting scholarship in subtle ways. As we move into the electronic age, scholarly journals will evolve and change. The role of librarians and scholars in guiding and nurturing the evolution of these journals into new forms is examined. *[Article copies available from The Haworth Document Delivery Service: 1-800-342-9678.]*

The workshop consisted of two presentations and a discussion group session. Ann Schaffner (Assistant Director, Science Library, Brandeis University) presented a historical overview of the evolution of the scholarly print journal from the seventeenth century to the present. Neil Calkin (Assistant Professor, School of Mathematics, Georgia Institute of Technology) spoke about the current "communication paradigm shift" with the advent of electronic journal

---

Rita Echt is Acquisitions Team Manager for Michigan State University Libraries, East Lansing, MI.

© 1996 by the North American Serials Interest Group, Inc. All rights reserved.

[Haworth co-indexing entry note]: "Scholarly Journals at the Crossroads." Echt, Rita. Co-published simultaneously in *The Serials Librarian* (The Haworth Press, Inc.) Vol. 28, No. 3/4, 1996, pp. 355-359; and *Serials to the Tenth Power: Tradition, Technology, and Transformation* (ed: Mary Ann Sheble, and Beth Holley) The Haworth Press, Inc., 1996, pp. 355-359. Single or multiple copies of this article are available from The Haworth Document Delivery Service [1-800-342-9678, 9:00 a.m. - 5:00 p.m. (EST)].

publishing. The third segment of the workshop organized the audience into small groups with a given topic for analysis. Following this analysis, the groups reported on their discussions to the workshop audience.

Schaffner described print journals as meandering down Vermont roads and meeting a highway, at which point one had to cross over or merge. Using historical overhead illustrations, she led the audience through the creation of scholarly journals. She began with a discussion about the publications of Bacon, Newton and Galileo, which were primarily in the form of letters that described work and experiments of the authors. They were written to convince readers of the veracity of the authors' claims. For quite a long time, journals mimicked letters, gradually evolving into what is now a standard journal format.

Schaffner itemized the basic functions of a journal as: building a knowledge base, coordinating information, validating quality as in peer review, distributing rewards, and building communities. By fulfilling these functions, journals fit into the big picture of scholarly communication.

Neil Calkin emphasized that we have entered the knowledge age, not the information age. We must learn how to handle information as it exists today. The overview of his talk provided a brief history of electronic journals, and preprint servers in mathematics and science. He examined the advantages and features of electronic publishing, gave a case history of the journal he produces, *The Journal of Combinatorics*, and posed some questions for the future of electronic publishing. He is an enthusiastic advocate for electronic publishing but clearly recognizes the drawbacks as well as the advantages of this medium. His discussion of advantages included: availability, timeliness from acceptance to publication, and the possibility of unlimited capacity. The discussion of drawbacks included: availability (depending on whether users had suitable equipment), lack of accessibility in less developed countries, a certain resistance from the academic community, speed and capacity leading to lower standards, and the possible impact on commercial publishers.

Calkin indicated that mathematics has been a little slower than a number of other disciplines in publishing electronic journals but is slowly catching up. The advent of preprints has made revolutionary changes in the access to scholarly information. Many scholarly societies are now becoming involved in making information available through the World Wide Web (WWW).

Schaffner distributed a bibliography and pointed out the citations she considered especially useful for the workshop discussion. Among these was the Andrew Odlyzko article "Tragic Loss or Good Riddance? The Impending Demise of Traditional Scholarly Journals." This article is available on the WWW with updates attached.

Calkin enumerated the traditional roles of scholars, publishers, and libraries, and enlarged on these roles for the future. In the world of electronic publishing, scholars will be authors, editors, readers, typesetters, copy editors, and distributors. Publishers will also be copy editors, typesetters, distributors, archivers, classifiers, and searchers. Libraries will continue to catalog these publications, but will have the added responsibilities of archiving, knowledge retrieval, searching, and increased inter-library cooperation.

Calkin gave the audience a prehistory of electronic publishing starting with language, writing, papyrus, the monks' use of parchment, and finally, paper and the invention of the printing press. In his discussion of recent history, Calkin traced the evolutionary process of electronic journals. He listed TeX and PostScript or document preparation by author, anonymous file transfer protocol (FTP) or electronic distribution of the document, gopher, hypertext with embedded links within the document and finally, Mosaic, Lynx, and Netscape.

According to Calkin, there are a number of features that are unique to electronic publishing. These features include automatic subscriptions, updating papers via "comments" files, the potential for full-text searches, dynamic surveys, hypertext bibliographies, mirror sites, and statistics gathering. The question is whether or not we are ready to tackle such dramatic "paradigm shifts."

Major problems relating to archiving and acceptability remain to be resolved. The problem of archiving is a challenging issue. How will materials be archived? Will archiving be in paper or electronic format and who will be responsible? Will authors and academic institutions recognize archiving as a legitimate form of publishing and communication? Calkin emphasized that a uniform searching tool is needed for accessing journals. Issues relating to distribution and fees will also need to be resolved. Should we pay per view or pay per journal? Should there be central distribution or local distribution centers and should we pay to view archives? Electronic publishing is still in its infancy and many issues remain unresolved.

Ann Schaffner organized the audience into groups. She asked each group to focus on two or three of the problems identified as key to the future of electronic journals. The workshop leaders participated in the small group discussions through responding to questions and comments. After some animated discussion within the groups, a reporter for each group gave a short presentation to the larger audience. Deana Astle (Assistant Dean of Libraries, Clemson University) reported on her group's discussion of standards and archiving. There was a concern that as technology changes, storage devices for archiving material will also change, necessitating a continuous alteration in how and where archived materials will remain. Her group proposed libraries and computer centers of the home institution or regional consortia as possible groups that could assume archiving responsibilities.

Chestalene Pintozzi (Science-Engineering Team Librarian, University of Arizona) reported for her group discussion on the value added function of commercial publishers. Her group questioned who would pay for editing. Universities could possibly use faculty for editing, which might maintain lower costs and, in turn, might keep subscription rates at a reasonable level.

Some participants expressed concern about libraries becoming too actively involved in the electronic journal life cycle. There were comments about dwindling human resources and about being asked to do more with less. Do we now have to add additional responsibilities to an already full plate? Several participants discussed the possibility of publishers becoming involved in archiving.

Other suggestions for archiving journals were multiple sites, the Library of Congress, and for math titles, the American Mathematical Society. The media used for archiving could be magnetic tapes, copied and reformatted on a regular basis. In addition, the most current version of the article should include all recent versions and updates.

Further discussion by the audience brought out that publishing in peer reviewed electronic journals has not hindered a faculty member's chances for tenure. Calkin verified that so far, this is the case.

In response to audience questions, Calkin gave a brief case history of how his *Electronic Journal of Combinatorics* was formed. The journal was first discussed in January, 1994. A mock-up was shown to prospective editors in February, with the first papers published in April, 1994. Three and one half months elapsed between conception and distribution. There are currently 650 subscribers from almost forty countries and all continents except Antarctica. The journal averages twenty accesses per hour, with papers accessed one to two times each per day. At this point, the journal is available free of charge.

The quick start-to-finish processing time for articles to appear in electronic format gave us all reason to reflect on the current time it takes for a print article to make its way to readers. Members of the audience clearly understood that the future has arrived but is still a work in progress, requiring the cooperation of authors, academic institutions, publishers, and of course, librarians. The workshop brought forward many problems and issues related to electronic journals. Schaffner and Calkin stressed that librarians are major contributors to the knowledge chain, and that they need to think ahead and remain positive about access to knowledge.

Implementing Teams for Technical Services Functions

Tim McAdam
Nancy Markle Stanley

Workshop Presenters

Cathy Tijerino

Recorder

SUMMARY. In the 1990s, librarians need to apply quality principles and techniques to allow more flexibility in service delivery. Many library technical services operations are reorganizing staff into teams. The promises and benefits of team-based organizations are increased employee empowerment and increased production with fewer employees. These benefits should result in high levels of staff satisfaction and reduce operational budgets. *[Article copies available from The Haworth Document Delivery Service: 1-800-342-9678.]*

An audience of about fifty, mostly technical services personnel and one or two vendors, gathered to listen to the first session of a presentation by Tim McAdam (Acquisitions Librarian, University of California, Irvine) and Nancy Markle Stanley (Joint Chief, Acquisitions Services, Pennsylvania State University) about the

---

Cathy Tijerino is Assistant Serials Librarian at the University of New Orleans, New Orleans, LA.

© 1996 by the North American Serials Interest Group, Inc. All rights reserved.

[Haworth co-indexing entry note]: "Implementing Teams for Technical Services Functions." Tijerino, Cathy. Co-published simultaneously in *The Serials Librarian* (The Haworth Press, Inc.) Vol. 28, No. 3/4, 1996, pp. 361-365; and *Serials to the Tenth Power: Tradition, Technology, and Transformation* (ed: Mary Ann Sheble, and Beth Holley) The Haworth Press, Inc., 1996, pp. 361-365. Single or multiple copies of this article are available from The Haworth Document Delivery Service [1-800-342-9678, 9:00 a.m. - 5:00 p.m. (EST)].

implementation of team-based structures in technical services. Outlines of the presentations were distributed, along with handouts describing job responsibilities, current organizational hierarchies, and a bibliography. Overhead projections provided a comparison of the two institutions on the number of full time employees, student enrollment, and other basic statistics.

Nancy Stanley began the workshop by explaining why her library and many other institutions have reorganized their work force using "quality techniques." Changes in technology, such as, the availability of high-speed desk top computing and the accessibility of the Internet, have changed the way librarians and staff interact with vendors and other library professionals, and the way librarians perform day-to-day activities. Economic forces are also causing institutions to compete in a global market, and this compels organizations to re-examine effectiveness and costs. An educated workforce has prompted a need to improve job satisfaction, to recognize and reward employees, and for organizational commitment to continuous training.

Stanley addressed the benefits for quality and team-based organizations. By streamlining operations, a team is able to streamline processes, cut costs, enhance communications, and provide for flexibility across functions. Streamlining often produces a "flattened organization" with few management positions. Stanley said that through training, teams are able to take advantage of technological developments and to satisfy needs of educated workers who want more control and flexibility in their jobs. Such changes usually lead to improved employee morale and increased commitment to the organization.

Stanley outlined some of the challenges of self-directed work teams, namely the drastic changes that take place in the work environment. While staff members become empowered, the organizational lines shift from hierarchical to horizontal. The staff must learn to focus commitment on the library rather than the local work unit. Most policies and procedures must be rewritten to accommodate the new team-based structure.

Stanley related the Penn State Experience in reorganizing technical services. The process began in 1992. As a result of a resignation at the highest level of the department, the Acquisitions Department staff was queried about the type of organization they would like to see in place. The staff expressed needs for improved communication and more involvement, and suggested a team-based structure. A steering committee, which included administrators, acquisitions librarians, a consultant in operations management, and a psychologist, conducted a survey. The committee concluded that self-directed teams would be feasible. The Acquisitions Management Team, a twelve-member design team of elected and appointed employees, developed a plan and assisted in preparing the staff for changes by providing training and techniques for improving communication and "new ways to work." The process took seven to eight months. The result included four teams that eventually became the Approval Plan/Monograph, Serials, Commonwealth Campus, and Support teams. A prioritized list of responsibilities was developed to gradually shift functions to the appropriate self-directed work team. Implementation of the process began with the staff members choosing preferred team assignments. Most individuals chose the team most aligned with their current skills. The first day of implementation was set for July 18, 1994. The Acquisitions Staff spent this day in the park, involved in team training, discussing current projects in process, and a picnic. As the teams became fully functional, a number of unresolved issues became apparent. For example, no one had been designated to sign time cards. The department secretary was quickly selected to sign time cards. To resolve issues that affect the entire department, the team elects representatives to various interest groups (e.g., equipment, space planning).

After a restructuring of this magnitude, human resource issues become the most profoundly affected components of an organization. A national trend is to have staff review processes focused on employees' development, rather than on evaluation or appraisal of past performance. Goals, standards, and job descriptions should be driven by the teams with management support. The descriptions should be reflective of the teams, and the departmental mission and goals. Stanley believes that self-directed teams should have at least two levels for job descriptions. Employees should expect upgrades once the job descriptions are established if the teams are truly empowered. Employees must be satisfied with their jobs. As most institutions cannot award bonuses, Stanley suggested some inexpensive rewards such as a free lunch, an afternoon off, or a book placed in the stacks honoring an employee's performance.

Stanley added that in the future, the acquisitions teams will need to work toward job training, streamlining procedures, and developing communication styles. The teams will also need to complete job descriptions, continue to do more with less money and personnel, and redirect their focus on the needs of the library as a whole.

Stanley completed her presentation by relating several anecdotes about the effects of the change on some of her longtime employees. She believes that most of the staff are finding their jobs to be much more rewarding under the new organizational structure.

Tim McAdam reported that his library began to plan for reorganization in December 1992, through the Library Wide Organizational Review and Design Project (OR & DP). The Association of Research Libraries Office of Management Services served as a consultant and there was a high level of staff participation in the OR & DP project. A seven person library-wide steering committee was formed. By May, 1994, the team structure for the Acquisitions Department had been finalized. During the next six months, there were two changes which would facilitate the reorganization of the library. On July 1, 1993, the Acquisitions and Serials Departments merged to form one department. The newly consolidated department moved into the new science library on June 15, 1994, placing all components of the department in one building. McAdam noted that this was an especially stressful time for employees.

The implementation of teams began, and workshops and training were provided for all staff. The final organizational structure for the teams was received from the OR & DP Steering Committee. The committee recommended a department head with three team leaders, plus a team called the Acquisitions Operations Management Team consisting of the department head and team leaders. The acquisitions staff identified all functions they thought the teams should perform, and each function was assigned to a team. The number of staff needed for each team was determined. Measures to simplify team tasks were implemented: increased use of vendors for all monographs and serials, beta test and implement claiming serials via the Internet, and establishing a schedule for approval books. Job descriptions were drafted for Acquisitions Team Leaders which would be "permanent" positions. After a search committee was selected, the interview process for the team leaders began. After team leaders were announced, team membership was finalized. Staff were asked to rank-order their choices of teams and everyone was able to get their first choice. The Acquisitions Department began the new team-based structure November 1, 1994.

McAdams outlined some of the benefits of team-based organizations. Operations shifted from format-based to function-based. Other benefits include: procuring standards for processes, reducing levels of management, streamlining staff, and improved employee morale. Like the employees at Penn State, University of California Irvine employees are discovering that they can do more with less staff and that there is more time to pursue broad work-related interests. Team members have realized a certain sense of control, as they are able to identify responsibilities and develop workflows. Communication has improved, greatly enhanced by all staff members having terminals on their desks and individual e-mail accounts.

McAdams closed his presentation by commenting on some fine-tuning needed for the new department. Currently, the four team leaders have different rankings and this has caused some minor obstacles in the level of participation in the management of the day-to-day operations of the department by the team leaders. McAdams believes it would be better if all team leaders had equal ranking. He realizes that the teams still need to establish their own goals and objectives, and update job descriptions. Currently, only team leaders have job descriptions. As in many libraries, there is a need to address the technical processing aspects of government publications, and to fully implement and maintain the Marcive Project.

Stanley and McAdams opened the floor for questions and were instantly confronted with raised hands. As expected, many questions concerned personnel issues, such as, rankings for paraprofessionals, the effect of turnover on the teams, upgrading positions, and the role of student workers in the teams. Other questions concerned the effect of government documents on the teams, and how serials staff relate to cataloging staff.

Changes to the Serial Item and Contribution Identifier and the Effects of Those on Publishers and Librarians

Fritz Schwartz

Workshop Presenter

Cindy Hepfer

Recorder

SUMMARY. ANSI/NISO Z39.56-1991 [SIC] is the only accredited standard for identifying serially published materials in a machine-readable context. This standard is currently under revision. This is an unusual NISO standard in that it was envisioned for established formats but has been eclipsed by new developments in the industry that were barely imagined in the 1980s. *[Article copies available from The Haworth Document Delivery Service: 1-800-342-9678.]*

Fritz Schwartz, Manager of Electronic Services and Standards for the Faxon Company, presented an extremely well-received workshop on a key standard for serialists, ANSI/NISO Z39.56, the Serial Item and Contribution Identifier (SICI). The SICI is currently

---

Cindy Hepfer is Head of the Serials and Bindery Department at the State University of New York at Buffalo, Health Sciences Library, Buffalo, NY.

© 1996 by the North American Serials Interest Group, Inc. All rights reserved.

[Haworth co-indexing entry note]: "Changes to the Serial Item and Contribution Identifier and the Effects of Those on Publishers and Librarians." Hepfer, Cindy. Co-published simultaneously in *The Serials Librarian* (The Haworth Press, Inc.) Vol. 28, No. 3/4, 1996, pp. 367-370; and *Serials to the Tenth Power: Tradition, Technology, and Transformation* (ed: Mary Ann Sheble, and Beth Holley) The Haworth Press, Inc., 1996, pp. 367-370. Single or multiple copies of this article are available from The Haworth Document Delivery Service [1-800-342-9678, 9:00 a.m. - 5:00 p.m. (EST)].

used for Electronic Data Interchange (EDI) transmissions, table of contents and A&I services, and in the SISAC Bar Code Symbol for serials check-in. Future uses are expected to include identification of royalty payments; identification of abstracts, tables of contents, and indexes of contributions; tracking manuscripts through review and production processes; and identification of serial images, sound files, and other binary files appearing within URLs.

Fritz noted the relationship between Z39.56, the SICI, and the SISAC Bar Code Symbol: Z39.56 is the American National Standard Institute/National Information Standard Organization (ANSI/NISO) standard for the Serial Item and Contribution Identifier. Another document, *Serial Item Identification: Bar Code Symbol Implementation Guidelines*, defines the requirements for a variable length bar code, which provides a unique identification of serial items. The SISAC Bar Code Symbol is a bar code, created in accordance with Z39.56, which an increasing number of periodicals include on their covers to enable automated systems to automatically scan and check-in serial issues or volumes.

The 1991 version of Z39.56 is under revision. Fritz chairs the revision committee which also includes Julia Blixrud, Peter Ciuffetti, Allen Dean, Tina Feick, Peter Foppen, Mary Jackson, Ted Koppel, Sue Malawski, Mark Needleman, Linda Richter, and George Wright. They represent a broad segment of the serials, library, and automation communities. Cecilia Preston serves as the editor.

Reviewing the Z39.56-1991 structure, Fritz explained that the SICI has three distinct parts: an item segment, which identifies the issue or other serial unit; a contribution segment, which indentifies the article, book review, obituary, letter to the editor, etc.; and a control segment, which provides information necessary for an automated system to process the SICI by permitting the receiving unit to interpret the string.

In Z39.56-1991 the item (or issue) segment consists of the ISSN (required element), the chronology or date (required if present) in the YYYYMMDD format, and the enumeration or number of the piece (also required if present) with all labels (such as vol. or no.) stripped. The control segment is a safety valve which shows the version of the Standard and provides a check character.

The following string constitutes a SISAC Bar Code Symbol created under Z39.56-1991:

1234-5679(19950221)21:2;1-X

In this example, 1234-5679 is the ISSN, (19950221) is the date from the issue, and 21:2 shows two levels of enumeration. Together these three pieces form the item segment. Following the semicolon is the control segment. The 1 shows that the string is formulated following version 1 of Z39.56. The X is the check character.

When the SICI includes article-level information, a third segment is added between the item segment and the control segment. The middle part is called the contribution segment. It consists of the first page of an article and is followed by a contribution abbreviation. In Z39.56-1991, the abbreviation consists of the first letter of each of the first four words. There are no stop words, but words of less than three characters are disregarded.

The following string constitutes a SICI to be used to describe an article for a table of contents or an abstracting and indexing service:

1234(19950221)21:2:L.123:ABCD;1-X

This example is exactly like the one above, except that it includes the contribution segment **L.123:ABCD**: L.123 is the location data, showing that the article in question starts on page 123 of the issue. ABCD are the first letters from each of the first four words of three or more characters.

Because one cannot help but wonder if these strings are unique, Fritz reported that Ted Koppel from Uncover did an analysis of approximately four million SICI strings in the Uncover database and found only twelve duplicates, a remarkably low rate of duplication.

The 1995 version of Z39.56 will differ from the 1991 version in a number of ways. In the contribution segment, the leading "L." is being dropped. The contribution abbreviation is being expanded to six characters, using the first letter from each of the first six words of any length. Any characters not in 8-bit ASCII will be spelled out in English. In the control segment, three new indicators are introduced. In the control segment, the standard version number will change from 1 to 2 but the check character will not change. The three new indicators in the control segment are: the Code Structure Identifier (CSI), the Derivitive Part Identifier (DPI), and the Medium/Format Identifier (MFI). Other changes to the standard include some choice of delimiters, the use of upper case in the contribution and control segments whenever possible, and leeway for the Z39.56 maintenance agency to make changes within the five-year review.

How will the SISAC Bar Code Symbol change? Continuing the example shown above, with Z39.56-1995 the bar code will read:

1234-5679(19950221)21:2<>1.0.TX;2-X

In the contribution segment we find the addition of angle brackets after the enumeration, where page numbers, etc. would go. There is also a Code Structure Indentifier (CSI) of 1 (for SISAC Bar Code Symbol) immediately after the angle bracket; a period; a Derivitive Part Identifier (DPI) of 0 (meaning the item itself); a period; and a Medium/Format Identifier (MFI) of TX (for printed text) prior to the control segment.

A SICI for a table of contents might look like this:

1234-5679(19950221)21:1<123:ABCDEF>2.0.TX;2-X

The information within the angle brackets in the contribution segment tells us that item ABCDEF starts on page 123. The CSI, 2, indicates a table of contents or A&I item; the DPI, 0, indicates the item itself; and the MFI, TX, again indicates printed text.

Clearly workshop participants had specific uses in mind for Z39.56, as they asked a number of questions about both the 1991 standard and the 1995 revisions. The workshop closed with an exercise in which participants were given items and asked to create the SICIs for them. Fritz plans to mount the exercises on the Faxon Web server, along with other information on Z39.56, at <http://www.faxon.com>.

If Publishers Perished, Just What Would Be Lost?

Steve Cohn
Mike Brondoli
Matthew Bedell

Workshop Leaders

Barbara Woodford

Recorder

SUMMARY. In an effort to increase awareness and understanding of how publishers add value to the scholarly information process, three members of Duke University Press describe operational, production, and marketing functions from a day-to-day perspective. They discuss how a high-quality university press journals publisher maintains the delicate equilibrium between revenues and expenses, how a "raw" manuscript is converted to a published journal article, and how the marketing department serves the functions of dissemination and distribution. Each presenter also touched on the question of how electronic publishing would impact their job. *[Article copies available from The Haworth Document Delivery Service: 1-800-342-9678.]*

The presenters began the workshop by circulating a number of journals currently published by Duke University Press so that participants could examine the final product of the publishing process they were about to hear described. Steve Cohn (Director of Publish-

---

Barbara Woodford is Account Services Manager at EBSCO Subscription Services, Denver, CO.

© 1996 by the North American Serials Interest Group, Inc. All rights reserved.

[Haworth co-indexing entry note]: "If Publishers Perished, Just What Would Be Lost." Woodford, Barbara. Co-published simultaneously in *The Serials Librarian* (The Haworth Press, Inc.) Vol. 28, No. 3/4, 1996, pp. 371-375; and *Serials to the Tenth Power: Tradition, Technology, and Transformation* (ed: Mary Ann Sheble, and Beth Holley) The Haworth Press, Inc., 1996, pp. 371-375. Single or multiple copies of this article are available from The Haworth Document Delivery Service [1-800-342-9678, 9:00 a.m. - 5:00 p.m. (EST)].

ing Operations, Duke University Press) began by asking, "How do publishers add value?" Most people do not understand what is involved in the publication of a scholarly journal. Much of the process is not glamorous.

Duke University Press publishes about twenty-five journals, mainly in the humanities and social sciences, with a few science-technology-medicine (STM) titles. These journals have circulations ranging from a few hundred to more than 5,000. Libraries are the primary subscribers to a number of these journals, but many are sent to individual subscribers. Cohn said that the Duke University Press publishing program is fairly representative of university press journals programs, although he cannot speak for all journal publishers. Duke publishes a number of journals that have been in existence for more than fifty years, has taken over publication of a number of journals, and has started three new journals in recent years. Much of their production is in-house on disk. However, some of their journals are sent to typesetters. Duke is a nonprofit press. Like most university presses, it is a break-even operation, with some of the older, stronger journals supporting investment into newer journals, or journals that may not be covering production costs. Since the Press is a break-even operation, some of the current production costs must be eliminated, if the cost of subscriptions is to be reduced.

At the Press, personnel expenses account for over half of the 2.5 million dollar annual budget. Employee overhead includes people that the Press employs on a freelance basis, the editorial staff, and people who work in the Press office. Roughly one-third of the budget goes towards production costs, which includes the cost of getting the journal ready for printing, and printing costs. Five percent of the budget goes toward direct marketing expenses, which includes printing and mailing brochures, and buying ad space. Between 5 and 10 percent of the budget is spent on postage and mailing. Given this breakdown, publishing journals in electronic format cannot be expected to significantly reduce publication costs. Because of this, Cohn did not know how soon the Press will move their journals into electronic format.

The value that publishers add can be found in what publishers call "first copy costs"–the cost to make one issue, as opposed to the cost to print and mail many copies. Cohn defined this added value as three things: gatekeeping or winnowing out the chaff and improvement of work through substantive revisions; refinement of the product by making the material reader friendly; and marketing and promotion, which includes pricing and making appropriate arrangements for delivery of the journal to readers. Without these functions, the process of scholarly communication would not work.

Cohn discussed how interaction and interdependence between a journal's academic editor and the Press varies from journal to journal, and even from editor to editor. It is the responsibility of the publisher to support and bolster the editorial office, and to ensure that there are enough staff, resources, and expertise to do the job. It is ultimately the job of the publisher to parlay editorial energy and enthusiasm into revenues. Revenues must be sufficient to create an ongoing enterprise that can attract good editors. Otherwise, journals will fade in quality and eventually need to be discontinued.

Cohn described the editorial review process as remarkable: the brightest and most experienced scholars in a field are volunteering their time to read, evaluate, and make suggestions for the manuscripts of their colleagues. He stressed that for the process to receive cooperation, it must be well managed by the publisher. Rarely does a manuscript arrive ready to print. Usually, a manuscript is read and discussed at length. It then goes back to the author for revisions and is resubmitted.

Mike Brondoli (Production Manager, Duke University Press), described the process of turning a manuscript into an issue of a journal. He discussed how the Press devotes attention to the construction of the integrity of the text, and the ultimate look and feel of journals. Manuscripts rarely arrive in perfect shape and will go through an extensive process of revision before publication. Hours go into the design of a journal, from selecting paper to copy editing to proofs to the final mailing of the journal. The *Modern Language Quarterly* is one of Duke's more labor intensive journals from a production standpoint. Mike used this as an example and walked the audience through the one-hundred and forty-three day production process.

Once a manuscript has been received from the editorial office, it is put through an in-house copy editing process before it is reviewed by the editors and author(s). This portion of the process takes roughly fifty days. After all of the manuscripts are returned to the Press, they are sent to a freelance keyboarder who converts them into a single word processing program and makes the copy edited changes. These updated disks are made into first proofs. The first proofs are read by a freelance proofreader. Once this has been done, they will be sent back to the typesetter who creates second proofs. Again, this portion of the process takes approximately fifty days. The second proofs are returned to the editor and the author(s). After the editor and the author(s) have signed-off on them, the copy editor crossmarks the proofs and the production coordinator checks page elements. A third set of proofs is created and these are read by the copy editor and the production coordinator. Finally, a fourth set of proofs is created. It is from these that a "repro" or galley is made. The repro is turned into "boards" and sent to the printer who creates the "bluelines" or final negative. When the final negative has been approved, "F & G's" are created to check the ink and the cover. Finally, the advances are done and the issues are mailed to the subscribers. This last portion of the process takes approximately forty-three days.

In response to a question from a publisher in the audience about why the Press proofs so many times, Mike noted that some publishers collapse some of the steps he described. Mike said that one of the most difficult parts of the process is tracking down the author(s) for revisions.

Touching briefly on the question of the electronic journal, Mike concluded that the printed copy is the perfected vehicle for written language, and that things will have to be developed differently for the electronic format. He does not see that electronic publishing will necessarily cost less. Mike summarized the production process by stating that production work takes thoughts and transmutes them into ideas.

Matthew Bedell (Marketing Manager, Duke University Press), described the difficult task of marketing scholarly journals by discussing how the process differs from marketing commercial periodicals. With commercial periodicals, marketing must assess the needs and patterns of different audiences and route this information to potential advertisers. With scholarly journals, content is determined by editors and editorial boards. Scholarly journals are not market or advertising driven. Marketing within the university press environment is the final link in the dissemination chain in that it provides readers and members of the academic community the opportunity to make use of the knowledge.

Bedell discussed two different market types that scholarly journals target: individual subscribers (which include dedicated readers of a particular field and can include student and membership subscribers) and single copy sales to bookstores and news distributors. He noted that the marketing department is responsible for finding other revenue streams like journal issues that are repackaged as books, and advertising in other scholarly journals.

Markets and revenue sources vary greatly between different types of journals. In a handout, Bedell compared the following elements of six journals currently published by Duke to illustrate the different approaches the Press might take to market a journal:

- Percentage of library subscribers
- Bookstore sales
- Journals into books projects
- Newsstand distribution
- Percentage of total advertising sales
- Individual subscriber profile

The heaviest marketing activity tends to occur in new journals and journals with a high percent of individual subscribers. With the exception of new journals, the Press does not market to libraries. Even with new journals, marketing efforts tend to be focused on getting individuals to recommend titles to their libraries. The marketing department spends time developing other income sources, creating and maintaining an advertising database, administering the placement and billing of ads, and negotiating and fulfilling distributer contracts. Bedell stated that university press marketing departments are uniquely qualified to perform these services because they have the ability to combine resources to ensure that the journals that they publish are kept in the public eye.

This workshop was attended by a wide variety of participants including librarians, publishers, and vendors. It ended with a lively discussion about the impact an out-of-sequence inaugural issue can have on a library's automated system and how publishers can help libraries by putting SISAC barcodes on journals.

10th Annual NASIG Conference Registrants, Duke University, June 1995

Conference Registrants   *Institution*

Conference Registrants	Institution
Aaron, Amira	Readmore, Inc.
Aiello, Helen M.	Wesleyan University
Aitchison, Jada	University of Arkansas at Little Rock
Alexander, Adrian	Faxon
Alexander, Whitney	Louisiana State University
Allerton, Beth	University of Florida
Amiran, Eyal	Postmodern Culture
Anderson, Amy F.	Southwestern University
Anderson, Elma	Marywood College
Andrews, Susan	East Texas State University
Anemaet, Josephine	Ohio State University
Ashby, John	Faxon Canada
Ashton, Jonathan	Dawson Subscription Services
Ashton-Pritting, Randi L.	University of Hartford
Astle, Deana	Clemson University
Badger, Bob	Springer Verlag
Baker, Jeanne	University of Maryland
Baker, Mary Ellen	California Polytechnic University
Baker, Theresa	University of Kansas Medical Center
Banas-Marti, Kathy	University of Connecticut
Banks, Jennifer	MIT
Barnas, Ed	Raven Press
Basch, Buzzy	Basch Associates
Beach, Regina	Mississippi State University
Beckett, Chris	B. H. Blackwell

© 1996 by the North American Serials Interest Group, Inc. All rights reserved.

Bell, Carole	Northwestern University
Benham, Corie	Blackwell North America
Benson, Polly	George Mason University
Bergholz, Donna C.	Duke University
Bernards, Dennis	Brigham Young University
Black, Bob	Princeton University
Black, Leah	Michigan State University
Blaes, Evelyn R.	American University
Bland, Robert	University of North Carolina–Asheville
Blatchley, Jeremy	Bryn Mawr College
Blessing, Kathy	Johnson & Wales University
Blixrud, Julia	Council on Library Resources
Bloss, Alex	University of Illinois
Blosser, John	Northwestern University
Bolman, Pieter	Academic Press
Bordeianu, Sever	University of New Mexico
Born, Kathleen	EBSCO Information Services
Bowes, Frederick	Cadmus Digital Solutions
Braden, Patty	University of Michigan
Brannon, Kathy	Louisiana State University
Breed, Luellen	University of Wisconsin–Parkside
Breedlove, Rebecca	University of Massachusetts–Boston
Breithaupt, John	Allen Press
Brennan, Des	Harcourt Brace & Company
Broadwater, Deborah	Vanderbilt University
Broadway, Rita	University of Memphis
Bross, Valerie	California State University–Stanislaus
Broussard, Camille	New York Law School
Brown, Ladd	Georgia State University
Brown, Liz	Georgia Institute of Technology
Buell, Vivian	State University of New York
Bueter, Rita	Blackwell North America
Bull, David	Chapman & Hall

Burgos, Mary	Columbia University
Burk, Martha	Babson College
Burton, Pam	East Carolina University
Bustion, Marifran	George Washington University
Button, Leslie	University of Massachusetts
Caelleigh, Addeane	Academic Medicine
Calkin, Neil	Georgia Institute of Technology
Callaghan, Jean	Wheaton College
Caplan, Priscilla	University of Chicago
Cargille, Karen	University of California–San Diego
Carlson, Bobbie	Medical University of South Carolina
Carrigan, Ashley	University of North Carolina–Charlotte
Case, Candice	Harrisburg Area Community College
Cassidy, Vincent	Academic Press
Chaffin, Nancy	Arizona State University West
Champagne, Thomas	University of Michigan
Chang, Bao Chu	North Carolina State University
Chang, Ling-li	Loyola University
Chen, Abby	University of Illinois at Urbana-Champaign
Chou, Charlene	Columbia University
Chressanth, June	Mississippi State University
Christians, Christine	University of Miami
Clack, Mary Beth	Harvard College
Clark, Stephen D.	College of William & Mary
Clay, Genevieve J.	Eastern Kentucky University
Cleary, Robert	University of Missouri
Clendennin, Lynda	University of Virginia
Cochenour, Donnice	Colorado State University
Cole, Jim	*Serials Librarian*, Editor
Collins, Dorothy	Readmore, Inc.
Collins, Michelle	Center for Research Libraries

Collver, Mitsi	State University of New York at Stonybrook
Commodore, Paula	American Chemical Society
Compton, Bruce	VTLS, Inc.
Conger, Mary Jane	University of North Carolina at Greensboro
Congleton, Robert	Temple University
Connolly, Jo	Blackwell's Periodicals
Conway, Bernard C.	West Virginia University
Cook, Eleanor	Appalachian State University
Coombs, Mary	EBSCO Information Services
Copeland, Nora S.	Colorado State University
Corbett, Gloria	NRC–CISTI
Cordle, Alan	New Hanover Public Library
Courtney, Keith	Taylor & Francis
Cox, Brian	Elsevier Science Ltd.
Cox, John	Carfax Publishing Company
Creamer, Marilyn	Haverford College
Crews, Lucy A.	Mary Baldwin College
Crooker, Cynthia	Yale University
Crump, Michele	University of Florida
Cuesta, Emerita	Hofstra University
Curtis, Jerry	Springer Verlag
Czech, Isabel	ISI
D'Agostino, Angela	Reed Reference Publishing
Dabkowski, Charles	Niagara University
Dalton, Bobbie Lou	Davidson College
Dane, Stephen	Kluwer Academic Publishers
Darling, Karen	University of Oregon
Davis, Carroll	Columbia University
Davis, Eve	EBSCO Information Services
Davis, Susan	State University of New York–Buffalo
Davis, Susan M.	Gallaudet University
Dawson, Julie Eng	Princeton Theological Seminary
DeBuse, Judy	Washington State
Deeken, JoAnne	Clemson University

Degener, Christie	University of North Carolina–Chapel Hill
DeHart, Miyuki	Duke University Marine Lab
Denning, Peter	George Mason University
Devlin, Mary	Blackwell's Periodicals
Dickerson, Gene	Villanova University
Diodato, Louise	Cardinal Stritch College
Dodd, Janet	Virginia Polytechnic Institute
Donovan, Joanne	University of California
Douglass, Janet	Texas Christian University
Drabek, Hilda L.	University of Connecticut
Drake, Paul	Kansas City Public Library
Drozdowski, Michelle	Western Michigan University
Druesedow, Elaine	Duke University
Drum, Carol	University of Florida
Drummond, Rebecca C.	Georgia State University
Dunn, Sandra C.	North Carolina State University
Dyer, Sandra	University of North Carolina
Dyer, Sue	EBSCO Information Services
Dykstra, Lorraine	Faxon Canada
Echt, Rita	Michigan State University
Edelman, Marla	University of North Carolina–Greensboro
Edwards, Jennifer L.	Kansas State University
Eichholtz, Lisa	Medical University of South Carolina
Elling, Laura	Elon College
Elliott, Maxine	Clemson University
Ellis, Katie	University of Tennessee
Elsherbini, Pamela	Pennsylvania State University–Simpson
Elswick, Rebecca	Mary Washington College
Emery, Jill	University of Texas–Austin
Ercelawn, Ann	Vanderbilt University
Estes, Marilyn	Gallaudet University
Fairfield, Jack	Information Conservation, Inc.
Fattig, Karl	Bowdoin College

Feick, Tina	Blackwell's Periodicals Division
Field, Kenneth	Trent University
Findley, Marcia	Loyola Marymount University
Fischer, Ruth	Yankee Book Peddler
Fisher, Janet	MIT Press
Fitchett, Christine	Vassar College
Flannery, Debra	Duke University
Fletcher, Marilyn	University of New Mexico
Flowers, Janet	University of North Carolina–Charlotte
Floyd, Rebecca	North Carolina A&T State University
Fogarty, Nancy	Chapman & Hall
Folsom, Sandy	Central Michigan University
Forrester, David	Blackwell Publishers
Forrester, Jim	Ontario College of Art
Fortney, Lynn	EBSCO Information Services
Foster, Connie	Western Kentucky University
Frade, Pat	Brigham Young University
Frankel, Norman	American Medical Association
Freund, Leilani	University of Florida
Frick, Rachel	Readmore, Inc.
Gammon, Julia	University of Akron
Gasser, Sharon	James Madison University
Geer-Butler, Beverley	Trinity University
Geller, Marilyn	Readmore, Inc.
Germain, J. Charles	Publishers Communication Group
Gettys, Martha	Innovative Interfaces, Inc.
Gibbs, Nancy	North Carolina State University
Giles, Wadad	Glaxo Wellcome
Gill, Linda	Middle Tennessee State University
Gillespie, E. Gaele	University of Kansas
Gimmi, Bob	Shippensburg University of Pennsylvania

Ginanni, Katy	EBSCO Information Services
Gobin, Kip	University of Virginia
Goble, David	North Carolina State University
Golian, Linda Marie	Florida Atlantic University
Gordon, Martin	Franklin & Marshall College
Gordon-Gilmore, Anita	Fort Hays State University
Gormley, Alice	Marquette University
Grande, Dolores	John Jay College
Greene, Phil	EBSCO Information Services
Griffith, Joan C.	University of New Mexico
Guernsey, Nancy	University of Wyoming
Gurshman, Sandy	Readmore, Inc.
Haas, Ruth	Harvard College
Haest, Ruth	University of New Mexico
Hall, Barbara	University of Southern California
Halpin, Lola	Emory University
Harmon, Amanda	University of North Carolina–Charlotte
Harrell, Debbie	West Georgia College
Harris, Jay	University of Alabama–Birmingham
Harris, Sandra R.	Linda Hall Library
Harrison, Colin	W H Everett & Son Ltd
Hart, Eileen B.	Berea College
Hauser, Gloria	North Carolina State University
Hawkins, Les	United States ISSN Center
Hawthorn, Margaret	University of Toronto-Erindale College
Haynes, John	Institute of Physics Publishing
Hedberg, Jane	Wellesley College
Heinze, Linda	Weber State University
Helinsky, Zuzana	BTJ Subscription Service
Helmetsie, Carolyn L.	NASA-Langley Research Center
Henderson, Charlotte	Southern University

Hepfer, Cindy	*Serials Review* & State University of New York
Heras, Elaine	Lewis & Clark College
Herzog, Kate	State University of New York–Buffalo
Heterick, Bruce	Faxon Company
Hillery, Leanne	Ball State University
Hing, Trevor	B. H. Blackwell, Ltd.
Hinger, Joseph	Detroit College of Law
Hirons, Jean	Library of Congress
Holley, Beth	University of Alabama
Holley, Sandra H.	University of Texas Health Center
Hollmann, Pauline	Georgia State University
Holloway, Carson	EBSCO Information Services
Hollyfield, Diane	Virginia Commonwealth University
Holt, Tom	Stanford University
Hor, Annie Y.	Williams College
Horiuchi, Linda	Washington State University
Horn, Maggie	Northern Arizona University
Hoyle, Mary Sue	EBSCO Information Services
Hughes, Carolyn	University of Southern Maine
Hughes, Katherine	Loyola University
Hulbert, Linda	St. Louis University
Hull, Peggy	Glaxo Wellcome
Impellitti, Agnes J.	Elsevier Science
Irvin, Judy	Louisiana Polytechnic University
Ivins, October	Louisiana 'State University
Jacoby, Beth	New York University
Jacox, Corinne	University of Nebraska
Jaeger, Don	Alfred Jaeger, Inc.
Janes, Jodith	Cleveland Clinic Foundation
Jareo, Peter	University of North Carolina–Charlotte
Jayes, Linda	University of Chicago
Jizba, Richard	Creighton University

Johnson, Judy — University of Nebraska
Johnson, Kay G. — Appalachian State University
Johnston, Judith A. — University of North Texas
Jones, Daniel — University of Texas
Julian, Gail — University of South Carolina
Jurries, Elaine — University of Colorado–Denver

Kan, Irene — State Library of North Carolina
Keely, Alan — Wake Forest University
Keen, Sherry — Brandeis University
Keeton, Barbara A. — Society of Behavioral Medicine
Kellum, Cathy — SOLINET
Kennedy, Kit — Readmore, Inc.
Kenreich, Mary Ellen — Portland State University
Khosh-khui, Sam — Southwest Texas State University
Kietzke, Naomi K. — University of North Carolina
Kilpatrick, Janet — East Carolina University
Kim, Sook-Hyun — University of Tennessee
Kimball, Merle — College of William & Mary
Kirkland, Kenneth L. — DePaul University
Knapp, Leslie — EBSCO Information Services
Knupp, Blaine E. — Indiana University of Pennsylvania
Kobyljanec, Kathleen — Case Western Reserve University
Kochoff, Steve — Readmore, Inc.
Krieg, Linda — International Publishers Distributor
Krishan, Kewal — University of Saskatchewan
Ladjen, Nadia — New York Public Library
LaGrange, Johanne — Columbia University
Lai, Janet — Loyola Marymount University
Lai, Sheila — California State University–Sacramento
Laird, Kim — ETSU Medical Library

Lamborn, Joan G.	University of Northern Colorado
Landesman, Betty	George Washington University
Landry, Maureen	Library of Congress
Lange, Janice	Sam Houston State University
Leadem, Ellen	NIEHS
Leathem, Cecilia	University of Miami
Leazer, Bill	EBSCO Information Services
Lee, Deborah	Mississippi State University
Lennie, Mike	Current Science Group
Lenville, Jean	University of Richmond
Lenzini, Becky	CARL Corporation
Leonhardt, Tom	University of Oklahoma
Lester, Mark	San Diego State University
Lin, Selina	University of Iowa
Lindquis, Janice	Rice University
Linton, Liz	Sweet Briar College
Liu, Joan	New York University
Lombardy, Dawn	R. R. Bowker/Reed Reference Publishing
Loughner, Bill	University of Georgia
Lovett, Pete	International Thompson Publishing Service, Ltd.
Lowry, Charles B.	Carnegie Mellon
Lucado, Dianne	Virginia Polytechnic University
Lucas, Ann	Cooley Law School
Lucas, John	University of Mississippi
Luce, Clarice	University of North Texas
Luther, Judy	ISI
Lutz, Linda	University of Western Ontario
Lynch, Clifford	University of California
Lynch, Paula	Thomas Jefferson University
Lysyk, Pat	University of British Columbia
MacAdam, Carol	Princeton University
MacAdam, Jeanette A.	Northeastern University
Macklin, Lisa	Georgia Institute of Technology

MacLennan, Birdie	University of Vermont
MacWithey, Mary	Texas Medical Center
Maddox, Jane	Harrassowitz
Magenau, Carol	Dartmouth College
Makinen, Ruth H.	University of Minnesota
Malawski, Susan	John Wiley & Sons, Inc.
Malinowski, Teresa	California State University
Mallett, Bobbie	University of Maryland
Man, Di	University of the Witwatersrand
Mann, Marjorie F.	National Library of Medicine
Mansheim, Renee	Eastern Virginia Medical School
Marill, Jennifer	Washington Research Library Consortium
Markley, Susan	Villanova University
Markwith, Michael	Swets Subscription Services
Marland, Sid	R. R. Donnelley & Sons
Marsh, Corrie	University Microfilms International
Marshall, David	Georgetown University
Masters, Debbie	Coalition for Networked Information
Matthes, Meg	Nova Southeastern University
May, Charles	New Hanover County Library
McAdam, Tim	University of California–Irvine
McCafferty, Pat	Case Western Reserve University
McCann, Jett	EBSCO Information Services
McCarthy, Connie	Duke University
McClary, Maryon	University of Alberta
McCutcheon, Dianne	National Library of Medicine
McDonald, Lynn	FEDLINK
McDonough, Joyce	Columbia University
McDougald, Barbara T.	U.S. Patent & Trademark Office
McGrath, Kat	University of British Columbia
McKay, Bea	Trinity University
McKay, Peter	Harcourt Brace & Company

McKee, Anne	The Faxon Company
McLaren, Mary	University of Kentucky
McShane, Kevin	National Library of Medicine
McSweeney, Marilyn	MIT
Medaglia, Victoria	Bates College
Meiseles, Linda	Hofstra University
Meldrum, Jan	National Library of Canada
Melton, Sonja	Michigan Technological University
Meneely, Kathleen	Case Western Reserve University
Mering, Margaret	University of Nebraska
Merrill-Oldham, Pete	Acme Bookbinding
Merriman, Faith	Central Connecticut State University
Merriman, John	U. K. Serials Group
Mershon, Loretta K.	North Carolina State University
Metz, Allan	Drury College
Middeldorp, Ineke	Martinus Nijhoff International
Milam, Barbara	Kennesaw State College
Miller, Heather	University at Albany
Mills, Pamela	University of Minnesota
Moles, Jean Ann	University of Arkansas for Medical Sciences
Molinek, Frank	Davidson College
Moore, Judy	East Carolina University
Moran, Sheila	Massachusetts General Hospital
More, Susan	Northeastern University
Morgan, Eric Lease	North Carolina State University
Morgenroth, Karen	University of Georgia
Mouw, James	University of Chicago
Mullins, Teresa	UnCover Company
Murden, Steve	Virginia Commonwealth University
Nadler, Judith	University of Chicago

Narayanan, Kamala	Queens University
Nasea, Melissa	East Carolina University
Nelson, Catherine	University of California
Newman, Euthena	North Carolina A&T State University
Nichols, Karen	Lamar University
Noel, Lauren	Center for Research Libraries
Nordman, Alan	Dawson Subscription Services
Norquist, Heather	San Jose State University
Novak, Denise	Carnegie Mellon University
O'Donnell, Jim	University of Pennsylvania
O'Leary, Susan	EBSCO Information Services
O'Malley, Terrence	Cleveland State University
O'Neill, Ann	University of South Carolina
Oberg, Steve	University of Chicago
Ogburn, Joyce	Yale University
Okerson, Ann	Association of Research Libraries
Olivieri, Rene	Blackwell Publishers
Owens, Debbie	CCIW Library Environment Canada
Palmiter, Sherry	University of Maryland
Paradis, Olga	Baylor University
Parang, Elizabeth	University of Nevada–Las Vegas
Park, Amey	Kent State University
Patrick, Carol	Cleveland State University
Pendergraf, Cindy	Davidson College
Perry, Cheryl	Glaxo Wellcome
Persing, Bob	University of Pennsylvania
Peters, Paul Evan	Coalition for Networked Information
Peterson, Gretchen	Academic Book Center
Peterson, Jan	Academic Press
Phillips, Patricia A.	University of the South
Pintozzi, Chestalene	University of Arizona
Porter, Sherry	University of North Texas

Pratt, Kathy	Los Alamos National Laboratory
Preisser, Julie	Sinclair Community College
Presley, Roger	Georgia State University
Price, Margaret	University of British Columbia
Pulsipher, Susan	Methodist College
Qualls, Jane	University of Memphis
Ralston, M. Joan	Villanova University
Ralston, Rick	Indiana University
Randall, Kevin M.	Northwestern University
Randall, Mike	University of California–Los Angeles
Rankin, Juliann	California State University–Chico
Rast, Elaine	Northern Illinois University
Ratsoy, Marye	University of Ottawa
Reaves, Jennifer	University of North Texas
Reinalda, Roy J.	Dawson Subscription Services
Reinke, Christa	University of Houston
Reynolds, Regina	Library of Congress
Riddick, John F.	Central Michigan University
Riley, Cheryl	Central Missouri State University
Rioux, Maggie	Woods Hole Oceanographic Institute
Risher, Carol	Association of American Publishers
River, Sandy	Texas Tech University
Roach, Dani	Macalester College
Robischon, Rose	United States Military Academy
Robnett, Bill	Vanderbilt University
Rodell, Nancy Tento	Academic Book Center
Rogers, Marilyn	University of Arkansas
Rosado, Cynthia	New York Public Research Library
Rosenberg, Frieda	University of North Carolina–Charlotte

Rossignol, Lu	Smithsonian Institute Libraries
Roth, Alison	Blackwell's Periodicals
Rothaug, Caroline	John Wiley & Sons
Roy, Virginia	Faxon Canada, Ltd.
Rumph, Virginia A.	Butler University
Russov, Olga	Kennesaw State College
Sak, Lida	Rutgers University
Salzer, Melodie	Connecticut College
Sanders, Bridgette	University of North Carolina–Charlotte
Sanders, Susan	National Institute of Standards & Technology
Saudargas, Thomas A.	College Center for Library Automation
Savage, Steve	University of Kentucky
Saxe, Minna	CUNY Graduate School
Sayler, Terry	University of Maryland
Schaffner, Ann	Brandeis University
Scheffler, Eckhart	Walter de Gruyter, Inc.
Schein, Anna	West Virginia University
Scheman, Rita	Churchill Livingstone
Schmitt, Brian	American Institute of Physics
Scholl, Miki	Hamline University
Schwartz, Marla	American University
Schwartzko, Becky	Mankato State University
Scott, Sharon	University of Nevada–Reno
Shadle, Steve	University of Washington
Shaw, Ward	CARL Corporation
Sheble, Mary Ann	University of Detroit Mercy
Shelton, Judith M.	Georgia State University
Sherer, Ree	EBSCO Information Services
Shugar, Chris	National Research Council
Sibley, Debbie	University of Massachusetts
Sievers, Arlene	Case Western Reserve University
Simon, Rebecca	University of California Press
Sinha, Reeta	Emory University
Sleeman, Allison M.	University of Virginia

Sleep, Esther L.	Brock University
Smets, Kristine	Center for Research Libraries
Smith, Alan	Blackwell's Periodicals
Smith, Jeff	Kluwer Academic Publishers
Smith, Jim	EBSCO Information Services
Smith, Susan A.	West Georgia College
Somers, Mike	Louisiana State University
Sonafrank, Steve	Heckman Bindery, Inc.
Soper, Mary Ellen	University of Washington
Sorensen, Sally	Texas Christian University
Southern, Diana	John Wiley & Sons Ltd.
Sozansky, Bill	University of Minnesota–Duluth
Spence, Duncan	Carfax Publishing Company
Squire, Jan S.	University of North Carolina–Charlotte
St. John, Gregory	John Wiley & Sons
Stamison, Christine	Blackwell's Periodicals
Stanley, Nancy M.	Pennsylvania State University
Steele, Heather	Blackwell's Periodicals
Stephens, Joan	Georgia State University
Stewart, Doug	University of North Carolina–Charlotte
Stickman, Jim	University of Washington
Sullenger, Paula	Auburn University
Sullivan, Gene	University of South Alabama
Sullivan, Kathryn	Winona State University
Sutherland, Laurie	University of Washington
Sweet, Kathy	Maricopa County Community College
Swetman, Barbara	Hamilton College
Swets, Ariane	Swets Subscription Service
Tagler, John	Elsevier Science
Talley, Kaye	University of Central Arkansas
Teague, Elaine E.	Glaxo Wellcome
Teaster, Gale	Winthrop University
Teel, Kay	New York University

Tenney, Joyce	University of Maryland–Baltimore County
Terry, Ana Arias	MCB University Press
Terry, Nancy	Grand Valley State University
Testi, Andrea R.	University of New Mexico
Thompson, Jane L.	University of Cincinnati
Thomson, Sarah	University of Massachusetts–Amherst
Thorne, Kathleen	San Jose State University
Thornton, Christopher	Case Western Reserve University
Tijerino, Cathy	University of New Orleans
Timberlake, Phoebe	University of New Orleans
Tong, Dieu Van	University of Alabama at Birmingham
Tonkery, Dan	Readmore, Inc.
Tonn, Anke	Tulane University
Toren, Beth	West Virginia University Libraries
Toth-Waddell, Annemarie	Ontario Legislative Library
Toussaint, Jo Ann	University of St. Thomas
Tribit, Donald	Millersville University
Tseng, Sally	University of California–Irvine
Tumlin, Markel	University of San Diego
Tusa, Sarah	Lamar University
Tuttle, Marcia	University of North Carolina
Van Auken, Gayle	Linda Hall Library
Van Dyck, Craig	Springer-Verlag
Van, Jeri	Duke University
Velzen, Antoon van	Swets Subscription Service
Vent, Marilyn	University of Nevada–Las Vegas
Vikor, Marlene	University of Maryland Libraries
Vladika, Patty	Dawson Subscription Service
Vogel, Ginny	Mack Printing Group
Vogt, Norm	Northern Illinois University

Wakeling, Will	UKSG & University of Birmingham
Walford, Leo	Blackwell Science
Wallace, Pat	University of Colorado
Waltner, Robb M.	University of Evansville
Wang, Margaret K.	University of Delaware
Ward, Jeannette	University of Central Florida
Ward, Sharon	National Library of Canada
Watkinson, Anthony	Chapman & Hall
Weigel, Friedemann	Harrassowitz
Weir, Barbara	Swarthmore College
Weiss, Paul J.	University of New Mexico
Weisser, Teresa	Lafayette College
Weng, Cathy	Temple University
Weston, Beth	University of Delaware
Westover, Keith	Brigham Young University
Weum, Colleen	University of Washington
Whipple, Marcia	Naval Command Control & Ocean Survival Center
Whitney, Marla J.	CARL Corporation
Whittaker, Martha	UnCover Company
Wiles-Young, Sharon	Lehigh University
Wiley, David	Allen Press, Inc.
Wilhelme, Judy	University of Michigan
Wilhite, Marjorie	University of Iowa
Wilke, Mary	University of Chicago
Wilkerson, Judy	University of Oklahoma
Wilkes, Helen	University of Georgia
Wilkinson, Fran	University of New Mexico
Williams, Charmone	Smithsonian Institution
Williams, Gerry	Northern Kentucky University
Williams, Martha	Minot State University
Williams, Marvin	University of West Florida
Williamson, Nancy	Nassau Community College
Willmering, Bill	National Library of Medicine
Wilson, Jenni	Readmore, Inc.
Wimer, Miles	American Phytopathological Society

Winchester, David	Washburn University
Wingenroth, Lee	Mack Printing Group
Winjum, Roberta	University of Hawaii at Manoa
Wisniewski, Deborah	Mount Sinai School of Medicine
Withington, Charles W.	Kluwer Academic Publishers
Witkovski, Ruth	Creighton University
Witsenhaus, Helen	John Wiley & Sons
Wood, Don	Southern Illinois University
Woodburn, Judy	Duke Medical Center
Woodford, Barbara	EBSCO Information Services
Woolson, Elizabeth	Swarthmore College
Youngen, Ralph	American Mathematical Society
Zhang, Wei	Northwestern University
Zilper, Nadia	University of North Carolina–Chapel Hill
Zuidema, Karen	University of Illinois
Zuriff, Sue	University of Minnesota

Index

AACR2 192,240,244,306,308,323, 339-340
AAP *See* Association of American Publishers
AAU *See* Association of American Universities
ABC Express 276-277,280
ABI/Inform 145,147,155-156, 258-259
Academic American Encyclopedia 145
ACM (Association for Computing Machinery) 57-61,64,71, 118-119
AcqWeb 20,320
Acrobat software 183,315
Africa One project 101
African National Congress *See* ANC
ALA *See* American Library Association
"Alarmists" 188-194
ALASA (African Library Association of South Africa) 94-95
ALCTS (Association for Library Collections & Technical Services) 251,264
Alcuin Project 230,233-237
Alex database 231,234
ALISE (Association for Library and Information Science Education) 292
America Online 118
American Heritage Dictionary 145
American Library Association (ALA) 14,27,32,35,245, 293,298
American Mathematical Society (AMS) 129-134,358
American National Standards Institute *See* ANSI

AMS *See* American Mathematical Society
ANC (African National Congress) 91,94,98
Anderson, Bill 310
Anderson, Charles W. 189
Andrew project 144
Angelou, Maya 243-244
ANSI (American National Standards Institute) 367-368
Anthropolgy of Cyberspace, The 321
Apple Computers 99,144,183
AppleScript 236
Archie 9
archiving 58,316,357-358
ARIEL 259,278,280-281
ARL *See* Association of Research Libraries
ARLIS-L 250
Article Reference Number (ARN) 147
ASCII 8,127,145-146,161,173, 216,266,313,315,369
ASEE/ELD 251
ASIS Journal *See* JASIS
Association for Computing Machinery *See* ACM
Association for Library Collections & Technical Services *See* ALCTS
Association of American Publishers (AAP) 77,124
Association of American Universities (AAU) 79-80
Association of Research Libraries (ARL) 14,33,64,81-82,217, 278-279,344-345,364
Astle, Deana 29
AT&T 101,116,181-184
Auburn University 270

AUTOCAT 322
Azen, Rebekah 344

back issues 250-255
BACKSERV 252-255
Bacon, Francis 356
Bakhtin, Mikhail 217-218
bandwidth 9
barcodes 284,299,350-353,368,370, 375
Barglow, Raymond 188
Barlow, John Perry 84,86
Beck, Melissa 307
Bell Atlantic 314
Bellcore 162
Berners-Lee, Tim 8
binding 163-164,344-348
Birdsall, William 191
Birkerts, Sven 213
bitmaps 145,172,316
Blackwell North America (BNA) 162
Blackwell, Richard 27
Blackwell's 27
Blixrud, Julia 368
Blosser, John 337-339
bookmarks 13
Books for College Libraries 192
Bophuthatswana 96
Bowker Annual 162
Bowker Award 29
Brandon-Hill list 352
Britannica Online 8-9,321
Brittle Books Project 344
Brock University 23,30
Brown University 24
browsers (software) 18-20,242
Bryn Mawr Classical Review 214, 223-228
Bryn Mawr College 23,29,31-33, 224,315
Bryn Mawr Commentaries 224
Bryn Mawr Medieval Review 225-228
Buchdruck in der freuhen Neuzeit, Der 69

budgeting 257-258
Bulletin of the AMS 132
Business Dateline 145
Business Periodicals Index 259
Business Periodicals Ondisc 147, 156-159
business on the Internet 8-9,107

Campbell, Jerry 83
cancellations 260-262
CancerLit 352
CARL 140,144,277
Carnegie Corporation 93
Carnegie Mellon University 144-168
Cassiodorus 215
"Cataloger's Toolbox" 321
Cataloging Distribution Service (CDS) 307
Cataloging Internet Resources 240, 264,335
cataloging 9,230-237,263-273, 306-310,320-321,331-342
CCC *See* Copyright Clearance Center
CD-ROM 102,116,147-148,162-163, 165,168,175,214, 284,299, 302
Cello 19
Center for Research Libraries (CRL) 144
CEPD (Centre for Education Policy Development) 94
CERN (European Organization for Nuclear Research) 8,19
CGI (Gommon Gateway Interface) scripts 21,235-236
change 48-49,197-207,297-304
Charlemagne 234
Charlotte's Web 20
Chicago Journal of Theoretical Computer Science (CJTCS) 135-138
Chisnell-Dunn-Sittig method (CDS) 352-353
Chronicle of Higher Education 182
CINAHL 352

Cisbei 96
City of Bits 138
Civilization and its Discontents 215
CJTCS *See Chicago Journal of Theoretical Computer Science*
Clearinghouse for Subject-Oriented Internet Resource Guides 9
client/server software 8,12,144, 148-149,234,236
Coalition for Networked Information (CNI) 124
Code Structure Identifier (CSI) 370
College & Research Libraries 188
COLIS (Community Library Information Services) 94
Cominsky Park 30
community service 44-45
computer files 331-336
CONFU (Conferences on Fair Use) 74,77
Confucius 192
CONSER 264,305-310,334
CONSER Cataloging Manual (CCM) 264,307-308,310,334
CONSER Editing Guide (CEG) 309-310
Constitutional Assembly (South Africa) 98
Constitutional News 98
Contemporary Neurology 138
CONTU guidelines 77,279
Copyright Clearance Center (CCC) 64-66
copyright 21-22,58,60-61,64-87,119, 279
core record 309
Cornell University 302-304
costs of digital resources 162-165
Courtney, Keith 24,28-31,34,71
Crawford, Walt 190-191,194,237
Crisis of the Self in the Age of Information 188
CSISAC (Canadian Serials Industry Systems Advisory Committee) 286-287
Current Mathematical Publications 133

Dawson 290
DDBJ 178
de Grazia, Margaret 211-212
de la Peña McCook, Kathleen 292
Dean, Allen 368
Deleuze, Gilles 215
DeLoughry, Thomas 182
Denison University 23,29,34
Denning, Peter 64,71
Derivative Part Identifier (DPI) 370
DEU *See* Duplicate Exchange Union
Dewey, Melvil 189-190
Digital Equipment Corp. (DEC) 8, 144,163
digital formats 41
digital library 146
Directory of Electronic Journals, Newsletters and Academic Discussion Groups 14
DISA (Data Interchange Standards Association) 287
document delivery 42,140,147,262, 275-281
document navigation 9
Document Type Definitions (DTD) 119,124,183
DOS 12,147,302-303
DRA 20,234,237,261
Drucker, Peter 188,199-200
DTDs *See* Document Type Definitions
"Dublin Core" 242-245
Duke University 24,83
Duke University Press 371-375
Duplicate Exchange Union (DEU) 251-252
DVI files 134

E-JADS (Enhanced-Journal Article Delivery Service) 147, 156-158,160
e-mail 148,182,224-225,252,254,

280,300,302,315,318-319,
    348,365
e-MATH 129-134
EDI (electronic data interchange)
    283-285,287-290,368
education 292-295
education, future of 43-44
Educom 67
Ehrenreich, Barbara 84
Electronic Communications
    Committee (ECC) 16
Electronic Journal of Combinatorics
    359
Electronic Library Project 316
*Electronic Research Announcements
    of the AMS* 132
electronic books 162
electronic data interchange *See* EDI
electronic journals 14,124-142,
    161-162,193,210,213-214,
    216,218-228,240,261,
    263-267,311-316,356-360,
    374
Elsevier 116,145,165,168,172-179
Elsevier Electronic Subscriptions
    172-176
EMBASE *See* Excerpta Medica
Encyclopedia Britannica 8-9,321
Enhanced-Journal Article Delivery
    Service *See* E-JADS
EPA (Environmental Protection
    Agency) 294
"Equilibrists" 188
Ercelawn, Ann 20,321
Ethernet 116,144
European Bioinformatics Institute
    (EBI) 178
European Serials Conference 28
Excerpta Medica (EMBASE)
    177-178

fair use 64-67,73,168
FAQ (frequently-asked questions)
    252

Fattig, Karl 339
Faulkner, William 210
Faxon 287,367,370
FCC (Federal Communications
    Commission) 38
Federal Express (FedEx) 8
Feick, Tina 24-25,368
file transfer protocol *See* FTP
Filemaker Pro 236-237
firewalls 110-112
FirstSearch 101,144,258,320
Foppen, Peter 368
Ford Foundation 100
format integration 306-307
Freud, Sigmund 215
FTP (file transfer protocol) 8,9,14,
    16,98,130,234,236-237,
    240,252,255,284,302,307,
    315,318-319,334,357

Galileo 354
Gasaway, Laura 80
Geller, Marilyn 237
GenBank 178
GENE-COMBIS 172,178-179
General Periodicals Ondisc (GPO)
    147,156-159
Giesecke, Michael 69
GIFTEX-L 250-251
"Global Information Infrastructure
    (GII)" 46,49-51
Goldstone Commission 100
Golian, Linda 292-294
Gopher 8-9,11-16,98,118,127,130,
    225,231,251-252,264-265,
    267,315,318,322,334,337,
    339-342,357
Gopher Jewels 13
Gopher Plus 12-13,15
Gorman, Michael 190-191,194
Government of National Unity
    (South Africa) 95
government documents 96
graphical user interface *See* GUI
Grateful Dead 84

"Green Paper" 74-76,82
"GREN (Global Research and Education Network)" 54-55
Grolier 145
Guattari, Felix 215
GUI (graphical user interface) 19, 144,320
Guidon 174

Hamaker, Chuck 29
Hamilton, Richard 223-224,227
Harris, Roma 191
Haworth Press 71
Health Reference Update 352
Heterick, Robert 67
HGopher 12-13
Hofstra University 259-262
Holquist, Michael 218
home page 18
HoTMetaL 21
HTML (Hypertext Markup Language) 10,18-20, 140-141,165,216,231, 234-236,267,303,315, 318-319,323
HTTP (Hypertext Transfer Protocol) 20,240,320,340
httpd (Hypertext Transfer Protocol Daemon) 21
Humanist 224
HyperCard 231-232
hypermedia 17,19
HyperTalk 231
hypertext 8,17,19-21,176-177, 266,319,357
Hypertext Markup Language *See* HTML
Hypertext Transfer Protocol *See* HTTP

IAC *See* Information Access Corp.
IBM 8,99,144,183

ICEDIS (International Committee for the Electronic Data Interchange of Serials) 286-287
IEEE (Institute of Electrical & Electronics Engineers) 116,145,161
IESCA (Interactive Electronic Serials Cataloging Aid) 338
IETF (Internet Engineering Task Force) 240
IFLA 95
ILL *See* interlibrary loan
ILS systems 284-288,299
Immunology Today Online 172,176-178
indexing 58,314-315
Indiana University School of Medicine 350-352
Infoact Database 100
Information Access Corp. (IAC) 78,161
"Information Age" 39-45
"information highway" or "information superhighway" 38,40,74,99,111
InfoSlug 14
Infotrac 277
Innopac 299
Innovacq 299
Inside Informaton 102
Institute for the Study of Public Violence 100
Intellectual Property Working Group 66-67
intellectual freedom 40,97
Intercat *See* OCLC Internet Cataloging Project
interfaces 283-287
interlibrary loan (ILL) 77,97,127, 168,258-259,277-281,351
International Development Research Centre 92,101
International Intellectual Property Alliance 76

International Telecommunications
  Union (BDT) 101
Internet 7-22,38-61,105-114,
  117-118,124-125,129-133,
  140-141,152,167,175,210,
  224-225,231-234,236,
  239-242,250-253,264,
  289-290,303,318-323,
  338-340,342,362,364
Internet for Everyone 8
Internet Assistant 21
Internet indexing tools 9
Internet protocols 7-9
Internet World 20
Internet Worm 110
internships 294-295
ISBN 204
ISI (Institute for Scientific
  Information) 161,312-316,
  352
ISO 124
ISSN 266-267,351,368-369

Jackson, Mary 368
*JASIS (Journal of the American
  Society for Information
  Science)* 98
Jefferson, Thomas 84
Journal of Combinatorics 356
*Journal of Functional and Logic
  Programming* 138
*Journal of Image Guided Surgery
  (JIGS)* 139-141
Journal of the AMS 132
Jughead 13
Jurassic Park 76

Kambitsch, Tim 230,237
Kanter, Rosabeth Moss 199
Kardex 193,298-299
Kellogg Foundation 100
Kerberos 147,153
Kilgour, Fred 190

Kinko's 71
"knowledge guilds" 47,52-54
"knowledge management" 46-55
knowledge workers 188-189
Koppel, Ted 368-369

Lamar University 258-259
Landmarks of Tomorrow 188
LaTeX 136-137
LC *See* Library of Congress
LC Marvel 14
LCRIs (Library of Congress Rule
    Interpretations) 306-308,
    323,339
LCSH *See* Library of Congress
    Subject Headings
Lehman, Bruce 74
Leiserson, Anna Bell 20
LeMay, Ford 34
Lenzini, Becky 24-25,35
Library Association (U.K.) 28
Library Binding Institute 346-347
Library Hotline 34
Library of Congress (LC) 8,14,97,
    102,237,240,306-310,321,
    358
Library of Congress Classification 261
Library of Congress Rule
    Interpretations *See* LCRIs
Library of Congress Subject
    Headings (LCSH)
    97,339-340
library schools 292
Line Mode 19
Lingua Franca 214
Linotron 137
LIS (Library Information System)
    144-167
LISDESA (Library and Information
    Services in Developing
    South Africa) 95
listservs 14,216,250-255,315,
    318-319,321-322
LIWO (Library and Information
    Workers Organisation) 94

LOCIS 321
Lor, Peter 93
Lowry, Anita 214
Lycos 9
Lyman, Peter 83
Lynx 19,130,319-320,357

MacHTTP 235
Macintosh 12-13,21,183,234
MacLennan, Birdie 321
MacWeb 19
Malawski, Sue 368
Mandela, Nelson 90,94,103
MARBI (Machine Readable
    Bibliographic Information)
    245,309,339
MARC (Machine Readable
    Cataloging) 20,230,
    233-237,242,244-245,272,
    299-300,334,338-342
MARC tags, specific 20,230-237,
    239-241,265-266,271-272,
    306-307,309-310,335,339
Marcive 365
Mathematical Association of
    America 131
Mathematical Reviews 133
Mathematics of Computation 132
MathSci 130,133
Maxwell, Robert 27
MBL/WHOI (Marine Biological
    Laboratory/Woods Hole
    Oceanographic Institution)
    18,22
McCarty, Willard 224
McGann, Jerome 214
McGarry, Jane 33
McPherson, Isaac 84
Mead Data Central 78
Medium/Format Identifier (MFI) 370
MEDLIB-L 250
Medline 183,352-353
Megaword 162
Mellon Foundation 124,226

Memorial Library of Newfoundland
    321
Mental Workload 312
mentoring 292-294
Mercury Project 144-145
Merriman, John 24-25,27-28,33
microfilm 260
MIT 136-138,147
MIT Press 135-138
Mitchell, William 138
Mitnick, Kevin 85
MLA 250
MLS degree 345
Modern Language Quarterly 373
Monroe, Hunter 231,233-234,237
"Moore's Law" 46
Morris, William 210
Mosaic 8,18-19,314,357
Motif 146
Mott Foundation 100
Mozambique 101
Mr. Serials 230

NACO (Name Authority
    Cooperative Project) 272
NASIG gopher 14,16
NASIG history 23-35
NASIG Newsletter 24,26
NASIG Student Grant 24,26
NASIGNet 12,15,24,335
National Center for Supercomputing
    Applications (NCSA) 8,18
National Library of Canada (NLC)
    14
National Library of Medicine (NLM)
    183
National Science Foundation (NSF)
    129
National Writers Union (NWU)
    77-78
NCAA 190
NCSA *See* National Center for
    Supercomputing
    Applications
Needleman, Mark 368

NEPI (National Education Policy
    Initiative) 94
Netscape 8,19,357
networked information and
    technology 40-55
New England Journal of Medicine 182
New York Times 78
New York Times Book Review 84
New Yorker 77
NewJour-L 14
Newton search engine 145
Newton, Isaac 356
NIEHS (National Institute of
    Environmental Health
    Sciences) 294-295
NII (National Information
    Infrastructure) 73-74,86
NII Working Group on Copyright 74
Nineteenth-Century Literature 127
NISO 347,367-368
NLM *See* National Library of
    Medicine
NM 272
nongovernment organizations
    (NGOs) 99-100
North Carolina State University
    (NCSU) 14,20,198-207,
    230-237
Northwestern University 338
Notes for Serials Catalogers 323
Notices of the AMS 132
NOTIS 265-266,270,298,314,
    351-352

O'Donnell, James 214-215
O'Neil, Rosana 34
OCLC 101-102,144,168,174,
    176-177,204,240,264-266,
    278,301,307,309-310,
    314-315,320,334,339,346
OCLC Internet Cataloging Project
    9,239-240,264,266,321
OCLC/NCSA Metadata Workshop
    242

Odlyzko, Andrew 357
Oglethorpe University 23,29-30
Ohiolink 167
Okerson, Ann 33,64-65
OLC *See* Pittsburgh Oakland Library
    Consortium
Olson, Nancy 240,264
*Online Journal of Current Clnical
    Trials* 313
*Online Journal of Knowledge
    Synthesis for Nursing* 314
OPACs 230-231,233-237,258,
    269-273,320-321,339
OVID Technologies 352
Oxford University 27
Oxford University Journals 216-217

PageMaker 140
PALS 287
Paradox (software) 350
Paramount Pictures 71
Pat (search tool) 216
PDF files 134
peer review 58-59
Penn State University 362-364
Pergamon 27
Periodical Abstracts 145,147,151,
    155-156,258-259
Pew Charitable Trust 144
Philosophical Transactions 312
Pittsburgh Oakland Library
    Consortium (OLC) 144,167
poetry 211-212
Politics of the Third Wave 84
Poole, William Frederick 297-298
Postmodern Culture 216-217
Postscript 134,136-137,140,266,357
Power Pages system 145,147,153,
    167-168
preprints 42,61,78,131-132,140,
    356-357
preservation 344-348
Preston, Cecilia 368
Price-Wilkin, John 225
pricing 31,81,117,125,133-134,

174,177,179,213,216-217,
315-316
Prince 212
printing from databases 156-160
privacy 118,153
Proceedings of the AMS 132
Prodigy 72
Program for Cooperative Cataloging 307,309-310
ProQuest 145-147,153,156,160,167, 258-259
publishers 58-61,65-66,358,371-375
"Purple Rain" 212

Quattro Pro 351

Reader's Guide 259
Readmore 253,320
Reconstruction and Development Programme (RDP) 91-95,98-100
Red Sage project 116,140,181-184
Remley, Paul 225
Request-for-Comments (RFC) documents 241,243
RFP (Request for Proposals) 290,326-329
"rhetoric of seriality" 210-218
Rice University 13
Richter, Linda 368
Riddick, John 24-27,31-32
RightPages software 182
RLIN 278
Rossetti Archive project 214
RTF (Rich-Text Format) 127

SABINET (South African Bibliographic and Information Network) 97,99,102
SAILIS (South African Institute for Librarianship and Information Science) 94-95
Sam Houston State University (SHSU) 251
SANB (South African National Bibliography) 97
sanctions 99-100
SANGONET (South African Nongovernmental Organisations Network) 100
SCAN (Scholarship from California on the Net) 123-128
Scarry, Elaine 211
scholarly communications 115-119
Schwartz, Fritz 368
Schwind, Penny 33
Science Citation Index (SCI) 277
Scripps College 23,30
security on Internet 108-112,118
Separate Amenities Act 94
Serendipity Systems 214
Serials 24,27-28
"Serials in Cyberspace" 20,321
Serials Librarian 24
SERIALST 250,322
server software 14,20-21,146-147
Seulend, Peter 214
SGML (Standard Generalized Markup Language) 59,119, 124-125,127,140,165-166, 172,177,244,315
Shakespeare, William 20
Shimomura, Tsutomu 107,109
SICI (Serials Item Contribution Identifier) 119,241,284, 367-370
SID (Simple Internet Database) 231-232
Sigl, Doris 237
Sigma Theta Tau International 314
SIRSI 149,167
SISAC (Serials Industry Systems Advisory Committee) 284, 286-287,290,368,370,375

site licenses 127
Site Search 145,174
"sniffers" 109
Social Sciences Citation Index (SSCI) 277
Social Science Index 258
Society for Industrial and Applied Mathematics (SIAM) 131
Son of SID (computer program) 234-237
Sony 162
South Africa 90-104
South African Library Association 94-95
Southern African Development Community (SADC) 100-101
Spinelli, Martin 210
Spitin' Image Productions 214
Springer-Verlag 116,181-184
St. Columba 70,85
staff 197-207,297-304
Standard Generalized Markup Language *See* SGML
standards 119
STM Group 77
Stubbs, Kendon 225
Sutton, Willie 107
Swann, Julie 339

teams 202-207,361-365
technical services 318-323,361-365
telephones 99
Telnet 12,15,130,318-321,334
TeX 130-131,357
Texaco 71,77
TEXSHARE 259
Text Encoding Initiative (TEI) 243
textual user interface *See* TUI
Thoreau, Henry David 192
TIFF images 145,147,156,163, 165,172
Toffler, Alvin and Heidi 84-85
"Tools for Serials Catalogers" 20,321,334

training 300-301,303-304
transaction logs 270-273
Transactions of the AMS 132
Transkei 96
TransLis (Transforming our Library and Information Services) 94
Triangle Research Library Network 79
Trinity University 23
TUI (textual user interface) 320
TULIP 116,145-147,153,155-156, 161-163,165,168,172,175
TurboGopher 13
Turner, Victor 199
Tuttle, Marcia 25,28-29

U.S. Dept. of Commerce 74,77,79
UKSG (United Kingdom Serials Group) 24-29,33,329
Ulmer, Greg 213
Ulrich's International Periodicals Directory 161
UMI (University Microfilms International) 145-168,258
UnCover 102,140,258-259,262,277, 279-281,369
Unesco 95
Uniform Resource Characteristics *See* URC
Uniform Resource Identifier *See* URI
Uniform Resource Identifier (URI) Working Group 240-241
Uniform Resource Locator *See* URL
UNINET 101
Union List of Serials 298
United Kingdom Serials Group *See* UKSG
University of British Columbia 19,24
University of California 116
University of California Libraries 124-125,127
University of California Press 124-128
University of California, Berkeley 83,107,124-128,193

University of California, Irvine 124-128,364-365
University of California, Los Angeles (UCLA) 124-128,183,307
University of California, San Francisco 116,181-184
University of California, Santa Clara 14
University of Chicago 137,321-322
University of Florida 279
University of Houston 14
University of Illinois, Chicago 24
University of Illinois, Urbana-Champaign 140
University of Michigan 9,214,225
University of Minnesota 12,14
University of Nebraska, Lincoln 339,341
University of Nevada 13
University of New Mexico 326
University of North Carolina, Chapel Hill 294
University of Oregon 298-299,301
University of Pennsylvania 102
University of South Alabama 298
University of South Florida (USF) 292
University of Surrey 28
University of the Witwatersand 98
University of Vermont 18
University of Virginia 214,225,264, 266-267,321
University of Washington 225
UNIX 12,21,146-147,183,302,322
UNIX Curses (gopher client) 12,15
Upham, Lois 293
Uprisings in Libertyville USA 214
URC (Uniform Resource Characteristics) 119,242-245
URI (Uniform Resource Identifier) 10
URL (Uniform Resource Locator) 8, 10,13,16,18,20,119, 132-134,230-231,233,235, 240-242,244,265-266,320, 368
URN (Uniform Resource Name) 119,241-244
usage 183,260-261,349-353
user studies 149-168
USMARC 14,233-234,236-237,239, 241,244-245,321,339
USMARC Advisory Group 245

VAN (value-added network) 289-290
Vance, Eugene 225
Vanderbilt University 20,320,350, 352-353
Vatican Library 106
Venda 96
Veronica 9,13
Viacom 71
viewer applications 13
Virginia Polytechnic Scholarly Communication Project 137
Virtual Library Project 145-168
Visual Basic 233
Visual Human Project 184
VMS 21
VT100 146
VTLS 314

WAIS (Wide Area Information Server) 9,225,228,254
War Games 107
Web *See* WWW
West Virginia Library Commission 314
West Virginia State Dept. of Education 314
West Virginia University 311-312, 314
"What's New" 21
White, E.B. 20
Wiley 139-141,315
Wilkas, Lenore 32

Williamson, David 237
H.W. Wilson Co. 298
Windows (operating system)
    12-13,233-234,320
Wired 84
Wordsworth, William 211
workflow 203-207
World Wide Web *See* WWW
Wright, George 368
WVNET 314
WWW (World Wide Web) 8-10,
    17-22,39,65,98,108,
    110-112,117,127,130-138,
    140-141,178,183,216,226,
    230-231,233-237,240,242,
    252-255,265,314-315,
318-322,334,337-339,
341-342,357,370

X11 111
X12 287-289

Yale University 34,102,297

Z39.50 314
Z39.56 368-370
Zambia 101
Zhang, Wei 338

For Product Safety Concerns and Information please contact our EU representative GPSR@taylorandfrancis.com
Taylor & Francis Verlag GmbH, Kaufingerstraße 24, 80331 München, Germany

www.ingramcontent.com/pod-product-compliance
Lightning Source LLC
Chambersburg PA
CBHW071236300426
44116CB00008B/1059